Frank Wood's Book-keeping and Accounts

Frank Wood **BSc(Econ), FCA**

Third Edition

PITMAN PUBLISHING
128 Long Acre, London WC2E 9AN

A Division of Pearson Professional Limited

First published in Great Britain 1992

British Library Cataloguing in Publication Data
A catalogue record for this book is available from the British Library.

ISBN 0-273-03770-6

10 9 8 7 6 5

Printed in England by Clays Ltd, St Ives plc

Contents

Preface to the Third Edition

This book was written specifically to cover four examination syllabuses. It covers the work to be done in the following courses:

- RSA Examinations Board, Book-keeping Stage 1 (Elementary)
- London Chamber of Commerce and Industry, Book-keeping First Level
- Pitman Examinations Institute, Book-keeping and Accounts Level 1
- Business and Technician Education Council, Book-keeping requirements.

There has been an extensive revision of text in this edition. The aim was to ensure that the book was easier to understand. More diagrams have been used to help the student and to give him a better understanding of the subject.

The answers at the back of the book are now fully displayed. This will make it easier for students to check their own work. They will be able to see if they have drawn up their accounts in the proper fashion as well as getting the correct figures. The questions without answers will enable lecturers and teachers to set classwork or homework to check on the progress of their students.

Many of the questions are from past examinations of the RSA Examinations Board, London Chamber of Commerce and Industry, or Pitman Examinations Institute. I would like to thank each of these examination bodies for their permission to reprint questions from their examinations.

The male pronoun 'he' is used throughout the book. However, in all cases, the words 'he' or 'she' are interchangeable.

Frank Wood
Stockport
Cheshire

Summer 1991

Matrix of Subjects Covered and Examining Bodies

Key: ✓ = included in syllabus × = not in syllabus *Chapters*		**RSA Stage 1**	**LCCI First Level**	**PEI Level 1**	**BTEC**
1–22	Basic Accounting	✓	✓	✓	✓
23	Bank Reconciliation Statements	✓	✓	✓	✓
24	The Journal	✓	✓	✓	✓
25	Petty Cash Book	✓	✓	✓	✓
26	Errors Not Affecting Trial Balance	✓	✓	✓	×
27	Suspense Accounts and Errors	✓	✓	✓	×
28	Control Accounts	✓	✓	×	×
29	Accounting Ratios	✓	✓	✓	✓
30	Single Entry	✓	✓	✓	✓
31	Income and Expenditure Accounts	✓	✓	✓	×
32	Manufacturing Accounts	×	✓	×	×
33	Wages and Salaries	✓	×	×	✓
34	The Valuation of Stock	✓	✓	×	✓
35	Analysis Books	✓	✓	×	×
36	Capital and Revenue Expenditure	✓	✓	✓	✓
37	Accounting Concepts and Conventions	✓	✓	✓	×

Note: As syllabuses do change from time to time check that the above details still apply to your examination.

1 · Introduction to Accounting

1.1 What is Accounting?

People and Businesses

Accounting is something that affects people in their personal lives just as much as it affects very large businesses. We all use accounting ideas when we plan what we are going to do with our money. We have to plan how much of it we will spend and how much we will save. We may write down a plan, known as a **budget**, or we may simply keep it in our minds.

Recording Accounting Data

However, when people normally talk about accounting it means the type used by businesses and other organisations. They cannot keep all the details in their minds so they have to write it all down.

They will not only record cash received and paid out. They will also record goods bought and sold, items bought to use rather than to sell, and so on. This part of accounting is usually called the *recording of data*.

Classifying and Summarising

When the data is being recorded it has to be sorted out so as to be most useful to the business. This is known as *classifying* and *summarising* data.

Following such classifications and summaries it will be possible to work out how much profit or loss has been made by the business during a period of time. It will also be possible to show what resources are owned by the business, and what is owed by it, on the closing date of the period.

Communicating Information

From the data, someone skilled in accounting should be able to tell whether or not the business is performing well financially. He should be able to work out what are the strengths and weaknesses of the business.

Finally, he should be able to tell or *communicate* his results to the owners of the business, or to others allowed to receive this information.

Accounting is, therefore, concerned with:

- Recording of data.
- Classifying and summarising data.
- Communicating what has been learned from the data.

1.2 What is Book-keeping?

The part of accounting that is concerned with recording data is often known as **book-keeping**. Until about one hundred years ago all accounting data was recorded in books, hence the term book-keeping.

Nowadays, although books may be used, quite obviously a lot of accounting data is recorded by using computers.

1.3 Users of Accounting Information

The possible users can be:

- Owner(s) of the business. They want to be able to see whether or not the business is profitable. In addition they want to know what the financial resources of the business are.
- A prospective buyer. When the owner wants to sell his business the buyer will want to see such information.
- The bank. If the owner wants to borrow money for use in the business then the bank will need such information.
- Tax inspectors. They need it to be able to calculate the taxes payable.
- A prospective partner. If the owner wants to share ownership with someone else, then the would-be partner will want it.

There could also be other users. It is obvious that without recorded accounting data a business would have many difficulties.

New Terms

Budget (p 1): A plan shown expressed in money.

Book-keeping (p 2): The recording of accounting data.

2 · The Accounting Equation and the Balance Sheet

2.1 The Accounting Equation

The whole of accounting is based upon a very simple idea. This is called the *accounting equation* which sounds complicated, but in fact it is easy to understand.

It can be explained by saying that if a firm is to set up, and start trading, then it needs resources. Let us assume that in the first place it is the owner of the business who has supplied all of the resources. This can be shown as:

Resources in the business = Resources supplied by the owner

In accounting, terms are used to describe things. The amount of the resources supplied by the owner is called **capital**. The actual resources that are then in the business are called **assets**. This means that the accounting equation above, when the owner has supplied all of the resources, can be shown as:

Assets = Capital

Usually, however, someone other than the owner has supplied some of the assets. **Liabilities** is the name given to the amount owing to this person for these assets. The equation has now changed to:

Assets = Capital + Liabilities

It can be seen that the two sides of the equation will have the same totals. This is because we are dealing with the same thing from two different points of view. It is:

Resources: what they are	=	Resources: who supplied them
(Assets)		(Capital + Liabilities)

It is a fact that the totals of each side will always equal one another, and that this will always be true no matter how many transactions there may be. The actual assets, capital and liabilities may change, but the total of the assets will always equal the total of capital + liabilities.

Assets consist of property of all kinds, such as buildings, machinery, stocks of goods and motor vehicles. Also benefits such as debts owed by customers and the amount of money in the bank account are included.

Liabilities consist of money owing for goods supplied to the firm and for expenses. Also loans made to the firm are included.

Capital is often called the owner's **equity** or net worth.

2.2 The Balance Sheet

The accounting equation is shown in a statement called the **balance sheet**. It is not the first book-keeping record to be made, but it is a good place to start to consider accounting.

The Introduction of Capital

On 1 May 19–7 B Blake started in business and put £5,000 into a bank account for the business. The balance sheet would appear:

B Blake
Balance Sheet as at 1 May 19–7

Assets	£		£
Cash at bank	5,000	Capital	5,000
	5,000		5,000

The Purchase of an Asset by Cheque

On 3 May 19–7 Blake buys fixtures for £3,000. The effect of this transaction is that the cash at the bank is reduced and a new asset, fixtures, appears.

B Blake
Balance Sheet as at 3 May 19–7

Assets	£		£
Fixtures	3,000	Capital	5,000
Cash at bank	2,000		
	5,000		5,000

The Purchase of an Asset and the Incurring of a Liability

On 6 May 19–7 Blake buys some goods for £500 from D Smith, and agrees to pay for them some time within the next two weeks. There is now a new asset, **stock** of goods, and there is also a new liability because Blake owes money to D Smith for the goods.

A person to whom money is owed for goods is known in accounting language as a **creditor**.

B Blake
Balance Sheet as at 6 May 19–7

Assets	£	*Capital and Liabilities*	£
Fixtures	3,000	Capital	5,000
Stock of goods	500	Creditor	500
Cash at bank	2,000		
	5,500		5,500

Sale of an Asset on Credit

On 10 May 19–7 goods which had cost £100 were sold to J Brown for the same amount, the money to be paid later. This means a reduction in the stock of goods and there will now be a new asset. A person who owes money to the firm is known in accounting language as a **debtor**. The balance sheet now appears as:

B Blake
Balance Sheet as at 10 May 19–7

Assets	£	*Capital and Liabilities*	£
Fixtures	3,000	Capital	5,000
Stock of goods	400	Creditor	500
Debtor	100		
Cash at bank	2,000		
	5,500		5,500

Sale of an Asset for Immediate Payment

On 13 May 19–7 goods which had cost £50 were sold to D Daley for the same amount, Daley paying for them immediately by cheque. Here one asset, stock of goods, is reduced, while another asset, bank, is increased. The balance sheet now appears:

B Blake
Balance Sheet as at 13 May 19–7

Assets	£	*Capital and Liabilities*	£
Fixtures	3,000	Capital	5,000
Stock of goods	350	Creditor	500
Debtor	100		
Cash at bank	2,050		
	5,500		5,500

The Payment of a Liability

On 15 May 19–7 Blake pays a cheque for £200 to D Smith in part payment of the amount owing. The asset of bank is therefore reduced, and the liability of the creditor is also reduced. The balance sheet now appears:

B Blake
Balance Sheet as at 15 May 19–7

Assets	£	*Capital and Liabilities*	£
Fixtures	3,000	Capital	5,000
Stock of goods	350	Creditor	300
Debtor	100		
Cash at bank	1,850		
	5,300		5,300

Collection of an Asset

On 31 May 19–7 J Brown, who owes Blake £100, makes a part payment of £75 by cheque. The effect is to reduce one asset, debtor, and to increase another asset, bank. This results in a balance sheet as follows:

B Blake
Balance Sheet as at 31 May 19–7

Assets	£	*Capital and Liabilities*	£
Fixtures	3,000	Capital	5,000
Stock of goods	350	Creditor	300
Debtor	25		
Cash at bank	1,925		
	5,300		5,300

It can be seen that every transaction has affected two items. Sometimes it has changed two assets by reducing one and increasing the other. Other times things have changed differently. A summary of the effect of transactions upon assets, liabilities and capital is shown below.

Example of transaction	Effect	
1 Buy goods on credit	↑ Increase asset (Stock of goods)	↑ Increase liability (Creditors)
2 Buy goods by cheque	↑ Increase asset (Stock of goods)	↓ Decrease asset (Bank)
3 Pay creditor by cheque	↓ Decrease asset (Bank)	↓ Decrease liability (Creditors)
4 Owner pays more capital into the bank	↑ Increase asset (Bank)	↑ Increase capital
5 Owner takes money out of the business bank account for his own use	↓ Decrease asset (Bank)	↓ Decrease capital
6 Owner pays creditor from private money outside the firm	↓ Decrease liability (Creditors)	↑ Increase capital

Each transaction has, therefore, maintained the same total for assets as that of capital + liabilities. This can be shown:

Number of transactions as above	Assets	Capital and Liabilities	Effect on balance sheet totals
1	+	+	Each side added to equally
2	+ –		A *plus* and a *minus* both on the assets side *cancelling out* each other
3	–	–	Each side has equal deductions
4	+	+	Each side has equal additions
5	–	–	Each side has equal deductions
6		– +	A plus and a minus both on the liabilities side cancelling out each other

New Terms

Capital (p 3): The total of resources supplied to a business by its owner.
Assets (p 3): Resources owned by the business.
Liabilities (p 3): Total of money owed for assets supplied to the business.
Equity (p 4): Another name for the capital of the owner.
Balance Sheet (p 4): A statement showing the assets, capital and liabilities of a business.
Stock (p 4): Unsold goods
Creditor (p 4): A person to whom money is owed for goods or services.
Debtor (p 5): A person who owes money to the business for goods or services supplied to him.

Notes:

(a) Anyone who has studied book-keeping or accounting previously may well question the validity of having assets on the left-hand side of the balance sheet and capital and liabilities on the right-hand side, as previously they used to be the opposite to that. However, the company law lays it down that in two-sided balance sheets assets must be shown on the left-hand side of the balance sheet and capital and liabilities on the right-hand side. In the interests of standardisation, and to avoid confusion, the balance sheets for sole traders and partnerships will also be drawn up in the same way.

In fact the new method does make book-keeping and accounting much easier to learn than previously. It is however a point to bear in mind when looking at other textbooks which have not been updated.

(*b*) Generally, the figures used for exhibits and for exercises have been kept down to relatively small amounts. This has been done deliberately to make the work of the user of this book that much easier. Constantly handling large figures does not add anything to the study of the principles of accounting, instead it simply wastes a lot of the student's time, and he/she will probably make far more errors if larger figures are used.

It could lead to the author being accused of not being 'realistic' with the figures given, but I believe that it is far more important to make learning easier for the student.

Exercises

Note: *Questions with the letter X shown after the question number* ***do not*** *have answers shown at the back of the book. Answers to the other questions are shown on page 356 onwards.*

2.1 You are to complete the gaps in the following table:

	Assets	*Liabilities*	*Capital*
	£	£	£
(a)	12,500	1,800	?
(b)	28,000	4,900	?
(c)	16,800	?	12,500
(d)	19,600	?	16,450
(e)	?	6,300	19,200
(f)	?	11,650	39,750

2.2X You are to complete the gaps in the following table:

	Assets	*Liabilities*	*Capital*
	£	£	£
(a)	55,000	16,900	?
(b)	?	17,200	34,400
(c)	36,100	?	28,500
(d)	119,500	15,400	?
(e)	88,000	?	62,000
(f)	?	49,000	110,000

2.3 From the following list show which are assets and which are liabilities:
(a) Office machinery
(b) Loan from C Shirley
(c) Fixtures and fittings
(d) Motor vehicles
(e) We owe for goods
(f) Bank balance

2.4X Which of the following are assets, and which are liabilities?
(a) Motor vehicles
(b) Premises
(c) Creditors for goods
(d) Stock of goods
(e) Debtors
(f) Owing to bank
(g) Cash in hand
(h) Loan from D Jones
(i) Machinery

2.5 State which of the following are shown under the wrong headings for J White's business:

Assets	*Liabilities*
Loan from C Smith	Stock of goods
Cash in hand	Debtors
Machinery	Money owing to bank
Creditors	
Premises	
Motor vehicles	

2.6X Which of the following are shown under the wrong headings:

Assets	*Liabilities*
Cash at bank	Loan from J Graham
Fixtures	Machinery
Creditors	Motor vehicles
Building	
Stock of goods	
Debtors	
Capital	

2.7 A Smart sets up a new business. Before he actually sells anything he has bought Motor Vehicles £2,000, Premises £5,000, Stock of goods £1,000. He did not pay in full for his stock of goods and still owes £400 in respect of them. He had borrowed £3,000 from D Bevan. After the events just described, and before trading starts, he has £100 cash in hand and £700 cash at bank. You are required to calculate the amount of his capital.

2.8X T Charles starts a business. Before he actually starts to sell anything he has bought, Fixtures £2,000, Motor Vehicles £5,000 and a stock of goods £3,500. Although he has paid in full for the fixtures and the motor vehicle, he still owes £1,400 for some of the goods. J Preston had lent him £3,000. Charles, after the above, has £2,800 in the business bank account and £100 cash in hand. You are required to calculate his capital.

2.9 Draw up A Foster's balance sheet from the following as at 31 December 19–4:

	£
Capital	23,750
Debtors	4,950
Motor vehicles	5,700
Creditors	2,450
Fixtures	5,500
Stock of goods	8,800
Cash at bank	1,250

2.10X Draw up Kelly's balance sheet as at 30 June 19–2 from the following items:

	£
Capital	13,000
Office machinery	9,000
Creditors	900
Stock of goods	1,550
Debtors	275
Cash at bank	5,075
Loan from C Smith	2,000

2.11 Look at this list:
(a) We pay a creditor £70 in cash.
(b) Bought fixtures £200 paying by cheque.
(c) Bought goods on credit £275.
(d) The proprietor introduces another £500 cash into the firm.
(e) J Walker lends the firm £200 in cash.
(f) A debtor pays us £50 by cheque.
(g) We return goods costing £60 to a supplier whose bill we had not paid.
(h) Bought additional shop premises paying £5,000 by cheque.

For each item shown, you are to state how it changes assets, capital or liabilities. For example the answer to *(a)* will be:

(a) – Assets £70
– Liabilities £70

2.12X Show how each item on the following list changes assets, capital and liabilities.
(a) Bought a motor van on credit £500
(b) Repaid by cash a loan owed to P Smith £1,000
(c) Bought goods for £150 paying by cheque
(d) The owner puts a further £5,000 cash into the business
(e) A debtor returns to us £80 goods. We agree to make an allowance for them.

(f) Bought goods on credit £220
(g) The owner takes out £100 cash for his personal use
(h) We pay a creditor £190 by cheque.

2.13 C Sangster has the following items in his balance sheet as on 30 April 19–4: Capital £18,900; Loan from T Sharples £2,000; Creditors £1,600; Fixtures £3,500; Motor Vehicle £4,200; Stock of Goods £4,950; Debtors £3,280; Cash at Bank £6,450; Cash in Hand £120.

During the first week of May 19–4 Sangster:
(a) Bought extra stock of goods £770 on credit.
(b) One of the debtors paid us £280 in cash.
(c) Bought extra fixtures by cheque £1,000.

You are to draw up a balance sheet as on 7 May 19–4 after the above transactions have been completed.

2.14X H Charles has the following balance sheet as at 31 March 19–5:

Balance Sheet as at 31 March 19–5

Assets	£	*Capital and Liabilities*	£
Buildings	6,000	Capital	14,400
Motor vehicle	4,000	Loan from W Young	2,000
Stock of goods	2,000	Creditors	1,600
Debtors	2,800		
Cash at bank	3,200		
	18,000		18,000

The following transactions occur:

2 April Paid a cheque of £500 to a creditor.
8 April A debtor paid H Charles £300 by chcquc.
10 April W Young is repaid £1,000 by cheque.

Write up a balance sheet on 10 April 19–5 after the transactions have been completed.

3 · The Double Entry System for Assets, Liabilities and Capital

3.1 The Double Entry System

We have seen that every transaction affects two items. If we want to show the effect of every transaction when we are doing our book-keeping, we will have to show the effect of a transaction on each of the two items. For each transaction this means that a book-keeping entry will have to be made to show an increase or decrease of that item, and another entry to show the increase or decrease of the other item. From this you will probably be able to see that the term **double entry system** of book-keeping is a good one, as each entry is made twice (double entry).

In Chapter 2 we drew up a new balance sheet after each transaction. You could do this easily if you had only a few transactions per day, but if there were hundreds of transactions each day it would become impossible for you to draw up hundreds of different balance sheets. You simply would not have enough time.

The double entry system has an **account** (meaning details of transactions in that item) for every asset, every liability and for capital. Thus there will be a shop premises account (for transactions in shop premises), a motor vans account (for transactions in motor vans), and so on for every asset, liability and for capital.

3.2 The Accounts for Double Entry

Each account should be shown on a separate page. The double entry system divides each page into two halves. The left-hand side of each page is called the **debit** side, while the right-hand side is called the **credit** side. The title of each account is written across the top of the account at the centre.

You must not think that the words 'debit' and 'credit' in book-keeping mean the same as the words 'debit' and 'credit' in normal language. If you do, you will become very confused.

This is a page of an accounts book:

Title of account written here	
Left-hand side of the page. This is the 'debit' side.	Right-hand side of the page. This is the 'credit' side.

If you have to make an entry of £10 on the debit side of the account, the instructions could say 'debit the account with £10' or 'the account needs debiting with £10'.

In Chapter 2 transactions were to increase or decrease assets, liabilities or capital. Double entry rules for accounts are:

Accounts	To record	Entry in the account
Assets	an increase a decrease	Debit Credit
Liabilities	an increase a decrease	Credit Debit
Capital	an increase a decrease	Credit Debit

Let us look once again at the accounting equation:

	Assets =	Liabilities and	Capital
To increase each item	Debit	Credit	Credit
To decrease each item	Credit	Debit	Debit

The double entry rules for liabilities and capital are the same, but they are the opposite of those for assets. This is because assets are on the opposite side of the equation and, therefore, follow opposite rules. Looking at the accounts the rules will appear as:

Any asset account		*Any liability account*		*Capital account*	
Increases	*Decreases*	*Decreases*	*Increases*	*Decreases*	*Increases*
+	−	−	+	−	+

We have not enough space in this book to put each account on a separate page, so we will have to list the accounts under each other. In a real firm at least one full page would be taken for each account.

3.3 Worked Examples

The entry of a few transactions can now be attempted:

1 The proprietor starts the firm with £1,000 in cash on 1 August 19–6.

Effect	Action
1 Increases the *asset* of cash 2 Increases the capital	Debit the cash account Credit the capital account

These are entered:

Cash

19–6		£		
Aug 1		1,000		

Capital

		19–6		£
		Aug 1		1,000

The date of the transaction has already been entered. Now there remains the description which is to be entered alongside the amount. The double entry to the item in the cash account is completed by an entry in the capital account, therefore the word 'Capital' will appear in the cash account. Similarly, the double entry to the item in the capital account is completed by an entry in the cash account, therefore the word 'Cash' will appear in the capital account.

The finally completed accounts are therefore:

Cash

19–6		£		
Aug 1	Capital	1,000		

Capital

		19–6		£
		Aug 1	Cash	1,000

This method of entering transactions therefore fulfils the requirements of the double entry rules as shown on page 13. Now let us look at the entry of some more transactions.

2 A motor van is bought for £275 cash on 2 August 19–6.

Effect	Action
1 Decreases the *asset* of cash	Credit the cash account
2 Increases the *asset* of motor van	Debit the motor van account

Cash

		19–6		£
		Aug 2	Motor van	275

Motor van

19–6	£		
Aug 2 Cash	275		

3 Fixtures bought on credit from Shop Fitters for £115 on 3 August 19–6.

Effect	Action
1 Increases the *asset* of fixtures	Debit the fixtures account
2 Increases the *liability* to Shop Fitters	Credit the Shop Fitters account

Fixtures

19–6	£		
Aug 3 Shop Fitters	115		

Shop Fitters

		19–6	£
		Aug 3 Fixtures	115

4 Paid the amount owing in cash to Shop Fitters on 17 August 19–6.

Effect	Action
1 Decreases the *asset* of cash	Credit the cash account
2 Decreases the *liability* to Shop Fitters	Debit the Shop Fitters account

Cash

		19–6	£
		Aug 17 Shop Fitters	115

Shop Fitters

19–6	£		
Aug 17 Cash	115		

5 Transactions to date.
Taking the transactions numbered **1** to **4** above, the records will now appear:

Cash

19–6	£	19–6	£
Aug 1 Capital	1,000	Aug 2 Motor van	275
		" 17 Shop Fitters	115

Capital

			19–6	£
			Aug 1 Cash	1,000

Motor van

19–6	£			
Aug 2 Cash	275			

Shop Fitters

19–6	£		19–6	£
Aug 17 Cash	115		Aug 3 Fixtures	115

Fixtures

19–6	£			
Aug 3 Shop Fitters	115			

Before you read further you are required to work through questions 3.1 and 3.2.

3.4 A Further Worked Example

Now you have actually made some entries in accounts you are to go carefully through the following example. Make certain you can understand every entry.

Transactions			Effect		Action
19–4					
May	1	Started an engineering business putting £1,000 into a business bank account.	↑	Increases *asset* of bank.	Debit bank account.
			↑	Increases *capital* of owner.	Credit capital account
"	3	Bought works machinery on credit from Unique Machines £275.	↑	Increases *asset* of machinery.	Debit machinery account.
			↑	Increases *liability* to Unique Machines.	Credit Unique Machines account.
"	4	Withdrew £200 cash from the bank and placed it in the cash box.	↓	Decreases *asset* of bank.	Credit bank account.
			↑	Increases *asset* of cash.	Debit cash account.
"	7	Bought a motor van paying in cash £180.	↓	Decreases *asset* of cash.	Credit cash account.
			↑	Increases *asset* of motor van.	Debit motor van account.
"	10	Sold some of the machinery for £15 on credit to B Barnes	↓	Decreases *asset* of machinery.	Credit machinery account.
			↑	Increases *asset* of money owing from B Barnes.	Debit B Barnes account.
"	21	Returned some of the machinery, value £27 to Unique Machines.	↓	Decreases *asset* of machinery.	Credit machinery account.
			↓	Decreases *liability* to Unique Machines.	Debit Unique Machines.
"	28	B Barnes pays the firm the amount owing, £15, by cheque.	↑	Increases *asset* of bank.	Debit bank account.
			↓	Decreases *asset* of money owing by B Barnes.	Credit B Barnes account.
"	30	Bought another motor van paying by cheque £420.	↓	Decreases *asset* of bank.	Credit bank account.
			↑	Increases *asset* of motor vans.	Debit motor van account.
"	31	Paid the amount of £248 to Unique Machines by cheque.	↓	Decreases *asset* of bank.	Credit bank account.
			↓	Decreases *liability* to Unique Machines.	Debit Unique Machines.

In account form this is shown as:

Bank

19–4		£	19–4		£
May	1 Capital	1,000	May	4 Cash	200
"	28 B Barnes	15	"	30 Motor van	420
				Unique Machines	248

Cash

19–4	£	19–4	£
May 4 Bank	200	May 7 Motor van	180

Capital

		19–4	£
		May 1 Bank	1,000

Machinery

19–4	£	19–4	£
May 3 Unique Machines	275	May 10 B Barnes	15
		" 21 Unique Machines	27

Motor van

19–4	£		
May 7 Cash	180		
" 30 Bank	420		

Unique Machines

19–4	£	19–4	£
May 21 Machinery	27	May 3 Machinery	275
" 31 Bank	248		

B Barnes

19–4	£	19–4	£
May 10 Machinery	15	May 28 Bank	15

3.5 Abbreviation of 'Limited'

In this book when we come across transactions with limited companies the letters 'Ltd' are used as the abbreviation for 'Limited Company'. So we will know that if we see the name of a firm as T Lee Ltd, then that firm will be a limited company. In our books the transactions with T Lee Ltd will be entered the same as for any other customer or supplier.

New Terms

Double Entry Book-keeping (p 12): A system where each transaction is entered twice, once on the debit side and once on the credit side.

Account (p 12): Part of double entry records, containing details of transactions for a specific item.

Debit (p 12): The left-hand side of the accounts in double entry.

Credit (p 12): The right-hand side of the accounts in double entry.

Exercises

3.1 Complete the following table showing which accounts are to be credited and which to be debited:

	Account to be debited	Account to be credited
(a) Bought motor van for cash		
(b) Bought office machinery on credit from J Grant & Son		
(c) Introduced capital in cash		
(d) A debtor, J Beach, pays us by cheque		
(e) Paid a creditor, A Barrett, in cash.		

3.2 The following table is also to be completed, showing the accounts to be debited and credited:

	Account to be debited	Account to be credited
(a) Bought machinery on credit from A Jackson & Son		
(b) Returned machinery to A Jackson & Son		
(c) A debtor, J Brown, pays us in cash		
(d) J Smith lends us money, giving it to us by cheque		
(e) Sold office machinery for cash.		

3.3X Complete the following table:

Account to be debited	Account to be credited

(*a*) Bought office machinery on credit from D Isaacs Ltd
(*b*) The proprietor paid a creditor, C Jones, from his private monies outside the firm
(*c*) A debtor, N Fox, paid us in cash
(*d*) Repaid part of loan from P Exeter by cheque
(*e*) Returned some of office machinery to D Isaacs Ltd
(*f*) A debtor, N Lyn, pays us by cheque
(*g*) Bought motor van by cash.

3.4X Complete the following table showing which accounts are to be debited and which to be credited:

Account to be debited	Account to be credited

(*a*) Bought motor lorry for cash
(*b*) Paid creditor, T Lake, by cheque
(*c*) Repaid P Logan's loan by cash
(*d*) Sold motor lorry for cash
(*e*) Bought office machinery on credit from Ultra Ltd
(*f*) A debtor, A Hill, pays us by cash
(*g*) A debtor, J Cross, pays us by cheque
(*h*) Proprietor puts a further amount into the business by cheque
(*i*) A loan of £200 in cash is received from L Lowe
(*j*) Paid a creditor, D Lord, by cash.

3.5 Write up the asset and liability accounts in the records of D Coy to record these transactions:

19–2
May 1 Started business with £1,000 cash
" 3 Bought a motor lorry on credit from Speed & Sons for £698
" 14 Bought office machinery by cash for £60
" 31 Paid Speed & Sons the amount owing to them, £698, in cash.

3.6 Write up the asset and liability and capital accounts to record the following transactions in the records of G Powell.

19–3
July 1 Started business with £2,500 in the bank
" 2 Bought office furniture by cheque £150
" 3 Bought machinery £750 on credit from Planers Ltd
" 5 Bought a motor van paying by cheque £600
" 8 Sold some of the office furniture—not suitable for the firm—for £60 on credit to J Walker & Sons
" 15 Paid the amount owing to Planers Ltd £750 by cheque
" 23 Received the amount due from J Walker £60 in cash
" 31 Bought more machinery by cheque £280.

3.7X You are required to open the asset and liability and capital accounts and record the following transactions for June 19–4 in the records of C Williams.

19–4
June 1 Started business with £2,000 in cash.
" 2 Paid £1,800 of the opening cash into a bank account for the business
" 5 Bought office furniture on credit from Betta-Built Ltd for £120
" 8 Bought a motor van paying by cheque £950
" 12 Bought works machinery from Evans & Sons on credit £560
" 18 Returned faulty office furniture costing £62 to Betta-Built Ltd
" 25 Sold some of the works machinery for £75 cash
" 26 Paid amount owing to Betta-Built Ltd £58 by cheque
" 28 Took £100 out of the bank and put it in the cash till
" 30 J Smith lent us £500 – giving us the money by cheque.

3.8 Write up the asset, capital and liability accounts in the books of C Walsh to record the following transactions:

19–5
June 1 Started business with £5,000 in the bank
" 2 Bought motor van paying by cheque £1,200
" 5 Bought office fixtures £400 on credit from Young Ltd
" 8 Bought motor van on credit from Super Motors £800
" 12 Took £100 out of the bank and put it into the cash till
" 15 Bought office fixtures paying by cash £60
" 19 Paid Super Motors a cheque for £800
" 21 A loan of £1,000 cash is received from J Jarvis
" 25 Paid £800 of the cash in hand into the bank account
" 30 Bought more office fixtures paying by cheque £300.

3.9X Write up the various accounts needed in the books of S Russell to record the following transactions:

19–4
April 1 Opened business with £10,000 in the bank
" 3 Bought office equipment £700 on credit from J Saunders Ltd
" 6 Bought motor van paying by cheque £3,000
" 8 Borrowed £1,000 from H Thompson – he gave us the money by cheque
" 11 Russell put further capital into the firm in the form of cash £500
" 12 Paid £350 of the cash in hand into the bank account
" 15 Returned some of the office equipment costing £200 – it was faulty – to J Saunders Ltd
" 17 Bought more office equipment, paying by cash £50
" 19 Sold the motor van, as it had proved unsuitable, to R Jones for £3,000. R Jones will settle for this by three payments later this month
" 21 Received a loan in cash from J Hawkins £400
" 22 R Jones paid us a cheque for £1,000
" 23 Bought a suitable motor van £3,600 on credit from Phillips Garages
" 26 R Jones paid us a cheque for £1,800
" 28 Paid £2,000 by cheque to Phillips Garages Ltd
" 30 R Jones paid us cash £200.

4 · The Asset of Stock

4.1 Stock Movements

The stock of goods in a business is constantly changing because some of it is bought, some of it is sold, some is returned to the suppliers and some is returned by the firm's customers.

To keep a check on the movement of stock, an account is opened for each type of dealing in goods. Thus we will have the following accounts:

Account	Reason
Purchases Account	For the purchase of goods
Sales Account	For the sale of goods
Returns Inwards Account	For goods returned to the firm by its customers
Returns Outwards Account	For goods returned by the firm to its suppliers

As stock is an asset, and these four accounts are all connected with this asset, the double entry rules are those used for assets.

We shall now look at some entries in the following sections.

4.2 Purchase of Stock on Credit

1 August 19–4. Goods costing £165 are bought on credit from D Henry.

First, the twofold effect of the transaction must be considered so that the book-keeping entries can be worked out.

1 The asset of stock is increased. An increase in an asset needs a debit entry in an account. Here the account is a stock account showing the particular movement of stock, in this case it is the 'purchases' movement so that the account must be the purchases account.

2 An increase in a liability. This is the liability of the firm to D Henry because the goods bought have not yet been paid for. An increase in a liability needs a credit entry, so that to enter this part of the transaction a credit entry is made in D Henry's account.

Purchases

19–4	£			
Aug 1 D Henry	165			

D Henry

			19–4	£
			Aug 1 Purchases	165

4.3 Purchases of Stock for Cash

2 August 19–4. Goods costing £22 are bought, cash being paid for them immediately.

1 The asset of stock is increased, so that a debit entry will be needed. The movement of stock is that of a purchase, so that it is the purchases account which needs dcbiting.

2 The asset of cash is decreased. To reduce an asset a credit entry is called for, and the asset is that of cash so that the cash account needs crediting.

Cash

			19–4	£
			Aug 2 Purchases	22

Purchases

19–4	£			
Aug 2 Cash	22			

4.4 Sales of Stock on Credit

3 August 19–4. Sold goods on credit for £250 to K Leach.

1 The asset of stock is decreased. For this a credit entry to reduce an asset is needed. The movement of stock is that of 'Sales' so the account credited is the sales account.

2 An asset account is increased. This is the account showing that K Leach is a debtor for the goods. The increase in the asset of debtors requires a debit and the debtor is K Leach, so that the account concerned is that of K Leach.

Sales

			19–4	£
			Aug 3 K Leach	250

K Leach

19–4	£		
Aug 3 Sales	250		

4.5 Sales of Stock for Cash

4 August 19–4. Goods are sold for £55, the cash being received at once upon sale.

1 The asset of cash is increased. A debit in the cash account is needed to show this.

2 The asset of stock is reduced. The reduction of an asset requires a credit and the movement of stock is represented by 'Sales'. So the entry needed is a credit in the sales account.

Sales

		19–4	£
		Aug 4 Cash	55

Cash

19–4	£		
Aug 4 Sales	55		

4.6 Returns Inwards

These represent goods sold which have now been returned. Just as the original sale was entered in a double entry fashion, so also is the return of those goods.

5 August 19–4. Goods which had previously been sold to F Lowe for £29 are now returned by him.

1 The asset of stock is increased by the goods returned. So a debit representing an increase of an asset is needed, and this time the movement of stock is that of 'Returns Inwards'. The entry required therefore is a debit in the returns inwards account.

2 A decrease in an asset. The debt of F Lowe to the firm is now reduced, and to record this a credit is needed in F Lowe's account.

Returns Inwards

19–4	£		
Aug 5 F Lowe	29		

F Lowe

			19–4	£
			Aug 5 Returns inwards	29

An alternative name for a returns inwards account is a sales returns account.

4.7 Returns Outwards

These represent goods which were purchased, and are now being returned to the supplier. As the original purchase was entered in a double entry fashion, so also is the return to the supplier of those goods.

6 August 19–4. Goods previously bought for £96 are returned by the firm to K Howe.

1 The asset of stock is decreased by the goods set out. So a credit representing a reduction in an asset is needed, and the movement of stock is that of 'Returns Outwards' so that the entry will be a credit in the returns outwards account.

2 The liability of the firm to K Howe is decreased by the value of the goods returned to him. The decrease in a liability needs a debit, this time in K Howe's account.

Returns Outwards

			19–4	£
			Aug 6 K Howe	96

K Howe

19–4	£			
Aug 6 Returns outwards	96			

An alternative name for a returns outwards account is a purchases returns account.

4.8 A Worked Example

Enter the following transactions in suitable double entry accounts:

19–5
May 1 Bought goods on credit £68 from D Small
" 2 Bought goods on credit £77 from A Lyon & Son
" 5 Sold goods on credit to D Hughes for £60
" 6 Sold goods on credit to M Spencer for £45
" 10 Returned goods £15 to D Small
" 12 Goods bought for cash £100

" 19 M Spencer returned £16 goods to us
" 21 Goods sold for cash £150
" 22 Paid cash to D Small £53
" 30 D Hughes paid the amount owing by him £60 in cash
" 31 Bought goods on credit £64 from A Lyon & Son.

The double entry accounts can now be shown as:

Purchases

19–5	£		
May 1 D Small	68		
" 2 A Lyon & Son	77		
" 12 Cash	100		
" 31 A Lyon & Son	64		

Sales

		19–5	£
		May 5 D Hughes	60
		" 6 M Spencer	45
		" 21 Cash	150

Returns Outwards

		19–5	£
		May 10 D Small	15

Returns Inwards

19–5	£		
May 19 M Spencer	16		

D Small

19–5	£	19–5	£
May 10 Returns outwards	15	May 1 Purchases	68
" 22 Cash	53		

A Lyon & Son

		19–5	£
		May 2 Purchases	77
		" 31 Purchases	64

D Hughes

	£		£
19–5		19–5	
May 5 Sales	60	May 30 Cash	60

M Spencer

	£		£
19–5		19–5	
May 6 Sales	45	May 19 Returns inwards	16

Cash

	£		£
19–5		19–5	
May 21 Sales	150	May 12 Purchases	100
" 30 D Hughes	60	" 22 D Small	53

4.9 Special Meaning of 'Sales' and 'Purchases'

It must be emphasised that 'Sales' and 'Purchases' have a special meaning in accounting language.

'Purchases' in accounting means *the purchase of those goods which the firm buys with the prime intention of selling*. Sometimes the goods may be altered, added to, or used in the manufacture of something else, but it is the element of *resale* that is important. To a firm that deals in typewriters for instance, typewriters are purchases. If something else is bought, such as a motor van, such an item cannot be called purchases, even though in ordinary language it may be said that a motor van has been purchased. The prime intention of *buying* the motor van is for use by the company and not for resale.

Similarly, 'Sales' means the *sale of those goods in which the firm normally deals and which were bought with the prime intention of resale*. The word 'Sales' must never be given to the disposal of other items.

If we did not keep to these meanings, it would result in the different kinds of stock accounts containing something other than goods sold or for resale.

4.10 Comparison of Cash and Credit Transactions for Purchases and Sales

The difference between the records needed for cash and credit transactions can now be seen.

The complete set of entries for purchases of goods where they are paid for immediately by cash would be:

1 Credit the cash account.

2 Debit the purchases account.

On the other hand the complete set of entries for the purchase of goods on credit can be broken down into two stages. First, the purchase of the goods and second, the payment for them.

The first part is:

1 Debit the purchases account.

2 Credit the supplier's account.

The second part is:

1 Credit the cash account.

2 Debit the supplier's account.

The difference can now be seen; with the cash purchase no record is kept of the supplier's account. This is because cash passes immediately and therefore there is no need to keep a check of indebtedness (money owing) to a supplier. On the other hand, in the credit purchase the records should show to whom money is owed until payment is made.

A study of cash sales and credit sales will reveal a similar difference.

Cash Sales	Credit Sales
Complete entry: Debit cash account Credit sales account	First part: Debit customer's account Credit sales account Second part: Debit cash account Credit customer's account

New Terms

Purchases (p 27): Goods bought by the business for the purpose of selling them again.

Sales (p 27): Goods sold by the business.

Returns Inwards (p 24): Goods returned to the business by its customers.

Returns Outwards (p 25): Goods returned by the business to its suppliers.

Exercises

4.1 Complete the following table showing which accounts are to be credited and which are to be debited:

	Account to be debited	Account to be credited
(a) Goods bought, cash being paid immediately		
(b) Goods bought on credit from E Flynn		
(c) Goods sold on credit to C Grant		
(d) A motor van sold for cash		
(e) Goods sold for cash.		

4.2X Similarly, complete this next table:

	Account to be debited	Account to be credited
(a) Goods returned to H Flynn		
(b) Goods bought on credit from P Franklin		
(c) Goods sold on credit to S Mullings		
(d) M Patterson returns goods to us		
(e) Goods bought being paid for by cheque immediately.		

4.3 Complete the following table showing which accounts are to be credited and which are to be debited:

	Account to be debited	Account to be credited
(a) Goods bought on credit from J Reid		
(b) Goods sold on credit to B Perkins		
(c) Motor vans bought on credit from H Thomas		
(d) Goods sold, a cheque being received immediately		
(e) Goods sold for cash		
(f) Goods we returned to H Hardy		
(g) Machinery sold for cash		
(h) Goods returned to us by J Nelson		
(i) Goods bought on credit from D Simpson		
(j) Goods we returned to H Forbes.		

4.4X Complete the following table:

	Account to be debited	Account to be credited
(a) Goods bought on credit from T Morgan		
(b) Goods returned to us by J Thomas		
(c) Machinery returned to L Jones Ltd		
(d) Goods bought for cash		
(e) Motor van bought on credit from D Davies Ltd		
(f) Goods returned by us to I Prince		
(g) D Picton paid us his account by cheque		
(h) Goods bought by cheque		
(i) We paid creditor, B Henry, by cheque		
(j) Goods sold on credit to J Mullings.		

4.5 You are to write up the following in the books:

19–4
July 1 Started business with £500 cash
" 3 Bought goods for cash £85
" 7 Bought goods on credit £116 from E Morgan
" 10 Sold goods for cash £42
" 14 Returned goods to E Morgan £28
" 18 Bought goods on credit £98 from A Moses
" 21 Returned goods to A Moses £19

" 24 Sold goods to A Knight £55 on credit
" 25 Paid E Morgan's account by cash £88
" 31 A Knight paid us his account in cash £55.

4.6 You are to enter the following in the accounts needed:

19–6
Aug 1 Started business with £1,000 cash
" 2 Paid £900 of the opening cash into the bank
" 4 Bought goods on credit £78 from S Holmes
" 5 Bought a motor van by cheque £500
" 7 Bought goods for cash £55
" 10 Sold goods on credit £98 to D Moore
" 12 Returned goods to S Holmes £18
" 19 Sold goods for cash £28
" 22 Bought fixtures on credit from Kingston Equipment Co £150
" 24 D Watson lent us £100 paying us the money by cheque
" 29 We paid S Holmes his account by cheque £60
" 31 We paid Kingston Equipment Co by cheque £150.

4.7 Enter up the following transactions in the records of E Sangster:

19–7
July 1 Started business with £10,000 in the bank
" 2 T Cooper lent us £400 in cash
" 3 Bought goods on credit from F Jones £840 and S Charles £3,600
" 4 Sold goods for cash £200
" 6 Took £250 of the cash and paid it into the bank
" 8 Sold goods on credit to C Moody £180
" 10 Sold goods on credit to J Newman £220
" 11 Bought goods on credit from F Jones £370
" 12 C Moody returned goods to us £40
" 14 Sold goods on credit to H Morgan £190 and J Peat £320
" 15 We returned goods to F Jones £140
" 17 Bought motor van on credit from Manchester Motors £2,600
" 18 Bought office furniture on credit from Faster Supplies Ltd £600
" 19 We returned goods to S Charles £110
" 20 Bought goods for cash £220
" 24 Goods sold for cash £70
" 25 Paid money owing to F Jones by cheque £1,070
" 26 Goods returned to us by H Morgan £30
" 27 Returned some of office furniture costing £160 to Faster Supplies Ltd
" 28 E Sangster put a further £500 into the business in the form of cash
" 29 Paid Manchester Motors £2,600 by cheque
" 31 Bought office furniture for cash £100.

4.8X Enter up the following transactions in the records:

19–5
May 1 Started business with £2,000 in the bank
" 2 Bought goods on credit from C Shaw £900
" 3 Bought goods on credit from F Hughes £250
" 5 Sold goods for cash £180
" 6 We returned goods to C Shaw £40
" 8 Bought goods on credit from F Hughes £190

″ 10 Sold goods on credit to G Wood £390
″ 12 Sold goods for cash £210
″ 18 Took £300 of the cash and paid it into the bank
″ 21 Bought machinery by cheque £550
″ 22 Sold goods on credit to L Moore £220
″ 23 G Wood returned goods to us £140
″ 25 L Moore returned goods to us £10
″ 28 We returned goods to F Hughes £30
″ 29 We paid Shaw by cheque £860
″ 31 Bought machinery on credit from D Lee £270.

4.9X You are to enter the following in the accounts needed:

June 1 Started business with £1,000 cash
″ 2 Paid £800 of the opening cash into a bank account for the firm
″ 3 Bought goods on credit from H Grant £330
″ 4 Bought goods on credit from D Clark £140
″ 8 Sold goods on credit to B Miller £90
″ 8 Bought office furniture on credit from Barrett's Ltd £400
″ 10 Sold goods for cash £120
″ 13 Bought goods for credit from H Grant £200
″ 14 Bought goods for cash £60
″ 15 Sold goods on credit to H Sharples £180
″ 16 We returned goods £50 to H Grant
″ 17 We returned some of the office furniture £30 to Barrett's Ltd
″ 18 Sold goods on credit to B Miller £400
″ 21 Paid H Grant's account by cheque £480
″ 23 B Miller paid us the amount owing in cash £490
″ 24 Sharples returned to us £50 goods
″ 25 Goods sold for cash £150
″ 28 Bought goods for cash £370
″ 30 Bought motor van on credit from J Kelly £600.

5 · The Double Entry System for Expenses. The Effect of Profit or Loss on Capital

5.1 The Calculation of Capital

On 1 January the assets and liabilities of a firm are:

Assets: Fixtures £10,000, Stock £7,000,
Cash at the bank £3,000.
Liabilities: Creditors £2,000.

The Capital is found by the formula

Assets – Liabilities = Capital

In this case capital works out at £10,000 + £7,000 + £3,000 – £2,000 = £18,000.

During January the whole of the £7,000 stock is sold for £11,000 cash. On 31 January the assets and liabilities have become:

Assets: Fixtures £10,000, Stock nil, Cash at the bank £14,000.
Liabilities: Creditors £2,000.

The capital can be calculated:

Assets £10,000 + £14,000 – liabilities £2,000 = £22,000

It can be seen that capital has increased from £18,000 to £22,000 = £4,000 increase because the £7,000 stock was sold for £11,000, a profit of £4,000. Profit, therefore, increases capital.

Old Capital + Profit = New Capital
£18,000 + £4,000 = £22,000

On the other hand a loss would reduce the capital so that it would become:

Old Capital – Loss = New Capital

5.2 Profit or Loss and Sales

Profit will be made when goods are sold at more than cost price, while the opposite will mean a **loss**.

5.3 Profit or Loss and Expenses

While the firm is selling its goods there will be other **expenses** on top of the cost of the goods being sold. Every firm has other expenses such as rent, salaries, wages, telephone expenses, motor expenses and so on. Every extra £1 of expenses will mean £1 less profit.

It would be possible simply to have one account with the title 'Expenses Account'. However, rather than just know that the total expenses were £50,000 it would be more useful if we knew exactly how much of that figure was for rent, how much for motor expenses and so on. An expense account is, therefore, opened for each type of expense.

5.4 Debit or Credit

We have to decide whether expense accounts are to be debited or credited with the costs involved. Assets involve expenditure by the firm and are shown as debit entries. Expenses also involve expenditure by the firm and therefore should also be debit entries.

An alternative explanation may also be used for expenses. Every expense results in a decrease in an asset or an increase in a liability, and because of the accounting equation this means that the capital is reduced by each expense. The decrease of capital needs a debit entry and therefore expense accounts contain debit entries for expenses.

5.5 Effect of Transactions

A few illustrations will demonstrate the double entry required.

1 The rent of £20 is paid in cash.
Here the twofold effect is:
(a) The asset of cash is decreased. This means crediting the cash account to show the decrease of the asset.
(b) The total of the expenses of rent is increased. As expense entries are shown as debits, and the expense is rent, so the action required is the debiting of the rent account.

Summary: Credit the cash account with £20.
Debit the rent account with £20.

2 Motor expenses are paid with a cheque for £55.
The twofold effect is:
(a) The asset of money in the bank is decreased. This means crediting the bank account to show the decrease of the asset.
(b) The total of the motor expenses paid is increased. To increase an expenses

account needs a debit, so the action required is to debit the motor expenses account.

Summary: Credit the bank account with £55.
Debit the motor expenses account with £55.

3 £60 cash is paid for telephone expenses.

(a) The asset of cash is decreased. This needs a credit in the cash account to decrease the asset.

(b) The total of telephone expenses is increased. Expenses are shown by a debit entry, therefore to increase the expense account in question the action required is to debit the telephone expenses account.

Summary: Credit the cash account with £60.
Debit telephone expenses account with £60.

It is now possible to study the effects of some more transactions showing the results in the form of a table:

		Increase	Action	Decrease	Action
19–6 June 1	Paid for postage stamps by cash £5	Expense of postages	Debit postages account	Asset of cash	Credit cash account
2	Paid for advertising by cheque £29	Expense of advertising	Debit advertising account	Asset of bank	Credit bank account
3	Paid wages by cash £90	Expense of wages	Debit wages account	Asset of cash	Credit cash account
4	Paid insurance by cheque £42	Expense of insurance	Debit insurance account	Asset of bank	Credit bank account

The above four examples can now be shown in account form:

Cash

	19–6			£
	June	1	Postages	5
		3	Wages	90

Bank

	19–6			£
	June	2	Advertising	29
	"	4	Insurance	42

Advertising

19–6	£		
June 2 Bank	29		

Insurance

19–6	£		
June 4 Bank	42		

Postages

19–6	£		
June 1 Cash	5		

Wages

19–6	£		
June 3 Cash	90		

Sometimes the owner will want to take cash out of the business for his private use. These are known as **drawings**. Any money taken out as drawings will reduce capital.

The capital account is a very important account. To help to stop it getting full of small details, each item of drawings is not entered in the capital account. Instead a drawings account is opened, and the debits are entered there.

The following example illustrates the entries for drawings.

5.6 A Worked Example

25 August 19–6. Proprietor takes £50 cash out of the business for his own use.

Effect	Action
1 Capital is decreased by £50	Debit the drawings account £50
2 Cash is decreased by £50	Credit the cash account £50

Cash

		19–6	£
		Aug 25 Drawings	50

Drawings

19–6	£		
Aug 25 Cash	50		

Sometimes goods are also taken for private use. These are also known as drawings. Entries for such transactions will be described later in the book.

New Terms

Profit (p 32): Result of selling goods for more than they cost.

Expenses (p 33): Costs of operating the business.

Drawings (p 35): Cash or goods taken out of a business by the owner for his private use.

Exercises

5.1 Complete the following table, showing the accounts to be debited and those to be credited:

	Account to be debited	Account to be credited
(a) Paid rates by cheque.		
(b) Paid wages by cash.		
(c) Rent received by cheque.		
(d) Received by cheque refund of insurance previously paid.		
(e) Paid general expenses by cash.		

5.2 Complete the following table:

	Account to be debited	Account to be credited
(a) Paid rent by cash.		
(b) Paid for goods by cash.		
(c) Received by cheque a refund of rates already paid.		
(d) Paid general expenses by cheque.		
(e) Received commissions in cash.		
(f) Goods returned by us to T Jones.		
(g) Goods sold for cash.		
(h) Bought office fixtures by cheque.		
(i) Paid wages in cash.		
(j) Took cash out of business for private use.		

5.3X Complete the following table, showing the accounts to be debited and those to be credited:

	Account to be debited	Account to be credited
(a) Paid insurance by cheque.		
(b) Paid motor expenses by cash.		
(c) Rent received in cash.		
(d) Paid rates by cheque.		
(e) Received refund of rates by cheque.		
(f) Paid for stationery expenses by cash.		
(g) Paid wages by cash.		
(h) Sold surplus stationery receiving proceeds by cheque.		
(i) Received sales commission by cheque.		
(j) Bought motor van by cheque.		

5.4X The following table should be completed:

	Account to be debited	Account to be credited
(a) Sold surplus stationery, receiving proceeds in cash.		
(b) Paid salaries by cheque.		
(c) Rent received for premises sub-let, by cheque.		
(d) Goods returned to us by Royal Products.		
(e) Commission received by us previously in error, we now refund this by cheque.		
(f) Bought machinery by cheque.		
(g) Paid lighting expenses in cash.		
(h) Insurance rebate received by cheque.		
(i) Buildings bought by cheque.		
(j) Building repairs paid in cash.		

5.5 Enter the following transactions in the necessary accounts in double entry:

19–8
Jan 1 Started business with £200 in the bank
" 2 U Surer lent us £1,000 giving us the money by cheque
" 3 Bought goods on credit £296 from T Parkin
" 5 Bought motor van by cheque £250
" 6 Cash sales £105
" 7 Paid motor expenses in cash £15
" 8 Paid wages in cash £18
" 10 Bought goods on credit from C Moore £85
" 12 Paid insurance by cheque £22
" 25 Received commission in cash £15
" 31 Paid electricity bill by cheque £17.

5.6 You are to enter the following transactions, completing double entry in the books for the month of May 19–7:

19–7
May 1 Started business with £2,000 in the bank
" 2 Purchased goods £175 on credit from M Mills

″ 3 Bought fixtures and fittings £150 paying by cheque
″ 5 Sold goods for cash £275
″ 6 Bought goods on credit £114 from S Waites
″ 10 Paid rent by cash £15
″ 12 Bought stationery £27, paying by cash
″ 18 Goods returned to M Mills £23
″ 21 Let off part of the premises receiving rent by cheque £5
″ 23 Sold goods on credit to U Henry for £77
″ 24 Bought a motor van paying by cheque £300
″ 30 Paid the month's wages by cash £117
″ 31 The proprietor took cash for himself £44.

5.7 Write up the following transactions in the books of L Thompson:

19–8
March 1 Started business with cash £1,500
″ 2 Bought goods on credit from A Hanson £296
″ 3 Paid rent by cash £28
″ 4 Paid £1,000 of the cash of the firm into a bank account
″ 5 Sold goods on credit to E Linton £54
″ 7 Bought stationery £15 paying by cheque
″ 11 Cash sales £49
″ 14 Goods returned by us to A Hanson £17
″ 17 Sold goods on credit to S Morgan £29
″ 20 Paid for repairs to the building by cash £18
″ 22 E Linton returned goods to us £14
″ 27 Paid Hanson by cheque £279
″ 28 Cash purchases £125
″ 29 Bought a motor van paying by cheque £395
″ 30 Paid motor expenses in cash £15
″ 31 Bought fixtures £120 on credit from A Webster.

5.8X Enter the following transactions in double entry:

July 1 Started business with £8,000 in the bank
″ 2 Bought stationery by cheque £30
″ 3 Bought goods on credit from I Walsh £900
″ 4 Sold goods for cash £180
″ 5 Paid insurance by cash £40
″ 7 Bought machinery on credit from H Morgan £500
″ 8 Paid for machinery expenses by cheque £50
″ 10 Sold goods on credit to D Small £320
″ 11 Returned goods to I Walsh £70
″ 14 Paid wages by cash £70
″ 17 Paid rent by cheque £100
″ 20 Received cheque £200 from D Small
″ 21 Paid H Morgan by cheque £500
″ 23 Bought stationery on credit from Express Ltd £80
″ 25 Sold goods on credit to N Thomas £230
″ 28 Received rent £20 in cash for part of premises sub-let
″ 31 Paid Express Ltd by cheque £80.

5.9X You are to enter the following transactions, completing double entry in the records of J Collins for the month of June 19–5:

June 1 Started business with £10,000 in the bank and £300 cash
" 1 Bought goods on credit from: J Carby £400; F McIntyre £1,188; C Morrison £1,344
" 2 Bought shop fittings by cheque £240
" 3 Bought shop fittings on credit from M Johnson Ltd £575
" 5 Paid insurance by cash £88
" 6 Bought motor van paying by cheque £3,200
" 7 Sold goods for cash £140
" 7 Sold goods on credit to: W Graham & Co £450; F Phillips Ltd £246; D R Edwards £80
" 8 Bought office stationery £180 on credit from D Ball & Co
" 9 Paid rent by cheque £75.
" 10 Paid rates by cheque £250
" 11 We returned goods to F McIntyre £168
" 12 Paid D Ball & Co £180 by cheque
" 13 Sold goods on credit to K P Prince & Co £220; F Phillips Ltd £154; Kay & Edwards Ltd £270
" 14 Goods returned to us by W Graham & Co £40
" 15 Paid wages by cash £120
" 16 Loan from D Clayton by cheque £500
" 17 W Graham & Co paid us the amount owing by cheque £410
" 18 Some of stationery was bought unwisely. We sell it for cash £15
" 20 We had overpaid insurance. A refund of £8 received by cheque
" 21 Paid motor expenses by cash £55.
" 23 Paid wages by cash £120
" 25 Cheques received from K P Prince & Co £220; F Phillips Ltd £100 (as part payment)
" 26 Some of shop fittings were unsuitable and were returned to M Johnson Ltd £25
" 28 Paid F McIntyre £1,188, rent £75
" 30 J Collins took drawings by cheque £200.

6 · Balancing off Accounts

6.1 Accounts for Debtors

Where Debtors Have Paid Their Accounts

What you have been reading so far is the recording of transactions in the books by means of debit and credit entries. At the end of each period we will have to look at each account to see what is shown by the entries.

Probably the most obvious reason for this is to find out how much our customers owe us for goods we have sold to them. In most firms this is done at the end of each month. Let us look at the account of one of our customers, K Tandy, for transactions in August 19–6:

K Tandy

19–6	£	19–6	£
Aug 1 Sales	144	Aug 22 Bank	144
Aug 19 Sales	300	Aug 28 Bank	300

This shows that during the month we sold a total of £444 goods to Tandy, and have been paid a total of £444 by him. At the close of business at the end of August he therefore owes us nothing. His account can be closed off on 31 August 19–6 by inserting the totals on each side, as follows:

K Tandy

19–6	£	19–6	£
Aug 1 Sales	144	Aug 22 Bank	144
Aug 19 Sales	300	Aug 28 Bank	300
	444		444

Notice that totals in accounting are shown with a single line above them, and a double line underneath. Totals on accounts at the end of a period are always shown on a level with one another, as shown in the following completed account for C Lee.

C Lee

19–6	£	19–6	£
Aug 11 Sales	177	Aug 30 Bank	480
Aug 19 Sales	203		
Aug 22 Sales	100		
	480		480

In this account, C Lee also owed us nothing at the end of August 19–6, as he had paid us for all sales to him.

If an account contains only one entry on each side and they are equal, totals are unnecessary. For example:

K Wood

19–6	£	19–6	£
Aug 6 Sales	214	Aug 12 Bank	214

Where Debtors Still Owe For Goods

On the other hand, some of our customers will still owe us something at the end of the month. In these cases the totals of each side would not equal one another. Let us look at the account of D Knight for August 19–6:

D Knight

19–6	£	19–6	£
Aug 1 Sales	158	Aug 28 Bank	158
Aug 15 Sales	206		
Aug 30 Sales	118		

If you add the figures you will see that the debit side adds up to £482 and the credit side adds up to £158. You should be able to see what the difference of £324 (i.e. £482 – £158) represents. It consists of sales of £206 and £118 not paid for and therefore owing to us on 31 August 19–6.

In double entry we only enter figures as totals if the totals on both sides of the account agree. We do, however, want to close off the account for August, but showing that Knight owes us £324. If he owes £324 at close of business on 31 August 19–6 then he will still owe us that same figure when the business opens on 1 September 19–6.

We show this by **balancing the account**. This is done in five stages:

1 Add up both sides to find out their totals. Do not write anything in the account at this stage.
2 Deduct the smaller total from the larger total to find the balance.
3 Now enter the balance on the side with the smallest total. This now means the totals will be equal.

4 Enter totals on a level with each other.
5 Now enter the balance on the line below the totals. The balance below the totals should be on the opposite side to the balance shown above the totals.

Against the balance above the totals, complete the date column by showing the last day of that period. Below the totals show the first day of the next period against the balance. The balance above the totals is described as balance *carried down*. The balance below the total is described as balance *brought down*.

Knight's account when 'balanced off' will appear as follows:

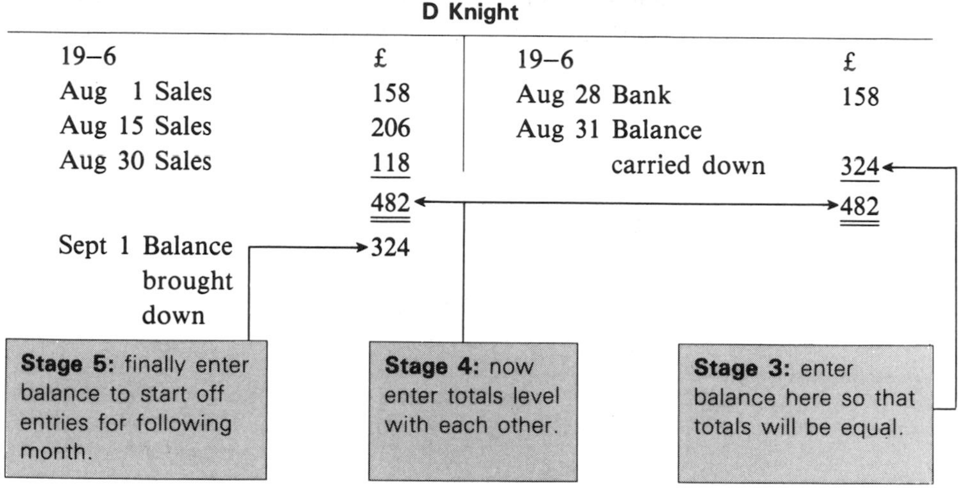

D Knight

19–6	£	19–6	£
Aug 1 Sales	158	Aug 28 Bank	158
Aug 15 Sales	206	Aug 31 Balance carried down	324
Aug 30 Sales	118		
	482		482
Sept 1 Balance brought down	324		

We can now look at another account prior to balancing:

H Henry

19–6	£	19–6	£
Aug 5 Sales	300	Aug 24 Returns inwards	50
Aug 28 Sales	540	Aug 29 Bank	250

We will abbreviate 'carried down' to 'c/d' and 'brought down' to 'b/d' from now on.

H Henry

19–6	£	19–6	£
Aug 5 Sales	300	Aug 24 Returns inwards	50
Aug 28 Sales	540	Aug 29 Bank	250
		Aug 31 Balance c/d	540
	840		840
Sept 1 Balance b/d	540		

Notes:

- The date given to balance c/d is the last day of the period which is finishing, and balance b/d is given the opening date of the next period.
- As the total of the debit side originally exceeded the total of the credit side, the balance is said to be a debit balance. This being a personal account (for a person), the person concerned is said to be a debtor – the accounting term for anyone who owes money to the firm. The use of the term debtor for a person whose account has a debit balance can again thus be seen.

If accounts contain only one entry it is unnecessary to enter the total. A double line ruled under the entry will mean that the entry is its own total. For example:

B Walters

19–6	£	19–6	£
Aug 18 Sales	51	Aug 31 Balance c/d	51
Sept 1 Balance b/d	51		

6.2 Account for Creditors

Exactly the same principles will apply when the balances are carried down to the credit side. We can look at two accounts of our suppliers which are to be balanced off.

E Williams

19–6	£	19–6	£
Aug 21 Bank	100	Aug 2 Purchases	248
		Aug 18 Purchases	116

K Patterson

19–6	£	19–6	£
Aug 14 Returns outwards	20	Aug 8 Purchases	620
Aug 28 Bank	600	Aug 15 Purchases	200

We now add up the totals and find the balance, i.e. stages 1 and 2.

When balanced these will appear as:

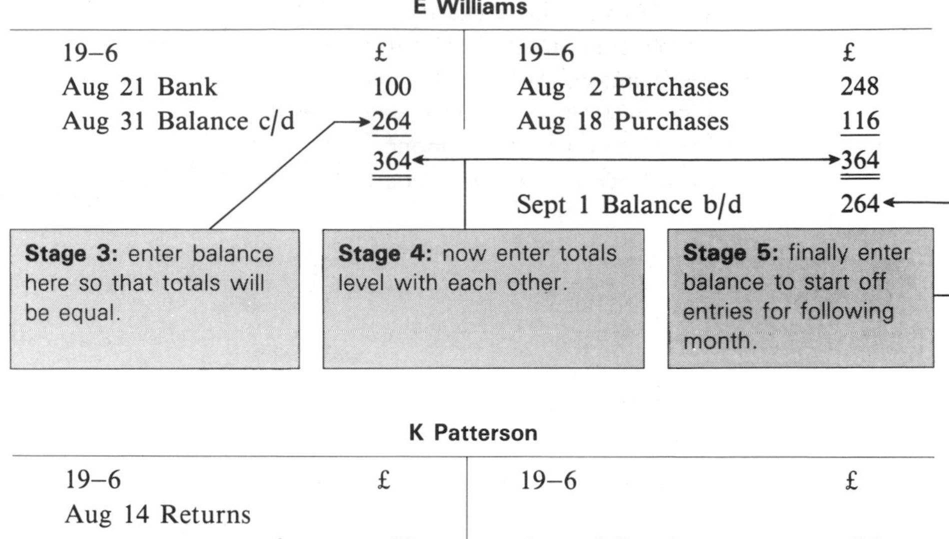

E Williams

19–6	£	19–6	£
Aug 21 Bank	100	Aug 2 Purchases	248
Aug 31 Balance c/d	264	Aug 18 Purchases	116
	364		364
		Sept 1 Balance b/d	264

K Patterson

19–6	£	19–6	£
Aug 14 Returns outwards	20	Aug 8 Purchases	620
Aug 28 Bank	600	Aug 15 Purchases	200
Aug 31 Balance c/d	200		
	820		820
		Sept 1 Balance b/d	200

The type of accounts which have been demonstrated so far are often known as *T accounts*. This is because the accounts are in the shape of a T, as now illustrated.

Account title here – the top stroke of the T

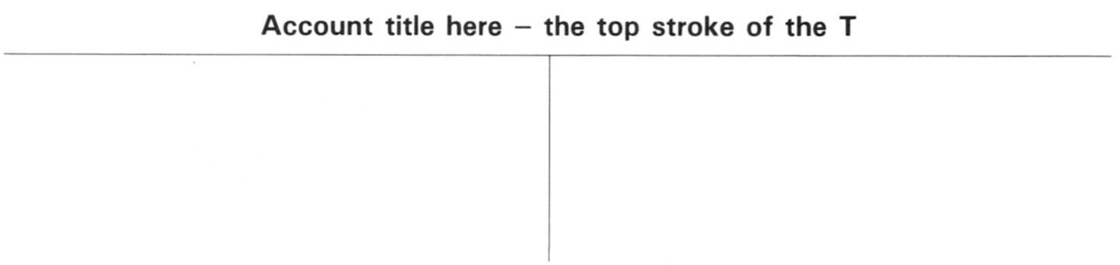

This line divides the two sides and is the downstroke of the T.

Before you read further attempt exercises 6.1, 6.2 and 6.3 on pages 46–47.

6.3 Computers and Accounts

Through the main part of this book the type of account used shows the left-hand side of the account as the debit side, and the right-hand side as the credit side. However, when most computers are used the style of the ledger account is different. It appears as three columns of figures, there being one column for debit entries, another column for credit entries, and the last column for the balance. If you have a current account at a bank your bank statements will normally be shown using this method.

The accounts used in this chapter will now be re-drafted to show the ledger accounts drawn up in this way.

K Tandy

	Debit	*Credit*	*Balance* (and whether debit or credit)
19–6	£	£	£
Aug 1 Sales	144		144 Dr
Aug 19 Sales	300		444 Dr
Aug 22 Bank		144	300 Dr
Aug 28 Bank		300	0

C Lee

	Debit	*Credit*	*Balance*
19–6	£	£	£
Aug 11 Sales	177		177 Dr
Aug 19 Sales	203		380 Dr
Aug 22 Sales	100		480 Dr
Aug 30 Bank		480	0

K Wood

	Debit	*Credit*	*Balance*
19–6	£	£	£
Aug 6 Sales	214		214 Dr
Aug 12 Bank		214	0

D Knight

	Debit	*Credit*	*Balance*
19–6	£	£	£
Aug 1 Sales	158		158 Dr
Aug 15 Sales	206		364 Dr
Aug 28 Cash		158	206 Dr
Aug 31 Sales	118		324 Dr

H Henry

	Debit	*Credit*	*Balance*
19–6	£	£	£
Aug 5 Sales	300		300 Dr
Aug 24 Returns		50	250 Dr
Aug 28 Sales	540		790 Dr
Aug 29 Bank		250	540 Dr

B Walters

	Debit	Credit	Balance
19–6	£	£	£
Aug 18 Sales	51		51 Dr

E Williams

	Debit	Credit	Balance
19–6	£	£	£
Aug 2 Purchases		248	248 Cr
Aug 18 Purchases		116	364 Cr
Aug 21 Bank	100		264 Cr

K Patterson

	Debit	Credit	Balance
19–6	£	£	£
Aug 8 Purchases		620	620 Cr
Aug 14 Returns	20		600 Cr
Aug 15 Purchases		200	800 Cr
Aug 28 Bank	600		200 Cr

It will be noticed that the balance is calculated again after every entry. This can be done quite simply when using a computer because it is the machine which calculates the new balance.

However, when manual methods are being used it is often too much work to have to calculate a new balance after each entry. It also means that the greater the number of calculations the greater the possibility of errors. For these reasons it is usual for students to use two-sided accounts. However, it is important to note that there is no difference in principle, the final balances are the same using either method.

New Terms

Balancing the account (p 41): Finding and entering the difference between the two sides of an account.

Exercises

6.1 Enter the following items in the necessary debtors and creditors accounts only, do *not* write up other accounts. Then balance down each personal account at the end of the month. (Keep your answer, it will be used as a basis for question 6.3.)

19–6
May 1 Sales on credit to H Harvey £690, N Morgan £153, J Lindo £420
" 4 Sales on credit to L Masters £418, H Harvey £66

″ 10 Returns inwards from H Harvey £40, J Lindo £20
″ 18 N Morgan paid us by cheque £153
″ 20 J Lindo paid us £400 by cheque
″ 24 H Harvey paid us £300 by cash
″ 31 Sales on credit to L Masters £203.

6.2 Enter the following in the personal accounts only. Do *not* write up the other accounts. Then balance down each personal account at the end of the month. (Keep your answer, it will be used as the basis of question 6.4X.)

19–8
June 1 Purchases on credit from J Young £458, L Williams £120, G Norman £708
″ 3 Purchases on credit from L Williams £77, T Harris £880
″ 10 We returned goods to G Norman £22, J Young £55
″ 15 Purchases on credit from J Young £80
″ 19 We paid T Harris by cheque £880
″ 28 We paid J Young by cash £250
″ 30 We returned goods to L Williams £17.

6.3 Redraft each of the accounts given in your answer to 6.1 in three column ledger style accounts.

6.4X Redraft each of the accounts given in your answer to 6.2 in three column ledger style accounts.

6.5 Enter the following in the personal accounts only, do *not* write up the other accounts. Balance down each personal account at the end of the month. After completing this state which of the balances represent debtors and those which are creditors.

19–4
Sept 1 Sales on credit to D Williams £458, J Moore £235, G Grant £98
″ 2 Purchases on credit A White £77, H Samuels £231, P Owen £65
″ 8 Sales on credit to J Moore £444, F Franklin £249
″ 10 Purchases on credit from H Samuels £12, O Oliver £222
″ 12 Returns inwards from G Grant £9, J Moore £26
″ 17 We returned goods to H Samuels £24, O Oliver £12
″ 20 We paid A White by cheque £77
″ 24 D Williams paid us by cheque £300
″ 26 We paid O Oliver by cash £210
″ 28 D Williams paid us by cash £100
″ 30 F Franklin pays us by cheque £249.

6.6X Enter the following in the necessary personal accounts. Do *not* write up the other accounts. Balance each personal account at the end of the month. (Keep your answer, it will be used as the basis of question 6.8X)

19–4
Aug 1 Sales on credit to L Sterling £445, L Lindo £480, R Spencer £221
″ 4 Goods returned to us by L Sterling £15, R Spencer £33
″ 8 Sales on credit to L Lindo £66, R Spencer £129, L Banks £465
″ 9 We received a cheque for £430 from L Sterling
″ 12 Sales on credit to R Spencer £235, L Banks £777
″ 19 Goods returned to us by L Banks £21, R Spencer £25

″ 22 We received cheques as follows: R Spencer £300, L Lindo £414
″ 31 Sales on credit to L Lindo £887, L Banks £442.

6.7X Enter the following, personal accounts only. Bring down balances at end of the month. After completing this state which of the balances represent debtors and those which are creditors.

19–7
May 1 Credit sales B Flynn £241, R Kelly £29, J Long £887, T Fryer £124
″ 2 Credit purchases from S Wood £148, T DuQuesnay £27, R Johnson £77, G Henriques £108
″ 8 Credit sales to R Kelly £74, J Long £132
″ 9 Credit purchases from T DuQuesnay £142, G Henriques £44
″ 10 Goods returned to us by J Long £17, T Fryer £44
″ 12 Cash paid to us by T Fryer £80
″ 15 We returned goods to S Wood £8, G Henriques £18
″ 19 We received cheques from J Long £500, B Flynn £241
″ 21 We sold goods on credit to B Flynn £44, R Kelly £280
″ 28 We paid by cheque the following: S Wood £140; G Henriques £50; R Johnson £60
″ 31 We returned goods to G Henriques £4.

6.8X Redraft each of the accounts given in your answer to 6.6X in three column style accounts.

7 · The Trial Balance

7.1 Total Debit Entries = Total Credit Entries

You have already seen that the method of book-keeping in use is that of the double entry method. This means:

- For each debit entry there is a credit entry
- For each credit entry there is a debit entry

All the items recorded in all the accounts on the debit side should equal in *total* all the items recorded on the credit side of the books. We need to check that for each debit entry there is also a credit entry. To see if the two totals are equal, usually known as seeing if the two sides of the books 'balance', a **trial balance** may be drawn up at the end of a period.

A form of a trial balance could be drawn up by listing all the accounts and adding together all the debit entries, at the same time adding together all the credit entries. Using the worked exercise on pages 25–27 such a trial balance would appear as below. Note that it could not be drawn up until after all the entries had been made. It will therefore be dated as on 31 May 19–5.

Trial Balance as on 31 May 19–5

	Dr.	*Cr.*
	£	£
Purchases	309	
Sales		255
Returns outwards		15
Returns inwards	16	
D Small	68	68
A Lyon & Son		141
D Hughes	60	60
M Spencer	45	16
Cash	210	153
	708	708

7.2 Total Debit Balances = Total Credit Balances

7.1 was not the normal method of drawing up a trial balance, but it is the easiest to understand at first. Usually, a trial balance is a list of balances only, arranged according to whether they are debit balances or credit balances. If the trial balance on page 49 had been drawn up using the normal balances method it would appear as below.

Trial Balance as on 31 May 19–5

	Dr.	*Cr.*
	£	£
Purchases	309	
Sales		255
Returns outwards		15
Returns inwards	16	
A Lyon & Son		141
M Spencer	29	
Cash	57	
	411	411

Here the two sides also 'balance'. The sums of £68 in D Small's account, £60 in D Hughes' account, £16 in M Spencer's account and £153 in the cash account have however been cancelled out from each side of these accounts by taking only the *balances* instead of *totals*. As equal amounts have been cancelled from each side, £297 in all, the new totals should still equal one another, as in fact they do at £411.

This form of trial balance is the easiest to extract when there are more than a few transactions during the period. Also the balances are either used later when the profits are being calculated, or else appear in a balance sheet. Trial balances, therefore, are not just done to find errors.

7.3 A Worked Example

The following accounts, for K Potter, have been entered up for May 19–1. They have not yet been balanced off.

K Potter's Books

Bank

19–1	£	19–1	£
May 1 Capital	9,000	May 21 Machinery	550
May 30 T Monk	300	May 29 T Wood	860

Cash

19–1	£	19–1	£
May 5 Sales	180	May 30 K Young	170
May 12 Sales	210		

T Wood

19–1	£	19–1	£
May 6 Returns outwards	40	May 2 Purchases	900
May 29 Bank	860		

K Young

19–1	£	19–1	£
May 28 Returns outwards	80	May 3 Purchases	250
May 30 Cash	170	May 18 Purchases	190

T Monk

19–1	£	19–1	£
May 10 Sales	590	May 23 Returns inwards	140
		May 30 Bank	300

C Howe

19–1	£	19–1	£
May 22 Sales	220	May 25 Returns inwards	10

AB Ltd

		19–1	£
		May 31 Machinery	2,700

Capital

		19–1	£
		May 1 Bank	9,000

Purchases

19–1	£		
May 2 T Wood	900		
May 3 K Young	250		
May 18 K Young	190		

Sales

		19–1		£
		May 5 Cash		180
		May 10 T Monk		590
		May 12 Cash		210
		May 22 C Howe		220

Returns Inwards

19–1	£		
May 23 T Monk	140		
May 25 C Howe	10		

Returns Outwards

		19–1	£
		May 6 T Wood	40
		May 28 K Young	80

Machinery

19–1	£		
May 21 Bank	550		
May 31 AB Ltd	2,700		

If the above accounts are balanced off, a trial balance would appear as follows:

K Potter
Trial Balance as on 31 May 19–1

	Dr	*Cr*
	£	£
Bank	7,890	
Cash	220	
K Young		190
T Monk	150	
C Howe	210	
AB Ltd		2,700
Capital		9,000
Purchases	1,340	
Sales		1,200
Returns inwards	150	
Returns outwards		120
Machinery	3,250	
	13,210	13,210

7.4 Multiple-choice Self-test Questions

A growing practice of examining boards is to set multiple-choice questions in Accounting.

Multiple-choice questions certainly give an examiner the opportunity to cover large parts of the syllabus briefly but in detail. Students who omit to study areas of the syllabus will be caught out by an examiner's use of multiple-choice questions. No longer will it be possible to say that it is highly probable a certain topic will not be tested – the examiner can easily cover it with a multiple-choice question.

We have deliberately set blocks of multiple-choice questions at given places in this textbook, rather than a few at the end of each chapter. Such questions are relatively easy to answer a few minutes after reading the chapter. By asking the questions later your powers of recall and understanding are far better tested. It also gives you practice at answering a few questions in one block, as in an examination.

Each multiple-choice question has a 'stem', this is a part which poses the problem, a 'key' which is the one correct answer, and a number of 'distractors', i.e. incorrect answers. The key plus the distractors are known as the 'options'.

If you do not know the answer you should guess. You may be right by chance, or you may remember something subconsciously. In any event, unless the examiner warns otherwise, he will expect you to guess if you don't know the answer.

You should now attempt Set No 1, which contains 20 multiple-choice questions, on page 341.

New Terms

Trial Balance (p 49): A list of balances in the books, shown in debit and credit columns.

Exercises

7.1 You are to enter up the necessary amounts for the month of May from the following details, and then balance off the accounts and extract a trial balance as at 31 May 19–6:

19–6
May 1 Started firm with capital in cash of £250
" 2 Bought goods on credit from the following persons: D Ellis £54; C Mendez £87; K Gibson £25; D Booth £76; L Lowe £64
" 4 Sold goods on credit to: C Bailey £43; B Hughes £62; H Spencer £176
" 6 Paid rent by cash £12
" 9 Bailey paid us his account by cheque £43
" 10 H Spencer paid us £150 by cheque

"	12	We paid the following by cheque: K Gibson £25; D Ellis £54
"	15	Paid carriage by cash £23
"	18	Bought goods on credit from C Mendez £43; D Booth £110
"	21	Sold goods on credit to B Hughes £67
"	31	Paid rent by cheque £18

7.2 Enter up the books from the following details for the month of March, and extract a trial balance as at 31 March 19–6:

19–6		
March	1	Started business with £800 in the bank
"	2	Bought goods on credit from the following persons: K Henriques £76; M Hyatt £27; T Braham £56
"	5	Cash sales £87
"	6	Paid wages in cash £14
"	7	Sold goods on credit to: H Elliott £35; L Lane £42; J Carlton £72
"	9	Bought goods for cash £46
"	10	Bought goods on credit from: M Hyatt £57; T Braham £98
"	12	Paid wages in cash £14
"	13	Sold goods on credit to: L Lane £32; J Carlton £23
"	15	Bought shop fixtures on credit from Betta Ltd £50
"	17	Paid M Hyatt by cheque £84
"	18	We returned goods to T Braham £20
"	21	Paid Betta Ltd a cheque for £50
"	24	J Carlton paid us his account by cheque £95
"	27	We returned goods to K Henriques £24
"	30	J King lent us £60 by cash
"	31	Bought a motor van paying by cheque £400.

7.3 The following transactions are to be entered up in the books for June, and accounts balanced off and a trial balance extracted as at 30 June 19–8:

19–8		
June	1	Started business with £600 in the bank and £50 cash in hand
"	2	Bought £500 goods on credit from C Jones
"	3	Credit sales: H Henry £66; N Neita £25; P Potter £43
"	4	Goods bought for cash £23
"	5	Bought motor van paying by cheque £256
"	7	Paid motor expenses by cheque £12
"	9	Credit sales: B Barnes £24; K Lyn £26; M Moore £65
"	11	Goods bought on credit: C Jones £240, N Moss £62; O Hughes £46
"	13	Goods returned by us to C Jones £25
"	15	Paid motor expenses by cash £5
"	19	Goods returned to us by N Neita £11
"	20	Cash taken for own use (drawings) £10
"	21	We paid the following by cheque: N Moss £62; O Hughes £46
"	23	H Henry paid us in cash £66
"	25	P Potter paid us by cheque £43
"	26	Cash sales £34
"	27	Cash taken for own use £24
"	28	Goods returned by us to C Jones £42
"	29	Paid for postage stamps by cash £4
"	30	Credit sales: N Neita £43; M Edgar £67; K Lyn £45.

7.4X Record the following transactions of D Chatsworth for the month of May 19–6, balance off all the accounts, and then extract a trial balance as on 31 May 19–6:

19–6
May 1 D Chatsworth started business with £8,000 cash
" 2 Put £7,500 of the cash into a bank account
" 2 Bought goods on credit from: Burton Brothers £180; Lyew & Co £560; P McDonald £380; K Black Ltd £410
" 3 Bought office fixtures by cheque £185
" 4 Bought goods for cash £190
" 5 Cash sales £110
" 6 Goods sold on credit: J Gayle & Son £190; P Gentles £340; T Sutherland £110; T Brown Ltd £300
" 7 Paid rent by cheque £100
" 8 Paid wages by cash £70
" 10 Bought goods on credit from: Lyew & Co £340; C Rose £160
" 11 Goods returned to us by J Gayle & Son £60
" 13 Goods sold on credit to: N Mattis £44; J Gayle & Son £300
" 14 Bought office fixtures on credit from Tru-kits Ltd £178
" 15 Bought office stationery for cash £90
" 16 Paid cheques to the following: Tru-kits Ltd £178; Burton Brothers £180
" 17 Paid wages by cash £90
" 18 D Chatsworth takes £100 drawings in cash
" 20 We returned goods to P McDonald £60; K Black Ltd £44
" 22 Bought office stationery £220 on credit from EP & Co
" 24 Received cheques from N Mattis £44; T Brown Ltd £180
" 26 Cash sales £140
" 29 D Chatsworth took cash drawings £150
" 31 Paid sundry expenses by cash £5.

7.5X Record the following details for the month of November 19–3 and extract a trial balance as at 30 November:

Nov 1 Started with £5,000 in the bank
" 3 Bought goods on credit from: T Henriques £160; J Smith £230; W Rogers £400; P Boone £310
" 5 Cash sales £240
" 6 Paid rent by cheque £20
" 7 Paid rates by cheque £190
" 11 Sold goods on credit to: L Matthews £48; K Allen £32; R Hall £1,170
" 17 Paid wages by cash £40
" 18 We returned goods to: T Henriques £14; P Boone £20
" 19 Bought goods on credit from: P Boone £80; W Rogers £270; D Diaz £130
" 20 Goods were returned to us by K Allen £2; L Matthews £4
" 21 Bought motor van on credit from UZ Motors £500
" 23 We paid the following by cheque: T Henriques £146; J Smith £230; W Rogers £300
" 25 Bought another motor van, paying by cheque immediately £700
" 26 Received a loan of £400 cash from A Williams
" 28 Received cheques from: L Matthews £44; K Allen £30
" 30 Proprietor brings a further £300 into the business, by a payment into the business bank account.

7.6X Record the following for the month of January, balance off all the accounts, and then extract a trial balance as at 31 January 19–4:

19–4
Jan 1 Started business with £3,500 cash
" 2 Put £2,800 of the cash into a bank account
" 3 Bought goods for cash £150
" 4 Bought goods on credit from: L Coke £360; M Burton £490; T Hill £110; C Small £340
" 5 Bought stationery on credit from: Swift Ltd £170
" 6 Sold goods on credit to: S Walters £90; T Binns £150; C Howard £190; P Peart £160
" 8 Paid rent by cheque £55
" 10 Bought fixtures on credit from Matalon Ltd £480
" 11 Paid salaries in cash £120
" 14 Returned goods to M Burton £40; T Hill £60
" 15 Bought motor van by cheque £700
" 16 Received loan from J Henry by cheque £600
" 18 Goods returned to us by: S Walters £20; C Howard £40
" 21 Cash sales £90
" 24 Sold goods on credit to: T Binns £100; P Peart £340; J Smart £115
" 26 We paid the following by cheque: M Burton £450; T Hill £50
" 29 Received cheques from: J Smart £115; T Binns £250
" 30 Received a further loan from J Henry by cash £200
" 30 Received £500 cash from P Peart.

8 · Trading and Profit and Loss Accounts: An Introduction

8.1 Purpose of Trading and Profit and Loss Account

People run businesses to try to make a profit. If they are not successful they may lose money. To calculate how much profit or loss has been made over a period of time a **trading and profit and loss account** is prepared.

Normally, all businesses prepare trading and profit and loss accounts at least once a year. They could be prepared for a lesser period if required.

The main purpose of a trading and profit and loss account is for the owners to be able to see how profitably the business is being run. It is also used for other purposes, for instance the Income Tax Inspector will want to see it so that he can work out the tax bill.

8.2 Format for the Trading and Profit and Loss Account

One of the most important uses of the trading and profit and loss account is the comparison of the results achieved with those of past periods. When doing this it is useful for traders, as you will see more fully later, to calculate two sorts of profits. These are:

Gross Profit (calculated in the **trading account**)	This is the difference between the figure of sales and the cost of goods sold in the period.
Net Profit (calculated in the **profit and loss account**)	This is what is left of the gross profit after all other expenses have been deducted.

It would be possible to have one account called a trading account, and another called a profit and loss account. Normally they are combined together to form one account called the trading and profit and loss account.

8.3 Information Needed

Before drawing up a trading and profit and loss account you should get out the trial balance. This contains nearly all the information needed. (Later on in this book you will see that certain adjustments have to be made, but we will ignore these at this stage.)

Our first look is at the preparation of a trading and profit and loss account for K Wade, after his first year's trading. His trial balance appears as Exhibit 8.1.

Exhibit 8.1

K Wade Trial Balance as on 31 December 19–3		
	Dr	*Cr*
	£	£
Sales		9,650
Purchases	7,150	
General expenses	550	
Fixtures and fittings	1,840	
Debtors	1,460	
Creditors		1,180
Capital		2,800
Drawings	1,750	
Bank	820	
Cash	60	
	13,630	13,630

We are going to assume that all the goods purchased were sold by 31 December 19–3, leaving no stock at that date.

8.4 Preparation of a Trading and Profit and Loss Account

To calculate gross profit

Remember that:

Sales – Cost of Goods Sold = Gross Profit

To do this in double entry, the following steps should be carried out.

1 Transfer the credit balance of the sales account to the credit of the trading account portion of the trading and profit and loss account.

Debit: Sales account
Credit: Trading account

2 Transfer the debit balance of the purchases account to the debit of the trading account.

Debit: Trading account
Credit: Purchases

Remember, in this case there is no stock of unsold goods. This means that Purchases = Cost of Goods Sold.

3 If sales are greater than the cost of goods sold the difference is gross profit. (If not, the answer would be a gross loss.) We will carry this gross profit figure from the trading account part down to the profit and loss part.

The double entry for gross profit is:

Debit: Trading account
Credit: Profit and loss account

Now we can see this done for Exhibit 8.1

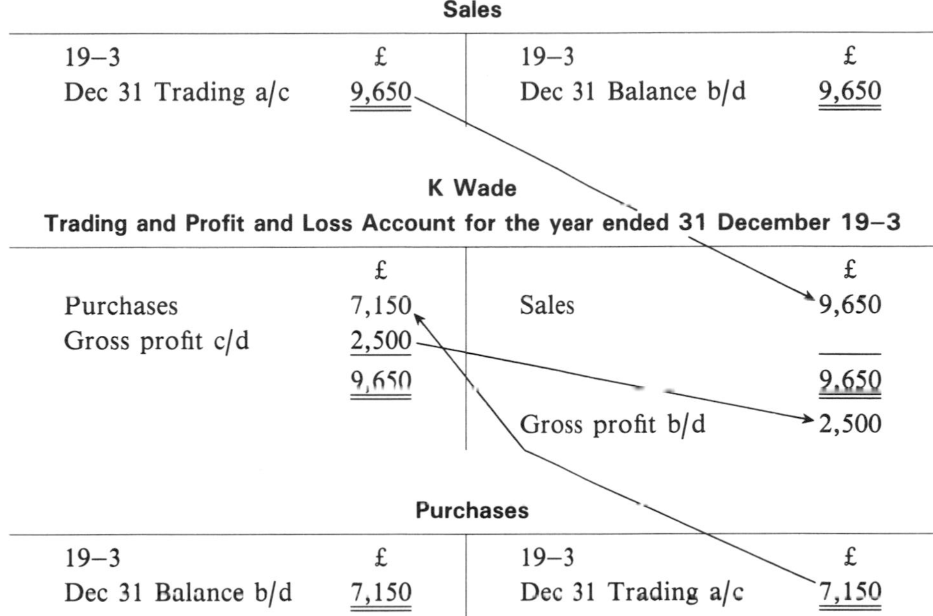

Sales

	£		£
19–3		19–3	
Dec 31 Trading a/c	9,650	Dec 31 Balance b/d	9,650

K Wade
Trading and Profit and Loss Account for the year ended 31 December 19–3

	£		£
Purchases	7,150	Sales	9,650
Gross profit c/d	2,500		
	9,650		9,650
		Gross profit b/d	2,500

Purchases

	£		£
19–3		19–3	
Dec 31 Balance b/d	7,150	Dec 31 Trading a/c	7,150

Notice that, after the trading account has been completed, there are no balances remaining in the sales and purchases accounts. They are now *closed*.

To calculate net profit and record it

Remember that:

Gross Profit – Expenses = Net Profit

Remember also that:

Old Capital + Net Profit = New Capital

Double entry needed to carry out these calculations:

1 Transfer the debit balances on expenses accounts to the debit of the profit and loss account.

Debit: Profit and loss account
Credit: Expenses accounts

2 Transfer the net profit, when found, to the capital account to show the increase in capital.

Debit: Profit and loss account
Credit: Capital account

K Wade
Trading and Profit and Loss Account for the year ended 31 December 19–3

	£		£
Purchases	7,150	Sales	9,650
Gross profit c/d	2,500		
	9,650		9,650
General expenses	550	Gross profit b/d	2,500
Net profit	1,950		
	2,500		2,500

General Expenses

	£		£
19–3		19–3	
Dec 31 Balance b/d	550	Dec 31 Profit and loss a/c	550

Capital

			£
		19–3	
		Dec 31 Balance b/d	2,800
		Dec 31 Net profit	1,950

8.5 Completion of Capital Account

You have seen that we credit the capital account with the amount of net profit. We have, therefore, recorded the increase in capital.

In the trial balance, Exhibit 8.1, we can see that there are drawings of £1,750. Drawings means withdrawals of capital.

After entering the net profit in the capital account we can now complete the account. To do this we transfer the drawings to the capital account.

Debit: Capital account
Credit: Drawings account

The completed capital and drawings accounts are as follows:

Drawings

	£		£
19–3		19–3	
Dec 31 Balance b/d	1,750	Dec 31 Capital	1,750

Capital

	£		£
19–3		19–3	
Dec 31 Drawings	1,750	Dec 31 Balance b/d	2,800
Dec 31 Balance c/d	3,000	Dec 31 Net Profit	1,950
	4,750		4,750
		19–4	
		Jan 1 Balance b/d	3,000

8.6 Stock of Unsold Goods at End of Period

Usually some of the goods bought (purchases) have not been sold by the end of the accounting period. We have already seen that gross profit is calculated as follows:

Sales – Cost of Goods Sold = Gross Profit

However, purchases only equals cost of goods sold if there is no stock at the end of a period. We can calculate cost of goods sold as follows:

What we bought in the period:	Purchases
less Goods bought but not sold in the period:	Closing Stock
	= Cost of Goods Sold

Let us look at the drawing up of a trading and profit and loss account for B Swift. His trial balance is shown as Exhibit 8.2 and was drawn up after his first year of trading:

Exhibit 8.2

B Swift
Trial Balance on 31 December 19–5

	Dr	*Cr*
	£	£
Sales		3,850
Purchases	2,900	
Rent	240	
Lighting	150	
General expenses	60	
Fixtures and fittings	500	
Debtors	680	
Creditors		910
Bank	1,510	
Cash	20	
Drawings	700	
Capital		2,000
	6,760	6,760

Note: On 31 December 19–5, at the close of trading, B Swift had goods costing £300 which were unsold.

The cost of goods sold figure will be:

	£
Purchases	2,900
less Closing stock	300
Cost of goods sold	2,600

Given the figure of sales £3,850, the gross profit can be calculated:

Sales – Cost of Goods Sold = Gross Profit
£3,850 – £2,600 = £1,250

The net profit will be:

Gross profit – Expenses = Net Profit
£1,250 – £(240 + 150 + 60)£450 = £800

We will now see this shown in double entry:

Sales

19–5	£	19–5	£
Dec 31 Trading a/c	3,850	Dec 31 Balance b/d	3,850

Purchases

19–5	£	19–5	£
Dec 31 Balance b/d	2,900	Dec 31 Trading a/c	2,900

Rent

19–5	£	19–5	£
Dec 31 Balance b/d	240	Dec 31 Profit and loss a/c	240

Lighting

19–5	£	19–5	£
Dec 31 Balance b/d	150	Dec 31 Profit and loss a/c	150

General Expenses

19–5	£	19–5	£
Dec 31 Balance b/d	60	Dec 31 Profit and loss a/c	60

Stock

19–5	£		
Dec 31 Trading a/c	300		

B Swift

Trading and Profit and Loss Account for the year ended 31 December 19–5

19–5	£	19–5	£
Purchases	2,900	Sales	3,850
Gross profit c/d	1,250	Closing stock	300
	4,150		4,150
Rent	240	Gross profit b/d	1,250
Lighting	150		
General expenses	60		
Net profit	800		
	1,250		1,250

To record the stock we have entered the following:

Debit: Stock account
Credit: Trading account

This means that there is now a balance on the stock account. We had to record it there because at 31 December 19–5 we had an asset, £300 of stock, but there was no record of that fact in our books. We have now brought our records up-to-date by showing the stock in our accounts. Without the stock accounts at 31 December 19–5 our records would have been incomplete.

8.7 The Capital Account

The capital account can now be completed.

Capital

19–5	£	19–5	£
Dec 31 Drawings	700	Jan 1 Cash	2,000
Dec 31 Balance c/d	2,100	Dec 31 Net profit from profit and loss a/c	800
	2,800		2,800
		19–6	
		Jan 1 Balance b/d	2,100

Drawings

19–5	£	19–5	£
Dec 31 Balance b/d	700	Dec 31 Capital	700

8.8 The Balances Still in Our Books

Taking Exhibit 8.3, but including the adjustment for closing stock of £300, we can now see which balances still exist. We can do this by drawing up a trial balance as it would appear once the trading and profit and loss account was completed. We will show it as Exhibit 8.3.

Accounts Closed

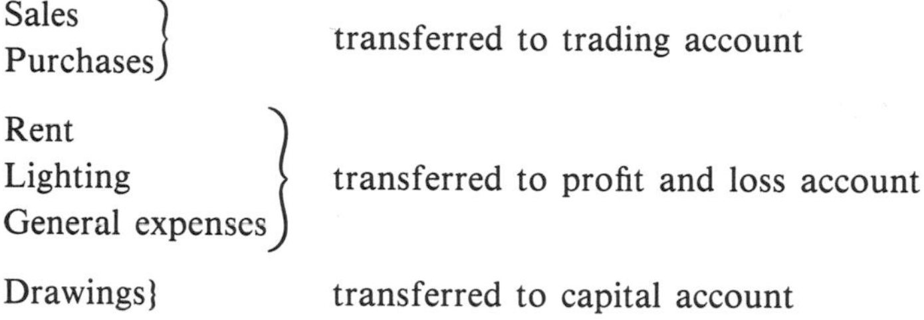

Sales Purchases	transferred to trading account
Rent Lighting General expenses	transferred to profit and loss account
Drawings	transferred to capital account

Accounts Not Closed

Exhibit 8.3

B Swift
Trial Balance as on 31 December 19–5
(after Trading and Profit and Loss Accounts completed)

	Dr	*Cr*
	£	£
Fixtures and fittings	500	
Debtors	680	
Creditors		910
Stock	300	
Bank	1,510	
Cash	20	
Capital		2,100
	3,010	3,010

The one account which was not in the original trial balance was stock account. It was not brought into our books until the trading account was prepared. These balances will be used by us when we look at the balance sheets.

New Terms

Trading and Profit and Loss Account (p 57): Combined account in which both gross and net profits are calculated.

Gross Profit (p 57): Found by deducting cost of goods sold from the figure of sales.

Net Profit (p 57): Gross profit less expenses.

Trading Account (p 57): Account in which gross profit is calculated.

Profit and Loss Account (p 57): Account in which net profit is calculated.

Exercises

8.1 From the following trial balance of B Webb, who has been in business for one year, extract a trading and profit and loss account for the year ended 31 December 19–6. A balance sheet is not required.

Trial Balance as at 31 December 19–6

	Dr £	*Cr* £
Sales		18,462
Purchases	14,629	
Salaries	2,150	
Motor expenses	520	
Rent and rates	670	
Insurance	111	
General expenses	105	
Premises	1,500	
Motor vehicles	1,200	
Debtors	1,950	
Creditors		1,538
Cash at bank	1,654	
Cash in hand	40	
Drawings	895	
Capital		5,424
	25,424	25,424

Stock at 31 December 19–6 was £2,548.
(Keep your answer – it will be used later in exercise 9.1.)

8.2 From the following trial balance of C Worth, who has been trading for one year, you are required to draw up a trading and profit and loss account for the year ended 30 June 19–4. A balance sheet is not required.

Trial Balance as at 31 December 19–4		
	Dr	*Cr*
	£	£
Sales		28,794
Purchases	23,803	
Rent and rates	854	
Lighting expenses	422	
Salaries and wages	3,164	
Insurance	105	
Shop buildings	50,000	
Shop fixtures	1,000	
Debtors	3,166	
Trade expenses	506	
Creditors		1,206
Cash at bank	3,847	
Drawings	2,400	
Motor vans	5,500	
Motor running expenses	1,133	
Capital		65,900
	95,900	95,900

Stock at 30 June 19–4 was £4,166.
(Keep your answer – it will be used later in exercise 9.2.)

8.3X From the following trial balance of F Chaplin draw up a trading and profit and loss account for the year ended 31 December 19–8. A balance sheet is not required. He has been in business for one year only.

Trial Balance as at 31 December 19–8		
	Dr	*Cr*
	£	£
General expenses	210	
Rent and rates	400	
Motor expenses	735	
Salaries	3,560	
Insurance	392	
Purchases	18,385	
Sales		26,815
Motor vehicle	2,800	
Creditors		5,160
Debtors	4,090	
Premises	20,000	
Cash at bank	1,375	
Cash in hand	25	
Capital		24,347
Drawings	4,350	
	56,322	56,322

Stock at 31 December 19–8 was £4,960.
(Keep your answer – it will be used later in exercise 9.3X.)

8.4X A business has been trading for one year. Extract a trading and profit and loss account for the year ended 30 June 19–4 for F Kidd. The trial balance as at 30 June 19–4 was as follows:

Trial Balance as at 30 June 19–4		
	Dr	*Cr*
	£	£
Rent and rates	1,560	
Insurance	305	
Lighting expenses	516	
Motor expenses	1,960	
Salaries and wages	4,850	
Sales		35,600
Purchases	30,970	
Trade expenses	806	
Motor vans	3,500	
Creditors		3,250
Debtors	6,810	
Shop fixtures	3,960	
Shop buildings	28,000	
Cash at bank	1,134	
Drawings	6,278	
Capital		51,799
	90,649	90,649

Stock at 30 June 19–4 was £9,960.
(Keep your answer – it will be used later in exercise 9.4X.)

9 · Balance Sheets

9.1 Contents of the Balance Sheet

You saw in Chapter 2 that balance sheets contain details of assets, capital and liabilities. These details have to be found in our records and then written out as a balance sheet.

It is easy to find these details. They consist of all the balances remaining in our records once the trading and profit and loss account for the period has been completed. All balances remaining have to be assets, capital or liabilities. All the other balances should have been closed off when the trading and profit and loss account was completed.

9.2 Drawing up a Balance Sheet

Let us now look at Exhibit 9.1, the trial balance of B Swift (from Exhibit 8.3) as on 31 December 19–5 *after* the trading and profit and loss account had been prepared.

Exhibit 9.1

B Swift
Trial Balance as on 31 December 19–5
(after Trading and Profit and Loss Accounts completed)

	Dr	*Cr*
	£	£
Fixtures and fittings	500	
Debtors	680	
Creditors		910
Stock	300	
Bank	1,510	
Cash	20	
Capital		2,100
	3,010	3,010

We can now draw up a balance sheet as at 31 December 19–5, Exhibit 9.2. You saw examples of balance sheets in Chapter 2. We will not worry at this point whether or not the balance sheet is set out in good style.

As you saw in Chapter 2, assets are shown on the left-hand side, and capital and liabilities are on the right-hand side.

Exhibit 9.2

B Swift
Balance Sheet as at 31 December 19–5

Assets	£	*Capital and liabilities*	£
Fixtures and fittings	500	Capital	2,100
Stock	300	Creditors	910
Debtors	680		
Bank	1,510		
Cash	20		
	3,010		3,010

9.3 No Double Entry in Balance Sheets

It may seem very strange to you to learn that balance sheets are *not* part of the double entry system.

When we draw up accounts such as cash account, rent account, sales account, trading and profit and loss account and so on, then we are writing up part of the double entry system. We make entries on the debit sides and the credit sides of these accounts.

In drawing up a balance sheet we do not enter anything in the various accounts. We do not actually transfer the fixtures balance or the stock balance, or any of the others, to the balance sheet.

All we do is to *list* the asset, capital and liabilities balances so as to form a balance sheet. This means that none of these accounts have been closed off. *Nothing is entered in the accounts.*

When the next accounting period starts, these accounts are still open containing balances. Entries are then made in them to add to, or deduct from the amounts shown in the accounts using normal double entry.

If you see the word 'account' you will know that it is part of the double entry system, and will include debit and credit entries. If the word 'account' cannot be used it is not part of double entry. For instance:

Trial balance: A list of balances to see if the records are correct.

Balance sheet: A list of balances arranged according to whether they are assets, capital or liabilities.

9.4 Balance Sheet Layout

You would not expect to go into a department store and see goods for sale all mixed up and not laid out properly. You would expect that the goods would be displayed so that you could easily find them. Similarly in balance sheets we do not want all the items shown in any order. We want them displayed so that useful information can easily be seen.

For people such as bank managers, accountants and investors who look at a lot of different balance sheets, we want to keep to one method so as to make a comparison of balance sheets easier. What you are going to look at now is a method for showing items in balance sheets.

Assets

Let us look at the assets side first. We are going to show the assets under two headings, **Fixed Assets** and **Current Assets**.

Assets are called fixed assets when they:
1 are of long life;
2 are to be used in the business; and
3 were not bought only for the purposes of resale.

Examples: buildings, machinery, motor vehicles, fixtures and fittings.

Fixed assets are listed starting with those we will keep the longest, down to those which will not be kept so long. For instance:

Fixed Assets
1 Land and buildings
2 Fixtures and fittings
3 Machinery
4 Motor vehicles

Current assets are cash in hand, cash at bank, items held for resale at a profit or items that have a short life.

These are listed starting with the asset furthest away from being turned into cash, finishing with cash itself. For instance:

Current Assets
1 Stock
2 Debtors
3 Cash at bank
4 Cash in hand

Capital and Liabilities

The order on the other side of the balance sheet is:

- Capital
- Long term liabilities: for instance, loans which do not have to be repaid in the near future.
- Current liabilities: items to be paid for in the near future.

9.5 A Properly Drawn Up Balance Sheet

Exhibit 9.3 shows Exhibit 9.2 drawn up in better style. Also read the notes following the exhibit.

Exhibit 9.3

B Swift

Balance Sheet as at 31 December 19–5

	£	£		£	£
Fixed Assets			*Capital*		
Furniture and fittings		500	Cash introduced	2,000	
			Add Net profit for the year	800	
Current Assets				2,800	
Stock	300		*Less* Drawings	700	
Debtors	680				2,100
Bank	1,510		*Current Liabilities*		
Cash	20		Creditors		910
		2,510			
		3,010			3,010

Notes to Exhibit 9.3

(a) A total for capital and for each class of liabilities should be shown. An example of this is the £2,510 total of current assets. To do this the figures for each asset are listed, and only the total is shown in the end column.

(b) You do not have to write the word 'account' after each item.

(c) The owner will be most interested in his capital. To show only the final balance of £2,100 means that the owner will not know how it was calculated. So we show the full details of his capital account.

(d) Look at the date on the balance sheet. Now compare it with the dates put on the top of the trading and profit and loss account. The balance sheet is a position statement, it is shown as being at one point in time, i.e. as at 31 December 19–5. The trading and profit and loss account is different. It is for a period of time, in this case for a whole year.

New Terms

Fixed Assets (p 70): Assets bought which have a long life and are to be used in the business.

Current Assets (p 70): Assets consisting of cash, goods for resale, or items having a short life.

Long-term Liabilities (p 71): Liabilities not having to be paid for in the near future.

Current Liabilities (p 71): Liabilities to be paid for in the near future.

Exercises

9.1 Complete exercise 8.1 by drawing up a balance sheet as at 31 December 19–6.

9.2 Complete exercise 8.2 by drawing up a balance sheet as at 31 December 19–4.

9.3X Complete exercise 8.3X by drawing up a balance sheet as at 31 December 19–8.

9.4X Complete exercise 8.4X by drawing up a balance sheet as at 31 December 19–4.

10 · Trading and Profit and Loss Accounts and Balance Sheets: Further Considerations

10.1 Carriage Inwards

Carriage (cost of transport of goods) into a firm is called **carriage inwards**.

When you buy goods the cost of carriage inwards may either be included as part of the price, or else the firm may have to pay separately for it. Suppose you were buying exactly the same goods. One supplier might sell them to you for £100, and he would deliver the goods and not send you a bill for carriage. Another supplier might sell the goods to you for £95, but you would have to pay £5 to a haulage firm for carriage inwards, i.e. a total cost of £100.

To keep the cost of buying goods shown on the same basis, carriage inwards is always added to the purchases in the trading account.

10.2 Carriage Outwards

Carriage from a firm out to its customers is called **carriage outwards**.

This is always treated as an expense to be transferred to the debit of the profit and loss account.

Exhibit 10.1 shows the items in a trial balance necessary for the trading and profit and loss account for the year ended 31 December 19–5.

Exhibit 10.1

Trial Balance as at 31 December 19–5 (extracts)		
	Dr	*Cr*
	£	£
Sales		6,000
Purchases	4,000	
Carriage inwards	350	
Carriage outwards	280	
Other expenses	220	

The closing stock on 31 December 19–5 was £650.

We can now show the trading and profit and loss account completed.

Trading and Profit and Loss Account for the year ended 31 December 19–5

	£		£
Purchases	4,000	Sales	6,000
Carriage inwards	350	Closing stock	650
	4,350		
Gross profit c/d	2,300		
	6,650		6,650
Carriage outwards	280	Gross profit b/d	2,300
Other expenses	220		
Net profit	1,800		
	2,300		2,300

10.3 The Second Year of a Business

Following on from Exhibit 9.3 in the last chapter, B Swift carries on his business for another year. He then extracts a trial balance as on 31 December 19–6, shown as Exhibit 10.2.

Exhibit 10.2

B Swift
Trial Balance as at 31 December 19–6

	Dr £	*Cr* £
Sales		6,700
Purchases	4,260	
Lighting	190	
Rent	240	
Wages: store assistant	520	
General expenses	70	
Carriage outwards	110	
Shop premises	2,000	
Fixtures and fittings	750	
Debtors	1,200	
Creditors		900
Bank	120	
Cash	40	
Loan from J Marsh		1,000
Drawings	900	
Capital		2,100
Stock (at 31 December 19–5)	300	
	10,700	10,700

Closing stock at 31 December 19–6 was £550.

Adjustments Needed for Stock

Previously we have done the accounts for new businesses only. They started without stock and therefore had closing stock only, as we were doing the first trading and profit and loss account.

When we prepare the trading and profit and loss account for the second year we can now see the difference. Looking at Exhibits 9.1 (on p. 68) and 10.2 for B Swift we can see the stock figures needed for the trading accounts:

Trading Account for period →	Year to 31 December 19–5	Year to 31 December 19–6
Opening stock 1.1.19–5	None	
Closing stock 31.12.19–5	£300	
Opening stock 1.1.19–6		£300
Closing stock 31.12.19–6		£550

This means that calculations for the first year of trading, to 31 December 19–5, had only one stock figure included in them. This was the closing stock. For the second year of trading, to 31 December 19–6, both opening and closing stock figures will be in the calculations.

The stock shown in the trial balance, Exhibit 10.2, is that brought forward from the previous year on 31 December 19–5; it is, therefore, the opening stock of 19–6. The closing stock at 31 December 19–6 can only be found by stock-taking. Assume it amounts at cost to be £550.

Let us first of all calculate the cost of goods sold for 19–6:

	£
Stock of goods at start of year	300
Add Purchases	4,260
Total goods available for sale	4,560
Less What remains at the end of the year:	
i.e. stock of goods at close	550
Therefore cost of goods that have been sold	4,010

We can look at a diagram to illustrate this, *see* Exhibit 10.3.

Exhibit 10.3

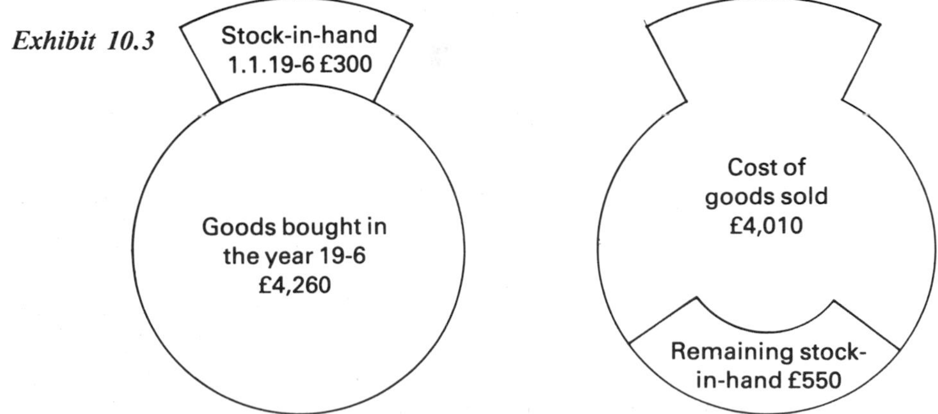

The sales were £6,700, so Sales £6,700 – Cost of Goods Sold £4,010 = Gross Profit £2,690.

Now the trading and profit and loss accounts can be drawn up using double entry, *see* Exhibit 10.4. For purposes of illustration the stock account will also be shown.

Exhibit 10.4

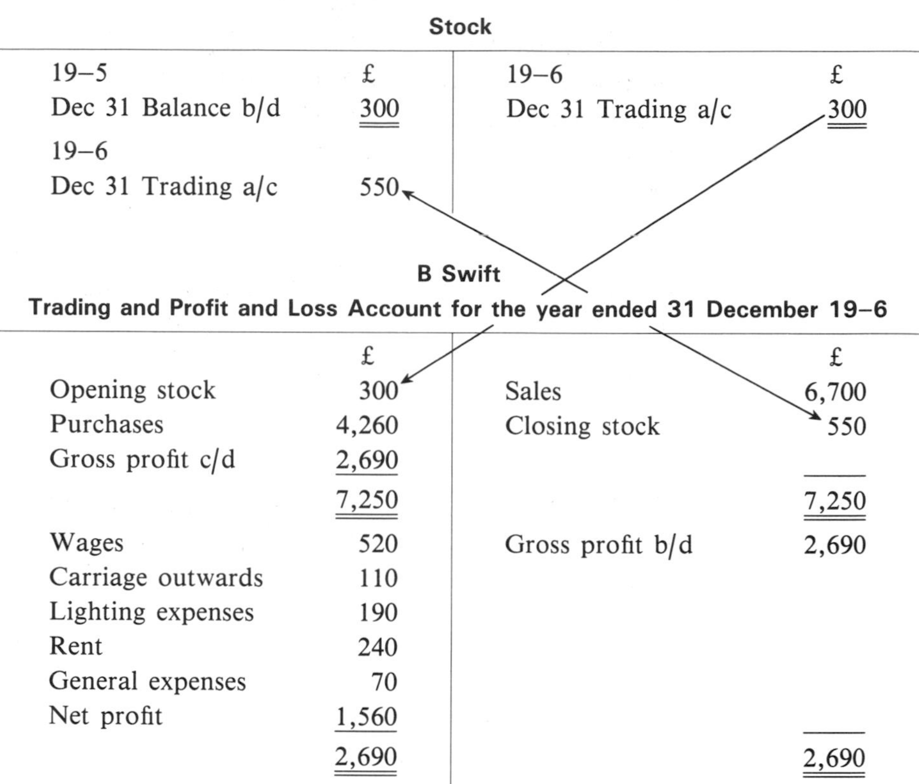

Stock

	£		£
19–5		19–6	
Dec 31 Balance b/d	300	Dec 31 Trading a/c	300
19–6			
Dec 31 Trading a/c	550		

B Swift
Trading and Profit and Loss Account for the year ended 31 December 19–6

	£		£
Opening stock	300	Sales	6,700
Purchases	4,260	Closing stock	550
Gross profit c/d	2,690		
	7,250		7,250
Wages	520	Gross profit b/d	2,690
Carriage outwards	110		
Lighting expenses	190		
Rent	240		
General expenses	70		
Net profit	1,560		
	2,690		2,690

The stock which at 31 December 19–6 is £550, and has not been previously shown in the accounts, has been entered using double entry:
Debit: Stock account £550
Credit: Trading account £550

Display of Cost of Goods Sold in the Trading Account

Accountants like to see a figure for **cost of goods sold** actually shown in the trading account. This is because they use it for various calculations to be described later in your course.

Exhibit 10.4 shows a trading account where the normal double entry is shown. However, although the stock account would stay exactly as in Exhibit 10.4, accountants would prefer to show the trading account part as in Exhibit 10.5. The figure of gross profit stays the same. The only difference is in display.

Exhibit 10.5

B Swift

Trading and Profit and Loss Account for the year ended 31 December 19–6

	£		£
Opening stock	300	Sales	6,700
Add Purchases	4,260		
	4,560		
Less Closing stock	550		
Cost of goods sold	4,010		
Gross profit c/d	2,690		
	6,700		6,700
Wages	520	Gross profit b/d	2,690
Carriage outwards	110		
Lighting expenses	190		
Rent	240		
General expenses	70		
Net profit	1,560		
	2,690		2,690

In future we will show trading accounts displayed by this method.

The balances remaining in the books, including the new balance on the stock account, are now drawn up in the form of a balance sheet, *see* Exhibit 10.6.

Exhibit 10.6

B Swift

Balance Sheet as at 31 December 19–6

Fixed Assets	£	£	*Capital*	£	£
Shop premises		2,000	Balance 1 Jan 19–6	2,100	
Fixtures and fittings		750	*Add* Net profit for year	1,560	
		2,750		3,660	
			Less Drawings	900	
Current Assets					2,760
Stock	550		*Long-term Liability*		
Debtors	1,200		Loan from J Marsh		1,000
Bank	120		*Current Liabilities*		
Cash	40		Creditors		900
		1,910			
		4,660			4,660

10.4 Final Accounts

The term **final accounts** is often used to mean the trading and profit and loss accounts and the balance sheet. The term can be misleading as the balance sheet is not an account.

10.5 Other Expenses in the Trading Account

Sometimes the goods you buy to sell have to have something done to them before they can be sold. An example of this is a trader who sells clocks packed in boxes. To do this he:

1 Buys clocks from one supplier.
2 Buys boxes from a different supplier.
3 Pays wages to a man to pack the clocks into the boxes.

Expenses **1**, **2** and **3** will be transferred to the trading account when calculating gross profit.

4 Wages of a man selling the clocks will *not* be transferred to the trading account. Instead these wages will be transferred to profit and loss account.

10.6 The Accountant as a Communicator

Quite often the impression is given that all that the accountant does is to produce figures, arranged in various ways. Naturally, such forms of computation do take up quite a lot of the accountant's time, but what then takes up the rest of his time is exactly how he communicates these figures to other people.

First of all, he can obviously arrange the figures in such a way as to present the information in as meaningful a way as possible. Suppose for instance that the figures he has produced are to be given to several people all of whom are very knowledgeable about accounting. He could, in such an instance, present the figures in a normal accounting way, knowing full well that the recipients of the information will understand it.

On the other hand, the accounting figures may well be needed by people who have absolutely no knowledge at all of accounting. In such a case a normal accounting statement would be no use to them at all, they would not understand it. In this case he might set out the figures in a completely different way to try to make it easy for them to grasp. For instance, instead of preparing a normal trading and profit and loss account he might show it as follows:

		£
In the year ended 31 December 19–6 you sold goods for		50,000
Now how much had those goods cost you to buy?		
At the start of the year you had stock costing	6,000	
+ You bought some more goods in the year costing	28,000	
So altogether you had goods available to sell of	34,000	
– At the end of the year you had stock of goods unsold of	3,000	
So the goods you had sold in the year had cost you	31,000	
Let us deduct this from what you had sold the goods for		31,000
This means that you had made a profit on buying and selling goods, before any other expenses had been paid, amounting to		19,000
(We call this sort of profit the Gross Profit)		
But you suffered other expenses such as wages, rent, lighting and so on, and during the year the amount of these expenses, not including anything taken for yourself, amounted to		9,000
So for this year your sales value exceeded all the costs involved in running the business, so that the sales could be made, by		£10,000
(We call this sort of profit the Net Profit)		

If an accountant cannot arrange the figures to make them meaningful to the recipient then he is failing in his task. His job is not just to produce figures for himself to look at, his job is to communicate these results to other people.

Very often the accountant will have to talk to people to explain the figures, or send a letter or write a report concerning them. He will also have to talk or write to people to find out exactly what sort of accounting information is needed by them or explain to them what sort of information he could provide. This means that if accounting examinations consist simply of computational type questions then they will not test the ability of the candidate to communicate in any other way than by writing down accounting figures. In recent years more attention has been paid by examining boards to these other aspects of an accountant's work.

New Terms

Carriage Inwards (p 73): Cost of transport of goods into a business.

Carriage Outwards (p 73): Cost of transport of goods to the customers of a business.

Cost of Goods Sold (p 76): Cost of goods sold to customers during an accounting period.

Final Accounts (p 78): Term which includes the trading and profit and loss accounts and balance sheet.

Exercises

10.1 From the following trial balance of R Graham draw up a trading and profit and loss account for the year ended 30 September 19–6, and a balance sheet as at that date.

	Dr	*Cr*
	£	£
Stock 1 October 19–5	2,368	
Carriage outwards	200	
Carriage inwards	310	
Returns inwards	205	
Returns outwards		322
Purchases	11,874	
Sales		18,600
Salaries and wages	3,862	
Rent and rates	304	
Insurance	78	
Motor expenses	664	
Office expenses	216	
Lighting and heating expenses	166	
General expenses	314	
Premises	5,000	
Motor vehicles	1,800	
Fixtures and fittings	350	
Debtors	3,896	
Creditors		1,731
Cash at bank	482	
Drawings	1,200	
Capital		12,636
	33,289	33,289

Stock at 30 September 19–6 was £2,946.

10.2 From the following details draw up the trading account for the year ended 31 December 19–3:

	£
Carriage inwards	670
Returns outwards	495
Returns inwards	890
Sales	38,742
Purchases	26,409
Stocks of goods: 1 January 19–3	6,924
31 December 19–3	7,489

10.3X The following trial balance was extracted from the books of B Jackson on 30 April 19–7. From it, and the notes, prepare his trading and profit and loss account for the year ended 30 April 19–7, and a balance sheet as at that date.

	Dr	*Cr*
	£	£
Sales		18,600
Purchases	11,556	
Stock 1 May 19–6	3,776	
Carriage outwards	326	
Carriage inwards	234	
Returns inwards	440	
Returns outwards		355
Salaries and wages	2,447	
Motor expenses	664	
Rent	456	
Rates	120	
Sundry expenses	1,202	
Motor vehicles	2,400	
Fixtures and fittings	600	
Debtors	4,577	
Creditors		3,045
Cash at bank	3,876	
Cash in hand	120	
Drawings	2,050	
Capital		12,844
	34,844	34,844

Stock at 30 April 19–7 was £4,998.

10.4X The following details for the year ended 31 March 19–8 are available. Draw up the trading account for that year.

	£
Stocks: 31 March 19–7	16,492
31 March 19–8	18,504
Returns inwards	1,372
Returns outwards	2,896
Purchases	36,905
Carriage inwards	1,122
Sales	54,600

10.5X The following is the trial balance of J Smailes as at 31 March 19–6. Draw up a set of final accounts for the year ended 31 March 19–6.

	Dr	*Cr*
	£	£
Stock 1 April 19–5	18,160	
Sales		92,340
Purchases	69,185	
Carriage inwards	420	
Carriage outwards	1,570	
Returns outwards		640
Wages and salaries	10,240	
Rent and rates	3,015	
Communication expenses	624	
Commissions payable	216	
Insurance	405	
Sundry expenses	318	
Buildings	20,000	
Debtors	14,320	
Creditors		8,160
Fixtures	2,850	
Cash at bank	2,970	
Cash in hand	115	
Loan from K Ball		10,000
Drawings	7,620	
Capital		40,888
	152,028	152,028

Stock at 31 March 19–6 was £22,390.

10.6X L Stokes drew up the following trial balance as at 30 September 19–8. You are to draft trading and profit and loss accounts for the year to 30 September 19–8 and a balance sheet as at that date.

	Dr	*Cr*
	£	£
Loan from P Owens		5,000
Capital		25,955
Drawings	8,420	
Cash at bank	3,115	
Cash in hand	295	
Debtors	12,300	
Creditors		9,370
Stock 30 September 19–7	23,910	
Motor van	4,100	
Office equipment	6,250	
Sales		130,900
Purchases	92,100	
Returns inwards	550	
Carriage inwards	215	
Returns outwards		307
Carriage outwards	309	
Motor expenses	1,630	
Rent	2,970	
Telephone charges	405	
Wages and salaries	12,810	
Insurance	492	
Office expenses	1,377	
Sundry expenses	284	
	171,532	171,532

Stock at 30 September 19–8 was £27,475.

11 · Books of Original Entry

11.1 The Growth of the Firm

While the firm is very small, all the double entry accounts can be kept in one book, which we would call the ledger. As the firm grows it would be impossible just to use one book, as the large number of pages needed for a lot of transactions would mean that the book would be too big to handle. Also, suppose we have several book-keepers. They could not all do their work properly if there was only one ledger.

The answer to this problem is for us to use more books. When we do this we put similar types of transactions together and have a book for that type. In each book we will not mix together transactions which are different from each other.

11.2 Books of Original Entry

These are books in which we record transactions first of all. We have a separate book for each different kind of transaction. The nature of the transaction affects which book it is entered into. Sales will be entered in one book, purchases in another book, cash in another book, and so on. We enter the transactions in these books giving the following details:

- Date. They should be shown in order of the date of transaction.
- Details column completed.
- Money column completed.

11.3 Types of Books of Original Entry

These are:

- **Sales Journal** – for credit sales.
- **Purchases Journal** – for credit purchases.
- **Returns Inwards Journal** – for returns inwards.
- **Returns Outwards Journal** – for returns outwards.
- **Cash Book** – for receipts and payments of cash.
- **General Journal** – for other items.

11.4 Using More than One Ledger

Although we have now made lists of transactions in the books of original entry, we still have more work to do. We have got to show the effect of the transactions by putting them into double entry accounts. Instead of keeping all the double entry accounts in one ledger, we have several ledgers. This again makes it easier to divide the work between different book-keepers.

11.5 Types of Ledgers

The different types of ledgers are:

- **Sales Ledger**. This is kept just for customers' personal accounts.
- **Purchases Ledger**. This is kept just for suppliers' personal accounts.
- **General Ledger**. This contains the remaining double entry accounts such as expenses, fixed assets, capital etc.

11.6 Diagram of Books Used

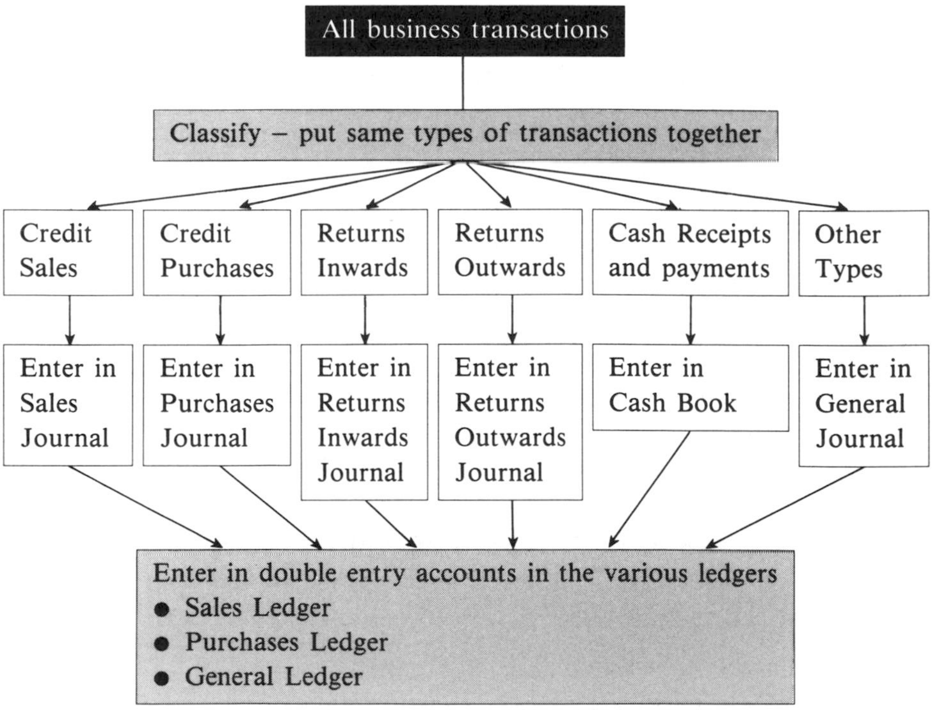

11.7 Description of Books Used

In the next few chapters we will look at the books used in more detail, except for the general journal which will be dealt with at a later stage.

11.8 Types of Accounts

Some people describe all accounts as **personal** accounts or as **impersonal** accounts.

- **Personal Accounts** – These are for debtors and creditors.
- **Impersonal Accounts** – Divided between real accounts and nominal accounts.
- **Real Accounts** – Accounts in which property is recorded. Examples are buildings, machinery, fixtures and stock.
- **Nominal Accounts** – Accounts in which expenses, income and capital are recorded.

A diagram may enable you to understand it better:

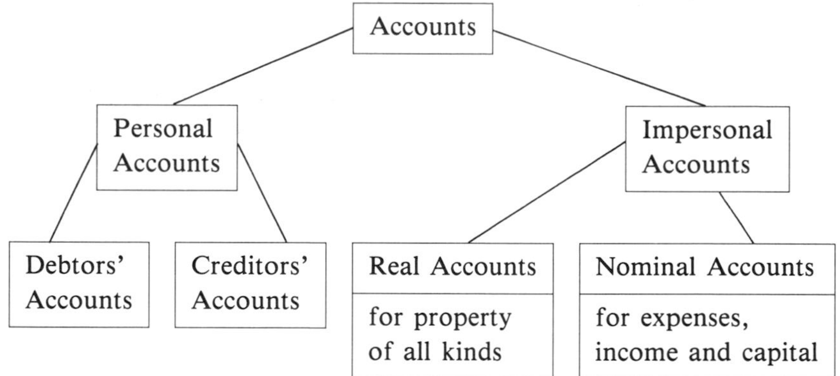

11.9 Nominal and Private Ledgers

The ledger in which the impersonal accounts are kept is known as the **nominal** (or general) **ledger**. Very often, to ensure privacy for the proprietor(s), the capital and drawing accounts and similar accounts are kept in a **private ledger**. By doing this office staff cannot see details of items which the proprietors want to keep a secret.

New Terms

Books of Original Entry (p 84): Books where the first entry of a transaction is made.

Sales Journal (p 84): Book of original entry for credit sales.

Purchases Journal (p 84): Book of original entry for credit purchases.

Returns Inwards Journal (p 84): Book of original entry for goods returned by customers.

Returns Outwards Journal (p 84): Book of original entry for goods returned to suppliers.

Cash Book (p 84): Book of original entry for cash and bank receipts and payments.

General Journal (p 84): Book of original entry for all items other than those for cash or goods.

Sales Ledger (p 85): A ledger for customers' personal accounts.

Purchases Ledger (p 85): A ledger for suppliers' personal accounts.

General Ledger (p 85): All accounts other than those for customers and suppliers.

Personal Accounts (p 86): Accounts for both creditors and debtors.

Impersonal Accounts (p 86): All accounts other than debtors' and creditors' accounts.

Real Accounts (p 86): Accounts in which property of all kinds is recorded.

Nominal Accounts (p 86): Accounts in which expenses, revenue and capital are recorded.

Nominal Ledger (p 86): Another name for the general ledger.

Private Ledger (p 86): Ledger for capital and drawings accounts.

Exercise

11.1 The following balances were taken from the ledger of Roger Craig at 31 December Year 3:

		£
(1)	Customer account balances	2,620
(2)	Drawings	4,210
(3)	Sales	36,340
(4)	Wages and salaries	8,310
(5)	Supplier account balances	1,730
(6)	Fixed assets at net book value	14,500
(7)	Cash in hand	15
(8)	Capital (at 1 January Year 3)	17,365
(9)	Cost of goods sold (Trading Account)	18,185
(10)	Rates and other local taxes	1,720
(11)	Insurances	680
(12)	Stock	1,836
(13)	Depreciation	1,010
(14)	General expenses	550
(15)	Bank	1,799

Required

(a) In your answer book, rule 3 columns headed respectively Personal Accounts, Real Accounts and Nominal Accounts. List each of the 15 accounts in its correct column.

(b) Calculate Roger Craig's **net** profit for the year.

(c) Prepare a Balance Sheet as at 31 December Year 3.
(LCCI)

12 · The Banking System

12.1 Introduction

We will be looking at payments into and out of bank accounts in Chapters 13 and 14. You therefore need to know some details about bank accounts.

12.2 Types of Account

There are two main types of bank account:

Current Accounts

Used for regular payments into and out of a bank account. A **cheque book** will be given by the bank to the holder of the account. He will use it to make payments to people to whom he owes money.

So that he can pay money into his current account, the holder will be given a paying-in book.

Deposit Accounts

Such a bank account is for putting money into the bank and not taking it out quickly.

Usually interest is given by the bank on money kept in deposit accounts. Current accounts do not usually earn interest.

12.3 Cheques

1 When the bank has agreed to let you open a current account it will ask you for a signature. This allows them to prove that your cheques are in fact signed by you, and have not been forged. You will then be issued with a cheque book.
2 You can then use the cheques to make payments out of the account. Normally you must make sure that you have more money in the account than the amount paid out. If you wish to pay out more money than you have banked, you will have to see the bank manager. You will then discuss the reasons for this with him, and if he agrees he will give his permission for you to 'overdraw' your account. This is known as a **bank overdraft**.

3 The person filling in the cheque and using it for payment is known as the **drawer**. The person to whom the cheque is paid is known as the **payee**.

We can now look at Exhibit 12.1, which is a blank cheque form before it is filled in.

Exhibit 12.1

19

PAYEE

£

914234

Cheshire Bank Ltd. 19 09-07-99

Stockport Branch

324 Low Road, Stockport, Cheshire SK6 8AP

PAY OR ORDER

£

J WOODSTOCK

⑈914234⑈ 09⑆07⑆99⑆ 058899⑈

This part is the counterfoil

On the face of the cheque are various sets of numbers. These are:

914234 Every cheque printed for the Cheshire Bank will be given a different number, so that individual items can be traced.

09-07-99 Each branch of each bank in the United Kingdom has a different number given to it. Thus this branch has a 'code' number 09-07-99.

058899 Each account with the bank is given a different number. This particular number is kept only for the account of J Woodstock at the Stockport branch.

When we fill in the cheque we copy the details on the counterfoil which we then detach and keep for our records.

We can now look at the completion of a cheque. Let us assume that we are paying seventy-two pounds and eighty-five pence to K Marsh on 22 May 19–5. Exhibit 12.2 shows the completed cheque.

Exhibit 12.2

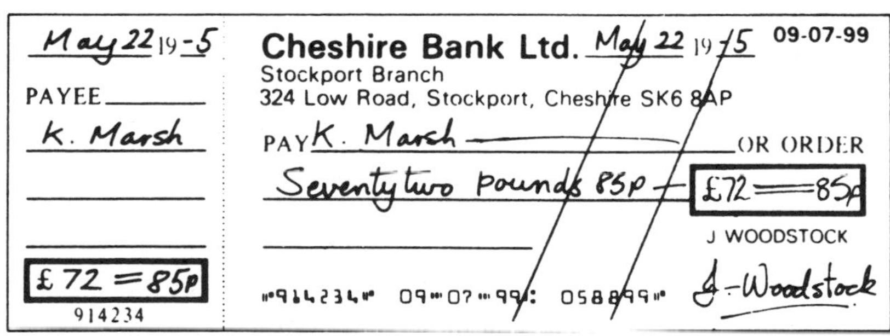

May 22 19-5

PAYEE

K. Marsh

£ 72 = 85p

914234

Cheshire Bank Ltd. May 22 19-5 09-07-99

Stockport Branch

324 Low Road, Stockport, Cheshire SK6 8AP

PAY K. Marsh OR ORDER

Seventy two pounds 85p £72 = 85p

J WOODSTOCK

⑈914234⑈ 09⑆07⑆99⑆ 058899⑈ J. Woodstock

In Exhibit 12.2:

The drawer is: J Woodstock
The payee is: K Marsh

The two parallel lines across the face of the cheque are drawn as a safeguard. If we had not done this the cheque would have been an 'uncrossed cheque'. If someone had stolen a signed uncrossed cheque he could have gone to the Stockport branch of the Cheshire Bank and obtained cash in exchange for the cheque. When the cheque is crossed it means it *must* be paid into a bank account, Post Office Giro bank or Savings Bank.

12.4 Cheque Crossings

Cheques can be further safeguarded by using specific crossing, i.e. writing a form of instruction within the crossing on the cheques as shown in Exhibit 12.3.

Exhibit 12.3

These are specific instructions to the banks about the use of the cheque. The use of 'A/c Payee only' means the cheques should be paid only into the account of the payee named. If cheques are lost or stolen the drawer must advise his bank immediately and confirm by letter. These cheques will be 'stopped', i.e. payment will not be made on these cheques, provided you act swiftly. The safest crossing is that of 'A/c Payee only, Not Negotiable'. If the cheque is lost or stolen it will be of no use to the thief or finder. This is because it is impossible for this cheque to be paid into any bank account other than that of the named payee.

12.5 Paying-in Slips

When we want to pay money into our current accounts, either cash or cheques, or both, we use a **paying-in slip**. One of these is shown as Exhibit 12.4.

J Woodstock has banked the following items:

Four	£5 notes
Three	£1 coins
One	50p coin
Other silver	30p
Bronze coins	12p

Cheques received from:		Code numbers:
E Kane & Son	£184.15	02-58-76
J Gale	£ 65.44	05-77-85

Exhibit 12.4

Face of paying in-slip

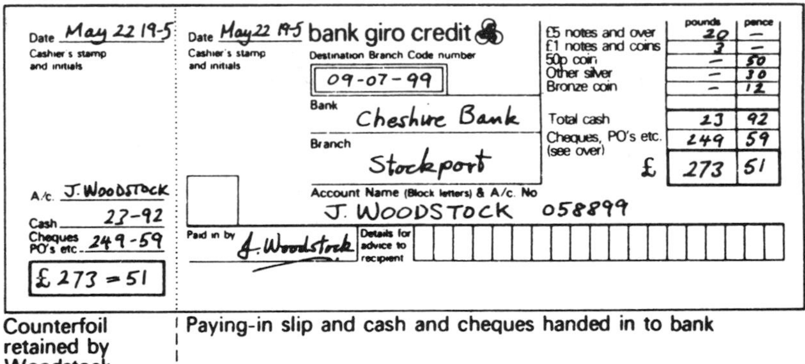

Date May 22 19-5
Cashier's stamp and initials
A/c. J. WOODSTOCK
Cash 23-92
Cheques PO's etc. 249-59
£ 273 = 51

Date May 22 19-5 bank giro credit
Cashier's stamp and initials
Destination Branch Code number 09-07-99
Bank Cheshire Bank
Branch Stockport
Account Name (Block letters) & A/c. No J. WOODSTOCK 058899
Paid in by J. Woodstock
Details for advice to recipient

	pounds	pence
£5 notes and over	20	—
£1 notes and coins	3	—
50p coin	—	50
Other silver	—	30
Bronze coin	—	12
Total cash	23	92
Cheques, PO's etc. (see over)	249	59
£	273	51

Counterfoil retained by Woodstock

Paying-in slip and cash and cheques handed in to bank

Reverse side of paying-in slip

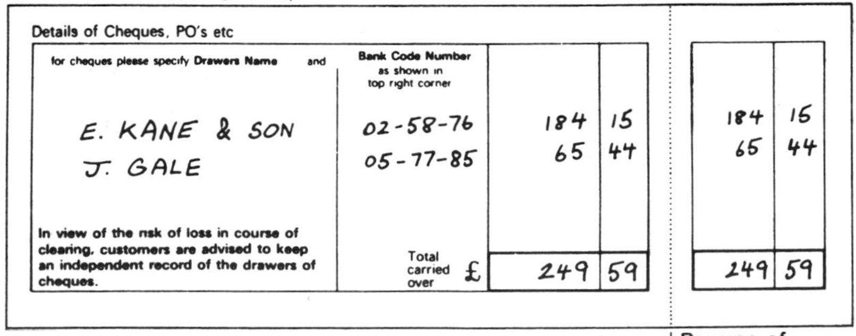

Details of Cheques, PO's etc

for cheques please specify Drawers Name and	Bank Code Number as shown in top right corner				
E. KANE & SON	02-58-76	184	15	184	15
J. GALE	05-77-85	65	44	65	44
In view of the risk of loss in course of clearing, customers are advised to keep an independent record of the drawers of cheques.	Total carried over £	249	59	249	59

Reverse of counterfoil

12.6 Cheque Clearings

We will now look at how cheques paid from one person's bank account pass into another person's bank account.

Let us look at the progress of the cheque in Exhibit 12.2. We will assume that the Post Office is being very efficient and delivering all letters the following day after being posted.

19–5	
May 22	Woodstock, in Stockport, sends the cheque to K Marsh, who lives in Leeds. Woodstock enters the payment in his cash book.
May 23	Cheque received by Marsh. He banks it the same day in his bank account at Barclays Bank in Leeds. Marsh shows the cheque in his cash book as being received and banked on 23 May.
May 24	Barclays in London receive it. They exchange it with the Head Office of the Cheshire Bank in London. The Cheshire bank send the cheque to their Stockport branch.
May 25	The Stockport branch of the Cheshire bank examine the cheque. If there is nothing wrong with it, the cheque can now be debited by the bank to J Woodstock's account.

In Chapter 22 we will be examining bank reconciliation statements. What we have looked at

19–5	
May 22	This is the day on which Woodstock has made the entry in his cash book.
May 25	This is the day when the bank makes an entry in Woodstock's account in respect of the cheque.

– will become an important part of your understanding such statements.

New Terms

Current Account (p 89): Bank account used for regular payments in and out of the bank.

Deposit Account (p 89): Bank account for money to be kept in for a long time. Interest is given on money deposited.

Cheque Book (p 89): Book containing forms (cheques) used to pay money out of a current account.

Bank Overdraft (p 89): When we have paid more out of our bank account than we have paid into it.

Drawer (p 90): The person making out a cheque and using it for payment.

Payee (p 90): The person to whom a cheque is paid.

Paying-in Slip (p 92): Form used for paying money into a bank account.

13 · Two-Column Cash Books

13.1 Introduction

The cash book consists of the cash account and the bank account put together in one book. We used to show these two accounts on different pages of the ledger. Now it is easier to put the two sets of account columns together. This means that we can record all money received and paid out on a particular date on the same page.

In the cash book the debit column for cash is put next to the debit column for bank. The credit column for cash is put next to the credit column for bank.

13.2 Drawing Up a Cash Book

We can now look at a cash account and a bank account in Exhibit 13.1 as they would appear if they had been kept separately. Then in Exhibit 13.2 they are shown as if the transactions had instead been kept in a cash book.

The bank column contains details of the payments made by cheque and of the money received and paid into the bank account. The bank will have a copy of the account in its own books.

The bank will send a copy of the account in its books to the firm, this copy usually being known as the **bank statement**. When the firm receives the bank statement, it will check it against the bank column in its own cash book to ensure that there are no errors.

Exhibit 13.1

Cash

19–5		£	19–5		£
Aug 2	T Moore	33	Aug 8	Rent	20
" 5	K Charles	25	" 12	C Potts	19
" 15	F Hughes	37	" 28	Wages	25
" 30	H Howe	18	" 31	Balance c/d	49
		113			113
Sept 1	Balance b/d	49			

Bank

19–5	£	19–5	£
Aug 1 Capital	1,000	Aug 7 Rates	105
" 3 W P Ltd	244	" 12 F Small Ltd	95
" 16 K Noone	408	" 26 K French	268
" 30 H Sanders	20	" 31 Balance c/d	1,204
	1,672		1,672
Sept 1 Balance b/d	1,204		

Exhibit 13.2

Cash Book

	Cash	*Bank*		*Cash*	*Bank*
19–5	£	£	19–5	£	£
Aug 1 Capital		1,000	Aug 7 Rates		105
" 2 T Moore	33		" 8 Rent	20	
" 3 W P Ltd		244	" 12 C Potts	19	
" 5 K Charles	25		" 12 F Small Ltd		95
" 15 F Hughes	37		" 26 K French		268
" 16 K Noone		408	" 28 Wages	25	
" 30 H Sanders		20	" 31 Balance c/d	49	1,204
" 30 H Howe	18				
	113	1,672		113	1,672
Sept 1 Balances b/d	49	1,204			

13.3 Cash Paid into the Bank

In Exhibit 13.2, the payments into the bank have been cheques received by the firm which have been banked immediately. We must now consider cash being paid into the bank.

1 Let us look at the position when a customer pays his account in cash, and later a part of this cash is paid into the bank. The receipt of the cash is debited to the cash column on the date received, the credit entry being in the customer's personal account. The cash banked has the following effect needing action as shown:

Effect	Action
1 Asset of cash is decreased	Credit the asset account, i.e. the cash account which is represented by the cash column in the cash book.
2 Asset of bank is increased	Debit the asset account, i.e. the bank account which is represented by the bank column in the cash book.

A cash receipt of £100 from M Davies on 1 August 19–5, later followed by the banking on 3 August of £80 of this amount would appear in the cash book as follows:

Cash Book					
	Cash	*Bank*		*Cash*	*Bank*
19–5	£	£	19–5	£	£
Aug 1 M Davies	100		Aug 3 Bank	80	
" 3 Cash		80			

The details column shows entries against each item stating the name of the account in which the completion of double entry has taken place. Against the cash payment of £80 appears the word 'bank', meaning that the debit £80 is to be found in the bank column, and the opposite applies.

2 Where the whole of the cash received is banked immediately the receipt can be treated in exactly the same manner as a cheque received, i.e. it can be entered directly in the bank column.

3 If the firm requires cash it may withdraw cash from the bank. This is done by making out a cheque to pay itself a certain amount in cash. The bank will give cash in exchange for the cheque.

The twofold effect and the action required may be shown:

Effect	Action
1 Asset of bank is decreased.	Credit the asset account, i.e. the bank column in the cash book.
2 Asset of cash is increased.	Debit the asset account, i.e. the cash column in the cash book.

A withdrawal of £75 cash on 1 June 19–5 from the bank would appear in the cash book thus:

Cash Book					
	Cash	*Bank*		*Cash*	*Bank*
19–5	£	£	19–5	£	£
June 1 Bank	75		June 1 Cash		75

Both the debit and credit entries for this item are in the same book. When this happens it is known as a **contra** item.

13.4 The Use of Folio Columns

As you have already seen, the details column in an account contains the name of the other account in which double entry has been completed. Anyone looking through the books would therefore be able to find where the other half of the double entry was.

However, when many books are being used, just to mention the name of the other account would not be enough information to find the other account quickly. More information is needed, and this is given by using **folio columns**.

In each account and in each book being used, a folio column is added, always shown on the left of the money columns. In this column the name of the other book, in abbreviated form, and the number of the page in the other book where double entry is completed is stated against each and every entry in the books.

An entry of receipt of cash from C Kelly whose account was on page 45 of the sales ledger, and the cash recorded on page 37 of the cash book, would use the folio column thus:

In the cash book. In the folio column would appear SL 45.

In the sales ledger. In the folio column would appear CB 37.

By this method full cross reference would be given. Each of the contra items, being shown on the same page of the cash book, would use the letter 'C' in the folio column.

13.5 Advantages of Folio Columns

These are:

- As described in 13.4 it speeds up reference to the other book where double entry for the item is completed.
- The folio column is filled in when double entry has been completed. If it has not been filled in, double entry will not have been made.

Looking through the folio columns to ensure they have all been filled in will help us to detect such errors.

13.6 Example of a Cash Book With Folio Columns

The following transactions are written up in the form of a cash book. The folio columns are filled in as though double entry had been completed to other accounts.

19–5			£
Sept	1	Proprietor puts capital into a bank account for the business.	940
"	2	Received cheque from M Boon.	115
"	4	Cash sales.	102
"	6	Paid rent by cash.	35
"	7	Banked £50 of the cash held by the firm.	50
"	15	Cash sales paid direct into the bank.	40
"	23	Paid cheque to S Wills.	277
"	29	Withdrew cash from bank for business use.	120
"	30	Paid wages in cash.	118

Cash Book

	Folio	Cash	Bank		Folio	Cash	Bank
19–5		£	£	19–5		£	£
Sept 1 Capital	GL1		940	Sept 6 Rent	GL65	35	
" 2 M Boon	SL98		115	" 7 Bank	C	50	
" 4 Sales	GL87	102		" 23 S Wills	PL23		277
" 7 Cash	C		50	" 29 Cash	C		120
" 15 Sales	GL87		40	" 30 Wages	GL39	118	
" 29 Bank	C	120		" 30 Balances	c/d	19	748
		222	1,145			222	1,145
Oct 1 Balances	b/d	19	748				

The abbreviations used in the folio column are as follows:
GL = General Ledger: SL = Sales Ledger: C = Contra: PL = Purchases Ledger.

13.7 Receipts

When a cash sale is made it is not necessary for a receipt to be given. This is a form stating how much cash has been received, and the date of payment. This is because the goods are handed over immediately and there is, therefore, no need to keep a check on the identity of the payer. However, quite a lot of businesses, for example Marks and Spencers, do give receipts in such cases even though it is not legally necessary. However, payment by cash for payments in respect of goods sold on credit would need the evidence of a receipt.

A receipt might be as follows:

Date ..15 May 19-1

Received from ...A Reader.......................

the sum of .....Fifty pounds 40p...........

in respect of ....Settlement of account..

Signed ....J. Hall................

on behalf of Johnson and Longden Ltd

When payment is made by cheque a receipt is not necessary, as the paid cheque will act as evidence of payment. Similarly payments by standing order and direct debit will mean that receipts are not needed.

New Terms

Bank Statement (p 94): Copy of our current account given to us by our bank.

Contra (p 96): A contra is where both the debit and credit entries are shown in the cash book.

Folio Columns (p 97): Columns used for entering reference numbers.

Exercises

13.1 Write up a two-column cash book from the following details, and balance off as at the end of the month:

19–5
May 1 Started business with capital in cash £100
" 2 Paid rent by cash £10
" 3 F Lake lent us £500, paying by cheque
" 4 We paid B McKenzie by cheque £65
" 5 Cash sales £98
" 7 N Miller paid us by cheque £62
" 9 We paid B Burton in cash £22
" 11 Cash sales paid direct into the bank £53
" 15 G Moores paid us in cash £65
" 16 We took £50 out of the cash till and paid it into the bank account
" 19 We repaid F Lake £100 by cheque
" 22 Cash sales paid direct into the bank £66
" 26 Paid motor expenses by cheque £12
" 30 Withdrew £100 cash from the bank for business use
" 31 Paid wages in cash £97.

13.2 Write up a two-column cash book from the following details, and balance off as at the end of the month:

19–6
Mar 1 Balances brought down from last month:
Cash in hand £56: Cash in bank £2,356
" 2 Paid rates by cheque £156
" 3 Paid for postage stamps in cash £5
" 5 Cash sales £74
" 7 Cash paid into bank £60
" 8 We paid T Lee by cheque £75: We paid C Brooks in cash £2
" 12 J Moores pays us £150, £50 being in cash and £100 by cheque
" 17 Cash drawings by proprietor £20
" 20 P Jones pays us by cheque £79
" 22 Withdrew £200 from the bank for business use
" 24 Bought a new motor van for £195 cash
" 28 Paid rent by cheque £40
" 31 Cash sales paid direct into the bank £105.

13.3X A two-column cash book is to be written up from the following, carrying the balances down to the following month:

19–4
Jan 1 Started business with £4,000 in the bank
" 2 Paid for fixtures by cheque £660
" 4 Cash sales £225: Paid rent by cash £140
" 6 T Thomas paid us by cheque £188
" 8 Cash sales paid direct into the bank £308
" 10 J King paid us in cash £300
" 12 Paid wages in cash £275
" 14 J Walters lent us £500 paying by cheque
" 15 Withdrew £200 from the bank for business use
" 20 Bought stationery paying by cash £60
" 22 We paid J French by cheque £166
" 28 Cash Drawings £100
" 30 J Scott paid us by cheque £277
" 31 Cash Sales £66.

13.4X Write up a two-column cash book from the following:

19–6
Nov 1 Balance brought forward from last month: Cash £105; Bank £2,164
" 2 Cash Sales £605
" 3 Took £500 out of the cash till and paid it into the bank
" 4 J Matthews paid us by cheque £217
" 5 We paid for postage stamps in cash £60
" 6 Bought office equipment by cheque £189
" 7 We paid J Lucas by cheque £50
" 9 Received rates refund by cheque £72
" 11 Withdrew £250 from the bank for business use
" 12 Paid wages in cash £239
" 14 Paid motor expenses by cheque £57
" 16 L Levy lent us £200 in cash
" 20 R Norman paid us by cheque £112
" 28 We paid general expenses in cash £22
" 30 Paid insurance by cheque £74.

14 · Cash Discounts and the Three-Column Cash Book

14.1 Cash Discounts

It is better if customers pay their accounts quickly. A firm may accept a smaller sum in full settlement if payment is made within a certain period of time. The amount of the reduction of the sum to be paid is known as a *cash discount*. The term 'cash discount' thus refers to the allowance given for quick payment. It is still called cash discount, even if the account is paid by cheque.

The rate of cash discount is usually stated as a percentage. Full details of the percentage allowed, and the period within which payment is to be made, are quoted on all sales documents by the selling company. A typical period during which discount may be allowed is one month from the date of the original transaction.

14.2 Discounts Allowed and Discounts Received

A firm may have two types of cash discounts in its books. These are:

1 **Discounts allowed**. Cash discounts allowed by a firm to its customers when they pay their accounts quickly.
2 **Discounts received**. Received by a firm from its suppliers when it pays their accounts quickly.

We can now see the effect of discounts by looking at two examples.

Example 1

W Clarke owed us £100. He pays on 2 September 19–5 by cash within the time limit laid down, and the firm allows him 5 per cent cash discount. So he will pay £100 – £5 = £95 in full settlement of his account.

Effect	Action
1 Of cash: Cash is increased by £95. Asset of debtors is decreased by £95.	 Debit cash account, i.e. enter £95 in debit column of cash book. Credit W Clarke £95.
2 Of discounts: Asset of debtors is decreased by £5. (After the cash was paid the balance of £5 still appeared. As the account has been paid this asset must now be cancelled.) Expenses of discounts allowed increased by £5.	 Credit W Clarke £5. Debit discounts allowed account £5.

Example 2

The firm owed S Small £400. It pays him on 3 September 19–5 by cheque within the time limit laid down by him and he allows $2\frac{1}{2}$ per cent cash discount. Thus the firm will pay £400 – £10 = £390 in full settlement of the account.

Effect	Action
1 Of cheque: Asset of bank is reduced by £390. Liability of creditors is reduced by £390.	 Credit bank, i.e. enter in credit bank column, £390. Debit S Small's account £390.
2 Of discounts: Liability of creditors is reduced by £10. (After the cheque was paid the balance of £10 remained. As the account has been paid the liability must now be cancelled.) Revenue of discounts received increased by £10.	 Debit S Small's account £10. Credit discounts received account £10.

The accounts in the firm's books would appear:

Cash Book (*page 32*)

	Cash	*Bank*		*Cash*	*Bank*
19–5	£	£	19–5	£	£
Sept 2 W Clarke SL12	95		Sept 3 S Small PL75		390

Discounts Received (General Ledger *page 18*)

	19–5	£
	Sept 2 S Small PL75	10

Discounts Allowed (General Ledger *page 17*)

19–5	£		
Sept 2 W Clarke SL12	5		

W Clarke (Sales Ledger *page 12*)

19–5	£	19–5	£
Sept 1 Balance b/d	100	Sept 2 Cash CB32	95
		〃 2 Discount GL17	5
	100		100

S Small (Purchases Ledger *page 75*)

19–5	£	19–5	£
Sept 3 Bank CB32	390	Sept 1 balance b/d	400
〃 3 Discounts GL18	10		
	400		400

It is the accounting custom to enter the word 'Discount' in the personal accounts, not stating whether it is a discount received or a discount allowed.

14.3 Discount Columns in Cash Book

The discounts allowed account and the discounts received account are in the general ledger along with all the other revenue and expense accounts. It has already been stated that every effort should be made to avoid too much reference to the general ledger.

In the case of discounts this is done by adding an extra column on each side of the cash book in which the amounts of discounts are entered. Discounts received are entered in the discounts column on the credit side of the cash book, and discounts allowed in the discounts column on the debit side of the cash book.

The cash book, if completed for the two examples so far dealt with, would appear:

Cash Book

	Discount	*Cash*	*Bank*		*Discount*	*Cash*	*Bank*
19–5	£	£	£	19–5	£	£	£
Sept 2 W Clarke SL12	5	95		Sept 3 S Small PL75	10		390

There is no alteration to the method of showing discounts in the personal accounts.

To Make Entries in the Discounts Accounts

Total of discounts column on receipts side of cash book	Enter on debit side of discounts allowed account
Total of discounts column on payments side of cash book	Enter on credit side of discounts received account

14.4 A Worked Example

19–5			£
May	1	Balances brought down from April:	
		Cash Balance	29
		Bank Balance	654
		Debtors accounts:	
		B King	120
		N Campbell	280
		D Shand	40
		Creditors accounts:	
		U Barrow	60
		A Allen	440
		R Long	100
"	2	B King pays us by cheque, having deducted $2\frac{1}{2}$ per cent cash discount £3	117
"	8	We pay R Long his account by cheque, deducting 5 per cent cash discount £5	95
"	11	We withdrew £100 cash from the bank for business use	100
"	16	N Campbell pays us his account by cheque, deducting $2\frac{1}{2}$ per cent discount £7	273
"	25	We paid wages in cash	92
"	28	D Shand pays us in cash after having deducted $2\frac{1}{2}$ per cent cash discount	38
"	29	We pay U Barrow by cheque less 5 per cent cash discount £3	57
"	30	We pay A Allen by cheque less $2\frac{1}{2}$ per cent cash discount £11	429

Cash Book — Page 64

	Folio	Discount	Cash	Bank		Folio	Discount	Cash	Bank
19–5		£	£	£	19–5		£	£	£
May 1					May 8				
Balances	b/d		29	654	R Long	PL58	5		95
May 2					May 11				
B King	SL13	3		117	Cash	C			100
May 11					May 25				
Bank	C		100		Wages	GL77		92	
May 16					May 29				
N Campbell	SL84	7		273	U Barrow	PL15	3		57
May 28					May 30				
D Shand	SL91	2	38		A Allen	PL98	11		429
					May 31				
					Balances	c/d		75	363
		12	167	1,044			19	167	1,044
Jun 1 Balances	b/d		75	363					

Sales Ledger

B King — *Page 13*

		£			£
19–5		£	19–5		£
May 1 Balance b/d		120	May 2 Bank	CB 64	117
			" 2 Discount	CB 64	3
		120			120

N Campbell — *Page 84*

		£			£
19–5		£	19–5		£
May 1 Balance b/d		280	May 16 Bank	CB 64	273
			" 16 Discount	CB 64	7
		280			280

D Shand — *Page 91*

		£			£
19–5		£	19–5		£
May 1 Balance b/d		40	May 28 Cash	CB 64	38
			" 28 Discount	CB 64	2
		40			40

Purchases Ledger

U Barrow — *Page 15*

		£			£
19–5		£	19–5		£
May 29 Bank	CB 64	57	May 1 Balance b/d		60
" 29 Discount	CB 64	3			
		60			60

R Long — *Page 58*

		£			£
19–5		£	19–5		£
May 8 Bank	CB 64	95	May 1 Balance b/d		100
" 8 Discount	CB 64	5			
		100			100

A Allen — *Page 98*

		£			£
19–5		£	19–5		£
May 30 Bank	CB 64	429	May 1 Balance b/d		440
" 30 Discount	CB 64	11			
		440			440

General Ledger

Wages — *Page 77*

		£			
19–5		£			
May 25 Cash	CB 64	92			

Discounts Received *Page 88*

				19–5		£
				May 31 Total for the month	CB64	19

Discounts Allowed

19–5		£			
May 31 Total for the month	CB64	12			

Is the above method of entering discounts correct?
You can easily check. See the following:

Discounts in Ledger Accounts	Debits		Credits	
		£		
Discounts Received	U Barrow	3	Discounts	
	R Long	5	received	
	A Allen	11	account	£19
		19		
				£
Discounts Allowed	Discounts		B King	3
	allowed		N Campbell	7
	account	£12	D Shand	2
				12

You can see that proper double entry has been carried out. Equal amounts, in total, have been entered on each side of the accounts.

14.5 Bank Overdrafts

A firm may borrow money from a bank by means of a bank overdraft. This means that the firm is allowed to pay more out of the bank account, by paying out cheques, than the total amount which is placed in the account.

Up to this point the bank balances have all been money at the bank, so they have all been assets, i.e. debit balances. When the account is overdrawn the firm owes money to the bank, so the account is a liability and the balance becomes a credit one.

Taking the cash book last shown, suppose that the amount payable to A Allen was £1,429 instead of £429. Thus the amount in the bank account, £1,044, is exceeded by the amount withdrawn. The cash book would appear as follows:

Cash Book

	Discount	Cash	Bank		Discount	Cash	Bank
19–5	£	£	£	19–5	£	£	£
May 1 Balances b/d		29	654	May 8 R Long	5		95
" 2 B King	3		117	" 11 Cash			100
" 11 Bank		100		" 25 Wages		92	
" 16 N Campbell	7		273	" 29 U Barrow	3		57
" 28 D Shand	2	38		" 30 A Allen	11		1,429
" 31 Balance c/d			637	" 31 Balance c/d		75	
	12	167	1,681		19	167	1,681
Jun 1 Balance b/d		75		Jun 1 Balance b/d			637

On a balance sheet a bank overdraft will be shown as an item included under the heading current liabilities.

14.6 Multiple-choice questions

Now attempt Set No 2 of multiple choice questions, *see* pages 345–7.

New Terms

Discounts Allowed (p 101): A reduction given to customers who pay their accounts within the time allowed.

Discounts Received (p 101): A reduction given to us by a supplier when we pay his account before the time allowed has elapsed.

Exercises

14.1 Enter up a three column cash book from the details following. Balance off at the end of the month, and show the relevant discount accounts as they would appear in the general ledger.

19–7
May 1 Started business with £6,000 in the bank
" 1 Bought fixtures paying by cheque £950
" 2 Bought goods paying by cheque £1,240
" 3 Cash Sales £407
" 4 Paid rent in cash £200
" 5 N Morgan paid us his account of £220 by a cheque for £210, we allowed him £10 discount
" 7 Paid S Thompson & Co £80 owing to them by means of a cheque £76, they allowed us £4 discount
" 9 We received a cheque for £380 from S Cooper, discount having been allowed £20
" 12 Paid rates by cheque £410
" 14 L Curtis pays us a cheque for £115
" 16 Paid M Monroe his account of £120 by cash £114, having deducted £6 cash discount
" 20 P Exeter pays us a cheque for £78, having deducted £2 cash discount
" 31 Cash Sales paid direct into the bank £88.

14.2 A three column cash book is to be written up from the following details, balanced off and the relevant discount accounts in the general ledger shown.

19–5

Mar 1 Balances brought forward: Cash £230; Bank £4,756

" 2 The following paid their accounts by cheque, in each case deducting 5 per cent cash discounts; Accounts: R Burton £140; E Taylor £220; R Harris £300

" 4 Paid rent by cheque £120

" 6 J Cotton lent us £1,000 paying by cheque

" 8 We paid the following accounts by cheque in each case deducting a $2\frac{1}{2}$ per cent cash discount; N Black £360; P Towers £480; C Rowse £800

" 10 Paid motor expenses in cash £44

" 12 H Hankins pays his account of £77 by cheque £74, deducting £3 cash discount

" 15 Paid wages in cash £160

" 18 The following paid their accounts by cheque, in each case deducting 5 per cent cash discount: Accounts: C Winston £260; R Wilson & Son £340; H Winter £460

" 21 Cash withdrawn from the bank £350 for business use

" 24 Cash Drawings £120

" 25 Paid T Briers his account of £140, by cash £133, having deducted £7 cash discount

" 29 Bought fixtures paying by cheque £650

" 31 Received commission by cheque £88.

14.3 From the following details write up a three-column cash book, balance off at the end of the month, and show the relevant discount accounts as they would appear in the general ledger:

19–3

Mar 1 Balances brought forward:
Cash in hand £211
Cash at bank £3,984

" 2 We paid each of the following accounts by cheque, in each case we deducted a 5 per cent discount: T Adams £80; C Bibby £260; D Clarke £440

" 4 C Potts pays us a cheque for £98

" 6 Cash Sales paid direct into the bank £49

" 7 Paid insurance by cash £65

" 9 The following persons pay us their accounts by cheque, in each case they deducted a discount of $2\frac{1}{2}$ per cent: R Smiley £160; J Turner £640; R Pimlott £520

" 12 Paid motor expenses by cash £100

" 18 Cash Sales £98

" 21 Paid salaries by cheque £120

" 23 Paid rent by cash £60

" 28 Received a cheque for £500 being a loan from R Godfrey

" 31 Paid for stationery by cheque £27.

14.4X Enter the following in a three-column cash book. Balance off the cash book at the end of the month and show the discount accounts in the general ledger.

19–8
June 1 Balances brought forward: Cash £97; Bank £2,186
" 2 The following paid us by cheque in each case deducting a 5 per cent cash discount: R Harris £1,000; C White £280; P Peers £180; O Hardy £600
" 3 Cash Sales paid direct into the bank £134
" 5 Paid rent by cash £88
" 6 We paid the following accounts by cheque, in each case deducting $2\frac{1}{2}$ per cent cash discount: J Charlton £400; H Sobers £640; D Shallcross £200
" 8 Withdrew cash from the bank for business use £250
" 10 Cash Sales £206
" 12 D Deeds paid us their account of £89 by cheque less £2 cash discount
" 14 Paid wages by cash £250
" 16 We paid the following accounts by cheque: L Lucas £117 less cash discount £6; D Fisher £206 less cash discount £8
" 20 Bought fixtures by cheque £8,000
" 24 Bought motor lorry paying by cheque £7,166
" 29 Received £169 cheque from D Steel
" 30 Cash Sales £116
" 30 Bought stationery paying by cash £60.

14.5X You are to write up a three-column cash book for M Pinero from the details which follow. Then balance off at the end of the month and show the discount accounts in the general ledger.

19–6
May 1 Balances brought forward:
Cash in hand £58
Bank overdraft £1,470
" 2 M Pinero pays further Capital into the bank £1,000
" 3 Bought office fixtures by cheque £780
" 4 Cash Sales £220
" 5 Banked cash £200
" 6 We paid the following by cheque, in each case deducting $2\frac{1}{2}$ per cent cash discount: B Barnes £80; T Horton £240; T Jacklin £400
" 8 Cash Sales £500
" 12 Paid motor expenses in cash £77
" 15 Cash withdrawn from the bank £400
" 16 Cash Drawings £120
" 18 The following firms paid us their accounts by cheque, in each case deducting a 5 per cent discount: L Graham £80; B Crenshaw £140; H Green £220
" 20 Salaries paid in cash £210
" 22 T Weiskopf paid us his account in cash £204
" 26 Paid insurance by cheque £150
" 28 We banked all the cash in our possession except for £20 in the cash till
" 31 Bought motor van, paying by cheque £4,920.

14.6 *(a)* List *three* ways in which a trader can pay debts other than by cash or cheque.
(b) On 1 July Year 7, the debit balances in the Cash Book of E Rich were:

Cash	£419
Bank	£3,685

His transactions for the month of July were:

2 July	Received cheque from A Wood £296
6 July	Paid wages in cash £102
9 July	Paid C Hill £211 by cheque in full settlement of his account of £224
12 July	Received £146 cash for sale of damaged stock
	Paid T Jarvis £1,023 by cheque in full settlement of his account of £1,051
13 July	Paid wages in cash £104
17 July	Received cheque for £500 from Atlas & Company
19 July	Paid £21 in cash for postage stamps
20 July	Paid wages in cash £102
23 July	Withdrew £200 from bank for office cash
25 July	Paid W Moore £429 by cheque
26 July	Paid wages in cash £105
28 July	Received £317 cash from T Phillips in full settlement of his account of £325, paid into bank the same day
31 July	Paid £260 cash into bank

Required
Prepare the three-column Cash Book for the month of July Year 7 and balance it at 31 July, bringing the balances down at 1 August.
(LCCI)

15 · The Sales Journal and the Sales Ledger

15.1 Introduction

In Chapter 11 we saw that the ledger had been split up into a set of journals and ledgers. This chapter explains about sales journals and sales ledgers.

15.2 Cash Sales

When goods are paid for immediately by cash there is no need to enter such sales in the sales journal. In such cases we do not need to know the names and addresses of customers and what has been sold to them.

15.3 Credit Sales

In many businesses most of the sales will be made on credit rather than for immediate cash. In fact, the sales of some businesses will consist entirely of credit sales.

For each credit sale the selling firm will send a document to the buyer showing full details of the goods sold and the prices of the goods. This document is known as an **invoice**, and to the seller it is known as a **sales invoice**. The seller will keep one or more copies of each sales invoice for his own use. Exhibit 15.1 is an example of an invoice.

Exhibit 15.1

Your Purchase Order 10/A/980		J Blake 7 Over Warehouse Leicester LE1 2AP 1 September 19–5
INVOICE No. 16554		
To: D Poole 45 Charles Street Manchester M1 5ZN		
	Per unit	Total
	£	£
21 cases McBrand Pears	20	420
5 cartons Kay's Flour	4	20
6 cases Joy's Vinegar	20	120
		560
Terms: $1\frac{1}{4}$% cash discount if paid within one month		

You must not think that all invoices will look exactly like the one chosen as Exhibit 15.1. Each business will have its own design. All invoices will be numbered, and they will contain the names and addresses both of the supplier and of the customer. In this case the supplier is J Blake and the customer is D Poole.

15.4 Copies of Sales Invoices

As soon as the sales invoices for the goods being sent have been made out, they are sent to the customer. The firm will keep copies of all these sales invoices. These copies will have been made at the same time as the original, usually by some kind of carbon paper or special copying paper.

15.5 Entering Into the Sales Journal

From the copy of the sales invoice the seller enters up his sales journal. This book is merely a list, showing the following:

- Date
- Name of customer
- Invoice number
- Final amount of invoice

There is no need to show details of the goods sold in the sales journal. This can be found by looking at copy invoices.

We can now look at Exhibit 15.2 which is a sales journal, starting with the record of the sales invoice already shown in Exhibit 15.1. Let us assume that the entries are on page 26 of the journal.

Exhibit 15.2

Sales Journal		
	Invoice No	*page 26*
19–5		£
Sept 1 D Poole	16554	560
8 T Cockburn	16555	1,640
28 C Carter	16556	220
30 D Stevens & Co	16557	1,100
		3,520

15.6 Posting Credit Sales to the Sales Ledger

Instead of having one ledger for all accounts, we now have a sales ledger. This was described in Chapter 11.

1 The credit sales are now posted, one by one, to the debit side of each customer's account in the sales ledger.
2 At the end of each period the total of the credit sales is posted to the credit of the sales account in the general ledger. This is now illustrated in Exhibit 15.3.

Exhibit 15.3 Posting Credit Sales

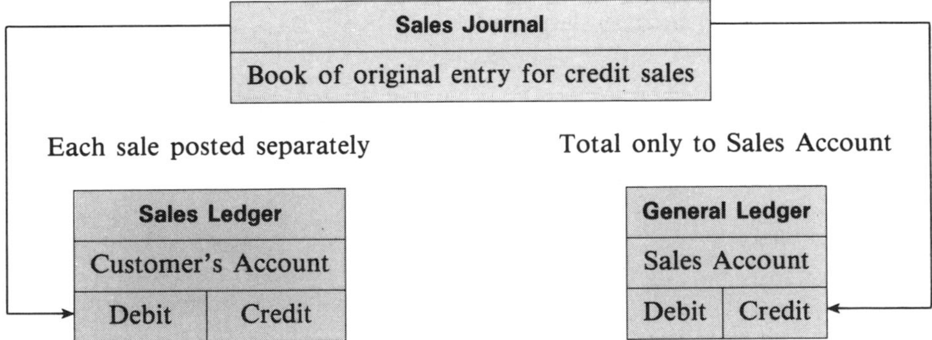

15.7 An Example of Posting Credit Sales

The sales journal in Exhibit 15.2 is now shown again. This time posting is made to the sales ledger and the general ledger. Notice the completion of the folio columns with the reference numbers.

Sales Journal

	Invoice No	Folio	(page 26)
19–5			£
Sept 1 D Poole	16554	SL 12	560
" 8 T Cockburn	16555	SL 39	1,640
" 28 C Carter	16556	SL 125	220
" 30 D Stevens & Co	16557	SL 249	1,100
Transferred to Sales Account		GL 44	3,520

Sales Ledger

D Poole *(page 12)*

19–5		£				
Sept 1 Sales	SJ 26	560				

T Cockburn *(page 39)*

19–5		£				
Sept 8 Sales	SJ 26	1,640				

C Carter *(page 125)*

19–5		£				
Sept 28 Sales	SJ 26	220				

D Stevens & Co *(page 249)*

19–5		£				
Sept 30 Sales	SJ 26	1,100				

General Ledger

Sales *(page 44)*

				19–5		£
				Sept 30 Credit Sales for the month	SJ 26	3,520

Alternative names for the sales journal are sales book and sales day book. Before you continue you should attempt exercise 15.1.

15.8 Trade Discounts

Suppose you are the proprietor of a business. You are selling to three different kinds of customers:

1 Traders who buy a lot of goods from you.
2 Traders who buy only a few items from you.
3 Direct to the general public.

The traders themselves have to sell the goods to the general public in their own areas. They have to make a profit to help finance their businesses, so they will want to pay you less than retail price.

The traders **1** who buy in large quantities will not want to pay as much as traders **2** who buy in small quantities. You want to attract such large customers, and so you are happy to sell to traders **1** at a lower price.

This means that your selling prices are at three levels: **1** to traders buying large quantities, **2** to traders buying small quantities, and **3** to the general public.

So that your staff does not need three different price lists, **1**, **2** and **3**, all goods are shown at the same price. However, a reduction (discount), called a **trade discount** is given to traders **1** and **2**. Exhibit 15.3 is an example.

Exhibit 15.3

You are selling a make of food mixing machine. The basic price is £200. Traders **1** are given 25 per cent trade discount, traders **2** 20 per cent, the general public get no trade discount. The prices paid by each type of customer would be:

		Trader 1		**Trader 2**	**General Public 3**
		£		**£**	**£**
Basic price		200		200	200
Less Trade discount	(25%)	50	(20%)	40	nil
Price to be paid by customer		150		160	200

Exhibit 15.4 is an invoice for goods sold to D Poole. It is for the same items as were shown in Exhibit 15.1, but this time the seller is R Grant and he uses trade discounts to get to the price paid by his customers.

Exhibit 15.4

Your Purchase Order 11/A/G80 INVOICE No. 30756 To: D Poole & Co 45 Charles Street Manchester M1 5ZN	R Grant Higher Side Preston PR1 2NL 2 September 19–5 Tel (0703) 33122 Fax (0703) 22331	
	Per unit	Total
	£	£
21 cases McBrand Pears	25	525
5 cartons Kay's Flour	5	25
6 cases Joy's Vinegar	25	150
		700
Less 20% Trade discount		140
		560

By comparing Exhibits 15.1 and 15.3 you can see that the prices paid by D Poole were the same. It is simply the method of calculating the price that is different.

15.9 No Double Entry for Trade Discounts

As trade discount is simply a way of calculating sales prices, no entry for trade discount should be made in the double entry records nor in the sales journal. The recording of Exhibit 15.4 in R Grant's Sales Journal and D Poole's personal account will appear:

Sales Journal			
	Invoice No	*Folio*	*(page 87)*
19–5			
Sept 2 D Poole	30756	SL 32	560

Sales Ledger *(page 32)*

D Poole

19–5		£	
Sept 2 Sales	SJ 87	560	

To compare with cash discounts:
Trade discounts: not shown in double entry accounts.
Cash discounts: are shown in double entry accounts.

15.10 Other Documentation

Each firm will have its own system of making out documents. All but the very smallest organisations will have their documents prepared via the computer.

The sales invoice is the document from which the book-keeping records are prepared. There will usually be several other documents prepared at the same time, so that the firm may properly organise the sending of the goods and ensuring that they are safely received.

These extra documents may be as follows:

1 Advice notes. These will be sent to the customer before the goods are dispatched. This means that the customer will know that the goods are on the way and when they should arrive. If the goods do not arrive within a reasonable time then the customer will notify the seller, so that enquiries may be made with the carrier to establish what has happened to the goods.

The document will look something like that shown in Exhibit 15.5. Compare it with the invoice sent out as Exhibit 15.4.

Exhibit 15.5

No 178554

ADVICE NOTE

R GRANT
Higher Side
Preston PR1 2NL

Tel (0703) 33122
Fax (0703) 22331

30 August 19–5
J Jones, Head Buyer
D Poole & Co
45 Charles Street
Manchester M1 5ZN

Your order No 11/A/G80
Despatch details: 27 cases and 5 cartons

Quantity	Cat No	Description	Price
21 cases	M566	McBrand Pears	£25 each
5 cartons	K776	Kay's Flour	£5 each
6 cases	J865	Joy's Vinegar	£25 each
			All less 20%

Delivery to:
Warehouse 2, D Poole & Co,
Longmills Trading Estate, Manchester M14 2TT

2 Delivery note. When the goods are sent out they usually have a delivery note to accompany them. This means that the customer can check immediately, and easily, what goods are being received. Very often a copy will be retained by the carrier, with the customer having to sign to say that he has received the goods as stated on the note.

In connection with the goods shown on the advice note in Exhibit 15.5, a delivery note may appear as in Exhibit 15.6.

Exhibit 15.6

DELIVERY NOTE No 194431

R GRANT
Higher Side
Preston PR1 2NL

Tel (0703) 33122
Fax (0703) 22331

1 September 19–5

J Jones, Head Buyer
D Poole & Co
45 Charles Street
Manchester M1 5ZN

Order No 11/A/G80
Despatch details: 27 cases, 5 cartons by road

Quantity	Cat No	Details
21 cases	M566	McBrand Pears
5 cartons	K776	Kay's Flour
6 cases	J865	Joy's Vinegar

Delivery to: Warehouse 2, Longmills Trading Estate,
Manchester M14 2TT

Received 27 cases and 5 cartons

Signed ....
On behalf of ....

3 Other documents. Each firm may vary in the type and number of documents used. Some of the other documents may be:

- *Despatch notes*. These will resemble the delivery notes, and are used by the despatch department.
- *Acknowledgement letters*. These may be sent to customers to show that their orders have been received, and whether delivery may be made as per the order.

15.11 Manufacturer's Recommended Retail Price

Looking at an item displayed in a shop window, you will frequently see something like the following:

Automatic Washer:	Manufacturer's Recommended Retail Price	£500
	less discount of 20 per cent	£100
	You pay only	£400

Very often the manufacturer's recommended retail price is a figure above what the manufacturer would expect the public to pay for its product. Probably, in the case shown the manufacturer would have expected the public to pay around £400 for its product.

The inflated figure used for the 'manufacturer's recommended retail price' is simply a sales gimmick. Most people like to feel they are getting a bargain. The salesmen know that someone usually would prefer to get '20 per cent discount' and pay £400, rather than the price simply be shown as £400 with no mention of a discount.

15.12 Credit Control

Any organisation which sells goods on credit should keep a close check to ensure that debtors pay their accounts on time. If this is not done properly, the amount of debtors can grow to an amount that will cripple the business.

The following procedures should be carried out:

1 For each debtor a limit should be set. They should then not be allowed to owe more than this limit. The amount of the limit will depend on the circumstances. Such things as the size of the customer's firm and the amount of business done with it, as well as its past record of payments, will help in choosing the limit figure.
2 As soon as the payment date has been reached it should be seen whether payment has been made or not. Failure to pay on time may mean you refusing to supply any more goods unless payment is made quickly.
3 Where payment is not forthcoming, after investigation it may be necessary to take legal action to sue the customer for the debt. This will depend on the circumstances.
4 It is important that the customer is aware as to what will happen if he does not pay his account by the correct date.

New Terms

Sales Invoice (p 111): A document showing details of goods sold and the prices of those goods.

Trade Discount (p 115): A reduction given to a customer when calculating the selling prices of goods.

Exercises

15.1 You are to enter up the sales journal from the following details. Post the items to the relevant accounts in the sales ledger and then show the transfer to the sales account in the general ledger.

19–6			
Mar	1	Credit sales to J Gordon	£187
"	3	Credit sales to G Abrahams	£166
"	6	Credit sales to V White	£12
"	10	Credit sales to J Gordon	£55
"	17	Credit sales to F Williams	£289
"	19	Credit sales to U Richards	£66
"	27	Credit sales to V Wood	£28
"	31	Credit sales to L Simes	£78

15.2X Enter up the sales journal from the following, then post the items to the relevant accounts in the sales ledger. Then show the transfer to the sales account in the general ledger.

19–8			
May	1	Credit sales to J Johnson	£305
"	3	Credit sales to T Royes	£164
"	5	Credit sales to B Howe	£45
"	7	Credit sales to M Lee	£100
"	16	Credit sales to J Jakes	£308
"	23	Credit sales to A Vinden	£212
"	30	Credit sales to J Samuels	£1,296

15.3 F Benjamin of 10 Lower Street, Plymouth, is selling the following items, the recommended retail prices as shown: white tape £10 per roll, green baize at £4 per metre, blue cotton at £6 per sheet, black silk at £20 per dress length. He makes the following sales:

19–7

May 1 To F Gray, 3 Keswick Road, Portsmouth: 3 rolls white tape, 5 sheets blue cotton, 1 dress length black silk. Less 25 per cent trade discount.

" 4 To A Gray, 1 Shilton Road, Preston: 6 rolls white tape, 30 metres green baize. Less $33\frac{1}{3}$ per cent trade discount.

" 8 To E Hines, 1 High Road, Malton: 1 dress length black silk. No trade discount.

" 20 To M Allen, 1 Knott Road, Southport: 10 rolls white tape, 6 sheets blue cotton, 3 dress lengths black silk, 11 metres green baize. Less 25 per cent trade discount.

" 31 To B Cooper, 1 Tops Lane, St Andrews: 12 rolls white tape, 14 sheets blue cotton, 9 metres green baize. Less $33\frac{1}{3}$ per cent trade discount.

You are to *(a)* draw up a sales invoice for each of the above sales, *(b)* enter them up in the Sales Journal, post to the personal accounts, *(c)* transfer the total to the Sales Account in the General Ledger.

15.4X J Fisher, White House, Bolton, is selling the following items, the retail prices as shown: plastic tubing at £1 per metre, polythene sheeting at £2 per length, vinyl padding at £5 per box, foam rubber at £3 per sheet. He makes the following sales:

19–5

June 1 To A Portsmouth, 5 Rockley Road, Worthing: 22 metres plastic tubing, 6 sheets foam rubber, 4 boxes vinyl padding. Less 25 per cent trade discount.

" 5 To B Butler, 1 Wembley Road, Colwyn Bay: 50 lengths polythene sheeting, 8 boxes vinyl padding, 20 sheets foam rubber. Less 20 per cent trade discount.

" 11 To A Gate, 1 Bristol Road, Hastings: 4 metres plastic tubing, 33 lengths of polythene sheeting, 30 sheets foam rubber. Less 25 per cent trade discount.

" 21 To L Mackeson, 5 Maine Road, Bath: 29 metres plastic tubing. No trade discount is given.

" 30 To M Alison, Daley Road, Box Hill: 32 metres plastic tubing, 24 lengths polythene sheeting, 20 boxes vinyl padding. Less $33\frac{1}{3}$ per cent trade discount.

Required

(a) Draw up a sales invoice for each of the above sales, *(b)* then enter up in the Sales Journal and post to the personal accounts, *(c)* transfer the total to the Sales Account in the general ledger.

15.5 James Grafton supplies heating and plumbing materials both to the trade (on credit) and to members of the public on a cash sales basis. Invoices are prepared for both cash and credit sales. Customers are grouped as follows:

	Price paid
Cash Customers	List
Credit Customers:	
Group A	List less 25% trade discount
B	List less 10% trade discount
C	List less 5% trade discount

At the end of each week, he summarises his sales (cash and credit) and posts the *total* to the sales account in the ledger.

In the week ended 31 January Year 4, Grafton made the following sales:

Invoice No	**List Price** £	**Customer Category**
1040	80	Cash
1041	420	Credit (A)
1042	30	Cash
1043	860	Credit (A)
1044	110	Credit (B)
1045	1,040	Credit (A)
1046	15	Cash
1047	32	Cash
1048	320	Credit (C)
1049	100	Credit (B)

Credit customers are offered 1% of the net invoice value as a cash discount for the settlement of accounts within 30 days of the invoice date.

Required

(a) In your answer book:

(i) Enter the above invoices in the Sales Day Book (Sales Journal) for the week, as follows:

Invoice	**List (£)**	**Trade Discount (£)**	**Net (£)**
1040	80	—	80

(ii) Show the posting to the Sales Account in the Nominal Ledger.

(b) Invoices 1043 and 1045 were for sales to PH Ltd. Invoice 1043 was settled by cheque within 30 days of the invoice date. Show the Personal Account for Customer PH Ltd.
(LCCI)

16 · The Purchases Journal and the Purchases Ledger

16.1 Purchases Invoices

An invoice is a **purchases invoice** when it is entered in the books of the firm purchasing the goods. The same invoice, in the books of the seller, would be a sales invoice. For example for 15.1 which is an invoice,

1 In the books of D Poole: it is a purchases invoice.
2 In the books of J Blake: it is a sales invoice.

16.2 Entering Into the Purchases Journal

From the purchases invoices for goods bought on credit, the purchaser enters the details in his purchases journal. This book is merely a list, showing the following:

- date
- name of supplier
- the reference number of the invoice
- final amount of invoice

There is no need to show details of the goods bought in the purchases journal. This can be found by looking at the invoices themselves. Exhibit 16.1 is an example of a purchases journal.

Exhibit 16.1

Purchases Journal			
	Invoice No	*Folio*	*(page 49)*
19–5			£
Sept 2 R Simpson	9/101		670
8 B Hamilton	9/102		1,380
19 C Brown	9/103		120
30 K Gabriel	9/104		510
			2,680

16.3 Posting Credit Purchases to the Purchases Ledger

We now have a separate purchases ledger. The double entry is as follows:
1 The credit purchases are posted one by one, to the credit of each supplier's account in the purchases ledger.
2 At the end of each period the total of the credit purchases is posted to the debit of the purchases account in the general ledger. This is now illustrated in Exhibit 16.2.

Exhibit 16.2 Posting Credit Purchases

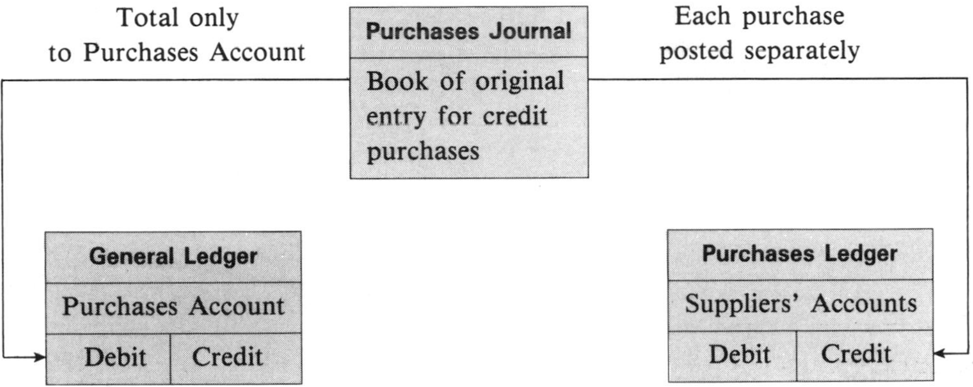

16.4 An Example of Posting Credit Purchases

The purchases journal in Exhibit 16.1 is now shown again. This time posting is made to the purchases ledger and the general ledger. Notice the completion of the folio columns.

Purchases Journal

	Invoice No	*Folio*	*(page 49)*
19–5			£
Sept 2 R Simpson	9/101	PL16	670
8 B Hamilton	9/102	PL29	1,380
19 C Brown	9/103	PL55	120
30 K Gabriel	9/104	PL89	510
Transferred to purchases account		GL63	2,680

Purchases Ledger

R Simpson *(page 16)*

	19–5			£
	Sept 2 Purchases		PJ 49	670

B Hamilton *(page 29)*

	19–5		£
	Sept 8 Purchases	PJ 49	1,380

C Brown *(page 55)*

	19–5		£
	Sept 19 Purchases	PJ 49	120

K Gabriel *(page 89)*

	19–5		£
	Sept 30 Purchases	PJ 49	510

General Ledger

Purchases *(page 63)*

19–5		£	
Sept 30 Credit purchases for the month	PJ 49	2,680	

The purchases journal is often known also as the purchases book or the purchases day book.

New Terms

Purchases Invoice (p 123): A document received by purchaser showing details of goods bought and their prices.

Exercises

16.1 B Mann has the following purchases for the month of May 19–4:

19–4
May 1 From K King: 4 radios at £30 each, 3 music centres at £160 each. Less 25 per cent trade discount.
" 3 From A Bell: 2 washing machines at £200 each, 5 vacuum cleaners at £60 each, 2 dish dryers at £150 each. Less 20 per cent trade discount.
" 15 From J Kelly: 1 music centre at £300 each, 2 washing machines at £250 each. Less 25 per cent trade discount.
" 20 From B Powell: 6 radios at £70 each, less $33\frac{1}{3}$ per cent trade discount.
" 30 From B Lewis: 4 dish dryers at £200 each, less 20 per cent trade discount.

Required

(a) Enter up the Purchases Journal for the month.
(b) Post the transactions to the suppliers' accounts.
(c) Transfer the total to the Purchases Account.

16.2X A Rowland has the following purchases for the month of June 19–9:

19–9
June 2 From C Lee: 2 sets golf clubs at £250 each, 5 footballs at £20 each. Less 25 per cent trade discount.
" 11 From M Elliott: 6 cricket bats at £20 each, 6 ice skates at £30 each, 4 rugby balls at £25 each. Less 25 per cent trade discount.
" 18 From B Wood: 6 sets golf trophies at £100 each, 4 sets golf clubs at £300 each. Less $33\frac{1}{3}$ per cent trade discount.
" 25 From B Parkinson: 5 cricket bats at £40 each. Less 25 per cent trade discount.
" 30 From N Francis: 8 goal posts at £70 each. Less 25 per cent trade discount.

Required

(a) Enter up the Purchases Journal for the month.
(b) Post the items to the suppliers' accounts.
(c) Transfer the total to the Purchases Account.

16.3 C Phillips, a sole trader, has the following purchases and sales for March 19–5:

19–5
Mar 1 Bought from Smith Stores: silk £40, cotton £80, all less 25 per cent trade discount
" 8 Sold to A Grantley: linen goods £28, woollen items £44. No trade discount
" 15 Sold to A Henry: silk £36, linen £144, cotton goods £120. All less 20 per cent trade discount
" 23 Bought from C Kelly: cotton £88, linen £52. All less 25 per cent trade discount
" 24 Sold to D Sangster: linen goods £42, cotton £48. Less 10 per cent trade discount
" 31 Bought from J Hamilton: linen goods £270 less $33\frac{1}{3}$ per cent trade discount.

Required

(a) Prepare the Purchases and Sales Journals of C Phillips from the above.
(b) Post the items to the personal accounts.
(c) Post the totals of the journals to the Sales and Purchases Accounts.

16.4 G Bath, a retailer, purchased two items for resale in his shop, one of Product A and one of Product B. The following figures relate to these two items.

	Product A	*Product B*
Manufacturers Recommended Retail Price	£1500	£4000
Trade Discount allowed to retailers	20%	25%

It is G Bath's intention to sell these two products at the Recommended Retail Price.

You are required to:

(a) calculate the price which G Bath will pay for each product;

(b) calculate how much the gross profit will be on each product, if the products are sold at the Recommended Retail Price;

(c) calculate the gross profit as a percentage of cost price for each product.

(Ignore VAT)

(RSA)

16.5X *(a)* You work in the purchases department of a manufacturing firm, with responsibility for the approval of invoices, prior to settlement by monthly cheque.

List **five** steps which you would take in the processing of an invoice for approval.

(b) Your firm has received an invoice which shows the catalogue price of a small machine to be £360, subject to a trade discount of 25% and a further 5% cash discount if the invoice is settled within 14 days.

Your firm has purchased three of these machines and pays within seven days of receipt of the invoice. What is the total amount the firm should pay?

(Ignore VAT)

(RSA)

16.6 J Jarvis is a dealer in fancy goods who maintains Day Books.

4 August	Bought goods from G Mann with a list price of £400, subject to a Trade Discount of 25%
5 August	Sold goods to B Allen for £240, subject to a Cash Discount of 5% if paid within 14 days
11 August	Bought goods from B Jollie with a list price of £250, subject to a Trade Discount of 20% and a Cash Discount of 5% if paid within 14 days
12 August	Sold goods to G Parker for £360, subject to a Cash Discount of 10% if paid within 7 days
15 August	Paid cheque to B Jollie for goods bought on 11 August
18 August	Received cheque from G Parker for goods sold on 12 August
21 August	Sold goods to E Todd for £270, less Trade Discount of 10% and a Cash Discount of 5% if paid within 7 days
29 August	Paid G Mann a cheque for goods bought on 4 August
31 August	Received cheque from B Allen for goods sold on 5 August

Required

(a) Enter the above transactions in J Jarvis's Purchases Day Book, Sales Day Book and the Cash Book.

(b) What is Trade Discount?

(c) Why do traders allow Cash Discount?

(LCCI)

17 · The Returns Journals

17.1 Returns Inwards and Credit Notes

Sometimes we will agree to customers returning goods to us. This might be for reasons such as the following:

- Goods were of the wrong type
- They were the wrong colour
- Goods were faulty
- Customer had bought more than he needed

We might ask the customers to return the goods. Sometimes they may agree to keep the goods if an allowance is made to reduce the price of the goods.

In each of these cases a document known as a **credit note** will be sent to the customer, showing the amount of the allowance given by us for the returns or the faulty goods. It is called a credit note because the customer's account will be credited with the amount of the allowance, to show the reduction in the amount he owes. Exhibit 17.1 shows an example of a credit note.

Exhibit 17.1

R Grant
Higher Side
Preston PR1 2NL
8 September 19–5

To: D Poole
45 Charles Street,
Manchester M1 5ZN

CREDIT NOTE No 9/37

	Per Unit	Total
	£	£
2 cases McBrand Pears	25	50
Less 20% Trade Discount		10
		40

To stop them being mistaken for invoices, credit notes are often printed in red.

17.2 Returns Inwards Journal

The credit notes are listed in a returns inwards journal. This is then used for posting the items, as follows:

1 Sales ledger. Credit the amount of credit notes, one by one, to the accounts of the customers in the sales ledger.

2 General ledger. At the end of the period the total of the returns inwards journal is posted to the debit of the returns inwards account.

17.3 Example of a Returns Inwards Journal

An example of a returns inwards journal showing the items posted to the sales ledger and the general ledger is now shown:

Returns Inwards Journal

	Note No	*Folio*	*(page 10)*
19–5			£
Sept 2 D Poole	9/37	SL 12	40
17 A Brewster	9/38	SL 58	120
19 C Vickers	9/39	SL 99	290
29 M Nelson	9/40	SL 112	160
Transferred to returns inwards account		GL 114	610

Sales Ledger

D Poole *(page 12)*

	19–5	£
	Sept 8 Returns inwards RI 10	40

A Brewster *(page 58)*

	19–5	£
	Sept 17 Returns inwards RI 10	120

C Vickers *(page 99)*

	19–5	£
	Sept 19 Returns inwards RI 10	290

M Nelson *(page 112)*

	19–5	£
	Sept 29 Returns inwards RI 10	160

General Ledger
Returns Inwards *(page 114)*

19–5	£		
Sept 30 Returns for the month RI 10	610		

Alternative names in use for the returns inwards journal are returns inwards book or sales returns book.

17.4 Returns Outwards and Debit Notes

If the supplier agrees, goods bought previously may be returned. When this happens a **debit note** is sent to the supplier giving details of the goods and the reason for their return.

Also, an allowance might be given by the supplier for any faults in the goods. Here also, a debit note should be sent to the supplier. Exhibit 17.2 shows an example of a debit note.

Exhibit 17.2

R Grant
Higher Side
Preston PR1 2NL
11 September 19–5

To: B Hamilton
20 Fourth Street
Kidderminster KD2 4PP

DEBIT NOTE No 9/34

	Per Unit	Total
	£	£
4 cases	60	240
less 25% Trade Discount		60
		180

17.5 Returns Outwards Journals

The debit notes are listed in a returns outwards journal. This is then used for posting the items, as follows:

1 Purchases ledger. Debit the amounts of debit notes, one by one, to the accounts of the suppliers in the purchases ledger.
2 General ledger. At the end of the period, the total of the returns outwards journal is posted to the credit of the returns outwards account.

17.6 Example of a Returns Outwards Journal

An example of a returns outwards journal, showing the items posted to the purchases ledger and the general ledger, is now shown.

Returns Outwards Journal

	Note No	*Folio*	*(page 7)*
19–5			£
Sept 11 B Hamilton	9/34	PL 29	180
16 B Rose	9/35	PL 46	100
28 C Blake	9/36	PL 55	30
30 S Saunders	9/37	PL 87	360
Transferred to returns outwards account		GL 116	670

Purchases Ledger

B Hamilton *(page 29)*

		£		
19–5				
Sept 11 Returns outwards	RO 7	180		

B Rose *(page 46)*

		£		
19–5				
Sept 16 Returns outwards	RO 7	100		

C Blake *(page 55)*

		£		
19–5				
Sept 28 Returns outwards	RO 7	30		

S Saunders *(page 87)*

		£		
19–5				
Sept 30 Returns outwards	RO 7	360		

General Ledger
Returns Outwards *(page 116)*

		19–5	£
		Sept 30 Returns for the month RO 7	670

Other names in use for the returns outwards journal are returns outwards book or purchases returns book.

17.7 Double Entry and Returns

Exhibit 17.3 shows how double entry is made for both returns inwards and returns outwards.

Exhibit 17.3 Posting returns inwards and returns outwards

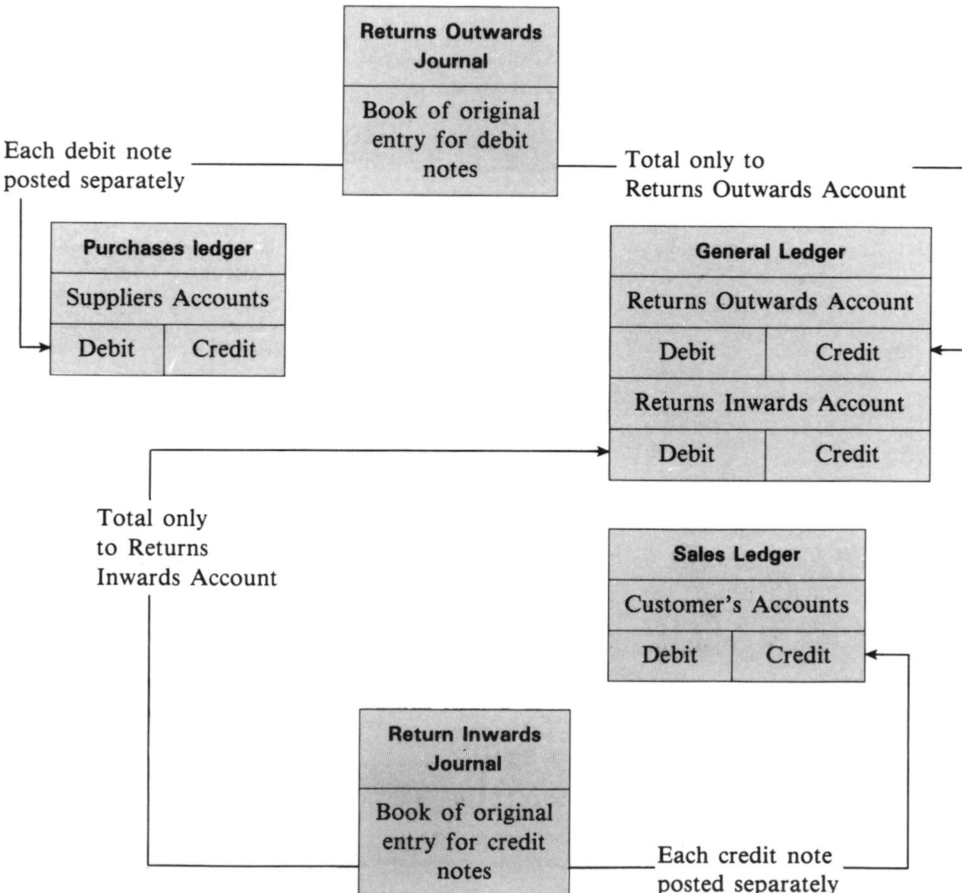

17.8 Statements

At the end of each month a **statement** should be sent to each debtor who owes money on the last day of each month. It is really a copy of his account in our books. It should show:

1 amount owing at start of month;
2 amount of each sales invoice sent to him during the month;
3 credit notes sent to him in the month;
4 cash and cheques received from him during the month;
5 finally, the amount due from him at the end of the month.

The debtor will use this to see if the account in his accounting records agrees with his account in our records. If in our books he is shown as owing £798 then, depending on items in transit between us, his books should show us as a creditor for £798. The statement also acts as a reminder to the debtor that he owes us money, and will show the date by which he should make payment.

An example of a statement might be as follows:

STATEMENT OF ACCOUNT

R GRANT
Higher Side
Preston PR1 2NL
Tel (0703) 33122
Fax (0703) 22331

Accounts Dept
D Poole & Co
45 Charles Street
Manchester M1 5ZN

Date	*Details*	*Debit*	*Credit*	*Balance*
19–5		£	£	£
Sept 1	Balance b/fwd			880
Sept 2	Invoice 30756	560		1,440
Sept 8	Returns 9/37		40	1,400
Sept 25	Bank		880	520
Sept 30	Balance owing c/f			520
All accounts due and payable within 1 month				

17.9 Sales and Purchases via Credit Cards

Various banks, building societies and other financial organisations issue credit cards to their customers. Examples are Visa, Access and American Express. The holder of the credit card purchases items or services without giving cash or cheques, but simply signs a special voucher used by the store or selling organisation. Later on, usually several weeks later, the credit card holder pays the organisation for which he holds the card, e.g. Visa, for all of his previous month's outgoings.

The sellers of the goods or services then present the vouchers to the credit card company and the total of the vouchers less commission is paid to them by that credit card company.

In effect the sales are 'cash sales' for as far as the purchaser is concerned he has seen goods (or obtained services) and has received them, and in his eyes he has paid for them by using his credit card. Such sales are very rarely sales to anyone other than the general public, as compared with professionals in a specific trade.

Once the customer has departed with his goods, or had the necessary services he does not become a debtor needing an entry for him in a sales ledger. All the selling company is then interested in, from a recording point of view, is collecting the money from the credit card company.

The double entry needed is:

Sale of items via credit cards:	Dr: credit card company
	Cr: cash sales
Receipt of money from credit card company:	Dr: Bank
	Cr: Credit card company
Commission charged by credit card company:	Dr: Selling expenses
	Cr: Credit card company

17.10 Internal Check

When sales invoices are being made out they should be scrutinised very carefully. A system is usually set up so that each stage of the preparation of the invoice is checked by someone other than the person whose job it is to send out the invoice. If this was not done then it would be possible for someone inside a firm to send out an invoice, as an instance, at a price less than the true price. Any difference could then be split between that person and the outside firm. If an invoice should have been sent to Ivor Twister & Co for £2,000, but the invoice clerk made it out deliberately for £200, then, if there was no cross-check, the difference of £1,800 could be split between the invoice clerk and Ivor Twister & Co.

Similarly outside firms could send invoices for goods which were never received by the firm. This might be in collaboration with an employee within the firm, but there are firms sending false invoices which rely on the firms receiving them being inefficient and paying for items never received. There have been firms sending invoices for such items as advertisements which have never been published. The cashier of the firm receiving the invoice, if the firm is an inefficient one, might possibly think that someone in the firm had authorised the advertisements and would pay the bill.

Besides these there are, of course, genuine errors, and these should also be detected. A system is, therefore, set up whereby the invoices have to be subject to scrutiny, at each stage, by someone other than the person who sends out the invoices or is responsible for paying them. Incoming invoices will be stamped with a rubber stamp, with spaces for each stage of the check.

The spaces in the stamp will be filled in by the people responsible for making the checks. For instance:

- Person certifying that the goods were actually received.
- Person certifying that the goods were ordered.
- Person certifying that the prices and calculations on the invoice are correct, and in accordance with the order originally placed and agreed.
- Person certifying that the goods are in good condition and suitable for the purpose for which ordered.

Naturally in a small firm, simply because the office staff might be quite small, this cross-check may be in the hands of only one person other than the person who will pay it. A similar sort of check will be made in respect of sales invoices being sent out.

17.11 The Basic Structure

Now that we have covered all aspects of book-keeping entries, we can now see the whole structure in the form of a diagram.

Exhibit 17.4 The basic structure of double entry book-keeping

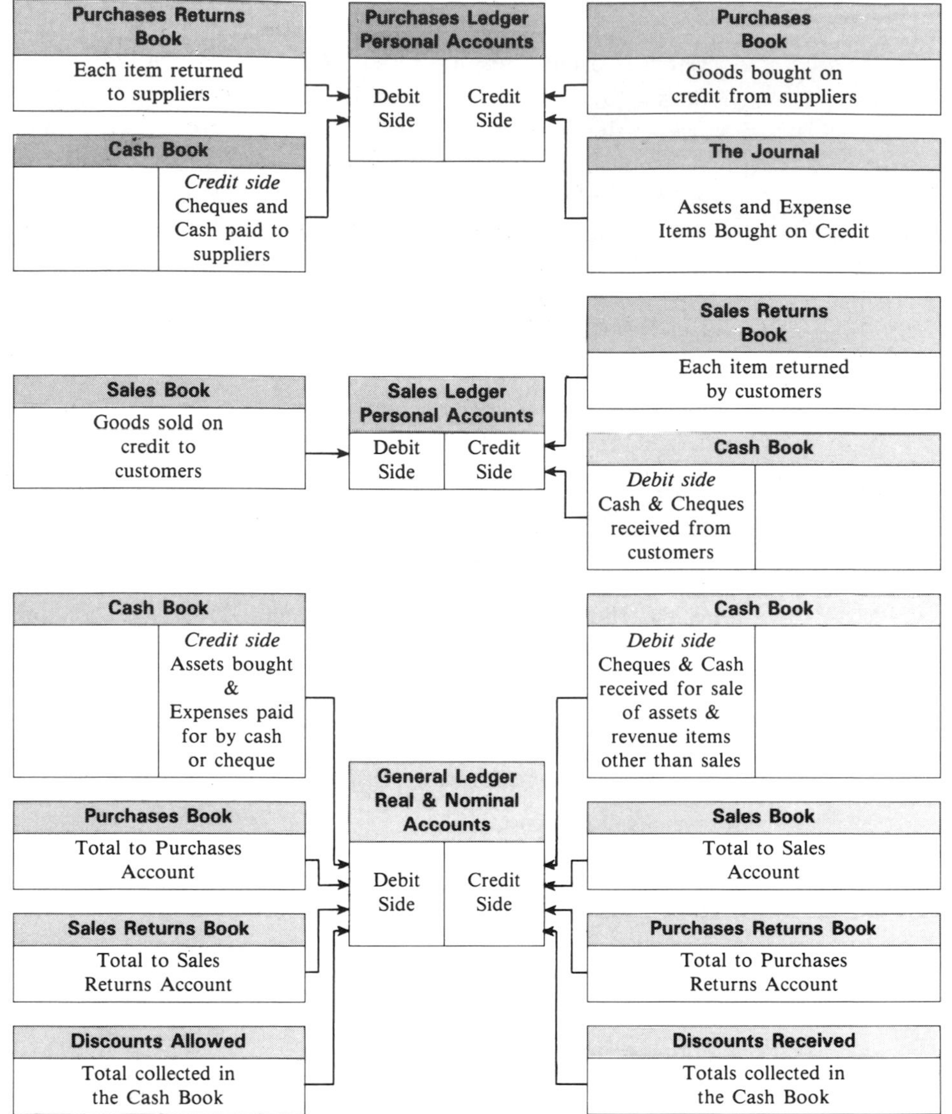

New Terms

Credit Note (p 128): A document sent to a customer showing allowance given by supplier in respect of unsatisfactory goods.

Debit Note (p 130): A document sent to a supplier showing allowance given for unsatisfactory goods.

Statement (p 133): A copy of a customer's personal account taken from the supplier's books.

Exercises

17.1 You are to enter up the purchases journal and the returns outwards journal from the following details, then to post the items to the relevant accounts in the purchases ledger and to show the transfers to the general ledger at the end of the month.

19–7
May 1 Credit purchase from H Lloyd £119
" 4 Credit purchases from the following: D Scott £98; A Simpson £114; A Williams £25; S Wood £56
" 7 Goods returned by us to the following: H Lloyd £16; D Scott £14
" 10 Credit purchase from A Simpson £59
" 18 Credit purchases from the following: M White £89; J Wong £67; H Miller £196; H Lewis £119
" 25 Goods returned by us to the following: J Wong £5; A Simpson £11
" 31 Credit purchases from: A Williams £56; C Cooper £98.

17.2X Enter up the sales journal and the returns inwards journal from the following details. Then post to the customer's accounts and show the transfers to the general ledger.

19–4
June 1 Credit sales to: A Simes £188, P Tulloch £60, J Flynn £77, B Lopez £88
" 6 Credit sales to: M Howells £114; S Thompson £118; J Flynn £66
" 10 Goods returned to us by: A Simes £12; B Lopez £17
" 20 Credit sales to M Barrow £970
" 24 Goods returned to us by S Thompson £5
" 30 Credit sales to M Parkin £91.

17.3 You are to enter the following items in the books, post to personal accounts, and show transfers to the general ledger:

19–5
July 1 Credit purchases from: K Hill £380; M Norman £500; N Senior £106
" 3 Credit sales to: E Rigby £510; E Phillips £246; F Thompson £356
" 5 Credit purchases from: R Morton £200; J Cook £180; D Edwards £410; C Davies £66
" 8 Credit sales to: A Green £307; H George £250; J Ferguson £185
" 12 Returns outwards to: M Norman £30; N Senior £16
" 14 Returns inwards from: E Phillips £18; F Thompson £22
" 20 Credit sales to: E Phillips £188; F Powell £310; E Lee £420
" 24 Credit purchases from: C Ferguson £550; K Ennevor £900
" 31 Returns inwards from E Phillips £27; E Rigby £30
" 31 Returns outwards to: J Cook £13; C Davies £11.

17.4 Post the following transactions from the sales day book and the sales returns day book to the ledgers.

Sales Day Book

Date		Folio	Details	£
January	3 M Jones	L2		60
"	7 B Buston	L3	200	
	less 10%		20	180
"	10 M Jones	L2		70
"	15 M White	L4	180	
	less 10%		18	162
"	21 M Jones			70
				542

Sales Returns Day Book

		Folio		£
January	20 M Jones	L2		12
				12

(PEI)

17.5X

STATEMENT

In account with J Hunt
24 Coventry Road
Nuneaton C4

Mr R J Cook
14 Thorn Street
Derby DE3

		£	£	£	31 March 19–4
February	1 Balance			130.42	
"	6 Invoice 512	140.64		271.06	
"	8 Cheque		127.16		
	Discount		3.26	140.64	
"	12 Returns		16.30	124.34	
"	26 Invoice 540	184.42		308.76	
"	28 Undercharge	3.60		312.36	

Study the statement above.

(a) Name the person who is supplying goods.

(b) Explain in simple terms the meaning of each item in the statement from February 1–26 and state the document used for the item on February 28 and the names of the sender and the receiver.

(c) Give the names of the debtor and the creditor and the amount owed on 28 February 19–4.

(RSA)

17.6X A Whitehead is a manufacturer of handbags. He keeps both a Purchases ledger and a Sales ledger. On 1 May he owed:

	£
Swade & Co	347
Fittings Ltd	264

Among his credit purchases during the month of May were:

4 May	Fittings Ltd	132
6 May	Swade & Co	202
14 May	Swade & Co	356
20 May	Fittings Ltd	118
26 May	Swade & Co	297
30 May	Swade & Co	145

Goods returned during the month were:

28 May	Swade & Co	28

Payments made during the month were:

10 May	Swade & Co	347
22 May	Fittings Ltd	257
	allowed discount	7

Among his credit sales during the month was:

21 May	Swade & Co	165

On 31 May, the balance of Swade & Co's account in the Sales ledger was transferred to Swade & Co's account in the Purchases ledger.

Required
Write up the accounts of Swade & Co and Fittings Ltd in Whitehead's ledgers, indicating clearly in which ledger you are entering the account.

Note: The accounts should be set out in three columns:
Dr Cr Balance
(LCCI)

17.7 On 30 September 19–0 the trial balance of Maurice Norman was as follows:

	Dr	*Cr*
	£	£
Capital		9,151
A Birch	4,251	
H Jameson	1,260	
Cash at Bank	7,200	
S Franklin		1,780
P Greenbank		670
E Oliver		1,110
	12,711	12,711

The following transactions, as shown in the books of original entry, took place during the month of October 19–0:

Sales Day Book

Oct		£
9	A Birch	1,095
15	H Jameson	740
19	H Jameson	205

Purchases Day Book

Oct		£
8	E Oliver	348
12	S Franklin	206
23	E Oliver	1,050

Returns Outwards Book

Oct		£
19	S Franklin	80

Returns Inwards Book

Oct		£
24	H Jameson	140

Payments Made by Cheque

Oct	To	Discounts Received £	Cheque Value £
2	P Greenbank	67	603
18	S Franklin	120	1,080
29	E Oliver		1,110

Payments Received by Cheque

Oct	From	Discounts Allowed £	Cheque Value £
7	A Birch	151	4,100
23	H Jameson		900

You are required to:

(a) open the accounts in the appropriate ledgers for all the above items shown in the trial balance (including Bank) and enter the balances shown as at 30 September 19–0;

(b) post the transactions indicated in the books of original entry direct to the appropriate ledger accounts, indicating the sub-divisions of the ledger involved;

(c) balance the personal accounts and bank accounts as at the end of the month.

(RSA)

18 · Value Added Tax

18.1 Introduction

Value Added Tax is a tax charged on the supply of most goods and services in the United Kingdom. Some goods and services are not taxable. Examples of these are food and postal services. In addition some persons and firms are exempted, these are dealt with later.

Value Added Tax is usually abbreviated as VAT.

18.2 Rate of Value Added Tax

The rate of VAT is decided by Parliament. It has been changed from time to time. At the time of writing it is 17.5 per cent. In this book the examples shown will be at the rate of 10 per cent. This is simply because it is easy to calculate. Most examining bodies have set VAT questions assuming a rate of 10 per cent to make the calculations easier for examination candidates.

The Government department which deals with VAT is the Customs and Excise department.

18.3 Taxable Firms

Imagine that Firm A takes raw materials it has grown. It sells some to the general public and some to traders.

1 Sale to the general public
A sells goods to Jones for £100 + VAT.

		£	
The sales invoice is for:	Price	100	
	+ VAT 10%	10	= Total Price £110

Firm A will then pay the £10 it has collected to the Customs and Excise.

2 Sale to another trader, who then sells to the general public
Firm A sells goods to Firm B for £100 + VAT.

		£	
The sales invoice is for:	Price	100	
	+ VAT 10%	10	= Total Price £110

Firm B alters the goods in some way, and then sells them to a member of the general public for £140 + VAT.

		£	
The sales invoice is for:	Price	140	
	+ VAT 10%	14	= Total Price £154

In this case Firm A will pay the Customs and Excise £10 for VAT collected. Firm B will pay the Customs and Excise a cheque for £4, being the amount collected £14 less the amount paid to A £10 = £4.

In the above cases you can see that the full amount of VAT has fallen on the person who finally buys the goods. Firms A and B have merely acted as collectors of the tax.

The value of goods sold by us or of services supplied by us is known as our **outputs**. Thus VAT on such items may be called **output tax**. The value of goods bought by us or of services supplied to us is known as **inputs**. The VAT on these items is, therefore, **input tax**.

18.4 Exempted Firms

Some firms do not have to add VAT on to the price at which they sell their products or services. Such firms will not get a refund of the VAT they have themselves paid on goods and services bought by them.

The types of firms exempted can be listed under two headings:

1 Nature of business. Various types of businesses do not have to add VAT to charges for goods or services. Two examples are banks and insurance companies. A bank does not have to add VAT on to its bank charges, and an insurance company does not have to add VAT to its insurance premiums.

2 Small firms. Firms with a turnover of less than a certain amount do not have to register for VAT if they do not want to. The turnover limit is changed from time to time, and so is not given here. This means that if they do not register they do not have to add VAT to the value of their sales invoices.

If small firms do register for VAT then they will have to keep full VAT records in addition to charging out VAT. To save very small businesses the costs and effort of keeping such records the Government, therefore, allows them not to register unless they want to.

18.5 Zero Rated Firms

This special category of firm:

1 Does not have to add VAT on to the selling price of products, and
2 Can obtain a refund of all VAT paid on the purchase of goods or services

If, therefore, £100,000 of goods are sold by the firm nothing has to be added for VAT, but if £8,000 VAT had been paid by it on goods or services bought then the firm would be able to claim a full refund of the £8,000 paid.

It is **2** above which distinguishes it from an exempted firm. A zero rated firm is, therefore, in a better position than an exempted firm. Examples of zero rated firms are publishers and firms selling food.

18.6 Partly Exempt Traders

Some traders will find that they are selling some goods which are exempt and some which are zero rated and others which are standard rated. These traders will have to apportion their turnover accordingly, and follow the rules already described for each separate part of their turnover.

18.7 Different Methods of Accounting for VAT

We can see from what has been said already that the accounting needed will vary between:

1 Firms which can recover VAT paid. All firms except exempted firms do not suffer VAT as an expense. They either:

- Get a refund of whatever VAT they have paid, as in the case of a zero rated firm
- Collect VAT from their customers, deduct the VAT paid on goods and services bought by them, and simply remit the balance owing to the Customs and Excise.

2 Firms which cannot recover VAT paid. This applies to all firms which are treated as exempted firms, and, therefore, suffer the tax as they cannot get refunds from it. The following discussion of the accounting entries needed will, therefore, distinguish between those two types of firms, those which do not suffer VAT as an expense, and those firms to whom VAT is an expense.

18.8 Firms Which Can Recover VAT Paid

1 Taxable Firms

Value Added Tax and Sales Invoices

A taxable firm will have to add VAT to the value of the Sales invoices. It must be pointed out that this is based on the amount of the invoice *after* any trade discount has been deducted. Exhibit 18.1 is an invoice drawn up from the following details:

On 2 March 19–2, W Frank & Co, Hayburn Road, Stockport, sold the following goods to R Bainbridge Ltd, 267 Star Road, Colchester: Bainbridge's order No was A/4/559, for the following items:

220 Rolls T56 Black Tape at £6 per 10 rolls
600 Sheets R64 Polythene at £10 per 100 sheets
7,000 Blank Perspex B49 Markers at £20 per 1,000

All of these goods are subject to VAT at the rate of 10 per cent.

A trade discount of 25 per cent is given by Frank & Co. The sales invoice is numbered 8851.

Exhibit 18.1

W Frank & Co
Hayburn Road
Stockport SK2 5DB

INVOICE No 8851 Date: 2 March 19–2

To: R Bainbridge
267 Star Road
Colchester CO1 1BT

Your order no A/4/559

	£
200 Rolls T56 Black Tape @ £6 per 10 rolls	120
600 Sheets R64 Polythene @ £10 per 100 sheets	60
7,000 Blank Perspex B49 Markers @ £20 per 1,000	140
	320
Less Trade Discount 25%	80
	240
Add VAT 10%	24
	264

Where a cash discount is offered for speedy payment, VAT is calculated on an amount represented by the value of the invoice less such a discount. Even if the cash discount is lost because of late payments, the VAT will not change.

The Sales Book will normally have an extra column for the VAT contents of the Sales Invoice. This is needed to make it easier to account for VAT. The entry of several sales invoices in the Sales Book and in the ledger accounts can now be examined:

W Frank & Co sold the following goods during the month of March 19–2:

		Total of Invoice, after trade discount deducted but before VAT added	VAT 10%
19–2		£	£
March	2 R Bainbridge Ltd (*see* Exhibit 18.1)	240	24
"	10 S Lange & Son	300	30
"	17 K Bishop	160	16
"	31 R Andrews & Associates	100	10

Sales Book *Page 58*

	Invoice No	Folio	Net	VAT
19–2			£	£
March 2 R Bainbridge Ltd	8851	SL 77	240	24
" 10 S Lange & Son	8852	SL 119	300	30
" 17 K Bishop	8853	SL 185	160	16
" 31 R Andrews & Associates	8854	SL 221	100	10
Transferred to General Ledger			GL 76 800	GL 90 80

Now that the Sales Book has been written up, the next task is to enter the amounts of the invoices in the individual customer's accounts in the Sales Ledger. These are simply charged with the full amounts of the invoices including VAT.

As an instance of this K Bishop will be shown as owing £176. When he pays his account he will pay £176. It will then be the responsibility of W Frank & Co to ensure that the figure of £16 VAT in respect of this item is included in the total cheque payable to the Customs and Excise.

Sales Ledger

R Bainbridge Ltd *Page 77*

19–2	£	
March 2 Sales SB 58	264	

S Lange & Son *Page 119*

19–2	£	
March 10 Sales SB 58	330	

K Bishop *Page 185*

19–2	£	
March 17 Sales SB 58	176	

R Andrews & Associates *Page 221*

19–2	£		
March 31 Sales SB 58	110		

In total, therefore, the personal accounts have been debited with £880, this being the total of the amounts which the customers will have to pay. The actual sales of the firm are not £880, the amount which is actually sales is £800, the other £80 being simply the VAT that W Frank & Co are collecting on behalf of the Government.

The double entry is made in the General Ledger:

1 Credit the Sales account with the sales content only, i.e. £800
2 Credit the Value Added Tax account with the VAT content only, i.e. £80

These are shown as:

General Ledger

Sales *Page 76*

		19–2	£
		March 31 Credit Sales for the month SB 58	800

Value Added Tax *Page 90*

		19–2	£
		March 31 Sales Book: VAT content SB 58	80

Value Added Tax and Purchases

In the case of a taxable firm, the firm will have to add VAT to its sales invoices, but it will *also* be able to get a refund of the VAT which it pays on its purchases.

Instead of paying VAT to the Inland Revenue, and then claiming a refund of the VAT on purchases, the firm can set off the amount paid as VAT on purchases against the amount payable as VAT on sales. This means that only the difference has to be paid to the Customs and Excise. It is shown as:

	£
(a) VAT collected on sales invoices	xxx
(b) Less VAT already paid on purchases	xxx
(c) Net amount to be paid to the Customs and Excise	xxx

In certain fairly rare circumstances *(a)* may be less than *(b)*. If that was the case then it would be the Customs and Excise that would refund the difference *(c)* to the firm. Such a settlement between the firm and the Customs and Excise will take place at least every three months.

The recording of Purchases in the Purchases Book and Purchases Ledger follows a similar method to that of Sales, but with the personal accounts being debited instead of credited. We can now look at the records of purchases for the same firm whose sales have been dealt with, W Frank & Co. The firm made the following purchases for March 19–2:

		Total invoice, after trade discount deducted but before VAT added	*VAT 10%*
19–2		£	£
March 1	E Lyal Ltd (*see* Exhibit 18.2)	180	18
" 11	P Portsmouth & Co	120	12
" 24	J Davidson	40	4
" 29	B Cofie & Son Ltd	70	7

Before looking at the recording of these in the Purchases Records, compare the first entry for E Lyal Ltd with Exhibit 18.2, to ensure that the correct amounts have been shown.

Exhibit 18.2

E Lyal Ltd
College Avenue
St Albans
Hertfordshire ST2 4JA

INVOICE No. K453/A

Date: 1/3/19–2
Your order no BB/667

To: W Frank & Co
Hayburn Road
Stockport

Terms: Strictly net 30 days

	£
50 metres of BYC plastic 1 metre wide × £3 per metre	150
1,200 metal tags 500 mm × 10p each	120
	270
Less Trade Discount at $33\frac{1}{3}\%$	90
	180
Add VAT 10%	18
	198

The Purchases Book can now be entered up.

Purchases Book			*Page 38*
	Folio	*Net*	*VAT*
19–2		£	£
March 1 E Lyal Ltd	PL 15	180	18
〃 11 P Portsmouth & Co	PL 70	120	12
〃 24 J Davidson	PL 114	40	4
〃 29 B Cofie & Son Ltd	PL 166	70	7
Transferred to General Ledger		GL 54 410	GL 90 41

These are entered in the Purchases Ledger. Once again there is no need for the VAT to be shown as separate amounts in the accounts of the suppliers.

Purchases Ledger

E Lyal Ltd *Page 15*

	19–2		£
	March 1 Purchases	PB 38	198

P Portsmouth & Co *Page 70*

	19–2		£
	March 11 Purchases	PB 38	132

J Davidson *Page 114*

	19–2		£
	March 24 Purchases	PB 38	44

B Cofie & Son Ltd *Page 166*

	19–2		£
	March 29 Purchases	PB 38	77

The personal accounts have been credited with a total of £451, this being the total of the amounts which W Frank & Co will have to pay to them.

The actual cost of purchases is not, however, £451. You can see that the correct amount is £410. The other £41 is the VAT which the various firms are collecting for the Customs and Excise. This amount is also the figure for VAT which is reclaimable from the Customs and Excise by W Frank & Co. The debit entry in the Purchases account is, therefore, £410, as this is the actual cost of the goods to the firm. The other £41 is entered on the debit side of the VAT account.

Notice that there is already a credit of £80 in the VAT account in respect of the VAT added to Sales.

General Ledger

Purchases *Page 54*

		£			£
19–2					
March 31	Credit Purchases for the month	410			

Value Added Tax *Page 90*

		£			£
19–2			19–2		
March 31	Purchase Book: VAT content PB 38	41	March 31	Sales Book: VAT content SB 58	80
" 31	Balance c/d	39			
		80			80
			April 1	Balance b/d	39

In the final accounts of W Frank & Co, the following entries would be made:

Trading Account for the month ended 31 March 19–2:
Debited with £410 as a transfer from the Purchases account
Credited with £800 as a transfer from the Sales account

Balance Sheet as at 31 March 19–2:
Balance of £39 (credit) on the VAT account would be shown as a current liability, as it represents the amount owing to the Customs and Excise for VAT.

2 Zero Rated Firms

These firms:

(a) Do not have to add VAT on to their sales invoices, as their rate of VAT is zero or nil.
(b) They can however reclaim from the Customs and Excise any VAT paid on goods or services bought.

Accordingly, because of *(a)* no VAT is entered in the Sales Book. VAT on sales does not exist. Because of *(b)* the Purchases Book and Purchases Ledger will appear exactly in the same manner as for taxable firms, as already shown in the case of W Frank & Co.

The VAT account will only have debits in it, being the VAT on Purchases. Any balance on this account will be shown in the Balance Sheet as a debtor.

18.9 Firms Which Cannot Get Refunds of VAT Paid

As these firms do not add VAT on to the value of their Sales Invoices there is obviously no entry for VAT in the Sales Book or the Sales Ledger. They do not get a refund of VAT on Purchases. This means that there will not be a VAT account. All that will happen is that VAT paid is included as part of the cost of the goods bought.

In the Purchases Book, goods bought for £80 + VAT £8 will simply appear as Purchases £88. The double entry will show a credit of £88 in the supplier's account.

Both the Sales and Purchases records will, therefore, not show anything separately for VAT. For comparison let us look at the accounting records of two firms for an item which costs £120 + VAT £12, the item being bought from D Oswald Ltd. The records for the month of May 19–4 would appear as follows:

1 Firm which cannot recover VAT:

Purchases Book

19–4	£
May 16 D Oswald Ltd	132

Purchases Ledger

D Oswald Ltd

		19–4	£
		May 16 D Oswald Ltd	132

General Ledger

Purchases

19–4	£	19–4	£
May 31 Credit Purchases for the month	132	May 31 Transfer to Trading Account	132

Trading Account for the month ended 31 May 19–4 (extract)

	£	
Purchases	132	

2 Firm which can recover VAT (e.g. zero rated firm):

Purchases Book

	Net	*VAT*
19–4	£	£
May 16 D Oswald Ltd	120	12

Purchases Ledger

D Oswald Ltd

		19–4	£
		May 16 Purchases	132

General Ledger

Purchases

19–4	£	19–4	£
May 31 Credit Purchases for the month	120	May 31 Transfer to Trading Account	120

Value Added Tax

19–4	£		
May 31 Purchases Book	12		

Trading Account for the month ended 31 May 19–4 (extract)

	£	
Purchases	120	

Balance Sheet as at 31 May 19–4 (extract)

	£	
Debtor	12	

18.10 VAT Included in Gross Amount

You will often know only the gross amount of an item, this figure will in fact be made up of the net amount plus VAT. To find the amount of VAT which has been added to the net amount, a formula capable of being used with any rate of VAT can be used. It is:

$$\frac{\text{\% rate of VAT}}{100 + \text{\% Rate of VAT}} \times \text{Gross Amount} = \text{VAT in £}$$

Suppose that the gross amount of sales was £1,650 and the rate of VAT was 10 per cent. Find the amount of VAT and the net amount before VAT was added. Using the formula:

$$\frac{10}{100 + 10} \times £1{,}650 = \frac{10}{110} \times £1{,}650 = £150.$$

Therefore, the net amount was £1,500, which with VAT £150 added, becomes £1,650 gross.

Given a rate of 17.5 per cent VAT, to find the amount of VAT in a gross price of £705, the calculation is:

$$\frac{17.5}{100 + 17.5} \times £705 = \frac{7}{47} \times £705 = £105.$$

18.11 VAT On Items Other Than Sales and Purchases

VAT is not just paid on purchases. It is also payable on many items of expense and on the purchase of fixed assets.

Firms which *can* get refunds of VAT paid will not include VAT as part of the cost of the expense or fixed asset. Firms which *cannot* get refunds of VAT paid will include the VAT cost as part of the expense or fixed asset. For example, two firms buying similar items would treat the following items as shown:

	Firm which can reclaim VAT		*Firm which cannot reclaim VAT*	
Buys Machinery	Debit Machinery	£200	Debit Machinery	£220
£200 + VAT £20	Debit VAT Account	£20		
Buys Stationery	Debit Stationery	£150	Debit Stationery	£165
£150 + VAT £15	Debit VAT Account	£15		

18.12 VAT Owing

VAT owing by or to the firm can be included with debtors or creditors, as the case may be. There is no need to show the amount(s) owing as separate items.

New Terms

Exempted Firms (p 142): Firms which do *not* have to add VAT to the price of goods and services supplied by them, but which *cannot* obtain a refund of VAT paid on goods and services received by them.

Inputs (p 142): value of goods and services *received by* our firm from others.

Input Tax (p 142): VAT added on to the price of inputs received.

Outputs (p 142): Value of goods and services *supplied by* our firm to others.

Output Tax (p 142): VAT added on to the prices of outputs by our firm.

Value Added Tax (VAT) (p 141): A tax charged on the supply of most goods and services.

Zero Rated Firms (p 143): Firms which do not have to add VAT to goods and services supplied by them to others, but which also receive a *refund* of VAT on goods and services received by them.

Exercises

18.1 On 1 May 19–7, D Wilson Ltd, 1 Hawk Green Road, Stockport, sold the following goods on credit to G Christie & Son, The Golf Shop, Hole-in-One Lane, Marple, Cheshire:

Order No. A/496
3 sets of 'Boy Michael' golf clubs at £270 per set.
150 Watson golf balls at £8 per 10 balls.
4 Faldo golf bags at £30 per bag.
Trade discount is given at the rate of $33\frac{1}{3}$%.
All goods are subject to VAT at 10%.

(a) Prepare the Sales Invoice to be sent to G Christie & Son. The invoice number will be 10586.
(b) Show the entries in the Personal Ledgers of D Wilson Ltd and G Christie & Son.

18.2 The following sales have been made by S Thompson Ltd during the month of June 19–5. All the figures are shown net after deducting trade discount, but before adding VAT at the rate of 10 per cent.

19–5			
August	1	to M Sinclair & Co	£150
"	8	to M Brown & Associates	£260
"	19	to A Axton Ltd	£80
"	31	to T Christie	£30

You are required to enter up the Sales Book, Sales Ledger and General Ledger in respect of the above items for the month.

18.3 The following sales and purchases were made by R Colman Ltd during the month of May 19–6.

		Net	*VAT added*
19–6		£	£
May 1	Sold goods on credit to B Davies & Co	150	15
" 4	Sold goods on credit to C Grant Ltd	220	22
" 10	Bought goods on credit from:		
	G Cooper & Son	400	40
	J Wayne Ltd	190	19
" 14	Bought goods on credit from B Lugosi	50	5
" 16	Sold goods on credit to C Grant Ltd	140	14
" 23	Bought goods on credit from S Hayward	60	6
" 31	Sold goods on credit to B Karloff	80	8

Enter up the Sales and Purchases Books, Sales and Purchases Ledgers and the General Ledger for the month of May 19–6. Carry the balance down on the VAT account.

18.4X On 1 March 19–6, C Black, Curzon Road, Stockport, sold the following goods on credit to J Booth, 89 Andrew Lane, Stockport. Order No 1697.

20,000 Coils Sealing Tape @ £4.46 per 1,000 coils
40,000 Sheets Bank A5 @ £4.50 per 1,000 sheets
24,000 Sheets Bank A4 @ £4.20 per 1,000 sheets
All goods are subject to VAT at 10%.

(a) Prepare the Sales Invoice to be sent to J Booth.
(b) Show the entries in the Personal Ledgers of J Booth, and C Black.

18.5 C Emberson, a sole trader, buys and sells goods on credit. A bank account is kept through which all amounts received and paid are entered. On 30 November 19–9 the following balances remain in the books:

	£	£
C Hills		154
L Howe		275
K Harris	330	
Bank	740	
Capital		641
	1070	1070

You are required to:
(a) open appropriate ledger accounts for the above and enter the balances as at 1 December 19–9;
(b) post the transactions indicated in the subsidiary books direct to the ledger and open any other accounts which may be required;
(c) balance the accounts where necessary and extract a trial balance on 31 December 19–9.

Purchases Day Book

December	£	*VAT*	*TOTAL*
13 C Hills	100	10	110
20 C Hills	150	15	165
21 H Lowe	60	6	66
	310	31	341

Sales Day Book

December	£	*VAT*	*TOTAL*
11 K Harris	240	24	264
15 K Harris	80	8	88
	320	32	352

Payments Received

December	£
16 K Harris	594

Payments Made

December	£
8 C Hills	154
15 Printing	20

(RSA)

18.6X At 1st February 19–5 K Murphy's debtors included D Hanson £103.30 and P Newbury £48.60. His creditors included E Goodman £178.20. The balance on Murphy's Value Added Tax account was £237.14 credit. During February his credit transactions with those named above were as follows:

Sales			*Purchases*		
Feb 4	P Newbury	£217.10	Feb 6	E Goodman	£83.00
Feb 20	D Hanson	£133.50			

All of these transactions were subject to Value Added Tax at 10%.
In the bank account in Murphy's books were recorded the following:

Debit			*Credit*		
Feb 8	P Newbury	£48.60	Feb 10	E Goodman	£178.20

You are required to write up in the books of Murphy the accounts of Hanson, Newbury and Goodman, and thc VAT account, all for the month of February 19–5.
(RSA)

18.7 The following is a summary of purchases and sales and the relevant figures for VAT for the three months ended 31 March 19–4.

Purchases			*VAT*
		£	£
19–4	January	20,000	2,000
	February	21,000	2,100
	March	22,000	2,200
Sales			
	January	21,000	2,100
	February	20,000	2,000
	March	15,000	1,500

Required

(a) Write up and balance the VAT account for the three months to 31 March 19–4.

(b) Explain briefly the significance of the balance and how it will be cleared.

(RSA)

19 · Depreciation of Fixed Assets: Nature and Calculations

19.1 Nature of Fixed Assets

Fixed assets are those assets which are:

- of long life, and
- to be used in the business, and
- not bought with the main purpose of resale.

19.2 Depreciation of Fixed Assets

However, fixed assets such as machinery, motor vans, fixtures and even buildings, do not last forever. If the amount received (if any) on disposal is deducted from the cost of buying them, the difference is called depreciation.

The only time that depreciation can be calculated accurately is when the fixed asset is disposed of, and the difference between the cost to its owner and the amount received on disposal is then calculated. If a motor van was bought for £1,000 and sold five years later for £20, then the amount of depreciation is £1,000 – £20 = £980.

19.3 Depreciation is an Expense

Depreciation is the part of the cost of the fixed asset consumed during its period of use by the firm. It is an expense for services consumed in the same way as expenses for items such as wages, rent or electricity. Because it is an expense, depreciation will have to be charged to the profit and loss account, and will therefore reduce net profit.

You can see that the only real difference between the cost of depreciation for a motor vehicle, and the cost of petrol for the motor vehicle, is that the petrol cost is used up in a day or two, whereas the cost for the motor vehicle is spread over several years. Both costs are costs of the business.

19.4 Causes of Depreciation

These can be divided up between (i) physical deterioration, (ii) economic factors, (iii) the time factor, (iv) depletion. Let us look at these in more detail.

Physical Depreciation

1 **Wear and tear**. When a motor vehicle or machinery or fixtures and fittings are used they eventually wear out. Some last many years, others last only a few years. This is true of buildings, although some may last for a long time.
2 **Erosion, rust, rot and decay**. Land may be eroded or wasted away by the action of wind, rain, sun and other elements of nature. Similarly, the metals in motor vehicles or machinery will rust away. Wood will rot eventually. Decay is a process which will also be present due to the elements of nature and the lack of proper attention.

Economic Factors

These may be said to be the reasons for an asset being put out of use even though it is in good physical condition. The two main factors are usually **obsolescence** and **inadequacy**.

1 **Obsolescence**. This is the process of becoming obsolete or out of date. An example of this was the propeller-driven aeroplanes, which, although in good physical condition, were made obsolete by the introduction of jet aircraft. The propeller-driven aircraft were put out of use by large airlines when they still had quite a few more years of potential use, because the newer aircraft were suited far better to the needs of the airlines.
2 **Inadequacy**. This is when an asset is no longer used because of the growth and changes in the size of firm. For instance, a small ferryboat that is operated by a firm at a seaside resort is entirely inadequate when the resort becomes more popular. It is found that it would be more efficient and economical to operate a large ferryboat, and so the smaller boat is put out of use by the firm.

Both obsolescence and inadequacy do not necessarily mean that the asset is destroyed. It is merely put out of use by the firm. Another firm will often buy it. For example, many of the aeroplanes no longer used by large airlines are bought by smaller firms.

The Time Factor

Obviously time is needed for wear and tear, erosion etc., and for obsolescence and inadequacy to take place. However, there are fixed assets to which the time factor is connected in a different way. These are assets which have a legal life fixed in terms of years.

For instance, you may agree to rent some buildings for 10 years. This is normally called a lease. When the years are finished the lease is worth nothing to you, as it has finished. Whatever you paid for the lease is now of no value.

A similar asset is where you buy a patent with complete rights so that only you are able to produce something. When the patent's time has finished it then has no value.

Instead of using the term depreciation, the term *amortisation* is often used for these assets.

Depletion

Other assets are of wasting character, perhaps due to the extraction of raw materials from them. These materials are then either used by the firm to make something else, or are sold in their raw state to other firms. Natural resources such as mines, quarries and oil wells come under this heading. To provide for the consumption of an asset of a wasting character is called provision for **depletion**.

19.5 Methods of Calculating Depreciation Charges

The two main methods in use are the **straight line method** and the **reducing balance method**. Most accountants think that, although other methods may be needed in certain cases, the straight line method is the one that is generally most suitable.

Straight Line Method

By this method, sometimes also called the fixed instalment method, the number of years of use is estimated. The cost is then divided by the number of years, to give the depreciation charge each year.

For instance, if a motor lorry was bought for £22,000, we thought we would keep it for four years and then sell it for £2,000, the depreciation to be charged would be:

$$\frac{\text{Cost (£22,000)} - \text{Disposal value (£2,000)}}{\text{Number of years of use (4)}} = \frac{\text{£20,000}}{4}$$

$$= \text{£5,000 depreciation each year for four years.}$$

If, after four years, the motor lorry would have had no disposal value, the charge for depreciation would have been:

$$\frac{\text{Cost (£22,000)}}{\text{Number of years use (4)}} = \frac{\text{£22,000}}{4}$$

$$= \text{£5,500 depreciation each year for four years.}$$

Reducing Balance Method

By this method a fixed percentage for depreciation is deducted from the cost in the first year. In the second or later years the same percentage is taken of the reduced balance (i.e. cost *less* depreciation already charged). This method is also known as the diminishing balance method.

If a machine is bought for £10,000, and depreciation is to be charged at 20 per cent, the calculations for the first three years would be as follows:

	£
Cost	10,000
First year: depreciation (20%)	2,000
	8,000
Second year: depreciation (20% of £8,000)	1,600
	6,400
Third year: depreciation (20% of £6,400)	1,280
	5,120

Using this method much larger amounts are charged in the earlier years of use as compared with the last years of use. It is often said that repairs and upkeep in the early years will not cost as much as when the asset becomes old.

This means that:

In the early years		**In the later years**
A higher charge for depreciation + A lower charge for repairs and upkeep	will tend to be fairly equal to	A lower charge for depreciation + A higher charge for repairs and upkeep

Exhibit 19.1 gives a comparison of the calculations using the two methods, if the same cost is given for the two methods.

Exhibit 19.1

A firm has just bought a machine for £8,000. It will be kept in use for four years, then it will be disposed of for an estimated amount of £500. They ask for a comparison of the amounts charged as depreciation using both methods.

For the straight line method a figure of (£8,000 − £500) ÷ 4 = £7,500 ÷ 4 = £1,875 per annum is to be used. For the reducing balance method a percentage figure of 50 per cent will be used.

	Method 1 Straight Line		**Method 2 Reducing Balance**
	£		£
Cost	8,000		8,000
Depreciation: year 1	1,875	(50% of £8,000)	4,000
	6,125		4,000
Depreciation: year 2	1,875	(50% of £4,000)	2,000
	4,250		2,000
Depreciation: year 3	1,875	(50% of £2,000)	1,000
	2,375		1,000
Depreciation: year 4	1,875	(50% of £1,000)	500
Disposal value	500		500

This illustrates the fact that using the reducing balance method there is a much higher charge for depreciation in the early years, and lower charges in the later years.

19.6 Other Methods of Calculating Depreciation

There are many more methods of calculating depreciation but they are outside the scope of this volume. Special methods are often used in particular industries where there are circumstances which are peculiar to that industry.

New Terms

Depreciation (p 156): The part of the cost of the fixed asset consumed during its period of use by the firm.

Obsolescence (p 157): Becoming out of date.

Depletion (p 158): The wasting away of an asset as it is used up.

Straight Line Method (p 158): Depreciation calculation which remains at an equal amount each year.

Reducing Balance Method (p 158): Depreciation calculation which is at a lesser amount every following period.

Exercises

19.1 D Sankey, a manufacturer, purchases a lathe for the sum of £4,000. It has an estimated life of five years and a scrap value of £500.

Sankey is not certain whether he should use the 'Straight Line' or the 'Reducing Balance' basis for the purpose of calculating depreciation on the machine.

You are required to calculate the depreciation on the lathe using both methods, showing clearly the balance remaining in the lathe account at the end of each of the five years for each method. (Assume that 40 per cent per annum is to be used for the Reducing Balance Method.)

(Calculations to the nearest £.)

19.2 A machine costs £12,500. It will be kept for four years, and then sold for an estimated figure of £5,120. Show the calculations of the figures for depreciation for each of the four years using *(a)* the straight line method, *(b)* the reducing balance method, for this method using a depreciation rate of 20 per cent.

19.3 A motor vehicle costs £6,400. It will be kept for five years, and then sold for scrap £200. Calculate the depreciation for each year using *(a)* the reducing balance method, using a depreciation rate of 50 per cent, *(b)* the straight line method.

19.4X A machine costs £5,120. It will be kept for five years, and then sold at an estimated figure of £1,215. Show the calculations of the figures for depreciation each year using *(a)* the straight line method, *(b)* the reducing balance method using a depreciation rate of 25 per cent.

19.5X A bulldozer costs £12,150. It will be kept in use for five years. At the end of that time agreement has already been made that it will be sold for £1,600. Show your calculation of the amount of depreciation each year if *(a)* the reducing method at a rate of $33\frac{1}{3}$ per cent was used, *(b)* the straight line method was used.

19.6X A tractor is bought for £6,000. It will be used for three years, and then sold back to the supplier for £3,072. Show the depreciation calculations for each year using *(a)* the reducing balance method with a rate of 20 per cent, *(b)* the straight line method.

19.7 A company, which makes up its accounts annually to 31 December, provides for depreciation of its machinery at the rate of 10 per cent per annum on the diminishing balance system.

On 31 December 19–6, the machinery consisted of three items purchased as under:

	£
On 1 January 19–4 Machine A	Cost 3,000
On 1 April 19–5 Machine B	Cost 2,000
On 1 July 19–6 Machine C	Cost 1,000

Required

Your calculations showing the depreciation provision for the year 19–6.

20 · Double Entry Records for Depreciation

20.1 The Old Method of Recording Depreciation

It used to be normal to show depreciation in the fixed asset accounts. This will be the first method to be shown, as it is the easiest to understand for a student.

Here the double entry for each year's depreciation charge is:

1 Debit the depreciation account.
2 Credit the asset account.

and then, this is transferred to the profit and loss account, by the following:

1 Debit the profit and loss account.
2 Credit the depreciation account.

Exhibit 20.1 shows the entries that would be needed during the first three years of use of a fixed asset.

Exhibit 20.1

A machine is bought on 1 January 19–5 for £2,000. It is to be depreciated at the rate of 20 per cent using the reducing balance method. The asset account, depreciation account, profit and loss account and balance sheet in respect of the first three years are now shown:

Machinery

	£		£
19–5	£	19–5	£
Jan 1 Cash	2,000	Dec 31 Depreciation	400
		Balance c/d	1,600
	2,000		2,000
19–6	£	19–6	£
Jan 1 Balance b/d	1,600	Dec 31 Depreciation	320
		Balance c/d	1,280
	1,600		1,600
19–7	£	19–7	£
Jan 1 Balance b/d	1,280	Dec 31 Depreciation	256
		Balance c/d	1,024
	1,280		1,280
19–8	£		
Jan 1 Balance b/d	1,024		

Depreciation Account

	£		£
19–5	£	19–5	£
Dec 31 Machinery	400	Dec 31 Profit and loss a/c	400
19–6	£	19–6	£
Dec 31 Machinery	320	Dec 31 Profit and loss a/c	320
19–7	£	19–7	£
Dec 31 Machinery	256	Dec 31 Profit and loss a/c	256

Profit and Loss Account for the year ended 31 December

	£	
19–5 Depreciation	400	
19–6 Depreciation	320	
19–7 Depreciation	256	

Usually shown on the balance sheet as follows:

Balance Sheets

	£	£
As at 31 December 19–5		
Machinery at cost	2,000	
Less Depreciation for the year	400	
		1,600
As at 31 December 19–6		
Machinery as at 1 January 19–6	1,600	
Less Depreciation for the year	320	
		1,280
As at 31 December 19–7		
Machinery as at 1 January 19–7	1,280	
Less Depreciation for the year	256	
		1,024

In larger firms the old method is not often found now. It is regarded as being out of date.

20.2 The Modern Method of Recording Depreciation

The method now normally used is where the fixed assets accounts are always kept for showing the assets at cost price. The depreciation is shown in a separate 'provision for depreciation' account. This method has been used by most limited companies for many years. This is because company balance sheets show fixed assets at cost less total depreciation to date.

When the depreciation calculations have taken place, the depreciation is then to be shown in a separate account. The double entry is:

1 Debit the profit and loss account.
2 Credit the provision for depreciation account.

Notice that no entry is made in the asset account for depreciation. This means that the fixed asset accounts will normally be shown at cost price.

The first example uses the same figures as Exhibit 20.1. In a business with financial years ended 31 December a machine is bought for £2,000 on 1 January 19–5. It is to be depreciated at the rate of 20 per cent using the reducing balance method. The records for the first three years are now shown in Exhibit 20.2.

Exhibit 20.2

Machinery

	£		
19–5	£		
Jan 1 Cash	2,000		

Provision for Depreciation – Machinery

	£		£
19–5	£	19–5	£
Dec 31 Balance c/d	400	Dec 31 Profit and loss a/c	400
19–6		19–6	
Dec 31 Balance c/d	720	Jan 1 Balance b/d	400
		Dec 31 Profit and loss a/c	320
	720		720
19–7		19–7	
Dec 31 Balance c/d	976	Jan 1 Balance b/d	720
		Dec 31 Profit and loss a/c	256
	976		976
		19–8	
		Jan 1 Balance b/d	976

Profit and Loss account for the year ended 31 December

	£		
	£		
19–5 Depreciation	400		
19–6 Depreciation	320		
19–7 Depreciation	256		

Now the balance on the machinery account is shown on the balance sheet at the end of each year less the balance on the provision for depreciation account.

Balance Sheets

	£	£
As at 31 December 19–5		
Machinery at cost	2,000	
Less Depreciation to date	400	
		1,600
As at 31 December 19–6		
Machinery at cost	2,000	
Less Depreciation to date	720	
		1,280
As at 31 December 19–7		
Machinery at cost	2,000	
Less Depreciation to date	976	
		1,024

Another example can now be given in Exhibit 20.3. This is of a business with financial years ended 30 June. A motor lorry is bought on 1 July 19–1 for £8,000. Another motor lorry is bought on 1 July 19–2 for £11,000. Each lorry is expected to be in use for five years, and the disposal value of the first lorry is expected to be £500 and the second lorry is expected to fetch £1,000 disposal value. The method of depreciation to be used is the straight line method. The first two years' accounts are shown.

Exhibit 20.3

Motor Lorries

	£		£
19–1		19–3	
Jul 1 Bank	8,000	Jun 30 Balance c/d	19,000
19–2			
Jul 1 Bank	11,000		
	19,000		19,000

Provision for Depreciation – Motor Lorries

	£		£
19–2		19–2	
Jun 30 Balance c/d	1,500	Jun 30 Profit and loss a/c	1,500
		Jul 1 Balance b/d	1,500
19–3		19–3	
Jun 30 Balance c/d	5,000	Jun 30 Profit and loss a/c	3,500
	5,000		5,000
		Jul 1 Balance b/d	5,000

Profit and Loss Account for the year ended 30 June (extracts)

	£	
19–2 Depreciation	1,500	
19–3 Depreciation	3,500	

Balance Sheet as at 30 June 19–2

	£	£
Motor lorry at cost	8,000	
Less Depreciation to date	1,500	6,500

Balance Sheet as at 30 June 19–3

	£	£
Motor lorries at cost	19,000	
Less Depreciation to date	5,000	14,000

You should note that examiners sometimes ask you to open a depreciation account as well as a provision for depreciation account. In this case the entries would be:

Dr Profit and Loss account with period's depreciation
Cr Depreciation account

Then transfer the balance of the Depreciation account to the Provision for Depreciation account thus:

Dr Depreciation account
Cr Provision for Depreciation account

This would not happen very often in practice, as it means extra book-keeping work which is not really necessary. But bear in mind that examiners are allowed to add their own requirements in examination questions. It can be useful to find out which examinees can reason things out instead of simply learning by memorising without understanding it. Question 20.6 is such a question. Compare your answer with that at the back of the book.

20.3 The Sale of an Asset

Reason for Accounting Entries

Upon the sale of an asset we will want to delete it from our accounts. This means that the cost of that asset needs to be taken out of the asset account. In addition, the depreciation of the sold asset will have to be taken out of the depreciation provision.

Finally, the profit or loss on sale, if any, will have to be calculated.

When we charge depreciation on a fixed asset we are having to make guesses.

We cannot be absolutely certain how long we will keep the asset in use, nor can we be certain at the date of purchase how much the asset will be sold for when we dispose of it. We will not often get our guesses correct. This means that when we dispose of an asset, the cash received for it is usually different from our original guess.

Accounting Entries Needed

On the sale of a fixed asset the following entries are needed; for instance, let us assume the sale of machinery.

(A)	Transfer the cost price of the asset sold to an assets disposal account (in this case a machinery disposals account).	Debit machinery disposals account. Credit machinery account.
(B)	Transfer the depreciation already charged to the assets disposal account.	Debit provision for depreciation – machinery. Credit machinery disposals account.
(C)	For remittance received on disposal.	Debit cash book. Credit machinery disposals account.
(D)	Transfer balance (difference on machinery disposals account) to the profit and loss account.	
	If the difference is on the debit side of the disposal account, it is a profit on sale.	Debit machinery disposals account. Credit profit and loss account.
	If the difference is on the credit side of the disposal account, it is a loss on sale.	Debit profit and loss account. Credit machinery disposals account.

We can now look at Exhibit 20.4 which shows the entries for an asset sold at a profit. In Exhibit 20.2 the machinery was bought for £2,000 and had been depreciated by £976 by 31 December 19–7, and then sold for £1,070. The entries shown in Exhibit 20.5 are those needed if the machinery was instead sold for £950 on 2 January 19–8. The letters (A) to (D) shown are references to the table of instructions shown above.

Exhibit 20.4 **Asset sold at a profit**

Machinery

		£			£
19–5			19–8		
Jan 1	Cash	2,000	Jan 2	Machinery disposals (A)	2,000

Provision for Depreciation: Machinery

		£			£
19–8			19–8		
Jan 2	Machinery disposals (B)	976	Jan 1	Balance b/d	976

Machinery Disposals

		£			£
19–8			19–8		
Jan 2	Machinery (A)	2,000	Jan 2	Cash (C)	1,070
Dec 31	Profit and loss a/c (D)	46	2	Provision for depreciation (B)	976
		2,046			2,046

Profit and Loss Account for the year ended 31 December 19–8

		£
	Profit on sale of machinery (D)	46

Exhibit 20.5 now shows what the entries would be for the same asset if, instead of being sold at a profit, the asset had been sold for £950 only, which would mean that a loss was incurred on sale.

Exhibit 20.5 **Asset sold at a loss**

Machinery

		£			£
19–5			19–8		
Jan 1	Cash	2,000	Jan 2	Machinery disposals (A)	2,000

Provision for Depreciation: Machinery

		£			£
19–8			19–8		
Jan 2	Machinery disposals (B)	976	Jan 1	Balance b/d	976

Machinery Disposals

		£			£
19–8			19–8		
Jan 2	Machinery (A)	2,000	Jan 2	Cash (C)	950
			2	Provision for depreciation (B)	976
			Dec 31	Profit and loss (D)	74
		2,000			2,000

Profit and Loss Account for the year ended 31 December 19–8

		£	
Loss on sale of machinery	(D)	74	

Exercises

20.1 On 1 July 19–2 R Burge, a greengrocer, purchased a motor delivery van for £2,000.

You are required to:

(a) Show how the 'Motor Delivery Van Account' would appear in the books of R Burge for the four years ending 30 June 19–6.
Depreciation is written off at the rate of 20 per cent on a 'Reducing Instalment' basis.

(b) Explain the difference between the 'Straight Line' method and the 'Reducing Instalment' method of Depreciation.

(RSA)

20.2 David Moore, who is a sole trader, decides to purchase a delivery van for the sum of £1,500. He cannot decide whether to write off depreciation of the new van on the 'straight line' method or the 'diminishing balance' method.

Required

In order to assist Moore in reaching a decision, draw up the Delivery Van Account for the first three years – taking a rate of 10 per cent for depreciation – as it would appear:

(a) Under the 'straight line' method.

(b) Under the 'diminishing balance' method.

(LCCI)

20.3 Charles Dudley, a sole trader, purchases on 1 November 19–7, a new delivery van for £1,200. His business year end is 31 October but he cannot decide which method of depreciation he should use in respect of the new van – the straight line method or the reducing balance method.

Required

In order to assist Charles Dudley in making his decision, draw up the Delivery Van Account for the three years from 1 November 19–7 using:

(a) the straight line method; and

(b) the reducing balance method.

Each account must indicate which method is being used and each account be balanced at the end of each of the three years.

Notes

(i) In both cases the rate of depreciation is to be 10 per cent.

(ii) Calculations should be made to the nearest £.

(LCCI)

20.4X *(a)* What is meant by depreciation and why is it important that a businessman should provide for depreciation in his accounts?

(b) On 1 January 19–6 A Swain, a haulage contractor, purchased three tipper lorries for £4,800 each. Mr Swain estimated that his lorries would have an effective working life of five years with a disposal value of £300 each. The straight line method of depreciation is to be used. The financial year ends on 31 December. One of the lorries kept breaking down and was sold on 1 January 19–8 for £2,500.

You are required to show the relevant entries for the years 19–6, 19–7 and 19–8 in the following ledger accounts:

(i) Lorries.
(ii) Lorries Disposal.
(iii) Provision for Depreciation on Lorries.

All workings are to be shown.
(RSA)

20.5X Reconstruct in good form the following balance sheet after taking into account the transactions for December.

Balance Sheet as at 30 November

Liabilities	£	*Assets*	£
Capital	3,000	Cash	500
+ Net Profit	1,000	Machinery	1,000
		Vans	2,000
	4,000	Debtors	1,500
− Drawings	300	Stock	1,000
	3,700		
Creditors	2,300		
	£6,000		£6,000

Dec 1 Received a cheque from Debtors £200
" 5 Took drawings in cash £150
" 10 Sold goods which cost £100 for £300 cash
" 15 Purchased goods on credit for £200
" 19 Depreciated machinery by £170
" 21 Took a loan from the bank to buy machine costing £2,000
" 31 Paid £25 cash into bank.

(PEI)

20.6 Philip Green purchased a machine for use in his business at a cost of £10,000 on 1 January Year 1.

He estimates that its working life will be three years and that, at the end of that period, its scrap value will be £700.

He has yet to decide which method of depreciation to adopt, the straight line method or the reducing balance method, using a rate of 60% on cost or written down balance.

Required

For years 1, 2 and 3, prepare for each depreciation method:

(a) The Machine Account (maintained at cost)
(b) The Machine Depreciation Account, showing the transfer to Profit and Loss Account at the end of each year
(c) The Accumulated Provision for Machine Depreciation Account, balancing the account at the end of each year

Note: Indicate clearly in your answer book which method you are using in each case.

21 · Bad Debts and Provisions for Bad Debts

21.1 Bad Debts

If a firm finds that it is impossible to collect a debt then that debt should be written off as a **bad debt**. This could happen if the debtor simply could not pay the debt.

An example of debts being written off as bad is shown in Exhibit 21.1.

Exhibit 21.1

We sold £50 goods to K Lee on 5 January 19–5, but he became bankrupt. On 16 February 19–5 we sold £240 goods to T Young. He managed to pay £200 on 17 May 19–5, but it became obvious that he would never be able to pay the final £40.

When drawing up our final accounts to 31 December 19–5 we decided to write these off as bad debts. The accounts would appear as follows:

K Lee

19–5	£	19–5	£
Jan 5 Sales	50	Dec 31 Bad debts	50

T Young

19–5	£	19–5	£
Feb 16 Sales	240	May 17 Cash	200
		Dec 31 Bad debts	40
	240		240

Bad Debts

19–5	£	19–5	£
Dec 31 K Lee	50	Dec 31 Profit and	
T Young	40	loss a/c	90
	90		90

Profit and Loss Account for the year ended 31 December 19–5

	£		
Bad debts	90		

21.2 Provision for Bad Debts

Why Provisions are Needed

The total of the debtors appears in the balance sheet as an asset. If they all paid their accounts then this would mean that the debtors figure was a correct figure. If some of the debtors do not pay, the figure of debtors has been overstated in the balance sheet. To try to get as accurate a figure as possible for debtors, a firm will make the best estimate it can of the number of debtors who will never pay their accounts. This estimate can be made:

1 By looking at each debt, and estimating which ones will be bad debts.
2 By estimating, on the basis of experience, what percentage of the debts will prove to be bad debts.

It is well known that the longer a debt is owing the more likely it will become a bad debt. Some firms draw up an ageing schedule, showing how long debts have been owing. Older debtors need higher percentage estimates of bad debts than do newer debts. Exhibit 21.2 gives an example of such an ageing schedule.

Exhibit 21.2

Ageing Schedule for Doubtful Debts			
Period debt owing	*Amount*	*Estimated percentage doubtful*	*Provision for bad debts*
	£		£
Less than one month	5,000	1	50
1 month to 2 months	3,000	3	90
2 months to 3 months	800	4	32
3 months to 1 year	200	5	10
Over 1 year	160	20	32
	9,160		214

Accounting Entries for Provisions for Bad Debts

When the decision has been taken as to the amount of the provision to be made, then the accounting entries needed for the provision are:

Year in which *provision first made*:
1 Debit profit and loss account with amount of provision.
2 Credit provision for bad debts account.

Exhibit 21.3 shows the entries needed for a provision for bad debts.

Exhibit 21.3

At 31 December 19–3 the debtors figure amounted to £10,000. It is estimated that two per cent of debts (i.e. £200) will prove to be bad debts, and it is decided to make a provision for these. The accounts would appear as follows:

Profit and Loss Account for the year ended 31 December 19–3

	£		
Provision for bad debts	200		

Provision for Bad Debts

			£
		19–3	
		Dec 31 Profit and loss a/c	200

In the balance sheet the balance on the provision for bad debts will be deducted from the total of debtors:

Balance Sheet (extracts) as on 31 December 19–3

Current Assets	£		
Debtors	10,000		
Less Provision for bad debts	200		
		9,800	

21.3 Increasing the Provision

Let us suppose that for the same firm as in Exhibit 21.2, at the end of the following year 31 December 19–4, the bad debts provision needed to be increased. This was because the provision was kept at two per cent, but the debtors had risen to £12,000. A provision of £200 had been brought forward from the *previous* year, but we now want a total provision of £240 (i.e. two per cent of £12,000). All that is needed is a provision for an extra £40.

The double entry will be:

1 Debit profit and loss account.
2 Credit provision for bad debts account.

Profit and Loss Account for the year ended 31 December 19–4

	£		
Provision for bad debts	40		

Provision for Bad Debts

	£		£
19–4		19–4	
Dec 31 Balance c/d	240	Jan 1 Balance b/d	200
		Dec 31 Profit and loss a/c	40
	240		240
		19–5	
		Jan 1 Balance b/d	240

The balance sheet as at 31 December 19–4 will appear as:

Balance Sheet (extract) as on 31 December 19–4

	£	
Current Assets		
Debtors	12,000	
Less Provision for bad debts	240	
		11,760

21.4 Reducing the Provision

The provision is shown as a credit balance. Therefore to reduce it we would need a debit entry in the provision account. The credit would be in the profit and loss account. Let us assume that at 31 December 19–5, in the firm already examined, the debtors figure had fallen to £10,500 but the provision remained at two per cent, i.e. £210 (two per cent of £10,500). Thus the provision needs a reduction of £30. The double entry is:

1 Debit provision for bad debts account.
2 Credit profit and loss account.

Profit and Loss Account for the year ended 31 December 19–5

			£
		Provision for bad debts: Reduction	30

Provision for Bad Debts

	£		£
19–5		19–5	
Dec 31 Profit and loss a/c	30	Jan 1 Balance b/d	240
" 31 Balance c/d	210		
	240		240
		19–6	
		Jan 1 Balance b/d	210

The balance sheet will appear:

Balance Sheet (extracts) as on 31 December 19–5

	£	£	
Current Assets			
Debtors	10,500		
Less Provision for bad debts	210		
		10,290	

Let us now look at a comprehensive example, Exhibit 21.4.

Exhibit 21.4

A business starts on 1 January 19–2 and its financial year end is 31 December annually. A table of the debtors, the bad debts written off and the estimated bad debts at the rate of two per cent of debtors at the end of each year is now given. The double entry accounts, and the extracts from the final accounts follow.

Year to 31 December	*Debtors at end of year (after bad debts written off)*	*Bad debts written off during year*	*Debts thought at end of year to be impossible to collect: 2% of debtors*
	£	£	£
19–2	6,000	423	120 (2% of £6,000)
19–3	7,000	510	140 (2% of £7,000)
19–4	7,750	604	155 (2% of £7,750)
19–5	6,500	610	130 (2% of £6,500)

Profit and Loss accounts for the year ended 31 December (extracts)

		£			£
19–2	Bad debts	423			
	Provision for bad debts	120			
19–3	Bad debts	510			
	Increase in provision for bad debts	20			
19–4	Bad debts	604			
	Increase in provision for bad debts	15			
19–5	Bad debts	610	19–5	Reduction in provision for bad debts	25

Provision for Bad Debts

		£			£
			19–2		
			Dec 31	Profit and loss a/c	120
19–3			19–3		
Dec 31	Balance c/d	140	Dec 31	Profit and loss a/c	20
		140			140
19–4			19–4		
Dec 31	Balance c/d	155	Jan 1	Balance b/d	140
			Dec 31	Profit and loss a/c	15
		155			155
19–5			19–5		
Dec 31	Profit and loss a/c	25	Jan 1	Balance b/d	155
	Balance c/d	130			
		155			155
			19–6		
			Jan 1	Balance b/d	130

Bad Debts

		£			£
19–2			19–2		
Dec 31	Various debtors	423	Dec 31	Profit and loss a/c	423
19–3			19–3		
Dec 31	Various debtors	510	Dec 31	Profit and loss a/c	510
19–4			19–4		
Dec 31	Various debtors	604	Dec 31	Profit and loss a/c	604
19–5			19–5		
Dec 31	Various debtors	610	Dec 31	Profit and loss a/c	610

Balance Sheets as at 31 December (extracts)

		£	£
19–2	Debtors	6,000	
	Less Provision for bad debts	120	5,880
19–3	Debtors	7,000	
	Less Provision for bad debts	140	6,860
19–4	Debtors	7,750	
	Less Provision for bad debts	155	7,595
19–5	Debtors	6,500	
	Less provision for bad debts	130	6,370

21.5 Diagram of Entries

Students often find it difficult to understand why there should be entries in the profit and loss account for bad debts and also a provision for bad debts. The following example should show why both of the items are needed:

T Kime starts a business. Let us look at some of the figures from his first year's trading:

1 He has sold £50,000 goods on credit.

2 Debtors have paid him £39,600.

3 Two debtors owing him a total of £400 have been made bankrupt. No money will ever be received from them.

4 There was still another £10,000 owing to him at the year end (does not include **3**).

5 Some of the £10,000 **4** will probably never be paid. Kime did not know exactly how much it would be. He estimates it at one per cent of debtors, i.e. £10,000 × 1% = £100. He decides to make a provision for bad debts account and extracts from the final accounts are now shown.

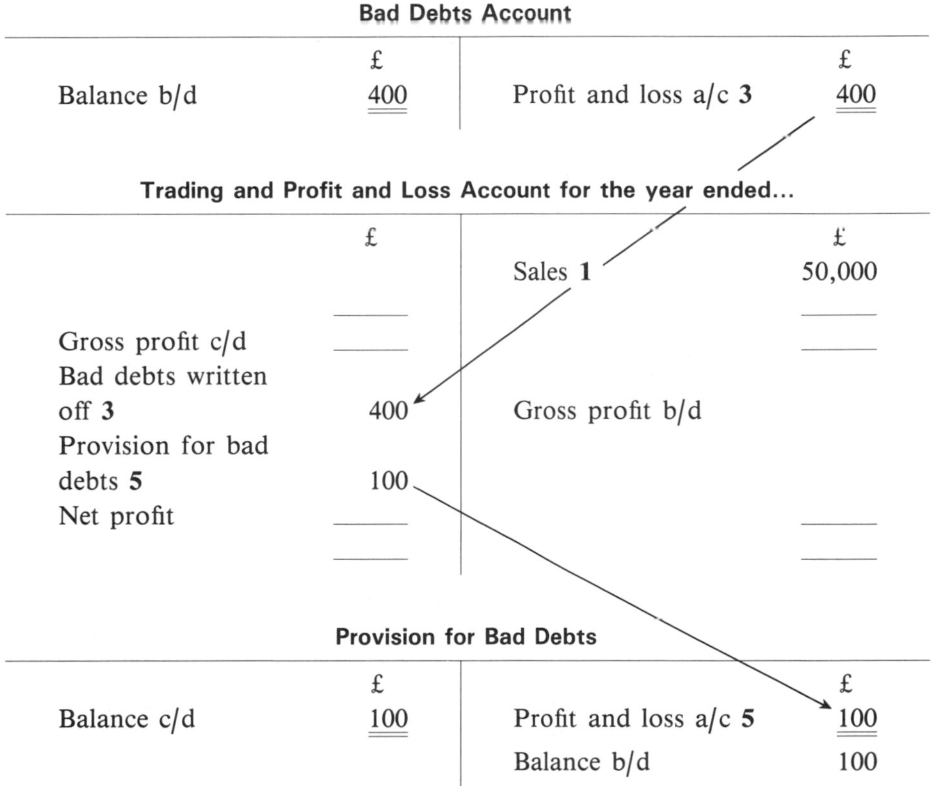

Bad Debts Account

	£		£
Balance b/d	400	Profit and loss a/c **3**	400

Trading and Profit and Loss Account for the year ended...

	£		£
		Sales **1**	50,000
Gross profit c/d			
Bad debts written off **3**	400	Gross profit b/d	
Provision for bad debts **5**	100		
Net profit			

Provision for Bad Debts

	£		£
Balance c/d	100	Profit and loss a/c **5**	100
		Balance b/d	100

For the balance sheet, the balances for debtors **4** and the provision for bad debts **5** have to be shown. There is no balance on the bad debts account, and therefore this will not appear.

Balance Sheet as at ......

	£	£
Current Assets		
Debtors **4**	10,000	
less Provision for bad debts **5**	100	9,900

To summarise:

Sales £50,000. Of this the amount that would not be paid, £400 (definite) + further £100 (estimated) = £500.	recorded in profit and loss account as	Bad debts £400, provision for bad debts £100 = £500 charged against profits	
Expected realisable value of debtors: Debtors £10,000 *less* £100 estimated not receivable = £9,900	shown in balance sheet as	Debtors	£10,000
		less Provision for bad debts	£100
			£9,900

21.6 Bad Debts Recovered

It is not uncommon for a debt written off in previous years to be recovered in later years. When this occurs, the book-keeping procedures are as follows:

First, re-instate the debt by making the following entries:

Dr Debtors Account
Cr Bad Debts Recovered Account.

The reason for re-instating the debt in the ledger account of the debtor is to have a detailed history of his/her account as a guide for granting credit in future. By the time a debt is written off as bad, it will be recorded in the debtor's ledger account. Therefore when such debt is recovered, it also must be shown in the debtor's ledger account.

When cash/cheque is later received from the debtor in settlement of the account or part thereof,

Dr Cash/Bank
Cr Debtor's Account

with the amount received.

At the end of the financial year, the credit balance in the Bad Debts Recovered Account will be transferred to either Bad Debts Account or direct to the credit side of the Profit and Loss Account. The effect is the same since the Bad Debts Account will in itself be transferred to the Profit and Loss Account at the end of the financial year.

21.7 Multiple-choice Questions

Now attempt Set No 3 consisting of 20 questions, shown on pages 347–50.

New Terms

Bad Debt (p 171): A debt which we will not be able to collect.

Exercises

21.1 On 1 January 19–7 the balances below appeared in the Sales ledger of S Sowerby:

	£
D Plim	200
C Mike	120

During the year the following events took place:

Feb 1 After negotiation Sowerby agreed to accept £150 cash from D Plim and regarded the outstanding balance as irrecoverable.

Mar 10 C Mike was declared bankrupt. A payment of 30 pence in the £ was received in full settlement.

Show how these matters would be dealt with in Sowerby's ledger assuming that the financial year ends on 30 June.

(RSA)

21.2 On 30 September 19–7 B Fox's debtors totalled £12,000. He decided to write off the following as bad debts:

	£
G Green	60
H Wilson	80

He further decided to make a provision for Doubtful Debts of 10 per cent on the remaining debtors.

Debtors on 30 September 19–8 totalled £10,000 when Fox decided to maintain the provision at 10 per cent.

You are required to show for each of the years ended 30 September 19–7 and 19–8:

(a) provision for Doubtful Debts Account;

(b) the appropriate entries in the Profit and Loss Account; and

(c) the necessary Balance Sheet entries on each of the above dates.

(RSA)

21.3

Date: 31 Dec	*Total Debtors*	*Profit and Loss*	*Dr/Cr*	*Final Figure for Balance Sheet*
	£	£		£
19–3	7,000			
19–4	8,000			
19–5	6,000			
19–6	7,000			

The above table shows the figure for debtors appearing in a trader's books on 31 December of each year from 19–3 to 19–6. The Provision for Doubtful Debts is to be one per cent of debtors from 31 December 19–3. Complete the above table indicating the amount to be debited or credited to the profit and loss account for the year ended on each 31 December, and the amount for the final figure of debtors to appear in the Balance Sheet on each date.
(RSA)

21.4X A business started on 1 January 19–5 and its financial year end is 31 December annually. A table of the debtors, the bad debts written off and the estimated bad debts at the end of the year is now given.

Year to 31 December	*Debtors at end of year (after bad debts written off)*	*Bad Debts written off during the year*	*Debts thought at end of year to be impossible to collect*
	£	£	£
19–5	12,000	298	100
19–6	15,000	386	130
19–7	14,000	344	115
19–8	18,000	477	150

You are required to show the above in the double entry accounts, as well as the extracts from the Profit and Loss Account for each year and the Balance Sheet extracts.

21.5X T Pitt owes you £59.00 on 1 January. He pays you £29.00 on 31 January but ignores all further requests for payment. On 6 May you hear that he has been made a bankrupt, and his trustee in bankruptcy announces that a dividend of 25% in the £ will be paid on 30 September. This payment was received in due course.

Show Pitt's ledger account and the bad debts account at 31 December, the end of your financial year.
(PEI)

21.6X The following data is available in relation to Thermogen Suppliers:

	£
(1) Balance of Debtors at 31 December Year 6 – *before* writing off bad debts	81,600
(2) Bad debts written off in Year 6	1,200
(3) A provision of 2% of debtors for doubtful debts was set up at 31 December Year 6	
(4) Bad debts written off in Year 7	1,800
(5) Balance of Debtors at 31 December Year 7 – *before* writing off bad debts	122,700
(6) The provision for doubtful debts is increased to 4% at 31 December Year 7	
(7) Bad debts written off in Year 8	2,100
(8) Balance of Debtors at 31 December Year 8 – *after* writing off bad debts	103,500
(9) The provision for doubtful debts is reduced to 3% at 31 December Year 8	

Required

(a) Prepare the following accounts for Years 6, 7 and 8, showing the transfer to Profit and Loss Account at the end of each year:
   (i) Bad Debts Account
   (ii) Provision for Doubtful Debts Account

(b) Show Balance Sheet extracts in respect of Debtors at the following dates:
   31 December Year 6
   31 December Year 7
   31 December Year 8

(c) If one of the debts, written off early in Year 8, was to be recovered later in Year 8, what accounting entries would you expect to be made?

(LCCI)

22 · Adjustments for Final Accounts

22.1 Final Accounts So Far

The trading and profit and loss accounts you have looked at have taken the sales for a period and deducted all the expenses for that period, the result being a nct profit (or a net loss).

Up to this part of the book it has always been assumed that the expenses belonged exactly to the period of the trading and profit and loss account. If the trading and profit and loss account for the year ended 31 December 19–5 was being drawn up, then the rent paid as shown in the trial balance was exactly for 19–5. There was no rent owing at the beginning of 19–5 nor any owing at the end of 19–5, nor had any rent been paid in advance.

This was done to make your first meeting with final accounts much easier for you.

22.2 Adjustments Needed

Let us look instead at two firms who pay rent for buildings in Oxford. The rent for each building is £1,200 a year.

1 Firm A pays £1,000 in the year. At the year end it owes £200 for rent.
Rent expense used up = £1,200
Rent paid for = £1,000

2 Firm B pays £1,300 in the year. This figure includes £100 in advance for the following year.
Rent expense used up = £1,200
Rent paid for = £1,300

A profit and loss account for 12 months needs 12 months' rent as an expense = £1,200.

This means that in both **1** and **2** the double entry accounts will have to be adjusted.

In all the examples following in this chapter the trading and profit and loss accounts are for the year ended 31st December 19–5.

22.3 Accrued Expenses

Assume that rent of £1,000 per year is payable at the end of every three months. The rent was not always paid on time. Details were:

Amount	Rent due	Rent paid
£250	31 March 19–5	31 March 19–5
£250	30 June 19–5	2 July 19–5
£250	30 September 19–5	4 October 19–5
£250	31 December 19–5	5 January 19–6

The rent account appeared as:

Rent

19–5	£		
Mar 31 Cash	250		
Jul 2 "	250		
Oct 4 "	250		

The rent paid 5 January 19–6 will appear in the books of the year 19–6 as part of the double entry.

The expenses for 19–5 are obviously £1,000, as that is the year's rent, and this is the amount needed to be transferred to the profit and loss account. But if £1,000 was put on the credit side of the rent account (the debit being in the profit and loss account) the account would not balance. We would have £1,000 on the credit side of the account and only £750 on the debit side.

To make the account balance the £250 rent owing for 19–5, but paid in 19–6, must be carried down to 19–6 as a credit balance because it is a liability on 31 December 19–5. Instead of rent owing it could be called rent accrued or just simply an accrual. The completed account can now be shown.

Rent

19–5	£	19–5	£
Mar 31 Cash	250	Dec 31 Profit and loss	1,000
Jul 2 "	250		
Oct 4 "	250		
Dec 31 Accrued c/d	250		
	1,000		1,000
		19–6	
		Jan 1 Accrued b/d	250

The balance c/d has been described as accrued c/d, rather than as a balance. This is to explain what the balance is for, it is for an **accrued expense**.

22.4 Prepaid Expenses

Insurance for a firm is at the rate of £840 a year, starting from 1 January 19–5. The firm has agreed to pay this at the rate of £210 every three months. However payments were not made at the correct times. Details were:

Amount	Insurance due	Insurance paid
£210	31 March 19–5	£210 28 February 19–5
£210	30 June 19–5	
£210	30 September 19–5	£420 31 August 19–5
£210	31 December 19–5	£420 18 November 19–5

The insurance account will be shown in the books:

Insurance

	£		
19–5	£		
Feb 28 Cash	210		
Aug 31 "	420		
Nov 18 "	420		

Now the last payment of £420 is not just for 19–5, it can be split as £210 for the three months to 31 December 19–5 and £210 for the three months ended 31 March 19–6. For a period of 12 months the cost of insurance is £840 and this is, therefore, the figure needing to be transferred to the profit and loss account.

The amount needed to balance the account will therefore be £210 and at 31 December 19–5 this is a benefit paid for but not used up; it is an asset and needs carrying forward as such to 19–6, i.e. as a debit balance. It is a **prepaid expense**.

The account can now be completed.

Insurance

	£		£
19–5		19–5	
Feb 28 Cash	210	Dec 31 Profit and loss A/c	840
Aug 31 "	420	" 31 Prepaid c/d	210
Nov 18 "	420		
	1,050		1,050
19–6			
Jan 1 Prepaid b/d	210		

Prepayment will also happen when items other than purchases are bought for use in the business, and they are not fully used up in the period.

For instance, packing materials are normally not entirely used up over the period in which they are bought, there being a stock of packing materials in hand at the end of the period. This stock is, therefore, a form of prepayment and needs carrying down to the following period in which it will be used.

This can be seen in the following example:

Year ended 31 December 19–5.
Packing materials bought in the year £2,200.
Stock of packing materials in hand as at 31 December 19–5 £400.

Looking at the example, it can be seen that in 19–5 the packing materials used up will have been £2,200 – £400 = £1,800. We will still have a stock of £400 packing materials at 31 December 19–5 to be carried forward to 19–6. The £400 stock of packing materials will be carried forward as an asset balance (debit balance) to 19–6.

Packing Materials

	£		£
19–5		19–5	
Dec 31 Cash	2,200	Dec 31 Profit and loss	1,800
		Stock c/d	400
	2,200		2,200
19–6			
Jan 1 Stock b/d	400		

The stock of packing materials is not added to the stock of unsold goods in hand in the balance sheet, but is added to the other prepayments of expenses.

22.5 Revenue Owing at the End of Period

The **revenue** owing for sales is already shown in the books. These are the debit balances on our customers' accounts, i.e. debtors. There may be other kinds of revenue, e.g. rent receivable. An example now follows:

22.6 Worked Example

Our warehouse is larger than we need. We rent part of it to another firm for £800 per annum. Details for the year ended 31 December were as follows:

Amount	Rent due	Rent received
£200	31 March 19–5	4 April 19–5
£200	30 June 19–5	6 July 19–5
£200	30 September 19–5	9 October 19–5
£200	31 December 19–5	7 January 19–6

The account for 19–5 appeared:

Rent Receivable

		19–5	£
		Apr 4 Bank	200
		Jul 6 Bank	200
		Oct 9 Bank	200

The rent received of £200 on 7 January 19–6 will be entered in the books in 19–6.

Any rent paid by the firm would be charged as a debit to the profit and loss account. Any rent received, being the opposite, is transferred to the credit of the profit and loss account.

The amount to be transferred for 19–5 is that earned for the twelve months, i.e. £800. The rent received account is completed by carrying down the balance owing as a debit balance to 19–6. The £200 owing is an asset on 31 December 19–5.

The rent receivable account can now be completed:

Rent Receivable

19–5	£	19–5	£
Dec 31 Profit and loss A/c	800	Apr 4 Bank	200
		Jul 6 Bank	200
		Oct 9 Bank	200
		Dec 31 Accrued c/d	200
	800		800
19–6			
Jan 1 Accrued b/d	200		

22.7 Expenses and Revenue Account Balances and the Balance Sheet

In all the cases listed dealing with adjustments in the final accounts, there will still be a balance on each account after the preparation of the trading and profit and loss accounts. All such balances remaining should appear in the balance sheet. The only question left is where and how they shall be shown.

The amounts owing for expenses are usually added together and shown as one figure. These could be called expense creditors, expenses owing, or accrued expenses. The item would appear under current liabilities as they are expenses which have to be discharged in the near future.

The items prepaid are also added together and called prepayments, prepaid expenses, or payments in advance. Often they are added to the debtors in the balance sheet, otherwise they are shown next under the debtors. Amounts owing for rents receivable or other revenue owing are usually added to debtors.

The balance sheet in respect of the accounts so far seen in this chapter would appear:

Balance Sheet as at 31 December 19–5

Current Assets	£	*Current Liabilities*	£
Stock		Trade creditors	
Debtors	200	Accrued expenses	250
Prepayments (400 + 210)	610		
Bank			
Cash			

22.8 Expenses and Revenue Accounts Covering More Than One Period

Students are often confused when asked to draw up an expense or revenue account for a full year, and there are amounts owing or prepaid at both the beginning and end of the year. We can now see how this is done.

Example A

The following details are available:

1 On 31 December 19–4 three months rent of £3,000 was owing.
2 The rent chargeable per year was £12,000.
3 The following payments were made in the year 19–5:
6 January £3,000; 4 April £3,000; 7 July £3,000; 18 October £3,000.
4 The final three months rent for 19–5 is still owing.

Now we can look at the completed rent account. The numbers **1** to **4** give reference to the details above.

Rent

19–5			£	19–5			£
Jan 6	Bank	3	3,000	Jan 1	Owing b/f	1	3,000
Apr 4	Bank	3	3,000	Dec 31	Profit and loss a/c	2	12,000
Jul 7	Bank	3	3,000				
Oct 18	Bank	3	3,000				
Dec 31	Owing c/d	4	3,000				
			15,000				15,000
				19–6			
				Jan 1	Owing b/d		3,000

Example B

The following details are available:

1 On 31 December 19–4 packing materials in hand amounted to £1,850.
2 During the year to 31 December 19–5 £27,480 was paid for packing materials.
3 There were no stocks of packing materials on 31 December 19–5.
4 On 31 December 19–5 we still owed £2,750 for packing materials already received and used.

The packing materials account will appear as:

Packing Materials

19–5	£	19–5	£
Jan 1 Stocks b/f **1**	1,850	Dec 31 Profit and loss a/c	32,080
Dec 31 Bank **2**	27,480		
Dec 31 Owing c/d **4**	2,750		
	32,080		32,080
		19–6	
		Jan 1 Owing b/d	2,750

The figure of £32,080 is the difference on the account, and is transferred to the profit and loss account.

We can prove it is correct:

	£	£
Stock at start of year		1,850
Add bought and used:		
Paid for	27,480	
Still owed for	2,750	30,230
Cost of packing materials used in the year		32,080

Example C

Where different expenses are put together in one account, it can get even more confusing. Let us look at where rent and rates are joined together.

Here are the details for the year ended 31 December 19–5:

1 Rent is payable of £6,000 per annum.
2 Rates of £4,000 per annum are payable by instalments.
3 At 1 January 19–5 rent £1,000 had been prepaid in 19–4.
4 On 1 January 19–5 rates were owed of £400.
5 During 19–5 rent was paid £4,500.
6 During 19–5 rates were paid £5,000.
7 On 31 December 19–5 rent £500 was owing.
8 On 31 December 19–5 rates of £600 had been prepaid.

A combined rent and rates account is to be drawn up for the year 19–5 showing the transfer to the profit and loss account, and balances are to be carried down to 19–6.

Rent and Rates

			£				£
19–5				19–5			
Jan 1	Rent prepaid b/f	**3**	1,000	Jan 1	Rates owing b/f	**4**	400
Dec 31	Bank: Rent	**5**	4,500	Dec 31	Profit and loss a/c	**1 + 2**	10,000
Dec 31	Rates	**6**	5,000	Dec 31	Rates prepaid c/d	**8**	600
Dec 31	Rent owing c/d	**7**	500				
			11,000				11,000
19–6				19–6			
Jan 1	Rates prepaid b/d	**8**	600	Jan 1	Rent owing b/d	**7**	500

22.9 Goodwill

When starting in business we could start from nothing. At that time we would have no customers at all. Over the years we might work hard, and then have a lot of customers who would buy or trade with us year after year.

Instead of this we might buy an existing business. We look at it and put a value on the items in the business.

These are:

	£
Premises	50,000
Equipment	20,000
Stock	12,000
	82,000

But the owner wants £100,000 for the business, an extra £18,000. He says it is worth £18,000 extra because he has made the business into a very good one, with a lot of customers. Many of the customers trade continually with him.

We agreed to pay the extra £18,000. This extra amount is known as **goodwill**. We will do this, because we will get a lot of customers immediately. It might take us many years to do this if we start from nothing.

In the balance sheet we will show goodwill as the first of the fixed assets.

22.10 Goods for Own Use

A trader will often take items out of his business stocks for his own use, without paying for them. There is nothing wrong about this, but an entry should be made

to record the event. This is done by:
1 Credit purchases account.
2 Debit drawings account.
Adjustments may also be needed for other private items. For instance, if a trader's private insurance had been incorrectly charged to the insurance account, then the correction would be:
1 Credit insurance account.
2 Debit drawings account.

22.11 Final Accounts for Non-traders

If the final accounts are for someone who is not trading in goods as such, for instance accountants, insurance agents, lawyers and the like, there will be no need for a trading account.

All of the revenue and expense items will be shown in a profit and loss account, disclosing a net profit (or net loss). Balance sheets for such providers of services (i.e. not goods) will be the same as for traders.

22.12 Vertical Form of Accounts

Final accounts are often shown in a vertical fashion. This is also said to be a narrative style, or a columnar presentation. When this is done, working capital is shown as a separate figure. Working capital is the term for the excess of the current assets over the current liabilities of a business.

The trading and profit and loss account shown as Exhibit 8.2 on page 63, and also the balance sheet shown as Exhibit 9.3 on page 71, are now shown in a vertical fashion in Exhibit 22.1. You will see that working capital £1,600 is shown as a separate figure.

Exhibit 22.1 **Vertical Form**

B Swift

Trading and Profit and Loss Account for the year ended 31 December 19–5

		£	£
Sales			3,850
Less	Cost of Goods Sold:		
	Purchases	2,900	
	Less Closing stock	300	2,600
Gross Profit			1,250
Less	Expenses:		
	Rent	240	
	Lighting and heating	150	
	General expenses	60	450
Net profit			800

B Swift
Balance Sheet as at 31 December 19–5

	£	£
Fixed assets		
Furniture and fittings		500
Current assets		
Stock	300	
Debtors	680	
Bank	1,510	
Cash	20	
	2,510	
Less Current liabilities		
Creditors	910	
Working Capital		1,600
		2,100
Financed by:		
Capital		
Cash introduced		2,000
Add Net profit for the year		800
		2,800
Less Drawings		700
		2,100

22.13 Definition of Accounting

In Chapter 1 we gave a definition of book-keeping as being concerned with the work of entering information into accounting records and afterwards maintaining such records properly. This definition does not need to be amended.

However, accounting was not fully defined in Chapter 1. It would not have meant much to the reader at that stage in his/her studies. The following is the most widely used definition – *The process of identifying, measuring, and communicating economic information to permit informed judgements and decisions by users of the information.*

New Terms

Accrued Expense (p 183): An expense which the firm has used, but which has not yet been paid for.

Prepaid Expense (p 184): An expense to be used up in a following period, but which has been paid for in advance.

Revenue (p 185): Money earned by the firm.

Goodwill (p 189): The extra amount paid for an existing firm above the value of its other assets.

Exercises

22.1 The financial year of H Saunders ended on 31 December 19–6. Show the ledger accounts for the following items including the balance transferred to the necessary part of the final accounts, also the balances carried down to 19–7:

(a) Motor Expenses: Paid in 19–6 £744; Owing at 31 December 19–6 £28.
(b) Insurance: Paid in 19–6 £420; Prepaid as at 31 December 19–6 £35.
(c) Stationery: Paid during 19–6 £1,800; Owing as at 31 December 19–5 £250; Owing as at 31 December 19–6 £490.
(d) Rent: Paid during 19–6 £950; Prepaid as at 31 December 19–5 £220; Prepaid as at 31 December £19–6 £290.
(e) Saunders sub-lets part of the premises. Receives £550 during the year ended 31 December 19–6. Tenant owed Saunders £180 on 31 December 19–5 and £210 on 31 December 19–6.

22.2X J Owen's year ended on 30 June 19–4. Write up the ledger accounts, showing the transfers to the final accounts and the balances carried down to the next year for the following:

(a) Stationery: Paid for the year to 30 June 19–4 £855; Stocks of stationery at 30 June 19–3 £290; at 30 June 19–4 £345.
(b) General expenses: Paid for the year to 30 June 19–4 £590; Owing at 30 June 19–3 £64; Owing at 30 June 19–4 £90.
(c) Rent and Rates (combined account): Paid in the year to 30 June 19–4 £3,890; Rent owing at 30 June 19–3 £160; Rent paid in advance at 30 June 19–4 £250; Rates owing 30 June 19–3 £205; Rates owing 30 June 19–4 £360.
(d) Motor Expenses: paid in the year to 30 June 19–4 £4,750; Owing as at 30 June 19–3 £180; Owing as at 30 June 19–4 £375.
(e) Owen earns commission from the sales of one item. Received for the year to 30 June 19–4 £850; Owing at 30 June 19–3 £80; Owing at 30 June 19–4 £145.

22.3 A Bush is a sole trader who occupies rented premises. The annual rental is £2,400 which he pays quarterly. His lease and financial year commenced on 1 August Year 1.
During his first financial year, A Bush made the following payments in respect of rent:

		£
Year 1	1 August	600
	4 November	600
Year 2	31 March	600
	8 August	600

He paid rates on the premises as follows:

Year 1	31 August	£75 for period 1 August to 30 September Year 1
	22 October	£220 for period 1 October to 31 March Year 2
Year 2	17 April	£270 for period 1 April to 30 September Year 2

He paid electricity bills as follows:

Year 1	17 October	£310
Year 2	21 January	£390
Year 2	10 April	£360

An electricity bill of £420 accrued due had not been paid.

Required

(a) Open the following accounts and, for the year ended 31 July Year 2, enter the payments and make the necessary year-end adjustments for prepayments or accruals. Enter the transfers to Profit and Loss Account and bring down balances at 1 August Year 2:
(i) Rent Payable
(ii) Rates
(iii) Electricity

(b) Show the relevant extracts covering the above items from the Balance Sheet of A Bush as at 31 July Year 2.

(LCCI)

22.4X The following are *some* of the balances existing in the ledger of P Danton at 31 March Year 7:

	£
Rent	1,265 (Debit balance)
Insurances	480 (Debit balance)
Loan from J Finniston	1,000 (Credit balance)
Motor Vehicle at cost	6,200 (Debit balance)
Provision for doubtful debts	820 (Credit balance)

The following additional information is ascertained:
1 One month's rent, amounting to £115, is due but unpaid.
2 Insurances consist of:

Property insurance	£120 for the year ended 31 March Year 7
Motor insurance	£360 for the year ended 30 June Year 7

3 Finniston's loan carries interest at 9% per annum. The first half year's interest has been paid and debited to the Loan Interest Account but the second half year's interest is to be provided for.
4 The motor vehicle was purchased on 1 July Year 6. However, a full year's depreciation is to be provided for at 25% per annum on cost.
5 The doubtful debts provision is to be adjusted to £865.

Required

Prepare Ledger Accounts for:
(a) Rent
(b) Insurances
(c) Loan Interest
(d) Provision for Depreciation of Motor Vehicle
(e) Provision for Doubtful Debts

Note: Show clearly in each case the transfer to Profit and Loss Account for the year ended 31 March Year 7.

(LCCI)

22.5 From the following particulars write up R Brown's rates account for the year ended 31 October 19–3 and show the amount transferred to Profit and Loss Account.

1 November 19–2. Rates owing for October 19–2 £10.
Payments for rates in year to 31 October 19–3:
4 November 19–2 for half-year to 31 March 19–3 £60.
11 April 19–3 for half-year to 30 September 19–3 £72.
26 October 19–3 for half-year to 31 March 19–4 £72.

(RSA)

22.6 The trial balance of Bilton Potteries prepared after calculation of the gross profit is shown below.

Bilton Potteries
Trial Balance as at 31 January 19–0

Details	*Debit* £	*Credit* £
Capital		7,000
Premises	5,000	
Bank	3,218	
Debtors	434	
Stock (31 January 19–0)	1,000	
Creditors		870
Drawings	3,800	
Insurance	450	
Rent Receivable		225
Rates	500	
Wages	5,200	
Gross Profit for year ended 31 January 19–0		11,507
	£19,602	£19,602

A detailed review by the accountant revealed that the following adjustments were outstanding:

1 Rates amounting to £100 had been paid in advance.
2 Rent receivable of £75 was still outstanding at 31 January 19–0.
3 The insurance total included the payment of £50 for private house contents insurance.
4 Wages owing amounted to £300.

Required

(a) Open up the appropriate ledger accounts and post the above adjustments. Balance off these ledger accounts.

(b) Prepare a profit and loss account for the year ended 31 January 19–0 and a balance sheet as at that date, after the above adjustments have been posted.

(RSA)

22.7 George Holt, a sole trader, extracted from his books the following Trial Balance as at the close of business on 31 October 19–6:

	Dr	*Cr*
	£	£
Stock 1 November 19–5	1,970	
Debtors and creditors	2,350	1,680
Wages and salaries	1,520	
Rent, rates and insurance	280	
Bad debts	110	
Discounts	130	90
Fixtures and fittings	400	
Purchases and sales	5,930	9,620
Bank overdraft		260
Cash in hand	30	
Capital Account 1 November 19–5		2,700
Drawings	1,440	
General office expenses	190	
	14,350	14,350

Notes:
(a) Rent prepaid at 31 October 19–6 £40.
(b) Stock 31 October 19–6 £1,780.
(c) Depreciation £100 for fixtures and fittings.

Required
Prepare the Trading and Profit and Loss Accounts for the year ending 31 October 19–6 together with a Balance Sheet as at that date.
(LCCI)

22.8 From the following Trial Balance of John Brown, a grocery shop owner, prepare a Trading Account and Profit and Loss Account, taking into consideration the adjustments shown below:

Trial Balance as at 31 December 19–7

	Dr	*Cr*
	£	£
Sales		40,000
Purchases	35,000	
Sales Returns	500	
Purchases Returns		620
Opening Stock at 1 January 19–7	10,000	
Provision for Bad Debt		80
Wages and salaries	3,000	
Rates	600	
Telephone	100	
Shop fittings at cost	4,000	
Van at cost	3,000	
Debtors and Creditors	980	700
Bad Debts	20	
Capital		17,900
Bank balance	300	
Drawings	1,800	
	59,300	59,300

Adjustments:
(a) Closing stock at 31 December 19–7 £12,000.
(b) Accrued wages £500.
(c) Rates prepaid £50.
(d) The Provision for Bad Debts to be increased to 10 per cent of Debtors.
(e) Telephone Account outstanding £22.
(f) Depreciate shop fittings at 10 per cent per annum, and van at 20 per cent per annum, on cost.

A Balance Sheet is not required.
(RSA adapted)

22.9X The following Trial Balance was extracted from the books of Adam Jenkins at the close of business on 28 February 19–7.

	Dr	*Cr*
	£	£
Purchases and sales	3,760	6,580
Cash at bank	380	
Cash in hand	70	
Capital Account 1 March 19–6		3,300
Drawings	950	
Office furniture	480	
Rent and rates	340	
Wages and salaries	860	
Discounts	230	120
Debtors and creditors	1,640	830
Stock 1 March 19–6	990	
Provision for Bad and Doubtful Debts 1 March 19–6		90
Delivery van	800	
Van running costs	150	
Bad Debts written off	270	
	10,920	10,920

Notes:
(a) Stock 28 February 19–7 £1,170.
(b) Wages and salaries accrued at 28 February 19–7 £30.
(c) Increase the provision for Bad and Doubtful Debts by £20.
(d) Provide for depreciation as follows: Office furniture £60; Delivery van £160.

Required
Draw up the Trading and Profit and Loss Accounts for the year ending 28 February 19–7 together with a Balance Sheet as on 28 February 19–7.
(LCCI)

22.10 Jane Jones is in business as a hairdresser. From the figures below prepare her Profit and Loss Account for the year ended 31 December 19–7 and a Balance

Sheet on that date.

	Dr	*Cr*
	£	£
Capital 1 January 19–7		9,740
Drawings	4,500	
Motor car (cost £1,800)	1,320	
Petty cash	40	
Cost of new hair dryer	120	
Equipment (cost £1,000)	600	
Freehold premises	6,000	
Advertising	230	
Cash at bank	5,400	
Motor car expenses	480	
Rates	140	
Telephone	110	
Revenue from hairdressing		10,400
Sundry expenses	1,200	
	20,140	20,140

The following should be taken into consideration.

(a) Rates prepaid 31 December 19–7 £30.

(b) One-third of motor car expenses including depreciation for the year is to be regarded as private use.

(c) Provide for cleaning costs £50.

(d) Depreciate all equipment on hand at 31 December 19–7 by 10 per cent of cost.

(e) Motor car is to be depreciated by 20 per cent on reduced balance.

(RSA)

22.11X Sandra Black operates a secretarial service to farmers and the following trial balance was extracted from her books on 31 May 19–0.

	£	£
Income from clients		32,500
Commissions from other sources		800
Discounts Received		150
Stationery	2,100	
Wages	7,600	
Equipment	4,500	
Vehicles	6,500	
Rent & Rates	2,350	
Vehicle Expenses	2,000	
Light and Heat	800	
Insurance	850	
Telephone	280	
Sundry Expenses	175	
Drawings	11,200	
Debtors	760	
Creditors		670
Bank Overdraft		250
Cash in Hand	175	
Capital		4,920
	39,290	39,290

Notes

(a) At 31 May 19–0 there is an unpaid telephone bill of £52 and an unpaid electricity bill of £45.
(b) Rates prepaid at 31 May 19–0 are £120.
(c) On 31 May 19–0 there is an unused stock of stationery valued at £150.

Required

Prepare a profit and loss account for Sandra Black for the year ended 31 May 19–0 and a balance sheet as at that date, showing clearly therein the value of her capital, fixed assets, current assets and current liabilities.
(RSA)

22.12 Thomas Williams, a sole trader, extracted the following Trial Balance from his books at the close of business on 31 March 19–9:

	Dr	*Cr*
	£	£
Purchases and sales	7,620	13,990
Stock 1 April 19–8	1,720	
Capital 1 April 19–8		2,400
Bank overdraft		1,450
Cash	30	
Discounts	480	310
Returns inwards	270	
Returns outwards		190
Carriage outwards	720	
Rent, rates and insurance	580	
Provision for Bad and Doubtful Debts		220
Fixtures and fittings	400	
Delivery van	700	
Debtors and creditors	3,970	2,020
Drawings	960	
Wages and salaries	2,980	
General office expenses	150	
	20,580	20,580

Notes

(a) Stock 31 March 19–9 £1,430.
(b) Wages and salaries accrued at 31 March 19–9 £70.
(c) Rates prepaid 31 March 19–9 £60.
(d) Increase the provision for Bad and Doubtful Debts by £50 to £270.
(e) Provide for depreciation as follows: Fixtures and fittings £40; Delivery van £100.

Required

Prepare the Trading and Profit and Loss Accounts for the year ended 31 March 19–9 together with a Balance Sheet as at that date.
(LCCI) (Keep your answer. It will be used as the basis for question 22.14X.)

22.13X Angus Brown is a retail trader. From the following information prepare a Trading and Profit and Loss Account for the year ended 31 December 19–4 and a Balance Sheet on that date.

Trial Balance – 31 December 19–4

	£	£
Capital 1 January 19–4		6,400
Land and buildings	5,000	
Motor vehicles (cost £1,200)	600	
Drawings	1,400	
Stock	910	
Bank overdraft		96
Sales		14,260
Purchases	11,100	
Motor expenses	310	
Sundry expenses	106	
Wages	1,560	
Debtors	820	
Creditors		1,210
Rates and insurance	160	
	21,966	21,966

The following items should be taken into consideration:

(a) Stock at 31 December 19–4 £1,820.
(b) A provision for doubtful debts of 5 per cent on the debtors at 31 December 19–4 is to be created.
(c) Depreciation is to be provided on motor vehicles at 20 per cent on cost.
(d) Rates prepaid at 31 December 19–4 £12.
(e) Motor expenses bill for December £26 is owing at 31 December 19–4.
(f) Sundry expenses includes £15 for a private telephone bill of Angus Brown.
(g) A cheque for £250 was paid to a creditor on 31 December 19–4 but had not been entered in the books at the time of extracting the trial balance.

(RSA) (Keep your answer. It will be used as the basis for question 22.15X.)

22.14X From your answer to question 22.12, draw up the final accounts in a vertical form.

22.15X From your answer to question 22.13X, draw up the final accounts in a vertical form.

22.16 The following balances remained in the books of G Williams, a sole trader, at 31 October 19–0:

	£
Trade Creditors	2,065
Stock, 31 October 19–0	3,073
Wages owing	225
Premises	27,400
Cash	500
Trade Debtors	5,127
Furniture and fittings	3,075
Vehicles	6,100
Plant and machinery	13,840
Bank overdraft	1,875
Insurance paid in advance	50
5-year loan from Loamshire Finance Co	7,500
Drawings	10,800
Net profit for year ended 31 October 19–0	12,970
Capital	?

Required

(a) Answer the following:
  (i) What is the meaning of the words 'as at' on a balance sheet heading?
  (ii) Why is the stock shown above as being at 31 October 19–0 rather than at 1 November 19–9?

(b) Prepare the balance sheet for G Williams, using the balances listed above, and thus calculate his capital at the balance sheet date. Pay particular attention to layout and presentation.

(c) Prepare Williams' capital account, as it would appear in his ledger for his financial year to 31 October 19–0.

(RSA)

23 · Bank Reconciliation Statements

23.1 The Need for Bank Reconciliation Statements

At the end of each period we will balance off our cash book. At the same time we should ask our bank for a copy of our bank statement. When we look at the closing balance in our cash book, and then compare with the balance on that date on the bank statement, we will usually find that the two balances are different.

We should then draw up a **bank reconciliation statement**, and the methods for doing this are shown in this chapter. This will either show:

1 that the reasons for the difference in balances are valid ones, showing that it has not been as a result of errors made by us or the bank, or
2 that there is not a good reason for the difference between the balances.

In the case of **2** we will have to find out exactly what the errors are. They can then be corrected.

23.2 A Worked Example

Let us assume that we have just written up our cash book. We call at the bank on 30 June 19–5 and get from the bank manager a copy of our bank statement. On our return we tick off in our cash book and on the bank statement the items that are similar. A copy of our cash book (bank columns only) and of our bank statement are now shown as Exhibit 23.1.

Exhibit 23.1

Cash Book
(bank columns only)

19–5			£	19–5			£
June 1 Balance b/f	✓		80	June 27 I Gordon	✓		35
" 28 D Jones	✓		100	" 29 B Tyrell			40
				" 30 Balance c/d			105
			180				180
July 1 Balance b/d			105				

Bank Statement

		Dr	*Cr*	*Balance*
19–5		£	£	£
June 26 Balance b/f	✓			80 Cr
" 28 Banking	✓		100	180 Cr
" 30 I Gordon	✓	35		145 Cr

By comparing the cash book and the bank statement, it can be seen that the only item that was not in both of these was the cheque payment to B Tyrell £40 in the cash book.

The reason this was in the cash book, but not on the bank statement, is simply one of timing. The cheque had been posted to B Tyrell on 29 June, but there had not been time for it to be banked by Tyrell and pass through the banking system. Such a cheque is called an **unpresented cheque** because it has not yet been presented at the drawer's bank.

To prove that, although they are different figures the balances are not different because of errors, a bank reconciliation statement is drawn up. This is as follows:

Bank Reconciliation Statement as at 30 June 19–5

	£
Balance in Hand as per Cash Book	105
Add unpresented cheque: Tyrell	40
Balance in Hand as per Bank Statement	145

It would have been possible for the bank reconciliation statement to have started with the bank statement balance:

Bank Reconciliation Statement as at 30 June 19–5

	£
Balance in Hand as per Bank Statement	145
Less unpresented cheque: Tyrell	40
Balance in Hand as per Cash Book	105

You should notice that the bank account is shown as a debit balance in the firm's cash book because to the firm it is an asset. In the bank's books the bank account is shown as a credit balance because this is a liability of the bank to the firm.

23.3 Some reasons for Differences in Balances

We can now look at a more complicated example in Exhibit 23.2. Similar items in both cash book and bank statement are shown ticked.

Exhibit 23.2

Cash Book

19–5		£	19–5		£
Dec 27 Total b/fwd		2,000	Dec 27 Total b/fwd		1,600
" 29 J Potter	✓	60	" 28 J Jacobs	✓	105
" 31 M Johnson (B)		220	" 30 M Chatwood (A)		15
			" 31 Balance c/d		560
		2,280			2,280
19–6					
Jan 1 Balance b/d		560			

Bank Statement

		Dr	*Cr*	*Balance*
19–5		£	£	£
Dec 27 Balance b/fwd				400 CR
" 29 Cheque	✓		60	460 CR
" 30 J Jacobs	✓	105		355 CR
" " Credit transfers: L Shaw (C)			70	425 CR
" " Bank Charges (D)		20		405 CR

The balance brought forward in the bank statement £400 is the same figure as that in the cash book, i.e. totals b/fwd £2,000 – £1,600 – £400. However, items (A) and (B) are in the cash book only, and (C) and (D) are on the bank statement only. We can now examine these in detail:

(A) This is a cheque sent by us yesterday to Mr Chatwood. It has not yet passed through the banking system and been presented to our bank, and is therefore an 'unpresented cheque'.

(B) This is a cheque banked by us on our visit to the bank when we collected the copy of our bank statement. As we handed this banking over the counter at the same time as the bank clerk gave us our bank statement, naturally it has not yet been entered on the statement.

(C) A customer, L Shaw, has paid his account by instructing his bank to pay us direct through the banking system, instead of paying by cheque. Such a transaction is usually called a **credit transfer**.

(D) The bank has charged us for the services given in keeping a bank account for us. It did not send us a bill: it simply takes the money from our account by debiting it and reducing the amount of our balance.

We can show these differences in the form of a table . This is followed by bank reconciliation statements drawn up both ways. This is for illustration only; we do not have to draw up a table or prepare two bank reconciliation statements. All we need in practice is one bank reconciliation statement, drawn up whichever way we prefer.

Items not in both sets of books	Effect on Cash Book balance	Effect on Bank Statement	Adjustment required to one balance to reconcile it with the other: To Cash Book balance	To Bank Statement balance
1. Payment M Chatwood £15	reduced by £15	none – not yet entered	add £15	deduct £15
2. Banking M Johnson £220	increased by £220	none – not yet entered	deduct £220	add £220
3. Bank Commission £20	none – not yet entered	reduced by £20	deduct £20	add £20
4. Credit Transfers £70	none – not yet entered	increased by £70	add £70	deduct £70

Bank Reconciliation Statement as on 31 December 19–5

	£	£
Balance in hand as per Cash Book		560
Add Unpresented cheque	15	
Credit transfers	70	
		85
		645
Less Bank commission	20	
Bank lodgement not yet entered on bank statement	220	
		240
Balance in hand as per bank statement		405

Bank Reconciliation Statement as on 31 December 19–5

	£	£
Balance in hand as per bank statement		405
Add Bank commission	20	
Bank lodgement not yet entered on bank statement	220	
		240
		645
Less Unpresented cheque	15	
Traders Credit Transfers	70	
		85
Balance in hand as per bank statement		560

23.4 Writing up the Cash Book Before Attempting a Reconciliation

The easiest way to do a reconciliation is to complete the cash book first. All items on the bank statement will then be in the cash book. This means that the only differences will be items in the cash book but not on the bank statement. In an examination it is possible that the examiner will ask you not to do it this way.

If, in Exhibit 23.2, the cash book had been written up before the bank reconciliation statement had been drawn up, then the cash book and reconciliation statement would have appeared as follows in Exhibit 23.3.

Exhibit 23.3

Cash Book

	£		£
19–5		19–5	
Dec 27 Total b/fwd	2,000	Dec 27 Total b/fwd	1,600
" 29 J Potter	60	" 28 J Jacobs	105
" 31 M Johnson	220	" 30 M Chatwood	15
" 31 Credit transfers		" 31 Bank commission	20
L Shaw	70	" 31 Balance c/d	610
	2,350		2,350
19–6			
Jan 1 Balance b/d	610		

Bank Reconciliation Statement as on 31 December 19–5

	£
Balance in hand as per cash book	610
Add Unpresented cheque	15
	625
Less Bank lodgement not yet entered on bank statement	220
Balance in hand as per bank statement	405

23.5 Bank Overdrafts

When there is a bank overdraft the adjustments needed for reconciliation work are opposite to those needed for a balance.

Exhibit 23.4 is of a cash book, and a bank statement, showing an overdraft. Only the cheque for G Cumberbatch (A) £106 and the cheque paid to J Kelly (B) £63 need adjusting. Work through the reconciliation statement and then see the note after it.

Exhibit 23.4

Cash Book

	£		£
19–4		19–4	
Dec 5 I Howe	308	Dec 1 Balance b/f	709
" 24 L Mason	120	" 9 P Davies	140
" 29 K King	124	" 27 J Kelly (B)	63
" 31 G Cumberbatch (A)	106	" 29 United Trust	77
" " Balance c/f	380	" 31 Bank Charges	49
	1,038		1,038

Bank Statement

	Dr.	Cr.	Balance
19–4	£	£	£
Dec 1 Balance b/f			709 O/D
" 5 Cheque		308	401 O/D
" 14 P Davies	140		541 O/D
" 24 Cheque		120	421 O/D
" 29 K King: Credit Transfer		124	297 O/D
" 29 United Trust: Standing order	77		374 O/D
" 31 Bank Charges	49		423 O/D

Note: an overdraft is often shown with the letters O/D following the amount.

Bank Reconciliation Statement as on 31 December 19–4

	£
Overdraft as per cash book	380
Add Bank lodgements not on bank statement	106
	486
Less Unpresented cheque	63
Overdraft per bank statement	423

Note: now compare the reconciliation statements in Exhibit 23.3 and 23.4. This shows:

	Exhibit 23.3 *Balances*	*Exhibit 23.4* *Overdrafts*
Balance/Overdraft per cash book	XXXX	XXXX
Adjustments		
Unpresented cheque	PLUS	LESS
Banking not entered	LESS	PLUS
Balance/Overdraft per bank statement	XXXX	XXXX

Adjustments are, therefore, made in the opposite way when there is an overdraft.

23.6 Dishonoured Cheques

When a cheque is received from a customer and paid into the bank, it is recorded on the debit side of the cash book. It is also shown on the bank statement as a banking by the bank. However, at a later date it may be found that his bank will not pay it. They will not let it go through his account. The bank has failed to honour the cheque. It is called a **dishonoured cheque**.

There are several possible reasons for this. Let us suppose that K King gave us a cheque for £5,000 on May 20th 19–2. We bank it, but a few days later our bank returns the cheque to us. Typical reasons are:

1 King had put £5,000 in figures on the cheque, but had written it in words as five thousand five hundred pounds. You will have to give the cheque back to King for amendment.
2 Normally cheques are considered *stale* six months after the date on the cheque, in other words the banks will not pay cheques over six months old. If King had put the year 19–1 on the cheque instead of 19–2, then the cheque would be returned to us by our bank.
3 King simply did not have sufficient funds in his bank account. Suppose he had previously only got a £2,000 balance and yet he has given us a cheque for £5,000. His bank has not allowed him to have an overdraft.

In such a case the cheque would be dishonoured. The bank would write on the cheque *refer to drawer*, and we would have to get in touch with King to see what he was going to do about it.

In all of these cases the bank would show the original banking as being cancelled, by showing the cheque paid out of our bank account. As soon as this happens they will notify us. We will then also show the cheque being cancelled by a credit in the cash book. We will then debit that amount to this account.

When King originally paid his account our records would appear as:

K King

19–2	£	19–2	£
May 1 Balance b/d	5,000	May 20 Bank	5,000

Bank Account

19–2	£		
May 20 K King	5,000		

After our recording the dishonour, the records will appear as:

K King

19–2	£	19–2	£
May 1 Balance b/d	5,000	May 20 Bank	5,000
May 25 Bank: cheque dishonoured	5,000		

Bank Account

19–2	£	19–2	£
May 20 K King	5,000	May 25 K King: cheque dishonoured	5,000

In other words King is once again shown as owing us £5,000.

23.7 Some Other Reasons for Differences in Balances

1 Standing Orders. A firm can instruct its bank to pay regular amounts of money at stated dates to persons or firms. For instance you may ask your bank to pay £200 a month to a building society to repay a mortgage.
2 Direct Debits. These are payments which have to be made, such as rates, insurance premiums and similar items. Instead of asking the bank to pay the money, as with standing orders, permission is given to the creditor to obtain the money direct out of their bank account. This is particularly useful if the amounts payable may vary from time to time, as it is the creditor who changes the payments, not you. With standing orders, if the amount is ever to be changed then you have to inform the bank. With direct debits it is the creditor who arranges that, not you.

As far as bank reconciliation statements are concerned, both of the above types of payments may have passed through the bank account but have not been entered in the cash book.

23.8 Reconciliation of Our Ledger Accounts with Suppliers' Statements

Because of differences in timing, the balance on a supplier's statement on a certain date can differ from the balance on that supplier's account in our purchases ledger. This is similar to the fact that a bank statement balance may differ from the cash book balance. In a similar fashion a reconciliation statement may also be necessary. This can now be shown.

Our Purchases Ledger

C Young

19–6	£	19–6	£
Jan 10 Bank	1,550	Jan 1 Balance b/d	1,550
" 29 Returns **1**	116	" 6 Purchases	885
" 31 Balance c/d	1,679	" 18 Purchases	910
	3,345		3,345
		Feb 1 Balance b/d	1,679

Supplier's Statement
A Hall Ltd

19–6			Debit £	Credit £	Balance £
Jan 1	Balance b/f				1,550 Dr
" 4	Sales		885		2,435 Dr
" 13	Bank			1,550	885 Dr
" 18	Sales		910		1,795 Dr
" 31	Sales	**2**	425		2,220 Dr

Comparing our purchases ledger account with the supplier's statement, two differences can be seen.

1 We sent returns £116 to C Young, but they had not received them and recorded them in their books by the end of January.
2 Our supplier has sent goods to A Hall Ltd (our company), but we had not received them and entered the £425 in our books by the end of January.

A reconciliation statement can be drawn up by us, A Hall Ltd, as on 31 January 19–6.

Reconciliation of Supplier's Statement
C Young as on 31 January 19–6

		£	£
Balance per our purchases ledger			1,679
Add Purchases not received by us	**2**	425	
Returns not received by supplier	**1**	116	541
Balance per supplier's statement			2,220

New Terms

Bank Reconciliation Statement (p 201): A calculation comparing the cash book balance with the bank statement balance.

Unpresented Cheque (p 202): A cheque which has been sent but has not yet gone through the bank account of the receiver of it.

Credit Transfer (p 203): An amount paid by someone direct into our bank account

Dishonoured Cheque (p 206): A cheque which is found to be worth nothing.

Exercises

23.1 From the following draw up a bank reconciliation statement from details as on 31 December 19–6:

	£
Cash at bank as per bank column of the Cash Book	678
Unpresented cheques	256
Cheques received and paid into the bank, but not yet entered on the bank statement	115
Credit transfers entered as banked on the bank statement but not entered in the Cash Book	56
Cash at bank as per bank statement	875

23.2X On 30 September 19.. George Snow's statement of account from his bank showed a credit balance in his favour of £1,024.66. On comparing the statement with his cash book he found the following entries in the cash book did not appear on the statement:

Cheques paid in 30 Sept	£342.51
Cheques drawn on 30 Sept	£297.82

The following entries on the statement did not appear in his cash book:

Bank charges to 30 Sept 19..	£15.48
Payment direct to the bank by one of his debtors	£230.17

Prepare a bank reconciliation statement to show the bank balance in his cash book on 30 September 19..
(PEI)

23.3 At the close of business on 31 March 19–9, William Robinson's bank balance according to his Cash Book was £787. This does not agree with the balance at the bank as shown by the Bank Statement, and the following items account for the entire difference:

(a) Frank Gibson, one of Robinson's debtors, had paid the sum of £73 direct into Robinson's banking account. This had not been entered in the Cash Book although it was recorded in the Bank Statement on 29 March 19–9.

(b) A bankers standing order for a trade subscription of £25 was paid by the bank during March but the transaction has not yet been shown in the Cash Book.

(c) The following cheques – drawn by Robinson during March 19–9 and entered in the Cash Book – had not been presented for payment at his bank by the close of business on 31 March 19–9: £34, £41 and £52.

(d) The sum of £112 was paid into his banking account by Robinson on 31 March 19–9 but this item did not appear on his Bank Statement until after that date.

Required
Prepare the Bank Reconciliation Statement as at 31 March 19–9, commencing with the Cash Book balance of £787 and ending with the Bank Statement balance.
(LCCI)

23.4X The bank columns of your cash book for the month of May 19–8 are shown below:

19–8		£	19–8		£
May	1 Balance	320	May	3 Rates	150
"	9 G Brown	300	"	9 D Lynch	75
"	12 R Williams	175	"	16 R Button	130
"	17 R Termatrie	54	"	31 J Cottam	210
"	31 K Jones	13	"	" P Black	150
			"	" Balance	147
		862			862
June	1 Balance	147			

The Rates were paid with cheque number 110, subsequent payments being made strictly in numerical order.

The bank statement for the month of May is below:

			£	£	£
May	1				370
"	2 Cheque no.	109	50		320
"	5	110	150		170
"	19	112	130		40
"	20 Sundries			529	569
"	31 Charges		10		559
"	" Credit transfer: J Rickman			40	599

(a) Make the necessary entries in the bank columns of the cash book, and find the correct balance.

(b) Reconcile the cash book bank columns with the bank statement.

(RSA)

23.5X William Kay's Cash Book on 28 February 19–6 showed a balance at the Bank of £456.48. On attempting a reconciliation with his Bank Statement the following matters were discovered:

(a) A payment from B Green to W Kay of £40 by direct bank transfer had not been recorded in the Cash Book.

(b) Cheques drawn but not presented to the bank were: A Roe £21.62; C Mills £36.55.

(c) A paying-in slip dated 27 February 19–6 totalling £372.31 was not credited by the bank until 1 March 19–6.

(d) A standing order for £21.58 payable on 20 February 19–6 for Fire Insurance had been paid by the bank but not entered in the Cash Book.

(e) Bank charges £15 had not been entered in the Cash Book.

(i) Open the Cash Book and make such additional entries as you consider necessary;

(ii) Prepare a statement reconciling your *revised* Cash Book balance with the balance shown by the Bank Statement.

(RSA)

23.6 Mitchell's cash book showed a balance of £2,200 as at 31 December and his bank statement showed a balance of £2,195. A comparison of the two records showed the following outstanding items:

non-presented cheques £250;
payments made by the bank out of his account under a standing order but not yet recorded in the cash book £40;
credit transfer from customer paid directly to bank account but not yet entered in cash book £175;
bank charges not in cash book £40;
takings deposited in night-safe on 31 December £300, but not recorded on bank statement.

Reconcile the two balances.
(PEI)

23.7 A Brook's cash book showed the following entries for June:

		£			£
June	1 To bank balance	500	June	6 By Jones	75
"	7 To Sundries	420	"	9 By Wages	40
"	11 To Sundries	90	"	12 By Foxton	28
"	21 To Sundries	400	"	18 By Shore	34
"	30 To Sundries	400	"	23 By Wages	40
			"	28 By Bates	70
			"	30 By Balances	1,523
		£1,810			£1,810

His account at the bank gave the following particulars:

		Dr £	*Cr* £	*Balance* £
June	1			500
"	8 Cheques		420	920
"	9 Cash	40		880
"	12 Cheques		90	970
"	13 Jones	75		895
"	22 Cheques		400	1,295
"	24 Foxton	28		1,267
"	Cash	40		1,227
"	30 Bates	70		1,157

Prepare a bank reconciliation as at 30 June.
(PEI)

23.8X On 31 October 19–5 the Cash Book of N Orange showed a balance at the bank of £570. An examination of his records located the following errors:
1 Orange paid to R Jones £175 by cheque on 15 October. This cheque was entered in the Cash Book as £195.
2 Bank charges not recorded in the Cash Book amounted to £25.
3 A cheque dated 19 October, value £150, payable to T Jack was not paid by the bank until 5 November.
4 Orange on 23 October received from W Green a cheque, value £125. This cheque was dishonoured on 29 October. No entry for the dishonour has been made in the Cash Book.
5 On 31 October a cheque, value £200, received from F Brown was banked; however, the bank statement was not credited until 1 November.

You are required to:

(a) Make the necessary entries in the Cash Book in order to show the revised Cash Book balance at 31 October 19–5.

(b) Prepare a statement reconciling the corrected Cash Book balance with the bank statement at 31 October 19–5.

(c) State the balance at bank at 31 October 19–5 as shown by the bank statements.

(RSA)

23.9X From the following cash book and bank statement draw up a statement reconciling the two balances.

Cash book (Bank columns only)

		£			£
April 1	Balance b/f	600.00	April 8	Rates	110.00
" 6	Cash paid in	75.20	" 15	Wages	40.00
" 12	Cheque from A	64.80	" 15	Electricity	60.42
" 18	Cheque from B	72.40	" 15	Paid X	72.15
" 28	Cash paid in	85.00	" 26	Rent	30.00
" 30	Cheque from C	54.62	" 26	Wages	40.00
			" 27	Paid Y	64.10
			" 30	Paid Z	24.10
			" 30	Balance c/f	511.25
		952.02			952.02
May 1	Balance b/f	511.25			

Bank statement

		Debit	*Credit*	*Balance*
April 1	Balance			600.00
" 6	Cash		75.20	675.20
" 12	A		64.80	740.00
" 12	Rates	110.00		630.00
" 15	Wages	40.00		590.00
" 18	B		72.40	662.40
" 19	Electricity	60.42		601.98
" 20	X	72.15		529.83
" 26	Wages	40.00		489.83
" 28	Cash		85.00	574.83

(PEI)

24 · The Journal

24.1 Main Books of Original Entry

We have seen in earlier chapters that most transactions are entered in one of the following books of original entry:

- Cash book
- Sales journal
- Purchases journal
- Returns inwards journal
- Returns outwards journal

These books have grouped together similar things, e.g. all credit sales are in the sales journal. To trace any of them would be relatively easy, as we know exactly which book would contain the item.

24.2 The Journal: the Other Book of Original Entry

The other items which do not pass through the above books are much less common, and sometimes much more complicated. It would be easy for a book-keeper to forget the details of these transactions.

If the book-keeper left the firm it could be impossible to understand such book-keeping entries.

What is needed is a form of diary to record such transactions, before the entries are made in the double entry accounts. This book is called *the journal.* It will contain, for each transaction:

- The date
- The name of account(s) to be debited and the amount(s)
- The name of the account(s) to be credited and the amount(s)
- A description of the transaction (this is called a 'narrative')
- A reference number should be given for the documents giving proof of the transaction

The use of the journal makes fraud by book-keepers more difficult. It also reduces the risk of entering the item once only instead of having double entry. Despite these advantages there are many firms which do not have such a book.

24.3 Typical Uses of the Journal

Some of the main uses of the journal are listed below. It must not be thought that this list is a fully detailed one.

- The purchase and sale of fixed assets on credit
- The correction of errors
- Writing off bad debts
- Opening entries. These are the entries needed to open a new set of books
- Other items:

The layout of the journal can be shown:

The Journal

Date	*Folio*	*Dr*	*Cr*
The name of the account to be debited.			
The name of the account to be credited.			
The narrative.			

You can see that we put on the first line the account to be debited. The second line gives the account to be credited. We do not write the name of the account to be credited directly under the name of the account to be debited. This makes it easier to see which is the debit and which is the credit.

We should remember that the journal is not a double entry account. It is a form of diary, and entering an item in the journal is not the same as recording an item in an account. Once the journal entry is made the entry in the double entry accounts can then be made. Examples of the uses of the journal are now given.

Purchase and Sale on Credit of Fixed Assets

1 A machine is bought on credit from Toolmakers for £550 on 1 July 19–5.

		Dr	*Cr*
19–5		£	£
July 1	Machinery	550	
	Toolmakers		550
	Purchase of milling machine on credit, Capital Purchases invoice no 7/159		

2 Sale of a motor vehicle for £300 on credit to K Lamb on 2 July 19–5

	Dr	Cr
19–5	£	£
July 2 K Lamb	300	
Motor vehicles disposal		300
Sales of motor vehicles per Capital		
Sales invoice no 7/43		

Correction of Errors

These are explained in detail in chapters twenty-six and twenty-seven.

Bad Debts

A debt of £78 owing to us from H Mander is written off as a bad debt on 31 August 19–5.

	Dr	Cr
19–5	£	£
Aug 31 Bad debts	78	
H Mander		78
Debt written off as bad. See letter in file 7/8906		

Opening Entries

J Brew, after being in business for some years without keeping proper records, now decides to keep a double entry set of books. On 1 July 19–6 he establishes that his assets and liabilities are as follows:

Assets: Motor Van £840, Fixtures £700, Stock £390,
Debtors – B Young £95, D Blake £45, Bank £80, Cash £20.
Liabilities: Creditors – M Quinn £129, C Walters £41.

The Assets therefore total £840 + £700 + £390 + £95 + £45 + £80 + £20 = £2,170; and the Liabilities total £129 + £41 = £170.

The Capital consists of: Assets – Liabilities, £2,170 – £170 = £2,000

We must start the writing up of the books on 1 July 19–6. To do this we:

1 Open asset accounts, one for each asset. Each opening asset is shown as a debit balance.
2 Open liability accounts, one for each liability. Each opening liability is shown as a credit balance.
3 Open an account for the capital. Show it as a credit balance.

The journal records what you are doing, and why.
Exhibit 24.1 shows:

- The journal.
- The opening entries in the double entry accounts.

Exhibit 24.1

The Journal Page 5

		Fol	Dr	Cr
19–6			£	£
July 1	Motor Van	GL 1	840	
	Fixtures	GL 2	700	
	Stock	GL 3	390	
	Debtors – B Young	SL 1	95	
	D Blake	SL 2	45	
	Bank	CB 1	80	
	Cash	CB 1	20	
	Creditors – M Quinn	PL 1		129
	C Walters	PL 2		41
	Capital	GL 4		2,000
	Assets and liabilities at the date entered to open the books.		2,170	2,170

General Ledger

Motor Van Page 1

19–6			£				
July 1	Balance	J 5	840				

Fixtures Page 2

19–6			£				
July 1	Balance	J 5	700				

Stock Page 3

19–6			£				
July 1	Balance	J 5	390				

Capital Page 4

				19–6			£
				July 1	Balance	J 5	2,000

Sales Ledger

B Young Page 1

19–6			£				
July 1	Balance	J 5	95				

D Blake Page 2

19–6		£			
July 1 Balance	J 5	45			

Purchases Ledger

M Quinn Page 1

			19–6		£
			July 1 Balance	J 5	129

C Walters Page 2

			19–6		£
			July 1 Balance	J 5	41

Cash Book

Cash Bank Page 1

		Cash	Bank	
19–6		£	£	
July 1 Balances	J 5	20	80	

Other Items

These can be of many kinds and it is impossible to write out a complete list. Several examples are now shown:

1 K Young, a debtor, owed £200 on 1 July. He was unable to pay his account in cash, but offers a motor car in full settlement of the debt. The offer is accepted on 5 July 19–6.

The personal account is, therefore, not now owed and needs crediting. On the other hand the firm now has an extra asset, a motor car, therefore the motor car account needs to be debited.

The Journal

	Dr	*Cr*
19–6	£	£
July 5 Motor Car	200	
K Young		200
Accepted motor car in full settlement of debt per letter dated 5/7/19–6		

2 T Jones is a creditor. On 10 July 19–6 his business is taken over by A Lee to whom the debt now is to be paid.

Here it is just one creditor being exchanged for another one. The action needed is to cancel the amount owing to T Jones by debiting his account, and to show it owing to Lee by opening an account for Lee and crediting it.

The Journal

	Dr	Cr
19–6	£	£
July 10 T Jones	150	
A Lee		150
Transfer of indebtedness as per letter ref G/1335		

3 We had previously bought an office typewriter for £310. It is faulty. On 12 July 19–6 we return it to the supplier, RS Ltd. An allowance of £310 is agreed, so that we will not have to pay for it.

The Journal

	Dr	Cr
19–6	£	£
July 12 RS Ltd	310	
Office Machinery		310
Faulty typewriter returned to supplier Full allowance given. See letter 10/7/19–6		

Exercises

24.1 You are to show the journal entries necessary to record the following items:

(a) 19–5 May 1 Bought a motor vehicle on credit from Kingston Garage for £6,790

(b) 19–5 May 3 A debt of £34 owing from H Newman was written off as a bad debt

(c) 19–5 May 8 Office furniture bought by us for £490 was returned to the supplier Unique Offices, as it was unsuitable. Full allowance will be given us

(d) 19–5 May 12 We are owed £150 by W Charles. He is declared bankrupt and we receive £39 in full settlement of the debt

(e) 19–5 May 14 We take £45 goods out of the business stock without paying for them

(f) 19–5 May 28 Some time ago we paid an insurance bill thinking that it was all in respect of the business. We now discover that £76 of the amount paid was in fact insurance of our private house

(g) 19–5 May 29 Bought machinery £980 on credit from Systems Accelerated.

24.2X Show the journal entries necessary to record the following items:

19–7

Apr 1 Bought fixtures on credit from J Harper £1,809

" 4 We take £500 goods out of the business stock without paying for them

" 9 £28 of the goods taken by us on 4 April is not returned back into stock by us. We do not take any money for the return of the goods

" 12 K Lamb owes us £500. He is unable to pay his debt. We agree to take some office equipment from him at the value and so cancel the debt

" 18 Some of the fixtures bought from J Harper, £65 worth, are found to be unsuitable and are returned to him for full allowance

" 24 A debt owing to us by J Brown of £68 is written off as a bad debt

" 30 Office equipment bought on credit from Super Offices for £2,190.

24.3 *(a)* On May 1st 19–0 the financial position of Carol Green was as follows:

Freehold Premises	45,000
Fixtures and Fittings	12,500
Motor Vehicles	9,500
Bank Overdraft	2,800
Cash in Hand	650
Stock in Hand	1,320
F Hardy (a trade debtor)	160
A Darby (a trade creditor)	270

Required

Make a journal entry for the above showing clearly the capital of Carol Green on May 1st 19–0.

(b) On examination of her books on 1 May Sue Baker discovered the following adjustments were necessary:

(i) When Parker a debtor for £350 paid his account he was allowed discount of 2% for prompt payment. The actual amount of cash received has been entered in Parker's account and in the cash book no entry having been made for the discount allowed.

(ii) The purchase of a motor van for £4,500 had not been entered in the books. The van was purchased from Supervans Ltd paying a deposit of 25% the balance being due in six months' time.

(iii) I M Broke a debtor for £250 has been declared bankrupt, on 1 May a payment of 20p in the pound was received with notification that it will be the only payment. The remaining balance on the account is therefore to be written off as a bad debt.

Required

(a) Make journal entries giving effect to all of the above transactions including the payment received from Broke and the writing off of the bad debt.

(b) Show I M Broke's account and the bad debts account in the ledger.

Note: Narratives must be given with all journal entries.

(RSA)

24.4X The following transactions relate to the business of Martin Cooper, a sole trader:

(a) A debtor, G Holt, was declared bankrupt, owing Cooper £250. On 1 May Year 8, he gave Cooper a cheque for £50, as a first and final payment. Cooper decided to write off the remainder of the debt as bad on the same day.

(b) During the month of June Year 8, Cooper had taken goods which had cost the business £180, for use outside the business.

(c) On 1 July Year 8, Cooper purchased on credit from Cousins & Co a motor car costing £3,850. He paid a deposit of £1,000 by cheque. He took out comprehensive insurance with Byline Insurance Company for the year from 1 July for £300. He settled the premium by cheque on that date.

(d) At the close of Cooper's financial year on 31 August Year 8, the following matters need adjustment, before final accounts can be prepared.

(i) Motor Insurance is prepaid 10 months [*see (c)* above].

(ii) Rent of £500 per month had not been paid for the month of August.

(iii) Bank charges amounting to £36, deducted by the Bank on their Statement for the month ended 31 August, had not been dealt with in the books.

Required

Draw up the Journal entries to record the above transactions and adjustments in the books of Martin Cooper.

Note: Cash entries should be journalised.

(LCCI)

24.5 Write the journal entries needed to effect the following:

(a) 1 July — Interest at 6% per annum charged to the account of James Crawford whose debit balance was due to be paid by the previous 31 March when he owed us £120.

(b) 30 Aug — Purchased on credit from 'Mechweights' a new weighing machine worth £1,500, less (i) 10% trade discount, and (ii) less a second-hand weighing machine from us worth £400, in part exchange.

(c) 10 Sept — A dividend of £0.35p in the £ received from the bankrupt estate of Thomas Watson whose debt of £150 had previously been written off as irrecoverable. The amount received had been entered in the cash book and posted to Thomas Watson's old account in the ledger, which had been re-opened for the purpose.

(d) 31 Dec — The proprietor of the business, A Walker, had taken stock from the shop for his own use to the value of £39.50.

(PEI)

24.6 You are to open the books of K Mullings, a trader, via the journal to record the assets and liabilities, and are then to record the daily transactions for the month of May. A trial balance is to be extracted as on 31 May 19–6.

19–6

May 1 *Assets* – Premises £2,000; Motor Van £450; Fixtures £600; Stock £1,289. Debtors – N Hardy £40; M Nelson £180. Cash at bank £1,254; Cash in hand £45.
Liabilities – Creditors; B Blake £60; V Reagan £200.

May 1 Paid rent by cheque £15
" 2 Goods bought on credit from B Blake £20; C Harris £56; H Gordon £38; N Lee £69
" 3 Goods sold on credit to: K O'Connor £56; M Benjamin £78; L Staines £98; N Duffy £48; B Green £118; M Nelson £40
" 4 Paid for motor expenses in cash £13
" 7 Cash drawings by proprietor £20
" 9 Goods sold on credit to: M Benjamin £22; L Pearson £67
" 11 Goods returned to Mullings by: K O'Connor £16; L Staines £18
" 14 Bought another motor van on credit from Better Motors Ltd £300
" 16 The following paid Mullings their accounts by cheque less 5 per cent cash discount: N Hardy; M Nelson; K O'Connor; L Staines
" 19 Goods returned by Mullings to N Lee £9
" 22 Goods bought on credit from: J Johnson £89; T Best £72
" 24 The following accounts were settled by Mullings by cheque less 5 per cent cash discount: B Blake; V Reagan; N Lee
" 27 Salaries paid by cheque £56
" 30 Paid rates by cheque £66
" 31 Paid Better Motors Ltd a cheque for £300.

25 · The Analytical Petty Cash Book and the Imprest System

25.1 Division of the Cash Book

With the growth of the firm it has been seen that it becomes necessary to have several books instead of just one ledger.

These ideas can be extended to the cash book. It is obvious that in almost any firm there will be many small cash payments to be made. It would be an advantage if the records of these payments could be kept separate from the main cash book. Where a separate book is kept it is known as a **petty cash book**.

The advantages of such an action can be summarised:

- The task of handling and recording the small cash payments could be given by the cashier to a junior member of staff. He would then be known as the petty cashier. The cashier, who is a higher paid member of staff, would be saved from routine work. This would then be done by the petty cashier who is a junior and lower paid member of staff.
- If small cash payments were entered into the main cash book, these items would then need posting one by one to the ledgers. If travelling expenses were paid to staff on a daily basis this could mean over 250 postings to the staff travelling expenses account during the year, i.e. 5 days per week × 50 working weeks per year. However, if a special form of a petty cash book is kept, it would only be the monthly totals for each period that need posting to the general ledger. If this was done, only 12 entries would be needed in the staff travelling expenses account instead of over 250.

When the petty cashier makes a payment to someone, then that person will have to fill in a voucher showing exactly what the payment was for. He may have to attach bills – e.g. bills for petrol – to the petty cash voucher. He would sign the voucher to certify that his expenses had been paid to him by the petty cashier.

25.2 The Imprest System

The **imprest system** is where the cashier gives the petty cashier enough cash to meet his needs for the following period. At the end of the period the cashier finds out the amounts spent by the petty cashier, and gives him an amount equal to that spent. The petty cash in hand should then be equal to the *original* amount with which the period was started. Exhibit 25.1 shows an example of this method.

Exhibit 25.1

		£
Period 1	The cashier gives the petty cashier	100
	The petty cashier pays out in the period	78
	Petty cash now in hand	22
	The cashier now gives the petty cashier the amount spent	78
	Petty cash in hand at the end of period 1	100
Period 2	The petty cashier pays out in the period	84
	Petty cash now in hand	16
	The cashier now gives the petty cashier the amount spent	84
	Petty cash in hand end of period 2	100

It may be necessary to increase the fixed sum, often called the cash 'float', to be held at the start of each period. In the above case if we had wanted to increase the 'float' at the end of the second period to £120, then the cashier would have given the petty cashier an extra £20, i.e. £84 + 20 = 104.

25.3 Illustration of an Analytical Cash Book

An analytical petty cash book is often used. One of these is shown as Exhibit 25.2.

The receipts column is the debit side of the petty cash book. On giving £50 to the petty cashier on 1 September the credit entry is made in the cash book while the debit entry is made in the petty cash book. A similar entry is made on 30 September for the £44 paid by the chief cashier to the petty cashier. This amount covers all expenses paid by the petty cashier.

On the credit side:

1 Enter date and details of each payment. Put amount in the total column.
2 For **1** also put the amount in the column for the type of expense.
3 At the end of each period, add up the totals column.
4 Now add up each of the expense columns. The total of **3** should equal the total of all the expense columns. In Exhibit 25.2 this is £44.

To complete double entry for petty cash expenses paid:

1 Total of each expense column is debited to the expense account in the general ledger.
2 Enter folio number of each general ledger page under each of the expense columns in the petty cash book.
3 The last column in the petty cash book is a ledger column. In this column items paid out of petty cash which need posting to a ledger other than the general ledger are shown.

This would happen if a purchases ledger account was settled out of petty cash, or if a refund was made out of the petty cash to a customer who had overpaid his account.

The double entry for all the items in Exhibit 25.2 appears as Exhibit 25.3.

19–4			£
Sept	1	The cashier gives £50 as float to the petty cashier	
		Payments out of petty cash during September:	
"	2	Petrol	6
"	3	J Green – travelling expenses	3
"	3	Postages	2
"	4	D Davies – travelling expenses	2
"	7	Cleaning expenses	1
"	9	Petrol	1
"	12	K Jones – travelling expenses	3
"	14	Petrol	3
"	15	L Black – travelling expenses	5
"	16	Cleaning expenses	1
"	18	Petrol	2
"	20	Postages	2
"	22	Cleaning expenses	1
"	24	G Wood – travelling expenses	7
"	27	Settlement of C Brown's account in the Purchases Ledger	3
"	29	Postages	2
"	30	The cashier reimburses the petty cashier the amount spent in the month.	

Exhibit 25.2

Petty Cash Book (page 31)

Receipts	*Folio*	*Date*	*Details*	*Voucher No*	*Total*	*Motor Expenses*	*Staff Travelling Expenses*	*Postages*	*Cleaning*	*Ledger Folio*	*Ledger Accounts*
£					£	£	£	£	£		£
50	CB 19	Sept 1	Cash								
		" 2	Petrol	1	6	6					
		" 3	J Green	2	3		3				
		" 3	Postages	3	2			2			
		" 4	D Davies	4	2		2				
		" 7	Cleaning	5	1				1		
		" 9	Petrol	6	1	1					
		" 12	K Jones	7	3		3				
		" 14	Petrol	8	3	3					
		" 15	L Black	9	5		5				
		" 16	Cleaning	10	1				1		
		" 18	Petrol	11	2	2					
		" 20	Postages	12	2			2			
		" 22	Cleaning	13	1				1		
		" 24	G Wood	14	7		7				
		" 27	C Brown	15	3					PL 18	3
		" 29	Postages	16	2			2			
					44	12	20	6	3		3
						GL 17	GL 29	GL 44	GL 64		
44	CB 22	" 30	Cash								
		" 30	Balance	c/d	50						
94					94						
50		Oct 1	Balance	b/d							

Exhibit 25.3

Cash Book (Bank Column only) Page 19

		19–4	£
		Sept 1 Petty Cash PCB 31	50
		" 30 Petty Cash PCB31	44

General Ledger

Motor Expenses Page 17

19–4	£		
Sept 30 Petty Cash PCB 31	12		

Staff Travelling Expenses Page 29

19–4	£		
Sept 30 Petty Cash PCB 31	20		

Postages Page 44

19–4	£		
Sept 30 Petty Cash PCB 31	6		

Cleaning Page 64

19–4	£		
Sept 30 Petty Cash PCB 31	3		

Purchases Ledger

C Brown Page 18

19–4	£	19–4	£
Sept 30 Petty Cash PCB 31	30	Sept 1 Balance b/d	3

25.4 Bank Cash Book

In a firm with both a cash book and a petty cash book, the cash book is often known as a bank cash book. This means that *all* cash payments are entered in the petty cash book, and the bank cash book will contain *only* bank columns and discount columns. In this type of firm any cash sales will be paid direct into the bank.

In such a cash book, as in fact could happen in an ordinary cash book, an extra column could be added. In this would be shown the details of the cheques banked, just the total of the banking being shown in the total column.

Exhibit 25.4 shows the receipts side of the Bank Cash Book. The totals of the banking made on the three days were £192, £381 and £1,218. The details column shows what the bankings are made up of.

Exhibit 25.4

Bank Cash Book (Receipts side)

Date	*Details*	*Discount*	*Items*	*Total banked*
19–6		£	£	£
May 14	G Archer	5	95	
〃 14	P Watts	3	57	
〃 14	C King		40	192
〃 20	K Dooley	6	114	
〃 20	Cash Sales		55	
〃 20	R Jones		60	
〃 20	P Mackie	8	152	381
〃 31	J Young		19	
〃 31	T Broome	50	950	
〃 31	Cash Sales		116	
〃 31	H Tiller	7	133	1,218

New Terms

Petty Cash Book (p 222): A cash book for small payments.

Imprest System (p 222): A system where a refund is made of the total paid out in a period.

Exercises

25.1 Thomas Jones, a sole trader, keeps his petty cash on the imprest system and the imprest amount is £50. The petty cash transactions for the month of February 19–8 were as follows:

19–8		
Feb	1	Petty cash in hand £4.67
"	"	Petty cash restored to imprest amount
"	3	Paid wages £8.76
"	7	Purchased postage stamps £2.94
"	10	Paid wages £9.11
"	14	Purchased envelopes £2.28
"	17	Paid wages £8.84
"	20	Paid cash to J Smith, a creditor, £4.16
"	21	Purchased stationery £2.75
"	24	Paid wages £8.48.

Required
Draw up Jones' petty cash book for the month of February 19–8. The analysis columns should be as follows:
(a) Wages
(b) Stationery
(c) Postage
(d) Ledger
On 1 March 19–8 show the restoration of the petty cash to the imprest amount.
(LCCI)

25.2X O Zone, a sole trader, uses an analysed petty cash book with columns for travelling, postage and stationery, motor expenses, cleaning, ledger accounts.

The petty cash system is based on an imprest of £100 which Zone replenishes on the Monday following the period of expenditure. O Zone supplies the following information for the month of August 19–9.

19–5			£
Aug	1	Petrol	4.00
"	3	Postage stamps	1.50
"	4	One ream of typing paper	3.00
"	6	H Wise – settlement of account	15.00
"	7	Office cleaning materials	2.00
"	8	Taxis	4.00
"	10	Refund of a clerk's bus fares	2.00
"	14	Car polish	3.00
"	16	Petrol and oil	7.00
"	18	Registered mail	2.00
"	20	Office carpet shampoo	1.00
"	21	Petrol	7.00
"	25	Petrol	7.00
"	27	J Brown – settlement of account	25.00
"	28	W Smith – settlement of account	6.00
"	29	Carbon paper (one packet)	4.00

Required
(a) Enter the above transactions into a suitably ruled Petty Cash Book.
(b) Replenish the imprest on Monday, 3 September 19–9.
(RSA)

25.3 I Markowska runs a small business where all receipts are paid into the firm's bank account at the end of each day and all payments are made by cheque except for those items costing less than £20 which are viewed as petty cash items.

You are required to:

(a) Rule up a suitable petty cash book and bank account for the month ending 31 December 1989;

(b) Record the following entries in the petty cash book and bank account of I Markowska;

(c) Balance accounts at the end of the month.

December		£
1	Balance at bank (Overdrawn)	1,125.50
	Petty cash balance	10.45
	Received an amount from the bank, in cash to restore the imprest of £100.	
3	A Cheque was received from N Etheridge	5,602.50
	Paid the office cleaner	15.00
	Paid motor expenses	6.00
	Cash sales	506.75
10	J Holland paid her account of £60 less cash discount of 5%	57.00
15	Paid sundry expenses	4.25
	Paid insurance	15.00
22	I Markowska's drawings	150.00
	Received a cheque for £91 from P Coleman in settlement of his balance outstanding of £100	
	Paid office cleaner	15.00
	Paid a cheque for the purchase of goods for resale	150.00
28	Cash sales	234.75
	Paid a cheque to C Ford	50.00
	Paid sundry expenses	3.50
	Paid a cheque to D White	75.00
30	A Cheque was received from J Holland	25.00

(RSA)

25.4X John Allison pays all receipts into the bank and makes all payments greater than £10 by cheque. All minor cash payments are made out of petty cash and at the end of each week the petty cashier is given a cheque to restore the imprest.

At the close of business on 23rd April 19–3 Allison's bank balance according to his cash book was £1,235.98 and his cash in hand stood at the imprest amount of £100.

The counterfoils of his paying-in book for the next week showed:

April 26 Total paid in £472.65 consisting of cash from sales £301.40, a cheque of £25 from G Lamb for one week's rent of the flat above the shop which Allison lets to him, and a cheque of £146.25 from D Stafford in full settlement of £150 owed by him.

" 28 Total paid in £495.30 consisting of cash from sales £295.30 and a cheque for £200 from G Lincoln who had purchased Allison's old delivery van.

" 29 Total paid in £400.90 consisting entirely of cash from sales.

During the week Allison drew the following cheques:

April 27	Grimchester County Council for rates	£248.00
" 28	D Stokes in settlement of £500 owing to them	£490.00
" 29	For own use	£200.00
	Petty cash	£47.40

Payments out of petty cash were as follows:

April	25	Paid petrol	£9.50
"	25	Paid postage stamps	£4.50
"	26	Paid cleaning lady	£5.60
"	27	Cleaning materials	£4.20
"	28	G Smith Ledger A/c	£8.00
"	29	Stationery	£6.40
"	29	Car repairs	£9.20

You are required to write up:

(a) The Bank Cash Book (the narrative columns of which should clearly indicate which ledger account is to be debited or credited in respect of each entry).

(b) The Petty Cash Book with analysis columns for cleaning, postage and stationery, motor expenses and ledger accounts.

(RSA)

25.5X R Barton has a Petty Cash Account which is used for all cash payments under £10 each. The 'float' of £100 is restored at the end of each week. All other money transactions are entered in his Bank Cash Book, and all receipts are paid into the bank.

At the start of business on 4th March 19–5 Barton's books showed a balance in hand at the bank of £780.65, and the £100 petty cash.

During the next week petty cash payments were as follows:

		Voucher No	
4th March	Stationery	601	£5.40
4th March	Window cleaner	602	£7.50
5th March	Bus fares	603	£1.10
5th March	H Adams (a creditor)	604	£8.40
6th March	Train fares	605	£6.80
7th March	Postage stamps	606	£8.00
8th March	Cleaning materials	607	£2.40

Cheques drawn during the week by Barton were as follows:

4th March	G Dyer (in settlement of £120 debt)	£114.40
6th March	Post Office (van tax)	£120.00
8th March	For wife's housekeeping	£60.00
8th March	Petty Cash	£ ?

The completed counterfoils of his bank paying-in book for the week showed the following:

4th March – Paid in £470.35, all in respect of cash sales.

6th March – Paid in total of £312.80, being cash sales of £165.80 and a cheque for £147 from W West in full settlement of his account of £150.

8th March – Paid in a total of £278.85. This consisted of cash sales £238.85, a cheque for £18 from C Ferncliff in payment for Barton's old cash register, and a cheque for £22, being commission received from a hire purchase company.

You are required to write up:

(a) The Petty Cash Book, with analysis columns for postage and stationery, cleaning, travel and ledger accounts.

(b) The Bank Cash Book. The narrative columns should clearly name the ledger account to be debited or credited in respect of each transaction.

(RSA)

25.6X Ida Rose is in business as a retailer of knitting wools. She occupies rented premises, the rent being £320 per quarter. On 1 January Year 7, she has an overdrawn bank balance of £260.76.

She has authorised her bank to make standing order payments as follows:

(a) 15th of each month – £26.75 to Fairclaim Insurance plc to cover business insurance premiums
(b) Annually on 28 January – £25 subscription to Retailers Association
(c) 2 January and quarterly thereafter – rent

Ida Rose has authorised Bellson Publishing to collect four payments of £12.15 each year from her account on a direct debit arrangement. The collection dates are to be 25 January, 25 April, 25 July, 25 October. She has one customer, Mrs R Bradwell, who makes payments to her by way of a standing order for £20, paid on the 20th of each month.

During the month ended 31 January Year 7, Ida Rose drew the following cheques:

		£	
00137500	3 January Year 7	124.00	Mather & Co
00137501	8 January Year 7	1,394.22	Parr Ltd
00137502	19 January Year 7	27.36	Blackstone News
00137503	27 January Year 7	2,210.00	Trend Motors Ltd

Takings banked in the same month were:

7 January	Cash £932.00	Cheque £15.00
14 January	Cash £739.00	
21 January	Cash £611.20	Cheque £28.00
28 January	Cash £846.00	

Required
Write up Ida Rose's Cash Book for the month ended 31 January Year 7.
Note: Entries should be in date order.
(LCCI)

26 · Errors Not Affecting Trial Balance Agreement

26.1 Trial Balance Agreement and Errors

There are two main classifications of errors:

Errors Not Affecting Trial Balance Agreement

These errors have resulted in the same amount of debits being entered as there were credits, or no entry has been made either on the debit or credit side. This means that if the trial balance would have balanced before the error, then it would also have balanced after the error.

Examples of the different types of errors which come under this heading are shown in sections 26.3 to 26.8 which follow. You are also shown how to correct this type of error.

Errors Affecting Trial Balance Agreement

Those which will mean that the total of the debit columns in the trial balance will not be the same as the total of the credit columns.

For instance, suppose we have made only one error in our books. We received cash £103 on 1 May 19–5 from H Lee. We enter it as:

Cash Book

19–5	*Cash*	*Bank*	
	£	£	
May 1 H Lee	103		

Sales Ledger

H Lee

	19–5	£
	May 1 Cash	13

We have put £103 on the debit side of our books, and £13 on the credit side. When we draw up a trial balance its totals will be different by £90, i.e. £103 – £13 = £90.

This will be true in every case where a debit entry does not equal a credit entry for the item.

The correction of these types of errors is shown in Chapter 27.

26.2 Correction of Errors

Most errors are found at a date later than the one on which they are first made. When we correct them we should not do so by crossing out items, tearing out accounts and throwing them away, or using chemicals to make the writing disappear.

We have to do corrections in double entry accounts by writing in the corrections in a double entry fashion.

We should:

1 Show the corrections by means of journal entries, and then
2 Show the corrections in the double entry set of accounts.

26.3 Errors of Commission (do not affect trial balance agreement)

These are where the correct amounts are entered, but in the wrong person's account.

Example: D Long paid us by cheque £50 on 18 May 19–5. It is correctly entered in the cash book, but it is entered by mistake in the account for D Lee.

This means that there has been both a debit of £50 and a credit of £50. It has appeared in the personal account as:

D Lee

		19–5	£
		May 18 Cash	50

The error was found on 31 May 19–5. We will now have to correct this. This needs two entries:

1 A debit of £50 in the account of D Lee to cancel out the error on the credit side in that account.

2 A credit of £50 in the account of D Long. This is where it should have been entered.

The accounts will now appear:

D Lee

19–5	£	19–5	£
May 31 D Long:		May 18 Cash	50
Error corrected **1**	50		

D Long

19–5	£	19–5	£
May 1 Balance b/d	50	May 31 Cash entered in error in D Lee's account 2	50

The Journal

The ways by which errors have been corrected should all be entered in the journal. The correction has already been shown above in double entry.

The journal entry will be:

The Journal

19–5		Dr	Cr
		£	£
May 31	D Lee	50	
	D Long		50
	Cash received...entered in wrong personal account, now corrected		

26.4 Errors of Principle (do not affect trial balance agreement)

This is where an item is entered in the wrong type of account.

For instance the purchase of a fixed asset should be debited to a fixed asset account. If in error it is debited to an expense account, then it has been entered in the wrong type of account.

Example: The purchase of a motor lorry £5,500 by cheque on 14 May 19–5 has been debited in error to a motor expenses account. In the cash book it is shown correctly. This means that there has been both a debit of £5,500 and a credit of £5,500.

It will have appeared in the expense account as:

Motor Expenses

19–5	£		
May 14 Bank	5,500		

The error is found on 31 May 19–5. We will now correct it. Two entries are needed:

1 A debit in the motor lorry account of £5,500 to put it where it should have been entered.

2 A credit of £5,500 in the motor expenses account to *cancel* the error. The accounts will now appear as:

Motor Expenses

19–5	£	19–5		£
May 14 Bank	5,500	May 31 Motor Lorry:		
		error corrected	**2**	5,500

Motor Lorry

19–5	£	
May 31 Bank: entered originally in Motor expenses **1**	5,500	

The Journal

The journal entries to correct the error will be shown as:

The Journal

		Dr	*Cr*
19–5		£	£
May 31	Motor lorry	5,500	
	Motor expenses		5,500
	Correction of error whereby purchase of motor lorry was debited to motor expenses account.		

26.5 Errors of Original Entry (do not affect trial balance agreement)

These happen when the original amount is incorrect.

This amount is then entered in double entry. For instance, if sales of £150 to T Higgins on 13 May 19–5 had been entered as both a debit and a credit as £130, the accounts would appear:

T Higgins

19–5	£	
May 13 Sales	130	

Sales

		19–5	£
		May 31 Sales journal	
		(part of total)	130

The error is found on 31 May 19–5. The entries to correct it are now shown:

T Higgins

19–5	£		
May 13 Sales	130		
" 31 Sales: error	20		

Sales

		19–5	£
		May 31 Sales journal	130
		31 T Higgins:	
		error corrected	20

The Journal

To correct the error the journal entries will be:

The Journal

		Dr	*Cr*
19–5		£	£
May 31	T Higgins	20	
	Sales account		20
	Correction of error. Sales of £150 had been incorrectly entered as £130		

26.6 Errors of Omission (do not affect trial balance agreement)

These errors are where transactions are not entered into the books at all.

For instance, if we purchased goods from T Hope for £250 but did not enter it in the accounts there would be nil debits and nil credits. We find the error on 31 May 19–5. The entries to record it will be:

Purchases

19–5	£		
May 13 T Hope:			
error corrected	250		

T Hope

		19–5	£
		May 31 Purchases:	
		error corrected	250

The Journal

The journal entries to correct the error will be:

The Journal

		Dr	*Cr*
19–5		£	£
May 31	Purchases	250	
	T Hope		250
	Correction of error. Purchases omitted from books.		

26.7 Compensating Errors (do not affect trial balance agreement)

These are where errors cancel each other out.

Let us take a case where the sales journal is added up to be £100 too much. In the same period the purchases journal is also added up to be £100 too much.

If these were the only errors in our books the trial balance totals would equal each other. Both totals would be wrong, they would both be £100 too much, but they would be equal totals.

If in fact the *incorrect* totals had purchases £7,900 and sales £9,900, the accounts would have appeared as:

Purchases

19–5	£		
May 13 Purchases			
journal	7,900		

Sales

			19–5	£
			May 31 Sales journal	9,900

When corrected, the accounts will appear as:

Purchases

19–5	£	19–5	£
May 13 Purchases	7,900	May 31 The Journal: error corrected	100

Sales

19–5	£	19–5	£
May 31 The Journal: error corrected	100	May 31 Sales journal	9,900

The Journal

Journal entries to correct these two errors will be:

The Journal

		Dr	*Cr*
19–5		£	£
May 31	Sales account	100	
	Purchases account		100
	Correction of compensating errors. Totals of both purchases and sales journals incorrectly added up £100 too much.		

26.8 Complete Reversal of Entries (do not affect trial balance agreement)

Where the correct amounts are entered in the correct accounts, but each item is shown on the wrong side of each account. There has therefore been both a debit and a credit of £200.

For instance we pay a cheque for £200 on 28 May 19–5 to D Charles. We enter it as follows in accounts with the letter (A).

Cash Book (A)

	Cash	Bank		Cash	Bank
19–5	£	£		£	£
May 28 D Charles		200			

D Charles (A)

		19–5	£
		May 28 Bank	200

This is incorrect. It should have been debit D Charles £200: credit Bank £200. Both items have been entered in the correct accounts, but each is on the wrong side of its account.

The way to correct this is more difficult to understand than with other errors. Let us look at how the items would have appeared if we had done it correctly in the first place. We will show the letter (B) behind the account names.

Cash Book (B)

	Cash	Bank		Cash	Bank
	£	£	19–5	£	£
			May 28 D Charles		200

D Charles (B)

19–5	£		
May 28 Bank	200		

We have found the error on May 31. By using double entry we have to make the amounts shown to cancel the error be twice the amount of the error. This is because:

1 First we have to cancel the error. This would mean entering these amounts:

Dr D Charles	£200	
Cr Bank		£200

2 Then we have to enter up the transaction:

Dr D Charles	£200	
Cr Bank		£200

All together then, the entries to correct the error are twice the amounts first entered.

When corrected the accounts appear as follows, marked (C).

Cash Book (C)

	Cash	*Bank*		*Cash*	*Bank*
19–5	£	£	19–5	£	£
May 28 D Charles		200	May 31 D Charles: error corrected		400

D Charles (C)

19–5	£	19–5	£
May 28 Bank: error corrected	400	May 28 Bank	200

You can see that accounts (C) give the same final answer as accounts (B).

	£	£
(B) Dr D Charles	200	
Cr Bank		200
(C) Dr D Charles (400 – 200)	200	
Cr Bank (400 – 200)		200

The Journal

Journal entries. These would be shown:

The Journal

		Dr	*Cr*
19–5		£	£
May 31	D Charles	400	
	Bank		400
	Payment of £200 on 28 May 19–5 to D Charles incorrectly credited to his account, and debited to bank. Error now corrected.		

26.9 Casting

You will often notice the use of the expression **to cast**, which means to add up. Overcasting means incorrectly adding up a column of figures to give an answer which is *greater* than it should be. Undercasting means incorrectly adding up a column of figures to give an answer which is *less* than it should be.

New Terms

Casting (p 239): Adding up figures.

Exercises

26.1 Show the journal entries necessary to correct the following errors:

(a) A sale of goods £678 to J Harkness had been entered in J Harker's account.
(b) The purchase of a machine on credit from L Pearson for £4,390 had been completely omitted from our books.
(c) The purchase of a motor van £3,800 had been entered in error in the Motor Expenses account.
(d) A sale of £221 to E Fletcher had been entered in the books, both debit and credit, as £212.
(e) Commission received £257 had been entered in error in the Sales Account.

26.2X Show the journal entries needed to correct the following errors:

(a) Purchases £699 on credit from K Webb had been entered in H Weld's account.
(b) A cheque of £189 paid for advertisements had been entered in the cash column of the cash book instead of in the bank column.
(c) Sale of goods £443 on credit to B Maxim had been entered in error in B Gunn's account.
(d) Purchase of goods on credit from K Innes £89 entered in two places in error as £99.
(e) Cash paid to H Mersey £89 entered on the debit side of the cash book and the credit side of H Mersey's account.

26.3X Redraft the following Balance Sheet, correcting the errors in it.

A Smith
Balance sheet for the year ending 31 December 19–6

	£		£
Drawings	20,000	Sundry debtors	43,200
Bank overdraft	9,000	Depreciation on furniture	
Provision for bad debts	2,160	and equipment	5,000
Cash in hand	1,000	Net profit	30,000
Stock at 31 December 19–6	38,500	Capital at 1 January 19–6	310,000
Furniture and equipment	97,400	Goodwill	14,000
Stock at 1 January 19–6	22,200	Rates prepaid	1,000
Creditors	39,680		
Premises	182,000		
Wages accrued	1,260		
	413,200		413,200

26.4 When Daniel Martin prepared his final accounts he calculated his net profit at £8,975. However, on more careful inspection of his accounts he found the following errors. Construct an adjustment of profit statement to show his true net profit.

(A) a bill for rates of £200 had not been recorded
(B) sales of £28 had not been recorded
(C) closing stock had been overvalued by £48
(D) depreciation of £200 had not been provided for
(E) rent receivable of £50 was outstanding
(F) sales returns of £22 had not been entered
(G) rent of £10 recorded in the profit and loss account related to next year

(H) a provision for bad debts of £20 should have been created.
(PEI)

26.5X The following trial balance was extracted from the books of J Sanders on 30 October 19–4.

	Debit	*Credit*
	£	£
Premises	84,000	
Office Equipment	2,190	
Fixtures and Fittings	1,240	
Trade Debtors	2,790	
Trade Creditors		1,870
Stock 1 November 19–3	2,455	
Purchases	41,000	
Sales		87,257
Wages	3,000	
Insurance	235	
Cash in Hand	384	
Bank Overdraft		583
Capital 1 November 19–3		47,584
	137,294	137,294

Further examination of the books revealed the following:
1 A typewriter bought on 5th October 19–4 for £85 had been posted to the purchases account.
2 A payment in cash of £25 had been made to a creditor, entries of £52 had been made in the books.
3 J Sanders had taken £200 from the firm's bank account, the amount had been debited to the wages account.
4 A standing order for £5 had been paid by the bank for insurance, no entry had been made in the cash book.

You are required to:
(a) Redraft the Trial Balance after making the corrections.
(b) Explain and give an example of each of the following:
(i) Compensating Error.
(ii) Error of Omission.
(RSA)

26.6 R James drew up the following Balance Sheet on 31 December 19–6:

Balance Sheet

	£	£		£	£
Fixed Assets			Capital 1 January 19–6	7,690	
Furniture and fittings	1,540		*Add* Net profit	3,040	
Motor vehicles	2,980				
		4,520		10,730	
Current Assets			*Less* Drawings	2,860	
Stock	2,724				7,870
Sundry debtors	1,241		Sundry creditors		1,850
Cash at bank	1,235				
		5,200			
		9,720			9,720

When checking the books, the following errors and omissions were found:
1 A purchase of fittings, £140, has been included in the purchases account.
2 Motor vehicles should have been depreciated by £280.
3 A debt of £41 included in sundry debtors was considered to be bad.
4 Closing stock had been overvalued by £124.

(a) Show your calculation of the correct net profit.
(b) Draw up a corrected Balance Sheet as at 31 December 19–6.
(RSA)

26.7X At the end of April 19–1 C Read extracted a trial balance as follows:

	£	£
Purchases	1,320	
Sales		4,675
Rent	50	
Wages	160	
General expenses	75	
Carriage inwards	100	
Carriage outwards	140	
Salaries	230	
Premises	10,000	
Fixtures and fittings	1,500	
Debtors		680
Creditors	1,050	
Bank overdraft		670
Cash	15	
Drawings	200	
Commission received		130
Capital		7,945
	14,840	14,100

An inspection revealed obvious errors. Further investigations revealed the following:
1 £30 for carriage inwards had been posted to the carriage outwards account.
2 Sales for cash had been entered incorrectly into the bank account instead of the cash account £40.
3 A Cheque for £10 from T Murphy had been entered into the S Murphy account. Both T Murphy and S Murphy are debtors.
4 No entry had been made in the books to record a cheque paid to P Sills, a creditor, £70.
5 General expenses included a payment of £10 which should have been entered into a motor expenses account.
6 Wages of £40 had been entered into salaries account.

You are required to:
(a) make journal entries to record items **1–6** above;
(b) extract a trial balance having taken notice of the obvious errors as well as the items **1–6** above.
(LCCI)

27 · Suspense Accounts and Errors

27.1 Errors and the Trial Balance

In the last chapter we looked at errors which still left equal totals in the trial balance. However, many errors will mean that trial balance totals will not be equal. Let us now look at some of these:

- Incorrect additions in any account.
- Making an entry on only one side of the accounts, e.g. a debit but no credit; a credit but no debit.
- Entering a different amount on the debit side from the amount on the credit side.

27.2 Suspense Account

We should try very hard to find errors immediately when the trial balance totals are not equal. When they cannot be found, the trial balance totals should be made to agree with each other by inserting the amount of the difference between the two sides in a **suspense account**. This occurs in Exhibit 27.1 where there is a £40 difference.

Exhibit 27.1

Trial Balance as on 31 December 19–5

	Dr	*Cr*
	£	£
Totals after all the accounts have been listed	100,000	99,960
Suspense account		40
	100,000	100,000

To make the two totals the same, a figure of £40 for the suspense account has been shown on the credit side. A suspense account is opened and the £40 difference is also shown there on the credit side.

Suspense Account

	19–5	£
	Dec 31 Difference per trial balance	40

27.3 Suspense Account and the Balance Sheet

If the errors are not found before the final accounts are prepared, the suspense account balance will be included in the balance sheet. Where the balance is a credit balance, it should be included on the capital and liabilities side of the balance sheet. When the balance is a debit balance it should be shown on the assets side of the balance sheet.

27.4 Correction of Errors

When the errors are found they must be corrected, using double entry. Each correction must also have an entry in the journal describing it.

One error only

We will look at two examples:

1 Assume that the error of £40 as shown in Exhibit 27.1 is found in the following year on 31 March 19–6. The error was that the sales account was undercast by £40. The action taken to correct this is:

Debit suspense account to close it: £40.

Credit sales account to show item where it should have been: £40.

The accounts now appear as Exhibit 27.2.

Exhibit 27.2

Suspense Account

	£		£
19–6		19–5	
Mar 31 Sales	40	Dec 31 Difference per trial balance	40

Sales

	£		£
		19–6	
		Mar 31 Suspense	40

This can be shown in journal form as:

The Journal

		Dr	*Cr*
		£	£
19–6			
Mar 31	Suspense	40	
	Sales		40
	Correction of undercasting of sales by £40 in last year's accounts.		

2 The trial balance on 31 December 19–6 had a difference of £168. It was a shortage on the debit side.
A suspense account is opened, the difference of £168 is entered on the debit side.
On May 19–7 the error was found. We had made a payment of £168 to K Leek to close his account. It was correctly entered in the cash book, but it was not entered in K Leek's account.
First of all, (A) the account of K Leek is debited with £168, as it should have been in 19–6. Second (B) the suspense account is credited with £168 so that the account can be closed.

K Leek

19–7		£	19–7		£
May 31 Bank	(A)	168	Jan 1 Balance b/d		168

The account of K Leek is now correct.

Suspense Account

19–6		£	19–7		£
May 31 Difference per trial balance		168	May 31 K Leek	(B)	168

The Journal entries are:

The Journal

		Dr	Cr
19–7		£	£
May 31	K Leek	168	
	Suspense		168
	Correction of non-entry of payment last year in K Leek's account.		

More than one error

We can now look at Exhibit 27.3 where the suspense account difference was caused by more than one error.

Exhibit 27.3

The trial balance at 31 December 19–7 showed a difference of £77, being a shortage on the debit side. A suspense account is opened, and the difference of £77 is entered on the debit side of the account.

On 28 February 19–8 all the errors from the previous year were found.

1 A cheque of £150 paid to L Kent had been correctly entered in the cash book, but had not been entered in Kent's account.

2 The purchases account had been undercast by £20.
3 A cheque of £93 received from K Sand had been correctly entered in the cash book, but had not been entered in Sand's account.

These three errors resulted in a net error of £77, shown by a debit of £77 on the debit side of the suspense account.

These are corrected as follows:
(a) Make correcting entries in accounts for **1**, **2** and **3**.
(b) Record double entry for these items in the suspense account.

L Kent

19–8	£		
Feb 28 Suspense **1**	150		

Purchases

19–8	£		
Feb 28 Suspense **2**	20		

K Sand

		19–8	£
		Feb 28 Suspense **3**	93

Suspense Account

19–8	£	19–8	£
Jan 1 Balance b/d	77	Feb 28 L Kent **1**	150
Feb 28 K Sand **3**	93	Feb 28 Purchases **2**	20
	170		170

The Journal

		Dr	*Cr*
19–8		£	£
Feb 28	L Kent	150	
	Suspense		150
	Cheque paid omitted from Kent's account		
Feb 28	Purchases	20	
	Suspense		20
	Undercasting of purchases by £20 in last year's accounts		
Feb 28	Suspense	93	
	K Sand		93
	Cheque received omitted from Sand's account		

Only those errors which make the trial balance totals different from each other have to be corrected via the suspense account.

27.5 The Effect of Errors on Profits

Some of the errors will have meant that original profits calculated will be wrong. Other errors will have no effect upon profits. We will use Exhibit 27.4 to illustrate the different kinds of errors.

Exhibit 27.4 shows a set of accounts in which errors have been made.

Exhibit 27.4

K Davis

Trading and Profit and Loss Account for the year ended 31 December 19–5

	£		£
Stock	500	Sales	8,000
Add Purchases	6,100		
	6,600		
Less Closing stock	700		
Cost of goods sold	5,900		
Gross profit c/d	2,100		
	8,000		8,000
Rent	200	Gross profit b/d	2,100
Insurance	120	Discounts received	250
Lighting	180		
Depreciation	250		
Net profit	1,600		
	2,350		2,350

Balance Sheet as at 31 December 19–5

	£	£		£	£
Fixed Assets			*Capital*		
Fixtures at cost	2,200		Balance as at		
Less Depreciation			1.1.19–5	1,800	
to date	800		*Add* Net profit	1,600	
		1,400		3,400	
Current Assets			*Less* Drawings	900	
Stock	700				2,500
Debtors	600		*Current Liabilities*		
Bank	340		Creditors		600
		1,640			
Suspense account		60			
		3,100			3,100

Errors Which Do Not Affect Profit Calculations

If an error affects items only in the balance sheet, then the original calculated profit will not need altering. Exhibit 27.5 shows this:

Exhibit 27.5

Assume that in Exhibit 27.4 the £60 debit balance on the suspense account was because of the following error:

1 November 19–5 we paid £60 to a creditor T Monk. It was correctly entered in the cash book. It was not entered anywhere else. The error was found on 1 June 19–6.

The journal entries to correct it will be:

The Journal

		Dr	*Cr*
19–6		£	£
Jun 1	T Monk	60	
	Suspense account		60
	Payment to T Monk on 1 November 19–5 not entered in his account. Correction now made.		

Both of these accounts appeared in the balance sheet only with T Monk as part of creditors. The net profit of £1,600 does not have to be changed.

Errors Which Do Affect Profit Calculations

If the error is in one of the figures shown in the trading and profit and loss account, then the original profit will need altering. Exhibit 27.6 shows this:

Exhibit 27.6

Assume that in Exhibit 27.4 the £60 debit balance was because the rent account was added up incorrectly. It should be shown as £260 instead of £200. The error was found on 1 June 19–6. The journal entries to correct it are:

The Journal

		Dr	*Cr*
19–5		£	£
Jun 1	Rent	60	
	Suspense		60
	Correction of rent undercast last year.		

Rent last year should have been increased by £60. This would have reduced net profit by £60. A statement of corrected profit for the year is now shown.

K Davis
Statement of Corrected Net Profit for the year ended 31 December 19–5

	£
Net profit per the accounts	1,600
Less Rent understated	60
	1,540

Where There Have Been Several Errors

If in Exhibit 27.4 there had been four errors in the accounts of K Davis, found on 31 March 19–6, their correction can now be seen. Assume that the net difference had also been £60.

1 Sales overcast by	£70
2 Insurance undercast by	£40
3 Cash received from a debtor entered in the cash book only	£50
4 A purchase of £59 is entered in the books, debit and credit entries, as	£95

The entries in the suspense account, and the journal entries will be as follows:

Suspense Account

19–6	£	19–6	£
Jan 1 Balance b/d	60	Mar 31 Sales	70
Mar 31 Debtor	50	" 31 Insurance	40
	110		110

The Journal

		Dr	*Cr*
19–6		£	£
1 Mar 31	Sales	70	
	Suspense		70
	Sales overcast of £70 in 19–5		
2 Mar 31	Insurance	40	
	Suspense		40
	Insurance expense undercast by £40 in 19–5		
3 Mar 31	Suspense	50	
	Debtor's account		50
	Cash received omitted from debtor's account in 19–5		
4 Mar 31	Creditor's account	36	
	Purchases		36
	Credit purchase of £59 entered both as debit and credit as £95 in 19–5		

Note: In **4**, the correction of the understatement of purchases does not pass through the suspense account.

Now we can calculate the corrected net profit for the year 19–5. Only items **1**, **2** and **4** affect figures in the trading and profit and loss account. These are the only adjustments to be made to profit.

K Davis
Statement of corrected Net Profit for the year ended 31 December 19–5

		£
Net profit per the accounts		1,600
Add Purchases overstated **4**		36
		1,636
Less Sales overcast **1**	70	
Rent undercast **2**	40	110
Corrected net profit for the year		1,526

Error **3**, the cash not posted to a debtor's account, did not affect profit calculations.

27.6 Suspense Accounts: Businesses and Examinations

Businesses

Every attempt should be made to find errors. Opening a suspense account should be done only if all other efforts have failed.

Examinations

Unless it is part of a question, do not make your balance sheet totals agree by using a suspense account. The same applies to trial balances. If you do, the examiner will be very angry and you will lose marks.

New Terms

Suspense Account (p 243): Account showing balance equal to difference in trial balance.

Exercises

27.1 Thomas Boyd, a sole trader, extracted a trial balance from his books at the close of business on 31 May 19–6. The trial balance did not agree and Boyd entered the difference in a suspense account and prepared the trading and profit and loss accounts in the normal manner. The profit and loss account showed a net profit of £1,170.

During June Boyd discovered the following errors and these accounted for the trial balance difference:

1 The purchases day book was overcast by £60.

2 Wages paid £76 had been debited to wages account but the workmen concerned had been engaged in installing new shelves in Boyd's office.

3 Discount allowed total of £97, as shown in the cash book, had been entered on the wrong side of discount account.

4 Cash £48 received from a debtor of Boyd – Samuel Lewis – had been correctly entered in the cash book but the double entry had not been completed.

Required

(a) Calculate the correct net profit.

Note: Calculations must be shown.

(b) Indicate the manner and extent to which the above errors affected the trial balance. Your answer should be given under the following headings:

Error	*Debit side overstated or credit side understated*	*Credit side overstated, or debit side understated*
(i)		
(ii)		
(iii)		
(iv)		

(LCCI)

27.2 For question 27.1, show the journal entries necessary to correct the errors.

27.3 The following is a trial balance which has been incorrectly drawn up:

Trial Balance – 31 January 19–9

	£	£
Capital 1 February 19–8	5,500	
Drawings	2,800	
Stock 1 February 19–8		2,597
Trade Debtors		2,130
Furniture and fittings	1,750	
Cash in hand	1,020	
Trade creditors		2,735
Sales		7,430
Returns inwards		85
Discount received	46	
Business expenses	950	
Purchases	4,380	
	16,446	14,977

As well as the mistakes evident above, the following errors were also discovered:

(a) A payment of £75 made to a creditor had not been posted from the cash book into the purchases ledger.

(b) A cheque for £56 received from a customer had been correctly entered in the cash book but posted to the customer's account as £50.
(c) A purchase of fittings £120 had been included in the purchases account.
(d) The total of discounts allowed column in the cash book of £38 had not been posted into the general ledger.
(e) A page of the sales day book was correctly totalled as £564 but had been carried forward as £456.

Show the trial balance as it would appear after all the errors had been corrected. You are required to show all workings.
(RSA)

27.4X At the close of business on 26 February 19–7, Alfred Bishop, a sole trader, extracted a trial balance from his books. The trial balance did not agree, but Bishop entered the difference in a suspense account. He then prepared his trading and profit and loss account for the year ending 26 February 19–7 in the normal way. The profit and loss account so prepared showed a net profit amounting to £2,370.

During March 19–7, Bishop discovered the following errors in his books and these accounted for the entire difference in the trial balance:
1 Bad debts account had been debited with items of £31 and £27 in respect of bad debts but the personal accounts of the individual debtors had not been credited.
2 The sales day book was overcast by £70.
3 Cash £36 received from Simon Jones had been correctly entered in the cash book but the double entry had been made on the wrong side of Jones' personal account in Alfred Bishop's ledger.
4 The discount allowed total in the cash book – £42 – had not been entered in the discount account.

Required
(a) State how, and to what extent, each of the above errors would have affected the trial balance, e.g. debit overstated £......
(b) Calculate the correct figure for net profit.
Note: Calculations must be shown.
(LCCI)

27.5X For question 27.4X, show the journal entries necessary to correct the errors.

27.6X J Jones extracted the following trial balance from his books on 31 January 19–2.

	£	£
Capital		7,450
Drawings	3,000	
Stock 1 February 19–1	2,500	
Trade debtors	2,950	
Trade creditors		2,684
Shop fittings	1,530	
Purchases	5,140	
Sales		7,460
General expenses	860	
Discount received		40
Cash at bank	1,660	
Returns outwards		40
	17,640	17,674

The following errors and omissions were subsequently discovered:

(a) A purchase of shop fittings £320 had been debited to purchases account.

(b) A sales invoice of £150 entered in the sales day book had not been posted to the customer's personal account.

(c) A credit note for £30 issued by J Jones to a customer had been completely omitted from the books.

(d) A credit balance of £16 in the purchases ledger had been omitted from the trial balance.

(e) The sales day book was undercast by £100 in December 19–1.

Draw up a corrected Trial Balance. Show all workings.

(RSA)

27.7X For question 27.6X, show the journal entries necessary to correct the errors.

28 · Control Accounts

28.1 Need for Control Accounts

When all the accounts were kept in one ledger a trial balance could be drawn up as a test of the arithmetical accuracy of the accounts. It must be remembered that certain errors were not revealed by such a trial balance. If the trial balance totals disagreed, for a small business the books could easily and quickly be checked so as to find the errors.

However, when the firm has grown and the accounting work has been so divided up that there are several or many ledgers, any errors could be very difficult to find. We could have to check every item in every ledger. What is required is a type of trial balance for each ledger, and this requirement is met by the **control account**. Thus it is only the ledgers whose control accounts do not balance that need detailed checking to find errors.

28.2 Principle of Control Accounts

The principle on which the control account is based is simple, and is as follows. If the opening balance of an account is known, together with information of the additions and deductions entered in the account, the closing balance can be calculated.

Applying this to a complete ledger, the total of opening balances together with the additions and deductions during the period should give the total of closing balances. This can be illustrated by reference to a sales ledger for entries for a month.

	£
Total of Opening Balances, 1 January 19–6	3,000
Add Total of entries which have increased the balances	9,500
	12,500
Less Total of entries which have reduced the balances	8,000
Total of closing balances should be	4,500

Because totals are used the accounts are often known as *total accounts*. Thus a control account for a sales ledger could be known as either a sales ledger control account or as a total debtors account.

Similarly, a control account for a purchases ledger could be known either as a purchases ledger control account or as a total creditors account.

It must be emphasised that control accounts are *not* necessarily a part of the double entry system. They are merely arithmetical proofs performing the same function as a trial balance to a particular ledger.

28.3 Form of Control Accounts

It is usual to find them in the same form as an account, with the totals of the debit entries in the ledger on the left-hand side of the control account, and the totals of the various credit entries in the ledger on the right-hand side of the control account.

Exhibit 28.1 shows an example of a sales ledger control account for a sales ledger in which all the entries are arithmetically correct.

Exhibit 28.1

Sales ledger	£
Debit balances on 1 January 19–6	1,894
Total credit sales for the month	10,290
Cheques received from customers in the month	7,284
Cash received from customers in the month	1,236
Returns inwards from customers during the month	296
Debit balances on 31 January as extracted from the sales ledger	3,368

Sales Ledger Control

19–6		£	19–6		£
Jan 1	Balances b/d	1,894	Jan 31	Bank	7,284
" 31	Sales	10,290		Cash	1,236
				Returns inwards	296
				Balances c/d	3,368
		12,184			12,184

We have proved the ledger to be arithmetically correct, because the totals of the control account equal each other. If the totals are not equal, then this proves there is an error somewhere.

Exhibit 28.2 shows an example where an error is found to exist in a purchases ledger. The ledger will have to be checked in detail, the error found, and the control account then corrected.

Exhibit 28.2

Purchases ledger	£
Credit balances on 1 January 19–6	3,890
Cheques paid to suppliers during the month	3,620
Returns outwards to suppliers in the month	95
Bought from suppliers in the month	4,936
Credit balances on 31 January as extracted from the purchases ledger	5,151

Purchases Ledger Control

19–6		£	19–6		£
Jan 31	Bank	3,620	Jan 1	Balances b/d	3,890
" 31	Returns outwards	95	" 31	Purchases	4,936
" 31	Balances c/d	5,151			
		8,866*			8,826*

* There is a £40 error in the purchases ledger. We will have to check that ledger in detail to find the error.

28.4 Information for Control Accounts

The following tables show where information is obtained from to draw up control accounts.

Sales Ledger Control	Source
1 Opening debtors	List of debtors drawn up at end of previous period
2 Credit sales	Total from Sales journal
3 Returns inwards	Total of Returns inwards journal
4 Cheques received	Cash book: bank column on received side. List extracted
5 Cash received	Cash book: cash column on received side. List extracted
6 Closing debtors	List of debtors drawn up at end of the period

Purchases Ledger Control	Source
1 Opening creditors	List of creditors drawn up at end of previous period
2 Credit purchases	Total from Purchases journal
3 Returns outwards	Total of Returns outwards journal
4 Cheques paid	Cash book: bank column on payments side. List extracted
5 Cash paid	Cash book: cash column on payments side. List extracted
6 Closing creditors	List of creditors drawn up at end of the period

28.5 Other Transfers

Transfers to bad debt accounts will have to be recorded in the sales ledger control account as they involve entries in the sales ledgers.

Similarly, a contra account whereby the same firm is both a supplier and a customer, and inter-indebtedness is set off, will also need entering in the control accounts. An example of this follows:

1 The firm has sold A Hughes £600 goods.
2 Hughes has supplied the firm with £880 goods.
3 The £600 owing by Hughes is set off against £880 owing to him.
4 This leaves £280 owing to Hughes.

Sales Ledger
A Hughes

		£			
Sales	**1**	600			

Purchases Ledger
A Hughes

					£
			Purchases	**2**	880

The set-off now takes place.

Sales Ledger
A Hughes

		£			£
Sales	**1**	600	Set-off Purchases ledger	**3**	600

Purchases Ledger
A Hughes

		£			£
Set-off: Sales ledger	**3**	600	Purchases	**2**	880
Balance c/d	**4**	280			
		880			880
			Balance b/d	**4**	280

The transfer of the £600 will therefore appear on the credit side of the sales ledger control account and on the debit side of the purchases ledger control account.

28.6 A More Complicated Example

Exhibit 28.3 shows a worked example of a more complicated control account.

You will see that there are sometimes credit balances in the sales ledger as well as debit balances. Suppose for instance we sold £500 goods to W Young, he then paid in full for them, and then afterwards he returned £40 goods to us. This would leave a credit balance of £40 on the account, whereas usually the balances in the sales ledger are debit balances.

Exhibit 28.3

19–6			£
Aug	1	Sales ledger – debit balances	3,816
"	1	Sales ledger – credit balances	22
"	31	Transactions for the month:	
		Cash received	104
		Cheques received	6,239
		Sales	7,090
		Bad debts written off	306
		Discounts allowed	298
		Returns inwards	664
		Cash refunded to a customer who had overpaid his account	37
		Dishonoured cheques	29
		Interest charged by us on overdue debt	50
		At the end of the month:	
		Sales ledger – debit balances	3,429
		Sales ledger – credit balances	40

Sales Ledger Control Account

19–6			£	19–6			£
Aug	1	Balances b/d	3,816	Aug	1	Balances b/d	22
"	31	Sales	7,090	"	31	Cash	104
		Cash refunded	37			Bank	6,239
		Bank: dishonoured cheques	29			Bad debts	306
		Interest on debt	50			Discounts allowed	298
		Balances c/d	40			Returns inwards	664
						Balances c/d	3,429
			11,062				11,062

New Terms

Control Account (p 254): An account which checks the arithmetical accuracy of a ledger.

Exercises

28.1 You are required to prepare a sales ledger control account from the following:

19–4		£
May 1	Sales ledger balances	4,560
	Total of entries for May:	
	Sales journal	10,870
	Returns inwards journal	460
	Cheques and cash received from customers	9,615
	Discounts allowed	305
May 31	Sales ledger balances	5,050

28.2 You are to prepare a sales ledger control account from the following. Deduce the closing figure of sales ledger balances as at 31 March 19–8.

19–8		£
Mar 1	Sales ledger balances	6,708
	Totals for March:	
	Discounts allowed	300
	Cash and cheques received from debtors	8,970
	Sales journal	11,500
	Bad debts written off	115
	Returns inwards journal	210
Mar 31	Sales ledger balances	?

28.3X Draw up a purchases ledger control account from the following:

19–2		£
June 1	Purchases ledger balances	3,890
	Totals for June:	
	Purchases journal	5,640
	Returns outwards journal	315
	Cash and cheques paid to creditors	5,230
	Discounts received	110
June 30	Purchases ledger balances	?

28.4X You are to prepare a purchases ledger control account from the following. As the final figure of purchases ledger balances at 30 November is missing, you will have to deduce that figure.

19–4		£
Nov 1	Purchases ledger balances	7,560
	Totals for November:	
	Discounts received	240
	Returns outwards journal	355
	Cash and cheques paid to creditors	9,850
	Purchases journal	11,100
Nov 30	Purchases ledger balances	?

28.5 The following balances have been extracted from the books of R Stevenson at 31 December 19–2:

1 January 19–2:	
Sales Ledger Balances	6,840
Further Balances:	
Sales	46,801
Discounts Allowed	420
Bad Debts written off	494
Receipts from Customers	43,780
Returns Inwards	296

Required

(a) Prepare the Sales Ledger Control Account for R Stevenson, showing clearly the balance carried forward at 31 December 19–2.

(b) An explanation of the meaning and use of the final balance.

(RSA)

28.6X The following balances are included in the purchase ledger of Ambrose Artichoke as at 1 January 19–0:

J Carrot	£86.14
F Parsnip	£20.28
B Sprout	£14.10
C Beetroot	£3.90

During January the following transactions took place:

3 January	Purchased stock on credit from F Parsnip £19.72 and from M Mushroom £55.90
10 January	Purchases on credit from C Beetroot £11.91, B Sprout £25.90 and M Mushroom £28.32
15 January	Returned goods to J Carrot £6.00 and B Sprout £7.40
25 January	Paid by cash J Carrot £20.00 on account
30 January	Paid F Parsnip by cheque the balance owing on her account after deducting a 5% cash discount.

You are required to:

(a) write up and balance off the personal accounts in the purchase ledger;

(b) prepare a purchase ledger control account as at 31 January 19–0;

(c) make up a simple reconciliation of the control account balance with the actual creditors as at 31 January 19–0.

(RSA)

29 · Introduction to Accounting Ratios

29.1 Mark-up and Margin

The purchase and sale of goods may be shown as

Cost Price + Profit = Selling Price

The profit when shown as a fraction, or percentage, of the cost price is known as the **mark-up**.

The profit when shown as a fraction, or percentage, of the selling price is known as the **margin**.

We can now calculate these using this example.

Cost Price + Profit = Selling Price
£4 + £1 = £5.

Mark-up = $\dfrac{\text{Profit}}{\text{Cost Price}}$ as a fraction, or if required as a percentage, multiply by 100:

$$\text{£}\tfrac{1}{4} = \tfrac{1}{4}, \text{ or } \tfrac{1}{4} \times 100 = 25 \text{ per cent.}$$

Margin = $\dfrac{\text{Profit}}{\text{Selling Price}}$ as a fraction, or if required as a percentage, multiply by 100:

$$\text{£}\tfrac{1}{5} = \tfrac{1}{5} \text{ or } \tfrac{1}{5} \times 100 = 20 \text{ per cent.}$$

29.2 Calculating Missing Figures

Now we can use these ratios to complete trading accounts where some of the figures are missing.

All examples in this chapter:

- assume that all the goods in a firm have the same rate of mark-ups, and
- ignore wastages and theft of goods.

1 The following figures are for the year 19–5:

	£
Stock 1 January 19–5	400
Stock 31 December 19–5	600
Purchases	5,200

A uniform rate of mark-up of 20 per cent is applied.

Find the gross profit and the sales figure.

First of all we enter the figures we already know in the trading account; the question marks show the places for the missing figures.

Trading Account

	£		£
Stock 1 January 19–5	400	Sales	?
Add Purchases	5,200		
	5,600		
Less Stock 31 December 19–5	600		
Cost of goods sold	5,000		
Gross profit	?		

Answer:

We know that: Cost of goods sold + Profit = Sales

and also that: Cost of goods sold + Percentage Mark-up = Sales

We do know the following figures: £5,000 + 20 per cent = Sales

After doing the arithmetic: £5,000 + £1,000 = £6,000

The trading account can be completed by inserting the gross profit £1,000 and £6,000 for Sales.

2 Another firm has the following figures for 19–6:

	£
Stock 1 January 19–6	500
Stock 31 December 19–6	800
Sales	6,400

A uniform rate of margin of 25 per cent is in use. Find the gross profit and the figure of purchases. First enter these figures in the trading account.

Trading Account

	£		£
Stock 1 January	500	Sales	6,400
Add Purchases	?		
Less Stock 31 December 19–6	800		
Cost of goods sold	?		
Gross profit	?		
	6,400		6,400

We know that: Cost of goods sold + Gross Profit = Sales
and, therefore: Sales – Gross Profit = Cost of Goods Sold

As we can say margin instead of gross profit, we know therefore that:
Sales – 25 per cent Margin = Cost of Goods Sold

This becomes:
£6,400 – £1,600 = £4,800

We can now fill in the figure of £4,800 for cost of goods sold. This leaves just two missing figures, **1** and **2**, as we can now see:

		£
Stock 1 January 19–6		500
Add Purchases	**1**	?
	2	?
Less Stock 31 December 19–6		800
Cost of goods sold		4,800

Figure **2** less £800 = £4,800. Therefore **2** must be £5,600.
Now that we know this, £500 + (**1**) = (**2**) £5,600. (**1**) is, therefore, £5,100.
In Exhibit 29.1 we can now show the completed trading account.

Exhibit 29.1

Trading Account

	£		£
Stock 1 January 19–6	500	Sales	6,400
Add Purchases	5,100		
	5,600		
Less Stock 31 December 19–6	800		
Cost of goods sold	4,800		
Gross Profit	1,600		
	6,400		6,400

This method can be very useful to retail stores. They may want to increase their sales, and to do this they need to know how much to buy in purchases. They can also estimate stock levels or sales figures.

29.3 Other Accounting Ratios

There are some ratios that are often used to compare one period's results against those of a previous period. Two ratios in most common use are the ratio of gross profit to sales and the rate of turnover or **stockturn**.

Gross Profit as Percentage of Sales

The basic formula is:

$$\frac{\text{Gross profit}}{\text{Sales}} \times 100 = \text{Gross profit as percentage of sales.}$$

This is the amount of gross profit for every £100 of sales. If the answer turned out to be 15 per cent, this would mean that for every £100 of sales £15 gross profit was made before any expenses were paid.

This ratio is used as a test of the profitability of the sales. Just because the sales are increased may not mean that the gross profit will increase. The trading accounts in Exhibit 29.2 illustrate this.

Exhibit 29.2

Trading Accounts for the year ended 31 December

	19–6	19–7		19–6	19–7
	£	£		£	£
Stock	500	900	Sales	7,000	8,000
Purchases	6,000	7,200			
	6,500	8,100			
Less Stock	900	1,100			
Cost of goods sold	5,600	7,000			
Gross profit	1,400	1,000			
	7,000	8,000		7,000	8,000

In the year 19–6 the gross profit as a percentage of sales was:

$$\frac{1,400}{7,000} \times 100 = 20 \text{ per cent.}$$

In the year 19–7 it became:

$$\frac{1,000}{8,000} \times 100 = 12\tfrac{1}{2} \text{ per cent.}$$

Sales had increased, but as the gross profit percentage had fallen by a relatively greater amount the gross profit has fallen. There can be many reasons for such a fall in the gross profit percentage. Some are now listed:

1 Perhaps the goods being sold have cost more, but the selling price of the goods has not risen to the same extent.

2 Perhaps in order to increase sales, reductions have been made in the selling price of goods.

3 There could be a difference in how much has been sold of each sort of goods, called the sales-mix, between this year and last, with different kinds of goods carrying different rates of gross profit per £100 of sales.

4 There may have been a greater wastage or theft of goods.

These are only some of the possible reasons for the decrease. The idea of calculating the ratio is to show that the profitability per £100 of sales has changed. The firm would then try to find out why and how such a change has taken place.

Stockturn or Rate of Turnover

If we always kept just £100 of stock at cost, which when we sold it would sell for £125, then if we sold this amount eight times in a year we would make 8 × £25 = £200 gross profit. The quicker we sell our stock (we could say the quicker we turn over our stock) the more the profit we will make, if our gross profit percentage stays the same.

To check on how quickly we are turning over our stock we can use the formula:

$$\frac{\text{Cost of goods sold}}{\text{Average stock}} = \text{Number of times stock is turned over within a period}$$

If would be best if the average stock held could be calculated by valuing the stock quite a few times each year, then dividing the totals of the figures obtained by the number of valuations. For instance, monthly stock figures are added up then divided by twelve.

However, it is quite common, especially in examinations or in cases where no other information is available, to calculate the average stock as the opening stock plus the closing stock and the answer divided by two. Using the figures in Exhibit 29.2 we can calculate the **stockturn** for 19–6 and 19–7:

19–6 $$\frac{5,600}{(500 + 900) \div 2} = \frac{5,600}{700} = 8 \text{ times per annum}$$

19–7 $$\frac{7,000}{(900 + 1,100) \div 2} = \frac{7,000}{1,000} = 7 \text{ times per annum}$$

Instead of saying that the stockturn is so many times per annum, we could instead say on average how long we keep stock before we sell it. We do this by the formula:

To express it in months:	$12 \div \text{Stockturn} = x$ months
To express it in days:	$365 \div \text{Stockturn} = x$ days

From Exhibit 29.2:

	19–6			19–7		
In months	$\frac{12}{8}$	=	1.5 months	$\frac{12}{7}$	=	1.7 months
In days	$\frac{365}{8}$	=	45.6 days	$\frac{365}{7}$	=	52.1 days

All the above figures are rounded off to the nearest decimal point.

29.4 The Relationship Between Mark-up and Margin

As both of these figures refer to the same profit, but are expressed as a fraction or a percentage of different figures, there is a relationship between them. If one is known as a fraction, the other can soon be found.

If the mark-up is known, to find the margin take the same numerator to be the numerator of the margin. Then for the denominator of the margin take the total of the mark-up's denominator plus the numerator. An example can now be shown:

Mark-up	**Margin**		
$\frac{1}{4}$	$\frac{1}{4+1}$	=	$\frac{1}{5}$
$\frac{2}{11}$	$\frac{2}{11+2}$	=	$\frac{2}{13}$

If the margin is known, to find the mark-up take the same numerator to be the numerator of the mark-up. Then for the denominator of the mark-up take the figure of the margin's denominator less the numerator:

Mark-up	**Margin**		
$\frac{1}{6}$	$\frac{1}{6-1}$	=	$\frac{1}{5}$
$\frac{3}{13}$	$\frac{3}{13-3}$	=	$\frac{3}{10}$

New Terms

Mark-up (p 261): Profit shown as a percentage or fraction of cost price.

Margin (p 261): Profit shown as a percentage or fraction of selling price.

Stockturn (p 265): Number of times we sell our stock in an accounting period.

Exercises

29.1 J Jackson is a trader who marks the selling price of his goods at 25 per cent above cost. His books give the following information at 31 July 19–3:

	£
Stock 1 August 19–2	4,936
Stock 31 July 19–3	6,310
Sales for year	30,000

You are required to:
(a) Find 'cost of goods sold'.
(b) Show the value of purchases during the year.
(c) Ascertain the profit Jackson made.
Note: Your answer should take the form of a trading account.
(RSA)

29.2 P R Match produces from his trial balance at 31 August 19–9 the following information.

	£
Stock 1 September 19–8	2,000
Purchases	18,000

Match has a 'mark-up' of 50 per cent on 'cost of sales'.
His average stock during the year was £4,000.

You are required to:
(a) Calculate the closing stock for P R Match at 31 August 19–9.
(b) Prepare his trading account for the year ended 31 August 19–9.
(c) Ascertain the total amount of profit and loss expenditure that Match must not exceed if he is to maintain a net profit on sales of 10 per cent.
(RSA)

29.3X A business has a rate of turnover of seven times. The average stock is £4,200. Trade discount allowed is $33\frac{1}{3}$ per cent off all selling prices. Expenses are given as 70 per cent of gross profit. Calculate:
(a) Cost of goods sold.
(b) Gross profit.
(c) Turnover.
(d) Total expenses.
(e) Net profit.
(RSA)

29.4X The following figures relate to the retail business of W Watson for the month of May 19–8. Goods which are on sale fall into two categories, A and B.

	Category A	Category B
Sales to the public at manufacturer's recommended list price	£3,000	£7,000
Trade discount allowed to retailers	20%	25%
Total expenses as a percentage of sales	10%	10%
Annual rate of stock turnover	12	20

Calculate for each category:

(a) Cost of goods sold.
(b) Gross profit.
(c) Total expenses.
(d) Net profit.
(e) Average stock at cost, assuming that sales are distributed evenly over the year, and that there are twelve equal months in the year.

(RSA)

30 · Single Entry and Incomplete Records

30.1 Why Double Entry is Not Used

For every small shopkeeper, market stall or other small business to keep its books using a full double entry system would be ridiculous. First of all, a large number of the owners of such firms would not know how to write up double entry records, even if they wanted to.

It is more likely that they would enter details of a transaction once only, using a single entry system. Also many of them would fail to record every transaction, resulting in incomplete records.

Somehow, however, the profits will have to be calculated. This could be for the purpose of calculating income tax payable. How can profits be calculated if the book-keeping records are inadequate or incomplete?

30.2 Profit as an Increase in Capital

Probably the way to start is to recall that, unless there has been an introduction of extra cash or resources into the firm, the only way that capital can be increased is by making profits. Therefore, profits can be found by comparing capital at the end of the last period with that at the end of this period.

Let us look at a firm where capital at the end of 19–4 was £2,000. During 19–5 there have been no drawings, and no extra capital has been brought in by the owner. At the end of 19–5 the capital was £3,000.

	This year's capital		Last year's capital	
Net profit =	£3,000	–	£2,000	= £1,000

If on the other hand the drawings had been £700, the profits must have been £1,700, calculated thus:

Last year's Capital	+	Profits	–	Drawings	=	This year's Capital
£2,000	+	?	–	£700	=	£3,000

We can see that £1,700 profits was the figure needed to complete the formula, filling in the missing figure by normal arithmetical deduction:

£2,000 + £1,700 – £700 = £3,000

Exhibit 30.1 shows the calculation of profit where insufficient information is available to draft a trading and profit and loss account, only information of assets and liabilities being known.

Exhibit 30.1

H Taylor provides information as to his assets and liabilities at certain dates.

At 31 December 19–5. *Assets:* Motor van £1,000; Fixtures £700; Stock £850; Debtors £950; Bank £1,100; Cash £100. *Liabilities:* Creditors £200; Loan from J Ogden £600.

At 31 December 19–6. *Assets:* Motor van (after depreciation) £800; Fixtures (after depreciation) £630; Stock £990; Debtors £1,240; Bank £1,700; Cash £200. *Liabilities:* Creditors £300; Loan from J Ogden £400; Drawings were £900.

Statement of Affairs as at 31 December 19–5

	£	£		£
Fixed Assets			*Capital (difference)*	3,900
Motor van		1,000	*Long-term Liability*	
Fixtures		700	Loan from J Ogden	600
		1,700	*Current Liabilities*	
Current Assets			Creditors	200
Stock	850			
Debtors	950			
Bank	1,100			
Cash	100			
		3,000		
		4,700		4,700

Statement of Affairs as at 31 December 19–6

Fixed Assets	£	£	*Capital*	£	£
Motor van		800	Balance at 1.1.19–6	3,900	
Fixtures		630	*Add* Net profit	?	
		1,430			
Current Assets			*Less* Drawings	900	
Stock	990				
Debtors	1,240		*Long-term Liability*		
Bank	1,700		Loan from J Ogden		400
Cash	200		*Current Liabilities*		
		4,130	Creditors		300
		5,560			5,560

First of all a statement of affairs is drawn as at 31 December 19–5, shown in Exhibit 30.1. This is the name given to what would have been called a balance sheet if it had been drawn up from a set of records. The capital is the difference between the assets and liabilities.

A statement of affairs is then drafted up at the end of 19–6. The formula of Opening capital + Profit – Drawings – Closing Capital is then used to deduce the figure of profit.

Deduction of net profit

Closing capital must be Assets – Liabilities = £5,560 – £400 – £300 = £4,860

Opening Capital + Net Profit – Drawings = Closing Capital

£3,900 + ? – £900 = £4,860

Therefore, net profit = £1,860

Obviously, this method of calculating profit is very unsatisfactory as it is much more informative when a trading and profit and loss account can be drawn up. Therefore, whenever possible the comparisons of capital method of ascertaining profits should be avoided and a full set of final accounts drawn up from the available records.

30.3 Deduction of Other Figures

To illustrate the deduction of sales and purchases, we shall use the figures from the firm of T Sands. We will then show the trading accounts for the first two years of trading.

Sales

We have seen that in double entry the figure of sales for the trading account is found in the sales account. If full double entry records are not kept, then the figure of sales may have to be deduced from other information.

Looking at the first year's records, we have the following information available for the year to 31 December 19–4:

	£
Received cash and cheques from debtors during the year	36,800
Amount owing by debtors at 31 December 19–4	7,600

If we consider that debtors represent sales which have been unpaid at the end of a year, we can say that:

Sales – Paid for Sales = Sales unpaid (i.e. debtors)

i.e. ? – £36,800 = £7,600

By arithmetical deduction and inserting the missing figure the sales answer is £44,400.

We can show this in the form of a control account representing all debtors. Enter the totals of items known on the same sides as you would enter single items in an *individual* debtor's account.

Total Debtors' Account

19–4		£	19–4		£
Dec 31	Sales for year	?	Dec 31	Cash received	36,800
				Balances c/d	7,600
		?			?
19–5					
Jan 1	Balances b/d	7,600			

We fill in the totals column which must be £44,400 each side, as the credit side totals £44,400 and there is no missing information on that side. On the debit side, therefore, the missing figures must also be £44,400.

When we look at the second year of the business we find the following:

	£
(a) Debtors at 1 January 19–5 (brought forward)	7,600
(b) Cash received from debtors during the year 19–5	43,500
(c) Debtors at 31 December 19–5	9,300

Arithmetically we can show this:

	£
Cash received from debtors	43,500
Less Cash received in respect of previous year's sales (i.e. debtors at 1 January 19–5 now paid)	7,600
	35,900
Add Sales during 19–5 but which have not been paid for (i.e. debtors at 31 December 19–5)	9,300
Therefore, sales for the year 19–5 are:	45,200

This can be shown instead like a control account, as a total debtors' account:

Total Debtors' Account

19–5		£	19–5		£
Jan 1	Balances b/fwd	7,600	Dec 31	Cash received	43,500
Dec 31	Sales (missing figure)	?		Balances c/d	9,300
		?			?
19–6					
Jan 1	Balance b/d	9,300			

The missing figure for sales is therefore £45,200.

If in the example just shown, there had also been bad debts of £180 and £240 discounts allowed, the total debtors' account would have shown a different figure of sales, as follows:

Total Debtors' Account

19–5		£	19–5		£
Jan 1	Balances b/fwd	7,600	Dec 31	Cash received	43,500
Dec 31	Sales (missing figure)	?		Discounts allowed	240
				Bad debts	180
				Balances c/d	9,300
		53,220			53,220

In this case the sales figure is £45,620.

Purchases

In double entry the figure of purchases for the trading account is obtained from the purchases account. When double entry records are not kept we will have to deduce the figure from other information.

Looking at the first year's records, we have the following information available for the year ended 31 December 19–4:

	£
Paid cheques and cash to creditors during the year	33,300
Amount owing to creditors at 31 December 19–4	5,400

Creditors represent purchases which have not been paid for by the end of the year. We can say that:

	Payments for purchases	+	owing for purchases	=	Purchases made during the year
i.e.	£33,300	+	£5,400	=	?

By arithmetical deduction and inserting the missing figure, the purchases are £38,700.

Instead of doing the calculations as shown, we could do it in the form of a control account. This would cover all creditors. The totals of items known would be entered on the same sides of this account as you would enter single items in an individual creditor's account.

Total Creditors' Accounts

19–4		£	19–4		£
Dec 31	Cash paid to suppliers	33,300	Dec 31	Purchases for year	?
31	Balances c/d	5,400			
		?			?

The totals column on each side must be £38,700, as the debt side totals £38,700 and there is no missing information on that side. On the credit side the missing figures must also be £38,700.

When we look at the second year of the business we find the following:

	£
Creditors at 1 January 19–5	5,400
Payments made to creditors in 19–5	37,200
Creditors at 31 December 19–5	5,650

We can arrive at the figure of purchases.

	£
Paid during the year	37,200
Less Payments made, but which were for goods which were purchases in a previous year (creditors 31.12.19–4)	5,400
	31,800
Add Purchases made in this year, but for which payment has not yet been made (creditors 31.12.19–5)	5,650
Goods bought in this year, i.e. purchases	37,450

The same answer could have been obtained if the information had been shown like a control account in the form of a total creditors' account. The figure of purchases is the amount required to make the account totals agree.

Total Creditors' Account

	£		£
Cash paid to suppliers	37,200	Balances b/d	5,400
Balances c/d	5,650	Purchases (missing figure)	37,450
	42,850		42,850

Completion of the Trading Accounts

We now know the sales and purchases figures for T Sands for his first two years of trading. All we now need to know are the stock figures. These are:

Stock as at 31 December 19–4	£6,300
Stock as at 31 December 19–5	£10,800

The trading accounts are now shown:

T Sands
Trading Account for the year ended 31 December 19–4

	£		£
Purchases	38,700	Sales	44,400
Less Closing stock	6,300		
Cost of goods sold	32,400		
Gross profit	12,000		
	44,400		44,400

T Sands
Trading Account for the year ended 31 December 19–5

	£		£
Opening stock	6,300	Sales	45,200
Add Purchases	37,450		
	43,750		
Less Closing stock	10,800		
Cost of goods sold	32,950		
Gross profit	12,250		
	45,200		45,200

Exercises

30.1 On 1 August 19–6 S Pea started his business with £1,000 in his bank account. After the end of his first year of trading he realised that because of his lack of book-keeping knowledge he was unable to prepare a balance sheet. S Pea was, however, able to produce the following data for the year ended 31 July 19–7:

	£
Furniture (cost £900)	800
Motor vehicles (cost £2,100)	1,600
Stock-in-trade	2,700
Creditors	3,300
Cash in hand	50
Balance at bank (overdrawn)	1,000
Debtors	1,600
Loan from B Smith	200
Drawings	3,000

You are required to:

(a) Ascertain S Pea's profit or loss for the year ended 31 July 19–7.

(b) Prepare S Pea's balance sheet as at 31 July 19–7, showing clearly all the totals and sub-totals normally found in a Balance Sheet.

(RSA)

30.2 Arthur Hobson is a sole trader who, although keeping very good records, does not operate a full double-entry system. The following figures have been taken from his records:

	31 March 19–8	*31 March 19–9*
	£	£
Cash at bank	730	870
Office furniture	300	250
Stock	1,160	1,310
Cash in hand	30	40

Debtors on 31 March 19–8 amounted to £1,490 and sales for the year ended 31 March 19–9 to £5,760. During the year ended 31 March 19–9 cash received from debtors amounted to £5,410.

Creditors on 31 March 19–8 amounted to £940 and purchases for the year ended 31 March 19–9 to £4,060. During the year ended 31 March 19–9 cash paid to creditors amounted to £3,890.

During the year to 31 March 19–9 no bad debts were incurred. Also during the same period there was neither discount allowed nor discount received.

Required

(a) Calculate debtors and creditors as at 31 March 19–9.
(b) Calculate Hobson's capital as at 31 March 19–8 and 31 March 19–9.
(c) Calculate Hobson's net profit for the year ended 31 March 19–9, allowing for the fact that during that year his drawings amounted to £1,270.

Note: Calculations must be shown.
(LCCI)

30.3 From the following information ascertain the profit made by C Cat during 19–1. On 1 January he started business with £4,000 in the bank. His position on the following 31 December was as follows:

	£		£
Sundry creditors	350	Machinery	2,000
Cash at bank	400	Furniture	1,500
Stock	1,000		
Debtors	350		

(PEI)

30.4 Joseph Adams is a sole trader who does not keep complete book-keeping entries on the double entry system. From his records, however, the following figures have been extracted:

	31 May 19–7	*31 May 19–8*
	£	£
Stock-in-trade	1,980	2,160
Debtors	7,250	8,080
Creditors	4,140	5,630

During the year ended 31 May 19–8 Adams received from his debtors cash amounting to £22,460. The debtors total of £8,080 at 31 May 19–8 was arrived at after writing off bad debts amounting to £410 and allowing for discount of £670.

Also during the year ended 31 May 19–8 Adams paid to his creditors cash amounting to £17,190. The creditors total of £5,630 at 31 May 19–8 was arrived at after allowing for discount received amounting to £470.

Required

For the year ended 31 May 19–8:
(a) Calculate the total of sales.
(b) Calculate the total of purchases.
(c) Draw up Adams' trading account.

Note: Calculations must be shown.
(LCCI)

30.5X

G Browning
Balance Sheet as at 31 May 19–7

	£		£
Fixtures	5,000	Capital	14,000
Motor vans	4,000	Creditors	1,500
Stock	3,000		
Debtors	1,300		
Bank	2,000		
Cash	200		
	15,500		15,500

The following transactions took place on 1 June 19–7:

	£
Purchases on credit	350
Sales on credit (cost £350)	500
Cash sales (cost £100)	150
A motor-van, book value £1,000, was sold for £950. A cheque was received in full settlement.	
Payment to creditors by cheque	800
Cheques received from debtors	700
A bad debt written off	100
Cash received from debtors	50
Stock taken by proprietor	150

Reconstruct the balance sheet as it would appear at close of business on 1 June 19–7. You should set out neatly all your calculations.
(RSA)

30.6X Malcolm Price is a sole trader who does not keep his books on the double entry system. From his records, however, the following information is available:

	31 March 19–6	*31 March 19–7*
	£	£
Fixed assets	3,120	3,400
Current assets	3,990	4,260
Current liabilities	1,960	1,880

During the year ending 31 March 19–7 Price used his private banking account to purchase additional office furniture costing £360, and this was brought into his business. Also during the same period Price made drawings of £1,280 in cash and £60 in goods (cost price).

Required

(a) Calculate the amount of Price's capital as at 31 March 19–6 and 31 March 19–7.

(b) Calculate his net profit for the year ending 31 March 19–7.

(c) Draw up his capital account for the year ending 31 March 19–7 as it would appear under the double entry system.

Note: Calculations must be shown.
(LCCI)

30.7X On 1 July 19–5 D Loss commenced business with £6,000 in his bank account. After trading for a full year, he ascertained that his position on 30 June 19–6 was as follows:

	£		£
Plant	3,600	Fixtures	360
Creditors	720	Bank balance	600
Debtors	930	Stock-in-trade	1,350
Cash in hand	135	Drawings	1,600

You are required to:

(a) Calculate D Loss's capital at 30 June 19–6.

(b) Prepare D Loss's balance sheet at 30 June 19–6 (assuming a profit of £1,855), set out in such a manner as to show clearly the totals normally shown in a balance sheet.

(RSA)

31 · Receipts and Payments Accounts and Income and Expenditure Accounts

31.1 Types of Organisations

Clubs, associations and other non-profit making organisations do not have trading and profit and loss accounts drawn up for them, as their main purpose is not trading or profit making. They are run so that their members can do things such as play football or chess. The kind of final accounts prepared by these organisations are either **receipts and payments accounts** or **income and expenditure accounts**.

31.2 Receipts and Payments Accounts

Receipts and payments accounts are a summary of the cash book for the period. Exhibit 31.1 is an example.

Exhibit 31.1

The Homers Running Club
Receipts and Payments Account for the year ended 31 December 19–5

Receipts	£	*Payments*	£
Bank balance 1.1.19–5	236	Groundsman's wages	728
Subscriptions received for 19–5	1,148	Sports stadium expenses	296
Rent received	116	Committee expenses	58
		Printing and stationery	33
		Bank balance 31.12.19–5	385
	1,500		1,500

31.3 Income and Expenditure Accounts

When assets are owned, and there are liabilities, the receipts and payments account is not a good way of drawing up final accounts. Other than the cash received and paid out, it shows only the cash balances. The other assets and liabilities are not shown at all.

What is required is:

1 a balance sheet, and

2 an account showing whether the association's capital has increased.

In a profit making firm, **2** would be a trading and profit and loss account. In a non-profit organisation **2** will be an income and expenditure account.

An income and expenditure account follows the same rules as trading and profit and loss accounts. The only differences are the terms used. A comparison now follows:

Terms used

Profit Making Firm	Non-profit Organisation
1 Trading and Profit and Loss Account	1 Income and Expenditure Account
2 Net Profit	2 Surplus of Income over Expenditure
3 Net Loss	3 Excess of Expenditure over Income

31.4 Profit or Loss for a Special Purpose

Sometimes there are reasons why a non-profit making organisation would want a profit and loss account.

This is where something is done to make a profit. The profit is not to be kept, but used to pay for the main purpose of the organisation.

For instance, a football club may have discos or dances which people pay to go to. Any profit from these helps to pay football expenses. For these discos and dances a trading and profit and loss account would be drawn up. Any profit (or loss) would be transferred to the income and expenditure account.

31.5 Accumulated Fund

A sole trader or a partnership would have capital accounts. A non-profit making organisation would instead have an **accumulated fund**. It is in effect the same as a capital account, as it is the difference between assets and liabilities.

In a sole trader or partnership:

Capital + Liabilities = Assets

In a non-profit making organisation:

Accumulated Fund + Liabilities = Assets

31.6 Drawing Up Income and Expenditure Accounts

We can now look at the preparation of an income and expenditure account and a balance sheet of a club. A separate trading account is to be prepared for a bar, where beer and alcohol is sold to make a profit.

Long Lane Football Club
Trial Balance as at 31 December 19–8

	Dr	*Cr*
	£	£
Sports equipment	8,500	
Club premises	29,600	
Subscriptions received		6,490
Wages of staff	4,750	
Furniture and fittings	5,260	
Rates and insurance	1,910	
General expenses	605	
Accumulated fund 1 January 19–8		42,016
Donations received		360
Telephone and postage	448	
Bank	2,040	
Bar purchases	9,572	
Creditors for bar supplies		1,040
Bar sales		14,825
Bar stocks 1 January 19–8	2,046	
	64,731	64,731

The following information is also available: **1** Bar stocks at 31 December 19–8 £2,362. **2** Provide for depreciation, Sports equipment £1,700: Furniture and fittings £1,315.

Long Lane Football Club Bar
Trading Account for the year ended 31 December 19–8

	£		£
Stock 1.1.19–8	2,046	Sales	14,825
Add Purchases	9,572		
	11,618		
Less Stock 31.12.19–8	2,362		
Cost of goods sold	9,256		
Gross profit to income and expenditure account	5,569		
	14,825		14,825

Income and Expenditure Account for the year ended 31 December 19–8

Expenditure		£	*Income*	£
Wages to staff		4,750	Subscriptions	6,490
Rates and insurance		1,910	Donations received	360
Telephone and postages		448	Gross profit from bar trading	5,569
General expenses		605		
Depreciation:				
Furniture	1,315			
Sports equipment	1,700	3,015		
Surplus of income over expenditure		1,691		
		12,419		12,419

Balance Sheet as at 31 December 19–8

Fixed Assets	£	£	*Accumulated Fund*	£	£
Club premises		29,600	Balance at 1.1.19–5	42,016	
Furniture and fittings	5,260		*Add* Surplus of income over expenditure	1,691	
Less Depreciation	1,315	3,945			43,707
Sports equipment	8,500				
Less Depreciation	1,700				
		6,800			
		40,345			
Current Assets			*Current Liabilities*		
Bar stocks	2,362		Creditors for bar supplies		1,040
Bank	2,040	4,402			
		44,747			44,747

31.7 Subscriptions

In an examination the examiner may tell you how to deal with subscriptions. You must follow his instructions.

Where the examiner does not give instructions, you are to follow normal accounting rules.

Let us take the following as an example:

Hightown Football Club has received the following subscriptions during the year ended 31 December 19–5:

Subscriptions for 19–4, received late	£55
Subscriptions for 19–5	£6,300

Subscriptions for 19–5, owing at 31 December 19–5, were £80.

The subscriptions to be shown in the income and expenditure account are those which should have been paid for membership for the year 19–5. This is £6,300 + £80 = £6,380. The amount owing at 31 December 19–5 £80 will be shown (as debtors would be in a business firm) as a current asset in the balance sheet at 31 December 19–5. The following illustrates this:

Hightown Football Club
Income and Expenditure Account for the year ended 31 December 19–5

Expenditure	£	*Income*	£
		Subscriptions	6,380

Balance Sheet as at 31 December 19–5

Current assets	£	
Debtors for subscriptions	80	

The £55 subscriptions received late for 19–4 will have been shown included in subscriptions for 19–4, and also shown as a debtor in the balance sheet as at 31 December 19–4.

31.8 Donations

Any donations received are shown as income in the year that they are received.

31.9 Entrance Fees

New members often have to pay an entrance fee in the year that they join, in addition to the membership fee for that year. Entrance fees are normally included as income in the year that they are received.

31.10 Life Membership

Sometimes members can pay one amount for membership, and they will never have to pay any more money. This membership will last for their lifetime.

The committee of the club will have to decide how to enter these in the accounts. In an examination you should follow the instructions of the examiner.

31.11 Multiple-choice questions

Now attempt Set No 4, to be found on pages 350–54.

New Terms

Receipts and Payments Account (p 279): A summary of the cash book of a non-profit making organisation.

Income and Expenditure Account (p 279): An account for a non-profit making organisation to find the surplus or loss made during a period.

Accumulated Fund (p 280): A form of capital account for a non-profit organisation.

Exercises

31.1 The Town Society was formed on 1 July 19–0 and at the end of the first year the Treasurer submitted the following statement to members:

Receipts and Payments Account for the Year Ended 30 June 19–1

	£		£
Subscriptions	320	Cost of refreshments	20
Sale of dance tickets	80	Printing and stationery	15
Proceeds of sales of		Rent	10
refreshments	30	Furniture	150
		Dance expenses	45
		Sundry expenses	15
		Balance	175
	430		430

You are required to prepare an Income and Expenditure Account for the year ended 30 June 19–1, and a Balance Sheet as at that date.

You are given the following information:
No Subscriptions were paid in advance;
No depreciation on the furniture;
Stock of stationery £5;
Rent owing £10.
(PEI)

31.2X From the following receipts and payments account and notes prepare the income and expenditure account, showing clearly within it the profit or loss on the bar and disco.

Receipts and Payments Account for the year ended 31 December 19–8

	£		£
Bar sales	5,000	Furniture	265
Sale of disco tickets	100	Loss on raffle	40
Subscriptions	2,350	Hire of disco equipment	400
		Rent	100
		Rates	625
		Purchases of bar stock	3,000
		Secretary's expenses	20
		Bar staff wages	2,000
		Balance	1,000
	£7,450		£7,450

Subscriptions due amounted to £45
Rent paid in advance was £25
Bar stock remaining was valued at £250
Depreciate furniture by 20%
Rates due amounted to £15.
(PEI)

31.3 The following receipts and payments account for the year ending 31 May 19–7 was prepared by the treasurer of the Down Town Sports and Social Club.

Receipts	£	*Payments*	£
Balance at bank 1 June 19–6	286	Purchases of new equipment	166
Subscriptions	135	Bar stocks purchased	397
Net proceeds of jumble sale	91	Hire of rooms	64
Net proceeds of dance	122	Wages of part-time staff	198
Sale of equipment	80	Balance at bank 31 May 19–7	352
Bar takings	463		
	1,177		1,177

Notes

(1) On 1 June 19–6 the club's equipment was valued at £340. Included in this total, valued at £92, was the equipment sold during the year for £80.

(2) Bar stocks were valued as follows:

31 May 19–6 £88 31 May 19–7 £101

There were no creditors for bar supplies on either of these dates.

(3) Allow £30 for depreciation of equipment during the year ending 31 May 19–7. This is additional to the loss on equipment sold during the year.

(4) No subscriptions were outstanding at 31 May 19–6, but on 31 May 19–7 subscriptions due but unpaid amounted to £14.

Required

(a) Calculate the accumulated fund of the club as at 1 June 19–6. (This is the equivalent of the capital account in the case of a sole trader.)

(b) Draw up the income and expenditure account of the Club for the year ending 31 May 19–7.

Note: Calculations must be shown.
(LCCI)

31.4 Shown below is the Balance Sheet of the Deepdale Church Youth Centre at 31 December 19–3.

Balance Sheet for the Deepdale Church Youth Centre at 31 December 19–3

Fixed Assets	£		£
Furniture and Fittings	1,500	Accumulated Fund at	
Games and Equipment	640	31 December 19–3	3,600
Motor Van	1,000		
	3,140		
Current Assets		*Current Liabilities*	
Cash at Bank and in Hand	460	Nil	–
	3,600		3,600

The following summarised transactions took place during the period 1 January 19–4 to 31 December 19–4.

Receipts	£	*Payments*	£
Subscriptions (160 members at £5 per annum)	800	Light and Heat	205
Donation (treated as a revenue receipt)	80	Expenses of Annual Fête	310
Sale of Tickets from Annual Fête	540	New Games Equipment	160
		Cleaner's Wages	104
		Repairs and Renewals	83
		Motor Van repairs	126

Note
An electricity bill of £45 was owing at 31 December 19–4 (analysed under Light and Heat).

Required
Prepare:
(a) A Receipts and Payments Account showing clearly the balance in hand at 1 January 19–5.
(b) An Income and Expenditure Account for the year ended 31 December 19–4.
(c) A Balance Sheet as at 31 December 19–4.
(RSA)

31.5X The Drones Sports and Social Club was formed on 1 January 19–2. The Treasurer kept the accounts by double entry and extracted the following trial balance on 31 December 19–2:

	£	£
Cash at Bank	320	
Cash in Hand	50	
Bar Takings		1,571
Lighting and Heating	172	
Sundry Expenses	63	
Bar Supplies Purchased	924	
Equipment	260	
Rates	180	
Rent	106	
Cleaning Expenses	96	
Caretaker's Wages	120	
Members' subscriptions		580
Christmas Dance Expenses	158	
Sales of Christmas Dance tickets		298
	2,449	2,449

The Treasurer has asked you to check his accounting records before the presentation of the annual accounts to the members. In doing this you find that account needs to be taken of the following:

1 Rates prepaid £40 at 31 December 19–2.
2 £14 was still outstanding for cleaning expenses, at 31 December 19–2.
3 Bar stock of refreshments at 31 December 19–2 was valued at £36.

Required
(a) An Income and Expenditure Account for the year ended 31 December 19–2, showing clearly the Profit or Loss on the Bar and the Christmas Dance.
(b) A Balance Sheet as at 31 December 19–2.
(RSA)

32 · Manufacturing Accounts

32.1 Manufacturing: not Retailing

We now have to deal with firms which are manufacturers. For these firms a **manufacturing account** is prepared in addition to the trading and profit and loss accounts.

32.2 Divisions of Costs

In a manufacturing firm the costs are divided into different types. These may be summarised in chart form as follows:

Direct materials Direct labour Direct expenses	Prime cost	Production cost	Total cost
Plus			
Factory or Work overhead expenses			
Plus			
Administrative expenses Selling and distribution expenses			

32.3 Direct and Indirect Costs

When you see the words **direct costs** you know that the costs of making an item have been able to be traced to the item being manufactured. If it cannot easily be traced to the item being manufactured then it is an indirect expense, and will be included under factory overhead expenses.

For example, the wages of a machine operator making a particular item will be direct labour. The wages of a foreman in charge of many men on different jobs will be indirect labour, and will be part of factory overhead expenses.

Other instances of costs being direct costs:

1 Cost of direct materials will include carriage inwards on raw materials.
2 Hire of special machinery for a job.

32.4 Factory Overhead Expenses

Factory overhead costs are all those costs which occur in the factory where production is being done, but which cannot easily be traced to the items being manufactured. Examples are:

- Wages of cleaners.
- Wages of crane drivers.
- Rent and rates of the factory.
- Depreciation of plant and machinery.
- Costs of operating fork-lift trucks.
- Factory power.
- Factory lighting.

32.5 Administration Expenses

Administration expenses consist of such items as managers' salaries, legal and accountancy charges, the depreciation of accounting machinery and secretarial salaries.

32.6 Selling and Distribution Expenses

Selling and distribution expenses are items such as sales staff's salaries and commission, carriage outwards, depreciation of delivery vans, advertising and display expenses.

32.7 Format of Final Accounts

Manufacturing Account Part

This is debited with the production cost of goods completed during the accounting period.
It contains costs of:

- Direct materials.
- Direct labour.
- Direct expenses.
- Factory overhead expenses.

When completed this account will show the total of production cost. This figure will then be transferred down to the trading account.

Trading Account Part

This account includes:

- Production cost brought down from the manufacturing account.
- Opening and closing stocks of finished goods.
- Sales.

When completed this account will disclose the gross profit. This will then be carried down to the profit and loss account part.

The Manufacturing Account and the Trading Account can be shown in the form of a diagram:

Manufacturing Account

	£		£
Various Production costs for the period →	xxx	Production cost of goods completed c/d	xxx
	xxx		xxx

Trading Account

	£		£
Opening Stock of finished goods (A)	xxx	Sales	xxx
→ Production cost of goods completed b/d	xxx		
	xxx		
Less closing stock of finished goods (B)	xxx		
Production cost of goods sold	xxx		
Gross Profit c/d	xxx		xxx
	xxx		xxx

(A) is production costs of goods unsold in previous period
(B) is production costs of goods unsold at end of the period

Profit and Loss Account Part

This account includes:

- Gross profit brought down from the trading account.
- All administration expenses.
- All selling and distribution expenses.

When completed, this account will show the net profit.

32.8 A Worked Example of a Manufacturing Account

Exhibit 32.1 shows the necessary details for a manufacturing account. It has been assumed that there were no partly completed units (known as **work in progress**) either at the beginning or end of the period.

Exhibit 32.1

Details of production cost for the year ended 31 December 19–7:

	£
1 January 19–7, stock of raw materials	500
31 December 19–7, stock of raw materials	700
Raw materials purchased	8,000
Manufacturing (direct) wages	21,000
Royalties	150
Indirect wages	9,000
Rent of factory – excluding administration and selling and distribution buildings	440
Depreciation of plant and machinery in factory	400
General indirect expenses	310

The production costs of goods completed, when calculated, is carried down to the trading account, to the place where normally purchases are shown.

Manufacturing Account for the year ended 31 December 19–7

	£	£		£
Stock of raw materials 1.1.19–7		500	Production cost of goods completed c/d	39,100
Add Purchases		8,000		
		8,500		
Less Stock of raw materials 31.12.19–7		700		
Cost of raw materials consumed		7,800		
Manufacturing wages		21,000		
Royalties		150		
Prime cost		28,950		
Factory Overhead Expenses				
Rent	440			
Indirect wages	9,000			
Depreciation	400			
General expenses	310			
		10,150		
		39,100		39,100

32.9 Work in Progress

The production cost to be carried down to the trading account is that of production cost of goods completed during the period. If items have not been completed they cannot be sold. Therefore, they should not appear in the trading account.

For instance, if we have the following information, we can calculate the transfer to the trading account:

	£
Total production costs expended during the year	5,000
Production costs last year on goods not completed last year, but completed in this year (work in progress)	300
Production costs this year on goods which were not completed by the year end (work in progress)	440

The calculation is:

Total production costs expended this year	5,000
Add Costs from last year, in respect of goods completed in this year (work in progress)	300
	5,300
Less Costs in this year, for goods to be completed next year (work in progress)	440
Production costs expended on goods completed this year	4,860

32.10 Another Worked Example

Exhibit 32.2

	£
1 January 19–7, Stock of raw materials	800
31 December 19–7, Stock of raw materials	1,050
1 January 19–7, Work in progress	350
31 December 19–7, Work in progress	420
Year to 31 December 19–7:	
Wages: Direct	3,960
Indirect	2,550
Purchase of raw materials	8,700
Fuel and power	990
Direct expenses	140
Lubricants	300
Carriage inwards on raw materials	200
Rent of factory	720
Depreciation of factory plant and machinery	420
Internal transport expenses	180
Insurance of factory buildings and plant	150
General factory expenses	330

Manufacturing Account for the year ended 31 December 19–7

	£	£		£
Stock of raw materials 1.1.19–7		800	Production costs of goods completed c/d	18,320
Add Purchases		8,700		
Carriage inwards		200		
		9,700		
Less Stock of raw materials 31.12.19–7		1,050		
Cost of raw materials consumed		8,650		
Direct wages		3,960		
Direct expenses		140		
Prime cost		12,750		
Factory Overhead Expenses	£			
Fuel and power	990			
Indirect wages	2,550			
Lubricants	300			
Rent	720			
Depreciation of plant	420			
Internal transport expenses	180			
Insurance	150			
General factory expenses	330			
		5,640		
		18,390		
Add Work in progress 1.1.19–7		350		
		18,740		
Less Work in progress 31.12.19–7		420		
		18,320		18,320

The trading account is concerned with finished goods. If in the foregoing exhibit there had been £3,500 stock of finished goods at 1 January 19–7 and £4,400 at 31 December 19–7, and the sales of finished goods amounted to £25,000, then the trading account would appear:

Trading Account for the year 31 December 19–7

	£		£
Stock of finished goods 1.1.19–7	3,500	Sales	25,000
Add Production cost of goods completed b/d	18,320		
	21,820		
Less Stock of finished goods 31.12.19–7	4,400		
	17,420		
Gross profit c/d	7,580		
	25,000		25,000

The profit and loss account is then constructed in the normal way.

32.11 A Full Set of Final Accounts

A complete worked example is now given. Note that in the profit and loss account the expenses have been separated so as to show whether they are administration expenses, selling and distribution expenses, or financial charges.

The trial balance Exhibit 32.3 has been extracted from the books of C Chinley, Toy Manufacturer, as on 31 December 19–7:

Exhibit 32.3 shows both the manufacturing, trading and profit and loss account, also the balance sheet, drawn up from the trial balance details.

Exhibit 32.3

C Chinley
Trial balance as on 31 December 19–7

	Dr	*Cr*
	£	£
Stock of raw materials 1.1.19–7	2,100	
Stock of finished goods 1.1.19–7	3,890	
Work in progress 1.1.19–7	1,350	
Wages (direct £18,000; Factory indirect £14,500)	32,500	
Royalties	700	
Carriage inwards (on raw materials)	350	
Purchases of raw materials	37,000	
Productive machinery (cost £28,000)	23,000	
Accounting machinery (cost £2,000)	1,200	
General factory expenses	3,100	
Lighting	750	
Factory power	1,370	
Administrative salaries	4,400	
Salesmen's salaries	3,000	
Commission on sales	1,150	
Rent	1,200	
Insurance	420	
General administration expenses	1,340	
Bank charges	230	
Discounts allowed	480	
Carriage outwards	590	
Sales		100,000
Debtors and creditors	14,230	12,500
Bank	5,680	
Cash	150	
Drawings	2,000	
Capital as at 1.1.19–7		29,680
	142,180	142,180

Notes at 31.12.19–7:

1 Stock of raw materials £2,400, stock of finished goods £4,000, work in progress £1,500.

2 Lighting, and rent and insurance are to be apportioned: factory 5/6ths, administration 1/6th.

3 Depreciation on productive and accounting machinery at 10 per cent per annum on cost.

C Chinley

Manufacturing, Trading and Profit and Loss Account for the year ended 31 December 19–7

	£	£		£
Stock of raw materials			Production cost of goods	
1.1.19–7		2,100	completed c/d	79,345
Add Purchases		37,000		
Carriage inwards		350		
		39,450		
Less Stock of raw materials				
31.12.19–7		2,400		
Cost of raw materials				
consumed		37,050		
Direct labour		18,000		
Royalties		700		
Prime cost		55,750		
Factory Overhead Expenses				
General factory expenses	3,100			
Lighting 5/6ths	625			
Power	1,370			
Rent 5/6ths	1,000			
Insurance 5/6ths	350			
Depreciation of plant	2,800			
Indirect labour	14,500			
		23,745		
		79,495		
Add Work in progress 1.1.19–7		1,350		
		80,845		
Less Work in progress				
31.12.19–7		1,500		
		79,345		79,345
		£		£
Stock of finished goods 1.1.19–7		3,890	Sales	100,000
Add Production cost of goods				
completed		79,345		
		83,235		
Less Stock of finished goods				
31.12.19–7		4,000		
		79,235		
Gross profit c/d		20,765		
		100,000		100,000
Administration Expenses	£	£		£
Administrative salaries	4,400		Gross profit b/d	20,765
Rent 1/6th	200			
Insurance 1/6th	70			
General expenses	1,340			
Lighting 1/6th	125			
Depreciation of				
accounting machinery	200	6,335		

	£	£		£
Selling and Distribution Expenses				
Salesmen's salaries	3,000			
Commission on sales	1,150			
Carriage outwards	590	4,740		
Financial Charges				
Bank charges	230			
Discounts allowed	480	710		
Net profit		8,980		
		20,765		20,765

C Chinley

Balance Sheet as at 31 December 19–7

	£	£		£	£
Fixed Assets			*Capital*		
Productive machinery at cost	28,000		Balance as at 1.1.19–7	29,680	
Less Depreciation to date	7,800		*Add* Net profit	8,980	
				38,660	
		20,200	*Less* Drawings	2,000	
					36,660
Accounting machinery at cost	2,000		*Current Liabilities*		
Less Depreciation to date	1,000		Creditors		12,500
		1,000			
		21,200			
Current Assets					
Stock:					
raw materials	2,400				
finished goods	4,000				
Work in progress	1,500				
Debtors	14,230				
Bank	5,680				
Cash	150	27,960			
		49,160			49,160

New Terms

Manufacturing Account (p 288): An account in which production cost is calculated.

Direct Costs (p 287): Costs which can be traced to the item being manufactured.

Factory Overhead Costs (p 288): Costs in the factory for production, but not traced to the item being manufactured.

Work in Progress (p 291): Items not completed at the end of a period.

Exercises

32.1 From the following information prepare the manufacturing and trading accounts of E Smith for the year ended 31 March 19–7.

	£
Stocks at 1 April 19–6:	
Finished goods	6,724
Raw materials	2,400
Work in progress	955
Carriage on purchases (raw materials)	321
Sales	69,830
Purchases of raw materials	21,340
Manufacturing wages	13,280
Factory power	6,220
Other manufacturing expenses	1,430
Factory rent and rates	2,300
Stocks at 31 March 19–7:	
Raw materials	2,620
Work in progress	870
Finished goods	7,230

32.2X From the following details you are to draw up a manufacturing, trading and profit and loss account of P Lucas for the year ended 30 September 19–4

	30.9.19–3	30.9.19–4
	£	£
Stocks of raw materials, at cost	8,460	10,970
Work in progress	3,070	2,460
Finished goods stock	12,380	14,570

	£
For the year	
Raw materials purchased	38,720
Manufacturing wages	20,970
Factory expenses	12,650
Depreciation:	
Plant and machinery	7,560
Delivery vans	3,040
Office equipment	807
Factory power	6,120
Advertising	5,080
Office and administration expenses	5,910
Salesmen's salaries and expenses	6,420
Delivery van expenses	5,890
Sales	134,610
Carriage inwards	2,720

32.3 Prepare manufacturing, trading and profit and loss accounts from the following balances of T Shaw for the year ended 31 December 19–7.

Stocks at 1 January 19–7:

	£
Raw materials	18,450
Work in progress	23,600
Finished goods	17,470
Purchases: raw materials	64,300
Carriage on raw materials	1,605
Direct labour	65,810
Office salaries	16,920
Rent	2,700
Office lighting and heating	5,760
Depreciation: Works machinery	8,300
Office equipment	1,950
Sales	200,600
Factory fuel and power	5,920

Rent is to be apportioned: Factory 2/3rds: Office 1/3rd. Stocks at 31 December 19–7 were: Raw materials £20,210, Work in progress £17,390, Finished goods £21,485.

32.4 The financial year of Excelsior Pressings, a manufacturer of small household equipment, ends on 31 December. The following balances are in the books of the firm as at 31 December Year 8:

	£
Stocks as at 1 January Year 8:	
Raw materials	28,315
Work in progress (at factory cost)	6,200
Finished goods	33,700
Heating and Lighting	3,450
Wages of indirect manufacturing personnel	45,820
Rent and Rates	16,400
Purchases of raw materials	172,300
Manufacturing wages	194,500
Factory expenses and maintenance	3,700
Salaries	32,400
Sales of finished goods	652,500
Advertising	60,800
Administration expenses	27,500

The following information is also available:

1 Stocks have been valued as at 31 December Year 8 as follows:

	£
Raw materials	30,200
Work in progress (at factory cost)	7,100
Finished goods	37,500

2 In respect of Year 8, the following apportionments are to be made:

	Factory	*General Office*
Heating and Lighting	4/5	1/5
Rent and Rates	3/4	1/4
Salaries	1/3	2/3

3 Depreciation is to be allowed as follows:

Plant and Machinery	£20,000
Office equipment	£4,000

Required
Prepare the Manufacturing, Trading and Profit and Loss Accounts of Excelsior Pressings for the year ended 31 December Year 8.
Note: A Balance Sheet is *not* required.
(LCCI)

32.5X Gordon Dace, a manufacturer, extracted the following Trial Balance at the end of his financial year, 30 September Year 7:

	Dr £	*Cr* £
Freehold Premises (cost)	120,000	
Plant and Machinery (cost)	60,000	
Provision for Depreciation – Plant and Machinery		18,000
Office Fixtures and Fittings (cost)	8,000	
Provision for Depreciation – Fixtures and Fittings		1,600
Stocks at 1 October Year 6:		
Raw Materials	8,500	
Finished Goods	6,320	
Purchases of Raw Materials	56,000	
Bad Debts	170	
Debtors and Creditors	4,820	2,780
Office Wages and Salaries	30,140	
Rates [Factory £610, Office £220]	830	
Insurance [Factory £450, Office £150]	600	
Light/Heat and Power [Factory £1,210, Office £210]	1,420	
Miscellaneous Expenses	350	
Repairs and Renewals [Factory £1,070, Office £230]	1,300	
Telephone [Factory £150, Office £250]	400	
Drawings	15,000	
Balance at Bank	12,170	
Cash in Hand	100	
Manufacturing Wages	62,000	
Sales		186,600
Capital Account		179,140
	£388,120	£388,120

The following additional information is available:

1 Closing Stocks at 30 September Year 7 are as follows:

Raw Materials	£10,500
Finished Goods	£7,410

2 Provide for Depreciation as follows:

Plant and Machinery [Factory]	£6,000
Fixtures and Fittings [Office]	£800

Required

Prepare Gordon Dace's Manufacturing, Trading and Profit and Loss Accounts for the year ended 30 September Year 7, using such information as is required from the above Trial Balance.

Note: A Balance Sheet is **not** required.

(LCCI)

33 · Wages and Salaries

33.1 Frequency of Payments

Wages are usually taken to be earnings paid on a weekly basis. Salaries are earnings paid monthly.

Wages can be paid on a time basis or on a piece-work basis.

33.2 Time Basis

This means being paid a given amount per hour for every hour worked. Usually a flat rate is paid per hour up to a given number of hours (normal time). Above that number of hours any extra time worked is called overtime. Overtime hours are paid at a higher rate than normal hours. The higher rates are usually stated as 'time and a quarter', 'time and a half', or 'double time'.

If normal time is £4 per hour, then

time and a quarter is $£4 \times 1\frac{1}{4} = £5$
time and a half is $£4 \times 1\frac{1}{2} = £6$
double time is $£4 \times 2 = £8$

We can look at the earnings of two workers. They are paid £4 per hour for a forty-hour week, time and a quarter for the next 10 hours, and time and a half for any hours in excess of that.

Chapel worked 48 hours:

	£
40 hours × £4 (normal time) =	160
8 hours × £5 (time and a quarter) =	40
Gross wages	200

Lake worked 55 hours:

	£
40 hours × £4 (normal time) =	160
10 hours × £5 (time and a quarter) =	50
5 hours × £6 (time and a half) =	30
Gross wages	240

33.3 Piece-work

- Payment is related to the work performed.
- The employers and employees agree a time in which one unit of work could be performed.
- An amount payable for each unit of work performed is agreed.

This means that if the agreed rate is £1 per unit, the payments for the week will be as follows for two employees:

- Hook, 96 units = 96 × £1 = £96 wages
- Long, 85 units = 85 × £1 = £85 wages

33.4 Deductions from Gross Wages

Income Tax

In the UK the wages and salaries of all employees are liable to have Income Tax deducted from them. This does not mean that everyone will pay Income Tax, but that if Income Tax is found to be payable then the employer will deduct the tax from the employee's wages or salary. The government department in charge of the collection of income tax is the Inland Revenue.

Each person in the UK is allowed to subtract various amounts from the earnings to see if he/she is liable to pay Income Tax. The amounts given for each person depend upon his or her personal circumstances. An extra amount can be deducted by a man who is married, as compared to a single man.

Further amounts can be deducted for things such as paying interest on money borrowed to buy a house, and so on. The amounts that can be deducted from wages or salaries, before tax is calculated, are known as 'reliefs'. Once these have been deducted any balance will have to suffer income tax. It is:

	£
Gross Pay	xxx
less reliefs	xxx
Pay which is taxable	xxx

Two men may, therefore, earn the same wages, but if one of them gets more reliefs than the other then he will have less taxable pay, and will pay less income tax than the other man.

Each year in his budget, the Chancellor of the Exchequer announces what the rates of income tax are going to be for the following year, and also how much is to be deducted in respect of each relief. Because of the annual changes the rates of income tax now shown are for illustration only, they are *not* the actual rates of income tax at the time you are reading this book.

For instance, assume that the rates of Income Tax are (on the amount actually exceeding the reliefs for each person):

On the first £1,000	Income Tax at 20 per cent
On the next £5,000	Income Tax at 30 per cent
On the remainder	Income Tax at 50 per cent

The Income Tax payable by each of four persons can now be looked at.
1 Miss Jones earns £1,500 per annum. Her personal reliefs amount to £1,700. Income Tax payable = Nil.
2 Mr Bland earns £4,000 per annum. His personal reliefs amount to £3,400. He therefore has £600 of his earnings on which he will have to pay Income Tax. As the rate on the first £1,000 taxable is 20 per cent, then he will pay £600 × 20 per cent = £120.
3 Mrs Hugo earns £6,500 per annum. She has personal reliefs amounting to £2,700. She will, therefore, pay Income Tax on the excess of £3,800. This will amount to:

		£
On the first £1,000 at 20 per cent	=	200
On the remaining £2,800 at 30 per cent	=	840
Total Income Tax for the year		£1,040

4 Mr Pleasance has a salary of £10,000 per annum. His personal reliefs amount to £3,560. He will therefore pay Income Tax on the excess of £6,440. This will amount to:

		£
On the first £1,000 at 20 per cent	=	200
On the next £5,000 at 30 per cent	=	1,500
On the next £440 at 50 per cent	=	220
Total Income Tax for the year		£1,920

The actual deduction of the Income Tax from the earnings of the employee is made by the employer. The tax is commonly called PAYE tax, which represents the initial letters for Pay As You Earn.

For every employee the Inland Revenue sends the employer a Notice of Coding and on this there is shown a 'code number'. The code number is based on the total of 'reliefs' available for each employee. The higher the reliefs, the higher the code number.

So far the amount of tax payable by everyone has been looked at on an annual basis. However, PAYE means just that, it has to be deducted on every pay date, be it weekly or monthly. To do this:

- The Inland Revenue sends a set of tax tables to each employer, showing taxes on both weekly and monthly bases.
- The employer then uses these tables to calculate the amount of PAYE income tax to be deducted from the wages or salary to be paid.
- The actual calculation is done by comparing both the amount of gross pay and the code number with the tax tables, which then shows how much PAYE tax is to be deducted.

Let us assume that in the cases of employees **1** to **4** already examined that **1** Miss Jones and **3** Mrs Hugo are paid weekly, and that **2** Mr Bland and **4** Mr Pleasance are paid monthly. If each payment to them during the year was of equal amounts, then we can calculate the amount of PAYE deducted from payment of earnings.

PAYE deducted on weekly basis:
1 Miss Jones. Tax for year = nil. Tax each week = nil.
3 Mrs Hugo. Tax for year = £1,040. Tax each week £1,040 ÷ 52 = £20.

PAYE deducted on monthly basis:
2 Mr Bland. Tax for year = £120. Tax each month £120 ÷ 12 = £10.
4 Mr Pleasance. Tax for year £1,920. Tax each month £1,920 ÷ 12 = £160.

National Insurance

In the UK employees are also liable to pay National Insurance contributions. The deduction of these is carried out by the employer at the same time as the PAYE Income Tax deductions are made.

The payment of such National Insurance contributions is to ensure that the payer will be able to claim benefits from the State, if and when he is in a position to claim, e.g. retirement and unemployment benefits.

Superannuation Contributions

Many firms have superannuation schemes. These are schemes whereby the employee will receive a pension on retiring from the firm, plus, very often, a lump sum payment in cash. They also usually include benefits which will be paid to an employee's wife or husband if the employee dies before reaching retirement age.

Other Deductions

Quite frequently deductions may be made for such items as subscriptions to the firm's social club, charitable donations, union subscriptions and so on.

Calculation of Net Wages/Salary Payable

Two illustrations of the calculation of the net pay to be made to various employees can now be looked at. The percentages used for National Insurance and superannuation are for illustration purposes only.

			£
(A) G Jarvis	Gross earnings for the week ended 8 May 19–4		100
	Income tax: found by consulting tax tables and employee's code number		12
	National Insurance 5%		

G Jarvis: Payslip week ended 8 May 19–4

	£	£
Gross pay for the week		100
Less Income tax	12	
" National Insurance	5	17
Net pay		83

		£
(B) H Reddish:	Gross earnings for the month of May 19–4	800
	Income tax (from tax tables)	150
	Superannuation: 6% of gross pay	
	National Insurance: 5% of gross pay	

H Reddish: Payslip month ended 31 May 19–4

	£	£
Gross pay for the month		800
Less Income tax	150	
" Superannuation	48	
" National Insurance	40	238
Net pay		562

Reference Number

In a large business each employee will be given a reference number, for easy identification.

Making Up Pay Packets

If there are more than one or two employees you should ensure that the notes and coins obtained from the bank will enable you to fill the wage packets with the correct amount. Quite obviously there will be local agreements with employees as to the number of different types of notes and coins to be put in each packet. An employee earning £100.01 in a week would probably object if the wages were given to him by five £20 notes plus a 1p coin. He would like to have his cash wages given to him so that he could easily use the cash once he had got it. Notes of larger amounts can be difficult to change. Imagine the man with only £20 notes and 1p in change taking a bus home and trying to pay the conductor with a £20 note!

Let us suppose that the following agreement has been reached:

1 £20 notes are not to be used, but £10 notes are acceptable;

2 each worker to be given a minimum of five £1 coins.

There are five employees earning the following:

(a) £85.08;
(b) £94.16;
(c) £109.66;
(d) £120.88;
(e) £94.27.

To carry out the calculation we should make a list of the note and coin values across the top, then list each employee down the side. After working out what is needed for each single employee, we can then add up the quantities required for all the workers. This is now shown:

	£10	*£5*	*£1*	*50p*	*10p*	*5p*	*2p*	*1p*	
(a)	8		5			1	1	1	(i.e. £85.08)
(b)	8	1	9		1	1		1	
(c)	10		9	1	1	1		1	
(d)	11	1	5	1	3	1	1	1	
(e)	8	1	9		2	1	1		
	45	3	37	2	7	5	3	4	

Now let us check that we have got the correct answer.

	Total wages required per employee	*Notes and coins requested*		
(a)	85.08	45 × £10	=	450.00
(b)	94.16	3 × £5	=	15.00
(c)	109.66	37 × £1	=	37.00
(d)	120.88	2 × 50p	=	1.00
(e)	94.27	7 × 10p	=	0.70
	£504.05	5 × 5p	=	0.25
		3 × 2p	=	0.06
		4 × 1p	=	0.04
				£504.05

We can also see that each employee will be given at least five £1 coins, as per agreement.

Exercises

33.1 H Smith is employed by a firm of carpenters at a rate of £1.50 per hour. During the week to 18 May 19–5 he worked his basic week of 40 hours. The income tax due on his wages was £8, and he is also liable to pay National Insurance contributions of 5 per cent. Calculate his net wages.

33.2 M Marchand works as an electrician with a basic rate of pay of £4.40 per hour for a 40 hour week, overtime is paid at a rate of $1\frac{1}{2}$ times the basic.

During the week ending 28 April 1990 M Marchand worked 50 hours. He pays National Insurance at 10% of the gross pay, pensions at 8% of the basic pay and income tax at 30% on all earnings after deducting £30 tax free pay. £2 is also paid in union contributions.

You are required to:
(a) calculate M Marchand's gross pay.
(b) calculate each of the deductions.
(c) show the amount M Marchand will take home.
(*Note:* Marks will be awarded if presented in the form of a pay slip.)
(RSA)

33.3 The following details relate to the earnings of two employees during the week ended 25 May 19–0.

Employee	J Brown	A White
Piecework rate per unit	120p	130p
Units produced	200	140
Hours worked	40	44
Hourly rate of pay	375p	410p

A 40 hour week is in operation and overtime is paid at time and a quarter.
If an employee's piecework earnings fall below his earnings at the hourly rate then the hourly rate earnings are paid.

Both employees have the following deductions:

Company Pension Scheme	2% of gross earnings
National Insurance	10% of gross earnings
PAYE	25% of all earnings in excess of £75 per week

You are required to calculate:
The gross and net wage of each employee showing clearly the amount of each deduction.
(RSA)

33.4 The wages of the five employees for the first week are: (1) £112.86; (2) £97.19; (3) £128.47; (4) £134.75; (5) £84.77. Bearing in mind that £20 notes are not to be used, and that each employee will have a minimum of five £1 coins in his wage packet, you are required to work out the quantities of the various coins and notes needed when paying out the wages.

33.5 As question 33.4 for the week following. This time the wages are: (1) £99.68; (2) £119.43; (3) £122.55; (4) £94.77; (5) £104.35.

33.6 As question 33.4 for the third week. The wages are: (1) £96.99; (2) £133.46; (3) £128.86; (4) £112.36; (5) £101.26.

33.7X C Ponsford manages a small firm employing four workers. During the week ending 31 December 19–9 each worker earned a take home pay as follows:

L Jennett	£160.56
J Smith	£90.75
J Grala	£100.20
G Thomas	£136.40

C Ponsford pays wages at the end of each week in cash using notes and coins of £10, £5, £1, 50p, 20p, 10p, 5p, 2p and 1p. C Ponsford insists that each worker receives at least one £1 coin.

You are required to:
(a) rule up and complete a note and coin analysis in table form using the least number of notes and coins permissible;
(b) reconcile the value of the total notes and coins with the total pay bill.
(RSA)

33.8X The wages to be paid to five employees is

	£
G Billison	74.63
P Farraday	91.17
H Oliver	82.53
R Watt	78.76
T Yoeman	87.80

Calculate the number of each denomination of note and coin required. £10 is the highest denomination of note used and each employee must receive the lowest number of coins or notes possible.
(RSA)

33.9X You are the general clerk in a small manufacturing business which employs four weekly paid assembly line workers.

The net wages for the week ending Saturday 27 October 19–4, which will be paid on Friday, 2 November 19–4 are as follows:

	£
C Ford	89.25
P Woodbine	76.90
J Swan	65.47
A Gill	101.22

You are required to:
(a) Rule up a note-coin analysis.
(b) Calculate the number and denominations of notes and coins required to pay the four workers.

The owner of the business will not pay with notes greater than £5 and insists that at least one £1 piece should be present in every pay packet. The least number of coins/notes should be used.
(RSA)

33.10X A firm employs John Jones at a standard rate of £1.10 per hour. Time and a half is paid for all hours worked in excess of 40. All employees pay a superannuation contribution of five per cent of all wages earned in a normal working week (40 hours). Time worked in excess of 40 hours is not subject to superannuation. National Insurance contributions are five per cent of gross wages. In the week ending 7 June John Jones has worked 45 hours. He pays income tax at 30 per cent on all he earns over £35 per week after superannuation has been deducted.

You are required to:
(a) calculate his gross wages.
(b) show the value of each deduction and calculate his net wages.
(RSA)

33.11X Ace Garden Services employs John Brooke and Philip Daly to lay turves on new housing estates. Each is paid £5 for every 100 turves laid and if any week a worker lays more than 2,000 turves he receives a bonus of 50% for laying the extra turves, in addition to the normal rate for all turves laid.

In the week ended 15 March 19–5 Brooke laid 2,200 turves and Daly laid 2,600 turves. Income tax of £18 is due from Brooke, and £32 from Daly. Five per cent of the gross earnings of each must be deducted for Social Security contributions. Each makes a voluntary contribution of £2 weekly to the Lawn Layers Union.

You are required to calculate the net pay of each employee and set out their pay slips for the week ended 15 March 19–5.

(RSA)

33.12X The information below appeared on the wages record of Miss E Wren for the week ending 5 March 19–2.

Name of employee: Miss E Wren — Grade: Machinist

Works No 3546

Piecework rates: Type A units £1 per 100
Type B units £1 per 150

Week ending: 5 March 19–2

	No of units produced	Type
Monday	1,600	A
Tuesday	1,400	A
Wednesday	1,800	B
Thursday	1,500	B
Friday	1,300	A

No of times late: Nil

Employees work 40 hours per week and an additional bonus of £3 per week is paid to those who commence work on time every day.

You are required to:

(a) calculate Miss Wren's total piecework earnings showing separately the amount earned for each type of unit produced;

(b) give the payroll entry for Miss Wren for the week ending 5 March 19–2 taking into account the additional information below:

Contribution to pension fund is at the rate of 5% of the employee's gross earnings

PAYE £7 — National Insurance £5.50

Cumulative deductions made up to the previous pay day were:

Income tax £359 — National Insurance £234.50

Pension fund £280

(RSA)

34 · The Valuation of Stock

34.1 Different Valuations of Stock

Most people would think that there can be only one figure for the valuation of stock. This is not true. We will examine in this chapter how we can calculate different figures for stock.

Assume that a firm has just completed its first financial year and is about to value stock at cost price. It has dealt in only one type of goods. A record of the transactions is now shown in Exhibit 34.1.

Exhibit 34.1

Bought			Sold		
19–5		£	19–5		£
January	10 at £30 each	300	May	8 for £50 each	£400
April	10 at £34 each	340	November	24 for £60 each	1,440
October	20 at £40 each	800			
	40	1,440		32	1,840

Still in stock at 31 December, 8 units.

The total figure of purchases is £1,440 and that of sales is £1,840. The trading account for the first year of trading can now be completed if the closing stock is brought into the calculations.

But what value do we put on each of the 8 units left in stock at the end of the year? If all of the units bought during the year had cost £30 each, then the closing stock would be $8 \times £30 = £240$. However, we have bought goods at different prices. This means that the valuation depends on which goods are taken for this calculation, the units at £30, or at £34, or at £40.

Many firms do not know exactly whether they have sold all the oldest units before they sell the newer units. For instance, a firm selling spanners may not know if the oldest spanners had been sold before the newest spanners.

The stock valuation will therefore be based on an accounting custom, and not on the facts of exactly which units were still in stock at the year end. The three main methods of doing this are now shown in sections 34.2, 34.3 and 34.4.

34.2 First In, First Out Method

This is usually known as **FIFO**, the first letters of each word.

This method says that the first goods to be received are the first to be issued.

Using the figures in Exhibit 34.1 we can now calculate the closing figure of stock as follows:

	Received	Issued	Stock after each transaction		
19–5				£	£
January	10 at £30 each		10 at £30 each		300
April	10 at £34 each		10 at £30 each	300	
			10 at £34 each	340	640
May		8 at £30 each	2 at £30 each	60	
			10 at £34 each	340	400
October	20 at £40 each		2 at £30 each	60	
			10 at £34 each	340	
			20 at £40 each	800	1,200
November		2 at £30 each			
		10 at £34 each			
		12 at £40 each			
		24	8 at £40 each		320

The closing stock at 31 December 19–5 is therefore valued at £320.

34.3 Last In, First Out Method

This is usually known as **LIFO**. As each issue of goods are made they are said to be from the last lot of goods received before that date. Where there is not enought left of the last lot of goods, then the balance of goods needed is said to come from the previous lot still unsold.

From the information shown in Exhibit 34.1 the calculation can now be shown.

	Received	Issued	Stock after each transaction		
19–5				£	£
January	10 at £30 each		10 at £30 each		300
April	10 at £34 each		10 at £30 each	300	
			10 at £34 each	340	640
May		8 at £34 each	10 at £30 each	300	
			2 at £34 each	68	368
October	20 at £40 each		10 at £30 each	300	
			2 at £34 each	68	
			20 at £40 each	800	1,168
November		20 at £40 each			
		2 at £34 each			
		2 at £30 each	8 at £30 each		240
		24			

The closing stock at 31 December 19–5 is, therefore, valued at £240.

34.4 Average Cost Method (AVCO)

Using the **AVCO** method, with each receipt of goods the average cost for each item of stock is recalculated. Further issues of goods are then at that figure, until another receipt of goods means that another recalculation is needed.

From the information is Exhibit 34.1 the calculation can be shown.

Received		Issued	Average cost per unit of stock held	Number of units in stock	Total value of stock
			£		£
January	10 at £30		30	10	300
April	10 at £34		32*	20	640
May		8 at £32	32	12	384
October	20 at £40		37*	32	1,184
November		24 at £37	37	8	296

The closing stock at 31 December 19–5 is therefore valued at £296.

* In April, this is calculated as follows: stock 10 × £30 = £300 + stock received (10 × £34) £340 = total £640. 20 units in stock, so the average is £640 ÷ 20 = £32. In October this is calculated as follows: stock 12 × £32 = £384 + stock received (20 × £40) £800 = £1,184. 32 units in stock, so the average is £1,184 ÷ 32 = £37.

34.5 Stock Valuation and the Calculation of Profits

Using the figures from Exhibit 34.1, with stock valuations shown by the three methods of FIFO, LIFO, and AVCO, the trading accounts would appear:

Trading Account for the year ended 31 December 19–5

	FIFO	*LIFO*	*AVCO*		*FIFO*	*LIFO*	*AVCO*
	£	£	£		£	£	£
Purchases	1,440	1,440	1,440	Sales	1,840	1,840	1,840
less Closing stock	320	240	296				
Cost of goods sold	1,120	1,200	1,144				
Gross profit	720	640	696				
	1,840	1,840	1,840		1,840	1,840	1,840

As you can see, different methods of stock valuation will mean that different profits are shown.

The choice of method depends on many factors. As the choice can involve many complicated economic factors it is not dealt with here. Students taking professional examinations later in their lives will deal with such matters.

34.6 Reduction to Net Realisable Value

The **net realisable value** of stock is calculated as follows:

Saleable value – expenses needed before completion of sale = Net realisable value

If saleable value is £300 and expenses needed would be £20, the net realisable value would be £280. Now if the net realisable value of stock is lower than the valuation at cost, the figure to be taken for the final accounts will be the net realisable value. If stock at cost valuation is £500 and net realisable value is £400, then the figure of £400 will be used in the trading account and the balance sheet.

34.7 Stock Groups and Valuation

If there is only one sort of goods in stock, calculating the lower of cost or net realisable value is easy. If we have several or many types of goods in stock we can use one of two ways of making the calculation.

From the information given in Exhibit 34.2 we will calculate the stock in two different ways.

Exhibit 34.2

Stock at 31 December 19–8			
Article	*Different categories*	*Cost*	*Net realisable value*
		£	£
1	A	100	80
2	A	120	150
3	A	300	400
4	B	180	170
5	B	150	130
6	B	260	210
7	C	410	540
8	C	360	410
9	C	420	310
		2,300	2,400

Articles 1, 2 and 3 are televisions. Articles 4, 5 and 6 are radios. Articles 7, 8 and 9 are videos.

The Category Method

The same sorts of items are put together in categories. Thus articles 1, 2 and 3 are televisions and shown as category A. Articles 4, 5 and 6 are radios and shown as category B. Articles 7, 8 and 9 are videos and shown as category C.

A calculation showing a comparison of cost valuation and net realisable value for each category is now shown.

Category	*Cost*	*Net Realisable Value*
A	£100 + £120 + £300 = £520	£80 + £150 + £400 = £630
B	£180 + £150 + £260 = £590	£170 + £130 + £210 = £510
C	£410 + £360 + £420 = £1,190	£540 + £410 + £310 = £1,260

The lower of cost and net realisable value is, therefore:

		£
Category A: lower of £520 or £630	=	520
Category B: lower of £590 or £510	=	510
Category C: lower of £1,190 or £1,260	=	1,190
Stock is valued for final accounts at		2,220

Article Method

By this method, the lower of cost or net realisable value for each article is compared and the lowest figure taken. From Exhibit 34.2 this gives us the following valuation:

Articles	**Valuation**
	£
1	80
2	120
3	300
4	170
5	130
6	210
7	410
8	360
9	310
	£2,090

34.8 Goods on Sale or Return

Goods Received on Sale or Return

Sometimes we may receive goods for one of our suppliers on a **sale or return** basis. What this means is that we do not have to pay for the goods until we sell them. If we do not sell them we have to return them to our supplier.

This means that the goods do not belong to us. If we have some goods on sale or return at the stocktaking date they should not be included in our stock valuation.

Goods Sent to Our Customers on Sale or Return

We may send goods on a sale or return basis to our customers. The stock will belong to us until it is sold. At our stocktaking date any goods held by our customers on sale or return should be included in our stock valuation.

34.9 Stocktaking and the Balance Sheet Date

Students often think that all the counting and valuing of stock is done on the last day of the accounting period. This might be true in a small business, but it is often impossible in larger businesses. There may be too many items of stock to do it so quickly.

This means that stocktaking may take place over a period of days. To get the figure of the stock valuation as on the last day of the accounting period, we will have to make adjustments. Exhibit 34.3 gives an example of such calculations.

Exhibit 34.3

Lee Ltd has a financial year which ends on 31 December 19–7. The stocktaking is not in fact done until 8 January 19–8. When the items in stock on that date are priced out, it is found that the stock value amounted to £28,850. The following information is available about transactions between 31 December 19–7 and 8 January 19–8:

1 Purchases since 31 December 19–7 amounted to £2,370 at cost.
2 Returns inwards since 31 December 19–7 were £350 at selling price.
3 Sales since 31 December 19–7 amounted to £3,800 at selling price.
4 The selling price is always cost price + 25 per cent.

Lee Ltd
Computation of stock as on 31 December 19–7

			£
Stock (at cost)			28,850
Add Items which were in stock on 31 December 19–7 (at cost)			
		£	
Sales		3,800	
Less Profit content (20 per cent of selling price)*		760	3,040
			31,890
Less Items which were not in stock on 31 December 19–7 (at cost)			
	£	£	
Returns inwards	350		
Less Profit content (20 per cent of selling price)*	70	280	
Purchases (at cost)		2,370	2,650
Stock in hand as on 31 December 19–7			29,240

* Stock at cost (or net realisable value), and not at selling price. As this calculation has a sales figure in it which includes profit, we must deduct the profit part to get to the cost price. This is true also for returns inwards.

34.10 Stock Records: Quantities Only

Quite often a firm will keep records of quantities only, to keep a check as to whether items are being stolen, broken, wasted or lost.

Exhibit 34.4 shows the stock quantity records for two items of stock, components FG and JK.

Exhibit 34.4

Component FG

19–6			*No of items*
Jan	1	Stock b/fwd	86
"	2	Received (invoice 5543)	20
"	4	Issue P67	16
"	6	Issue P68	29
"	10	Issue P132	19
"	21	Received (invoice 5874)	70
"	25	Issue P69	33
"	31	Issue P243	18

Component JK

19–6			*No of items*
Jan	1	Stock b/fwd	28
"	2	Received (invoice 5549)	300
"	3	Issue R323	44
"	5	Issue R324	23
"	9	Issue R129	107
"	11	Issue R325	79
"	13	Return in RA229	18
"	19	Received (invoice 5799)	200
"	22	Issue R354	96
"	29	Issue R130	64
"	31	Return in RA230	5

From these stock records we should be able to work out exactly how many of component FG and of component JK are in store on 31 January 19–6. We also do a physical stockcheck (i.e. we actually look at and count the items in the store) and find that we have 61 of FG and 134 of JK on that date.

We can now draft up a stock record card for each of these components. As each item is issued or received we alter the balance of stock in hand.

Component FG

Date		*Ref*	*In*	*Out*	*Balance*
19–6					
Jan	1	Opening balance			86
"	2	5543	20		106
"	4	P67		16	90
"	6	P68		29	61
"	10	P132		19	42
"	21	5874	70		112
"	25	P69		33	79
"	31	P243		18	61

With component FG the actual stock equals the stock per the stock card, verifying that there has been no stock losses.

With component JK we will see that the stock card records will disclose a stock loss of four items.

Component JK					
Date		*Ref*	*In*	*Out*	*Balance*
19–6					
Jan	1	Opening balance			28
"	2	5549	300		328
"	3	R323		44	284
"	5	R324		23	261
"	9	R129		107	154
"	11	R325		79	75
"	13	RA229	18		93
"	19	5799	200		293
"	22	R354		96	197
"	29	R130		64	133
"	31	RA230	5		138
"	31	Stock loss		4	134

The stock loss for four items of component JK will now have to be investigated. There may be a satisfactory explanation, or it might even be the case of theft with the police being called in to investigate. It is up to the individual firm to decide what course of action is to be taken, but the stock loss should be looked into to establish the reasons for the deficiency.

New Terms

FIFO (p 310): A method by which the first goods to be received are said to be the first to be sold.

LIFO (p 311): A method by which the goods sold are said to have come from the last lot of goods to be received.

AVCO (p 312): A method by which the goods used are priced out at average cost.

Net Realisable Value (p 313): The value of goods calculated as the selling price less expenses before sale.

Sale or Return (p 314): Goods that do not belong to the person holding them.

Exercises

34.1 From the following figures you are to calculate the figures for stock valuation, using *(a)* the category method, and *(b)* the article method.

Stock at 31 December 19–7			
Article	*Categories*	*Cost*	*Net Realisable Value*
		£	£
1	A	280	330
2	A	440	370
3	A	390	480
4	B	170	250
5	B	210	310
6	C	400	350
7	C	860	600
8	D	570	660
9	D	770	990

34.2X You are given the information as shown. From it you are to calculate the figures of stock valuation. Show the possible figures using *(a)* the category method, and *(b)* the article method.

Stock at 31 March 19–9			
Article	*Categories*	*Cost*	*Net Realisable Value*
		£	£
1	A	600	900
2	A	550	730
3	B	990	890
4	B	220	190
5	B	450	510
6	B	380	440
7	C	490	430
8	C	410	410
9	C	330	280

34.3 *(a)* From the following figures calculate the closing stock-in-trade that would be shown using (i) FIFO, (ii) LIFO, (iii) AVCO methods.

19–7	**Bought**	**Sold**	
January	24 at £10 each	June	30 at £16 each
April	16 at £12.50 each	November	34 at £18 each
October	30 at £13 each		

(b) Draw up trading accounts for 19–7 using each of the three methods for stock valuation.

34.4X *(a)* From the following figures calculate the closing stock-in-trade that would be shown using (i) FIFO, (ii) LIFO, (iii) AVCO methods

19–9	**Bought**	**Sold**	
January	30 at £12 each	July	24 at £15.50 each
May	30 at £14 each	November	16 at £18 each

(b) Draw up trading accounts for 19–9 using each of the three methods for stock valuation.

34.5 Edward Greenwood is a sole trader whose year end is 31 January each year. Owing to pressure of business, he is unable to value his stock in trade at the close of business on 31 January 19–4 but he does so on 7 February 19–4 when the value, *at cost price*, is calculated at £2,830.

For the period 1–7 February his purchases were £296, of which goods costing £54 were in transit at the time of stocktaking.

Sales for the period 1–7 February amounted to £460, all of which had left the warehouse at the time of stocktaking. Greenwood's gross profit is 20% of sales.

Also during the period 1–7 February, Greenwood took goods costing £38 for his personal use.

Included in the valuation figure of £2,830 given above were goods which cost £120, but which had a *market price* of £97 only at the date of the year end, i.e. 31 January 19–4.

Required
Calculate the figure which should be shown as 'Stock at 31 January 19–4' in Greenwood's Trading Account for the year ended 31 January 19–4.
Note: Calculations must be shown.
(RSA)

34.6 Chung Ltd make up their accounts to 31 December each year. The valuation of the stock, at cost, as at 31 December 19–8 was not attempted until 11 January 19–9 when a physical stock check revealed a total per stock sheets of £198,444 at cost.

Further investigation revealed that:

(a) All goods are sold at a uniform profit of 50 per cent on cost.
(b) Sales for the period 1 January 19–9 to 11 January 19–9, and for which goods had been despatched, amounted to £6,960.
(c) One stock sheet was undercast by £50 and another one overcast by £1,000.
(d) An extension of 660 articles at £0.80 each was shown as £560.
(e) The stock figure includes goods held on approval £3,000 and for which no invoices had been received, nor were the goods to be kept by Chung Ltd.
(f) A total at the bottom of one page, £105,680, had been carried forward to the next page as £106,850.

Calculate the figure of stock for the final accounts as at 31 December 19–8.

34.7 The accounting year of Ceramics Ltd ended on 30 June each year. Owing to holidays it was impossible to carry out stocktaking until 5 July 19–6. When this was done the total stock as per the stock sheets was £15,705 valued at cost. The normal rate of gross profit earned was $33\frac{1}{3}$% of selling price.

Adjustments were necessary to the stock sheet valuation to arrive at the stock figure for 30 June 19–6. While these adjustments were being made, certain errors came to light and the following matters had to be considered:

(a) A parcel of goods purchased in January at an enhanced price of £500 to complete a rush selling order was still in stock and the market price was now £390.
(b) An item valued at cost £500 was a standby generator for use if and when the electricity supply failed. It had been included on the stock sheets.
(c) Goods to the value of £900 had been received from suppliers in the period 1 to 4 July 19–6. These goods had been invoiced dated 30 June 19–6 and the amount included in creditors.
(d) Goods selling price £630 had been sent to Sang Ltd on approval. They had not been included in stock nor had any entries been made in the books.
(e) Sales for the period 1 to 4 July 19–6 and invoiced dated July 19–6 totalled £993.

(f) Sales credit notes issued before 30 June 19–6 totalling £150 had been omitted from the books in error.

(g) In the stocktaking sheets a sub-total of £240 had been wrongly carried forward as £420 and a sheet had been overcast by £100.

(h) Ceramics Ltd had agreed to take back from Wood goods invoiced at £540 but these were still in transit at 30 June 19–6 and no credit note had been issued.

(i) Goods valued at £600 cost were obsolete and it would cost £350 to convert them to 'good' stock. There would be no increase in the selling price obtainable.

Required:

Prepare a statement item by item to show the amount at which the stock should be shown in the accounts as at 30 June 19–6. State which, if any, of the items *(a)* to *(i)* above do not affect the stock.

(LCCI)

34.8 The following are four different business situations:

Business 1

R Simpson, a retail shopkeeper, determines his unsold stock at 31 December Year 4 to be £15,600, valued at normal selling prices. His normal selling prices are determined by adding 20% to the purchase cost of the goods.

Business 2

R Bendall's Manufacturing and Trading Account for the year ended 31 December Year 4 (in summarised form) showed:

	£
Opening stock raw materials	12,200
Raw material purchases	136,000
	148,200
Closing stock raw materials	14,700
	133,500
Direct Wages	205,700
	339,200
Production overhead	193,670
	532,870
Opening stock of work in progress	12,100
	544,970
Closing stock of work in progress	17,390
	527,580
Opening stock finished goods	23,262
	550,842
Closing stock finished goods	28,910
Cost of goods sold	521,932
Sales	620,000
Gross Profit	98,068

Business 3

J Gilbert took physical stock on 26 December Year 4 and this, valued at cost, amounted to £24,280. In the period 26 December to 31 December:

(a) Purchases delivered, at cost, amounted to £870.

(b) Sales, at a normal profit margin of 25% on cost, amounted to £500.

Business 4
Artimus Ltd has a stock of raw material X at 31 December Year 4 which had cost £3,730. It has a replacement price of £4,395. However, material X is no longer used by Artimus Ltd and it will have to be sold as scrap for £2,780.

Required
Calculate the stock valuation which should appear on the Balance Sheet for each of the businesses as at 31 December Year 4.
Note: All workings should be shown.
(LCCI)

34.9 Rule up a card suitable for the recording of the quantity of an item in stock.
The card should show receipts, issues, and balance. The name of suppliers should be shown against receipts, and the requisition number against issues.

Item number 24

1 May 19–9 Balance in stock		500
Receipts		
2 May 19–9 Starlight Co Ltd		300
8 May 19–9 Moonbeam & Sons		200
24 May 19–9 Starlight Co Ltd		350
Issues		
8 May 19–9 Requisition number	740	173
10 May 19–9	810	294
14 May 19–9	976	104
28 May 19–9	981	206

(RSA)

34.10 D Brown owns a petrol filling station. Petrol is sold at cost plus 25 per cent. The petrol pumps automatically record by meter the number of gallons sold. Stock of 4-star petrol on 1 January was 8,000 gallons valued at 60 pence per gallon.
During the month of January 19–9 Brown took delivery of 4-star petrol as follows:

19–9
Jan 8 6,000 gallons costing 60 pence per gallon
" 16 8,000 gallons costing 62 pence per gallon
" 24 12,000 gallons costing 64 pence per gallon

Meter readings taken from the 4-star petrol pump were:

19–9
Jan 1 35,609
" 31 56,609

You are required to calculate:
(a) The number of gallons of 4-star petrol in stock on 31 January 19–9.
(b) The value of that stock of petrol on 31 January 19–9.
(c) The number of gallons of 4-star petrol sold during January 19–9.
(d) The revenue from sales of 4-star petrol during January 19–9.
(e) The gross profit on sales of 4-star petrol for January 19–9.
Show your workings.
Ignore VAT.
(RSA)

34.11X Y Uck, a builders' merchant, has no reliable method of recording his stock receipts and issues. At the present time he has no means of obtaining a valuation for his stock-in-trade (without undertaking a lengthy and costly stocktaking).

Y Uck has produced the following data from the month ended 30 September 19–9.

Marble chippings stock	1 Sept 19–9	2 tonnes
Purchased from J Brown	4 "	8 "
Sold to T Williams	10 "	6 "
Purchased from B Green	14 "	9 "
Sold to W Thomas	20 "	2 "
Sold to B Dunstan	25 "	7 "

All stock and purchases are priced at £50 per tonne. All issues of stock are priced at £65 per tonne.

You are required to show:

Y Uck's trading account for the month ended 30 September 19–9.

(RSA)

35 · Sales and Purchases Analysis Books

35.1 Introduction

In many cases, just to know the total of the credit sales or of the credit purchases is not enough. We may wish to know more than that. We can look at some of the reasons why we would want more information.

35.2 Departmental Use

Our firm may have various departments. We may want to know how much of our sales and purchases were for each department. There would be a total column, in which the totals of each invoice would be entered. Then there would be extra columns, one for each department. Exhibit 35.1 is an example. Such a book could be called either an analysis book or a columnar book.

Exhibit 35.1

Columnar Sales Day Book

Date	*Name of Firm*	*Total*	*Sports Dept*	*Household Dept*	*Electrical Dept*
19–5		£	£	£	£
May 1	N Coward	190		190	
" 5	L Olivier	200	200		
" 8	R Colman & Co	307	102		205
" 16	A Smith	480			480
" 27	H Marshall	222	110	45	67
" 31	W Pratt	1,800		800	1,000
		3,199	412	1,035	1,752

In this exhibit the sales to N Coward were all goods of the Household Department. The sales to R Colman & Co were £102 of goods from the Sports Department and £205 goods from the Electrical Department. When added up at the end of the month we can find the total of sales for each department. The total of the total column should equal the sum of all the other totals, i.e. £412 + £1,035 + £1,752 = £3,199. A columnar purchases day book would be similarly drawn up.

35.3 Control Accounts Use

If we have control accounts (see Chapter 28), we may have more than one sales ledger or more than one purchases ledger. In this case we need to know the amount of sales or purchases and other items entered in each ledger.

If we had three purchases ledgers, one containing accounts for customers with name initials A to K, one G to O, and one P to Z, the purchases analysis or columnar book might be as in Exhibit 35.2.

Exhibit 35.2

Purchases Analysis Book

Date		*Details*	*Total*	*Ledgers*		
				A–F	G–O	P–Z
19–6			£	£	£	£
Feb	1	J Archer	58	58		
"	3	G Gaunt	103		103	
"	4	T Brown	116	116		
"	8	C Dunn	205	205		
"	10	A Smith	16			16
"	12	P Smith	114			114
"	15	D Owen	88		88	
"	18	B Blake	17	17		
"	22	T Green	1,396		1,396	
"	27	C Males	48		48	
			2,161	396	1,635	130

We now know that the purchases entered during February 19–6 in the A–F purchases ledger was £396, £1,635 in the G–O ledger, and £130 in the P–Z ledger.

35.4 Other Uses

Another way of keeping a columnar sales book would be to find the sales in each geographical area. For instance, we may sell goods to customers in Jamaica, in West Africa and in France. The sales book might be as in Exhibit 35.3.

Exhibit 35.3

Sales Analysis Book

Date	*Details*	*Total*	*Jamaica*	*West Africa*	*France*
19–4		£	£	£	£
May 1	R Smith	407	407		
" 5	T Ogunlade	116		116	
" 8	P Mitterand	210			210
" 12	T Sangster	1,165	1,165		
" 18	K Distel	180			180
" 22	J Onifade	307		307	
" 31	L Nwosu	416		416	
		2,801	1,572	839	390

The examples shown in this chapter do not cover all the possibilities, as we can use the analysis columns to obtain desirable information in any way that we may wish.

35.5 Advantages of Analysis Books

The advantages are that we are provided with exactly the information we need, at the time when we want it. Different firms have different needs, and, therefore, analyse their books in different ways.

They will enable us to do such things as to:

1 calculate the profit or loss made by each part of a business;
2 draw up control accounts for the sales and purchases ledgers;
3 keep a check on the sales of each type of goods;
4 keep a check on goods sold in the UK, and those sold overseas;
5 find the purchase of each type of goods.

Exercises

35.1 J Goode sub-divides his purchases ledger into three alphabetical sections: A–G, H–M and N–Z, the creditors' accounts being entered according to their surnames.

Draw up a purchases day book (or journal) with appropriate analysis columns and enter the following invoices. Rule and total for the period 1 to 6 February 19–9.

Date	*Supplier*	*Invoice No*	*Invoice Total*
19–9			£
Feb 1	F Archer	21	960
" 2	J Potter	22	360
" 3	J Harris	23	575
" 4	C Clay	24	106
" 5	B Sidwell	25	91
" 6	F Lake	26	450

Ignore VAT.

35.2X D Jewel, a hardware merchant, divides his business into three departments, namely: glass, china and miscellaneous. During October 19–6 Jewel made the following sales:

19–6		
Oct 4	To John Dove:	
	100 buckets	@ £6 per ten
	48 pans	@ £2 each
	100 jugs (china)	@ £10 each
	50 teapots (china)	@ £15 each
" 17	To D Brown:	
	150 glasses	@ £50 per hundred
" 20	To F James:	
	6 teapots (china)	@ £14 each
	25 buckets	@ £8 per ten
	18 glass flower bowls	@ £4 each

You are required to:

(a) Prepare D Jewel's tabular sales journal and to enter the above listed items therein, and

(b) Post from the sales journal to the nominal and the personal ledgers.

Note: Ignore VAT.

(RSA adapted)

35.3 T York has three sales ledgers, each one representing a particular geographical area. These are *(a)* UK, *(b)* The Far East, *(c)* USA.

Draw up a sales journal, with appropriate analysis columns, in respect of the following sales for May 19–6. Ignore VAT.

19–6		£
May 1	Hiram K Hiram, New York	119
" 3	P Osaki, Tokyo	288
" 5	B Hardcastle, Manchester	249
" 10	A Smith, London	44
" 15	T Roosevelt, Washington	387
" 17	L Nakamura, Tokyo	84
" 19	C Rockefeller, Los Angeles	219
" 28	I Aoki, Nagasaki	188
" 31	S Chang, Hong Kong	572

35.4X M Poynton has a sports store with four departments: *(a)* Golf; *(b)* Cricket; *(c)* Football; *(d)* Tennis. The following are the details of sales for the month of September 19–2. You are to write up a Sales Journal with appropriate analysis columns. VAT is ignored.

19–5		£
Sept 1	T Holton, golf clubs	388
" 3	M Naseby, cricket gear £165, footballs £99	264
" 5	P Moores, tennis nets	65
" 8	N Goodson, golf balls £67, football posts £432	499
" 11	H Harkness, tennis balls £44, golf clubs £66	110
" 12	T Holton, tennis racquets	70
" 18	P Oldham, cricket bats	55
" 21	P Chester, footballs £123, cricket balls £66	189
" 30	H Parton, football kits	111

35.5 C Berry, a retailer, divides his business into three departments: Kitchen Hardware; Electrical; and Garden.

During the month of June Year 6, he bought the following goods on credit:

4 June	Grofast Seeds Ltd	– 1,200 packets of garden seeds costing £5 per 100
6 June	E Gaze	– Various kitchen utensils for £240 list price less 20% Trade discount
16 June	Light & Shade Ltd	– 70 electric light shades at £5 each
20 June	E Gaze	– 50 Frying pans at £4 each 200 Peat flower pots for a total of £25
26 June	Lightning Wire Company	– 100 yards of electric wire at £120 list price less 10% Trade discount
29 June	The Rich Loam Company	– 60 bags of Garden compost at £6 per bag

Required

(a) Write up the Purchases Day Book of C Berry for the month of June Year 6, using the following columnar ruling:

Date	Name of Supplier	Ledger Folio	Total	Kitchen Hardware	Electrical	Garden

Note: Details of invoices need not be entered.

(b) Post the totals of the columns to the appropriate ledger accounts.

(LCCI)

35.6X C James manufactures office furniture and equipment.

His sales on credit and returns from customers during April 19–4 were:

April 2	Oakdene Office Supplies 4 typist's chairs	list price £70 each less trade discount 25%
April 14	Bewley Bros 2 desks	list price £120 each less trade discount 20%
April 21	Oakdene Office Supplies 1 typist's chair invoiced on April 2 returned damaged	
April 27	Tyrolean Agency 3 stapling machines	list price £10 each less trade discount 10%

All transactions are subject to Value Added Tax at 10%.

You are required to:

(a) Rule up and head appropriate day books suitable to record the above transactions with main columns headed:

Date	*Name and Details*	*List price less trade discount*		*VAT*	*Total*
		£	£	£	£

(b) Write up the day books in full detail so as to show clearly your calculations for trade discount and VAT and the individual totals for each day's transactions during April 19–4.

(c) Post the day books to the personal accounts and nominal accounts in the ledgers to complete the double entry.

(RSA)

36 · Capital and Revenue Expenditures

36.1 Capital Expenditure

Capital expenditure is made when a firm spends money to either:

1 Buy fixed assets, or
2 Add to the value of an existing fixed asset.

Included in such amounts should be those spent:

1 Acquiring fixed assets.
2 Bringing them into the firm.
3 Legal costs of buying buildings.
4 Carriage inwards on machinery bought.
5 Any other cost needed to get the fixed asset ready for use.

36.2 Revenue Expenditure

Expenditure which is not for increasing the value of fixed assets, but is for running the business on a day-to-day basis, is known as **revenue expenditure**.

The difference can be seen clearly with the total cost of using a motor van for a firm. To buy a new motor van is capital expenditure. The motor van will be in use for several years and is, therefore, a fixed asset.

To pay for petrol to use in the motor van for the next few days is revenue expenditure. This is because the expenditure is used up in a few days and does not add to the value of fixed assets.

36.3 Differences between Capital and Revenue Expenditure

A few instances will demonstrate the difference.

	Expenditure	Type of Expenditure
1	Buying motor van	Capital
2	Petrol costs for motor van	Revenue
3	Repairs to motor van	Revenue
4	Putting extra headlights on motor van	Capital
5	Buying machinery	Capital
6	Electricity costs of using machinery	Revenue
7	We spent £1,500 on machinery. £1,000 was for an item added to the machine: £500 for repairs	Capital £1,000 Revenue £500
8	Painting outside of new building	Capital
9	Three years later – repainting outside of building in (8)	Revenue

You can see that revenue expenditure is that chargeable to the trading or profit and loss account, while capital expenditure will result in increased figures for fixed assets in the balance sheet.

36.4 Joint Expenditure

Sometimes one item of expenditure will need dividing between capital and revenue expenditure.

A builder was engaged to tackle some work on your premises, the total bill being for £3,000. If one-third of this was for repair work and two-thirds for improvements, £1,000 should be charged in the profit and loss account as revenue expenditure, and £2,000 identified as capital expenditure and, therefore, added to the value of premises and shown as such in the balance sheet.

36.5 Incorrect Treatment of Expenditure

If one of the following occurs:

1 Capital expenditure is incorrectly treated as revenue expenditure, or
2 revenue expenditure is incorrectly treated as capital expenditure,

then both the balance sheet figures and trading and profit and loss account figures will be incorrect.

This means that the net profit figure will also be incorrect. If the expenditure affects items in the trading account, then the gross profit figure will also be incorrect.

36.6 Capital and Revenue Receipts

When an item of capital expenditure is sold, the receipt is called a capital receipt. Suppose a motor van is bought for £5,000, and sold five years later for £750. The £5,000 was treated as capital expenditure. The £750 received is treated as a capital receipt.

Revenue receipts are sales or other revenue items, such as rent receivable or commissions receivable.

New Terms

Capital Expenditure (p 328): When a firm spends money to buy or add value to a fixed asset.

Revenue Expenditure (p 328): Expenses needed for the day-to-day running of the business.

Exercises

36.1 For the business of K Thorne, wholesale chemist, classify the following between 'capital' and 'revenue' expenditure:

(a) Purchase of an extra motor van.
(b) Cost of rebuilding a warehouse wall which had fallen down.
(c) Building extension to the warehouse.
(d) Painting extension to warehouse when it is first built.
(e) Repainting extension to warehouse three years later than that done in *(d)*.
(f) Carriage costs on bricks for new warehouse extension.
(g) Carriage costs on purchases.
(h) Carriage costs on sales.
(i) Legal costs of collecting debts.
(j) Legal charges on acquiring new premises for office.
(k) Fire insurance premium.
(l) Costs of erecting new machine.

36.2X For the business of H Ward, a foodstore, classify the following between 'capital' and 'revenue' expenditure:

(a) Repairs to meat slicer.
(b) New tyre for van.
(c) Additional shop counter.
(d) Renewing signwriting on store.
(e) Fitting partitions in store.
(f) Roof repairs.
(g) Installing thief detection equipment.
(h) Wages of store assistant.
(i) Carriage on returns outwards.
(j) New cash register.
(k) Repairs to office safe.
(l) Installing extra toilet.

36.3 Explain clearly the difference between capital expenditure and revenue expenditure. State which of the following you would classify as capital expenditure, giving your reasons:

(a) Cost of building extension to factory.
(b) Purchases of filing cabinets for sales office.
(c) Cost of repairs to accounting machine.
(d) Cost of installing reconditioned engine in delivery van.
(e) Legal fees paid in connection with factory extension.

36.4 The following data was extracted from the books of account of H E Worth, a building contractor, on 31 March 19–9, his financial year end:

	£
(a) Wages (including wages of two of Worth's employees who worked on improvements to Worth's premises, amount involved £1,500)	8,000
(b) Light and heat (including new wiring £500, part of premises improvement)	2,000
(c) Purchase of extra cement mixer (includes £200 for repair of old dumper)	2,500
(d) Rent	400
(e) Carriage (includes £100 carriage on new cement mixer)	800
(f) Purchases of new lathe (extra)	4,000

You are required to:
Allocate each of the items listed above to either 'Capital' or 'Revenue' expenditure.
(RSA)

36.5X Mr Brown has recently started in business on his own account and is puzzled by the terms 'Capital Expenditure' and 'Revenue Expenditure'.

(a) Explain to him what Capital Expenditure is.
(b) Mr Brown has purchased a new van, the details of the account were as follows:

	£
Van	3,000
Seat Belts	24
Delivery Charges	42
Number Plates	15
Road Tax	90
Insurance	220
	3,391

He has also received an account from his local builder, details of which are as follows:

	£
Re-decorate shop front	400
Erect shelves in stock room	90
	490

You are required to list the items from both invoices under their respective headings of Capital and Revenue Expenditure.
(RSA)

36.6X Allocate the following debits between capital and revenue expenditure, giving reasons.

(a) Purchase of new vehicle
(b) Fuel for vehicles
(c) New tyres for vehicles
(d) Vehicles insurance
(e) Radio equipment fitted to vehicle.

(PEI)

36.7 Compupro is a small computer and data processing bureau. In a certain trading period it enters into the following transactions:

(a) The purchase of supplies of computer print-out paper, all of which is expected to be used within the current trading period.
(b) The renewal of insurance on the computer hardware.
(c) Expenditure on increasing the security to the building in which the bureau's facilities are situated.
(d) The wages of the computer operators.
(e) The adding of extra storage capacity to a mainframe computer used within the bureau.

Required

State in respect of each of the above whether you would treat the item as capital expenditure or revenue expenditure, giving the reason for your choice. Set out your answer in two columns as follows:

	Capital or Revenue Expenditure	**Reason**
(a)		
(b)		
(c)		
(d)		
(e)		

(LCCI)

36.8X Place the following outgoings under capital or revenue expenditure:

(a) purchase of premises.
(b) repairs to premises.
(c) legal costs connected with purchase of premises.
(d) payment of ground rent.
(e) purchase of second-hand motor van.
(f) payment for petrol.
(g) payment for telephone charges.
(h) depreciation on machinery.
(i) wages paid to staff.
(j) purchase of patent rights.

(PEI)

37 · Accounting Concepts and Conventions

37.1 Introduction

In this book we have been concerned with recording transactions in the books. While we have been making such records we have in fact been following certain *rules*. These rules under which we work are known as concepts and conventions.

The trading and profit and loss accounts and balance sheets shown in the previous chapters were drawn up for the owner of the business. As shown later in the book, businesses are often owned by more than just one person and these accounting statements are for the use of all the owners.

An owner of a business may not be the only person to see his final accounts. He may have to show them to his bank manager if he wants to borrow money. The Inspector of Taxes will want to see them for the calculation of taxes. He may also need them to show to someone when he sells his business.

37.2 One Set of Final Accounts for All Purposes

If it had always been the custom to draft different kinds of final accounts for different purposes, so that one type was given to a banker, another type to someone wishing to buy the business, etc., then Accounting would be different than it is today. However, copies of the same set of final accounts are given to all the different people.

This means that the banker, the prospective buyer of the business, the owner and the other people all see the same trading and profit and loss account and balance sheet. This is not a very good idea as the interests of each party are different and different kinds of information are needed from that wanted by the others. For instance, the bank manager would really like to know how much the assets would sell for if the firm ceased trading. He could then see what the possibility would be of the bank obtaining repayment of its loan. Other people would also like to see the information in the way that is most useful to them. Yet normally only one sort of final accounts is available for these different people.

This means that trading and profit and loss accounts and balance sheets have to be used for different needs, and to be of any use, the different parties have to agree to the way in which they are drawn up.

Assume that you are in a class of students and that you have the problem of valuing your assets, which consist of ten text books. The first value you decide is that of how much you could sell them for. Your own guess is £30, but the other members of the class may give figures from £15 to £50.

Suppose that you now decide to put a value on their use to you. You may well think that the use of these books will enable you to pass your examinations and so you will get a good job. Another person may have the opposite idea concerning the use of the books to him. The use value placed on the books by others in the class will be quite different.

Finally you decide to value them by reference to cost. You take out of your pocket the bills for the books, which show that you paid a total of £60 for the books. If the rest of the class do not think that you have altered the bills, then they also can all agree that the value expressed as cost is £60. As this is the only value that you can all agree to, then each of you decides to use the idea of showing the value of his asset of books at the cost price.

37.3 Objectivity and Subjectivity

The use of a method which all can agree to, instead of everyone using their own different method, is said to be **objective**. To use cost for the value of an asset is, therefore, a way to be objective.

When you are **subjective**, this means that you want to use your own method, even though no one else may agree to it.

Objectivity, using methods that all people can agree to, is what financial accounting ensures. The rules which state how the transactions are recorded are usually known as concepts.

37.4 Basic Concepts

The Cost Concept

The need for this has already been described. It means that assets are normally shown at cost price, and that this is the basis for valuation of the asset.

The Money Measurement Concept

Accounting is concerned only with those facts covered by **1** and **2** which follow:
1 it can be measured in money, and
2 most people will agree to the money value of the transaction.

This means that accounting can never tell you everything about a business. For example, accounting does not show the following:
1 whether the firm has good or bad managers,
2 that there are serious problems with the work force,
3 that a rival product is about to take away a lot of our best customers,
4 that the government is about to pass a law which will cost us a lot of extra expense in future.

The reason that **1** to **4** or similar items are not recorded is that it would be impossible to work out a money value for them which most people would agree to.

Some people think that accounting tells you everything you want to know. The above shows that this is not true.

Going Concern Concept

Normally we assume that a business will continue for a long time. Only if the business was going to be sold would we show how much the assets would sell for. This is because we use the cost concept. If businesses were not assumed to be **going concerns**, the cost concept could not be used. Should firms be treated as to be sold immediately, then the saleable value of assets would be used instead of cost.

The Business Entity Concept

The items recorded in a firm's books are limited to the transactions which affect the firm as a **business entity**. Suppose that a proprietor of a firm, from his personal monies outside the firm, buys a diamond necklace for his wife. As the money spent was not out of the firm's bank account or cash box, then this item will not be entered in the firm's books.

The only time that the personal resources of the proprietor affect the firm's accounting records is when he brings new capital into the firm, or takes drawings out of the firm.

The Realisation Concept

Normally, profit is said to be earned at the time when:

1 goods or services are passed to the customer, and
2 he then incurs liability for them.

This concept of profit is known as the **realisation concept**. Notice that is *not*

1 when the order is received, or
2 when the customer pays for the goods.

The Dual Aspect Concept

This states that there are two aspects of Accounting, one represented by the assets of the business and the other by the claims against them. The concept states that these two aspects are always equal to each other. In other words:

Assets = Capital + Liabilities

Double entry is the name given to the method of recording the transactions for the **dual aspect concept**.

The Accrual Concept

The **accrual concept** says that net profit is the difference between revenues and expenses, i.e.

Revenues – Expenses = Net Profit

Determining the expenses used up to obtain the revenues is referred to as *matching* expenses against revenues.

A lot of people who have not studied Accounting do not understand this concept. They think that receipts of a period, less payments of the period, equal net profit.

You know that expenses consist of the assets used up in a period. You also know that cash paid in a period and expenses of a period are usually different figures. This comes as a surprise to a lot of people.

You, however, know that we have to make adjustments for items such as expenses owing, payments in advance, depreciation and provisions for bad debts etc. Only then can we calculate net profit.

37.5 The Assumption of the Stability of Monetary Measures

One does not have to be very old to remember that a few years ago many goods could be bought with less money than today. If one listens to one's parents or grandparents then many stories will be heard of how little this item or the other could be bought for many years ago. The currencies of the countries of the world change in terms of what each unit of currency can buy over the years.

Accounting, however, uses the cost concept, which states that the asset is normally shown at its cost price. This means that accounting statements can be misleading because assets will be bought at different times at the prices then ruling, and the figures will be totalled up to show the value of the assets in cost terms.

For instance, suppose that you bought a building 20 years ago for £20,000. You now decide to buy an identical additional building, but the price has risen to £40,000. You buy it, and the buildings account now shows buildings at a figure of £60,000. One building is in the currency of 20 years ago, while the other is at today's currency value. The figure of a total of £60,000 is historically correct, but cannot be used for much else.

When we look at final accounts we must understand such problems. There are ways of adjusting accounts to make the figures more useful, but these are not in your syllabus. You will have to study them if you take accounting examinations at an advanced level.

37.6 The Conventions of Accounting

The concepts of Accounting have become accepted in the business world. The concepts, however, could be looked at in many ways if nothing had been done to bring about standard methods.

Accounting therefore has tried to make certain that similar items are dealt with in similar ways. As a result we have the conventions of Accounting.

The main conventions may be said to be: **1 materiality**, **2 prudence**, **3 consistency**.

Materiality

This convention is to try to stop you wasting time and effort doing completely unnecessary work. Accounting does not serve a useful purpose if the effort of recording a transaction in a certain way is not worthwhile. As an example, if a box of paperclips was bought it would be used over a period of time, and this cost is used up every time someone uses a paperclip. It is possible to record this as an expense every time it happens, but obviously the price of a box of paperclips is so little that it is not worth recording it in this way.

The box of paperclips is not a material item, and, therefore, would be charged as an expense in the period it was bought even though it could last for more than one accounting period. You should not waste your time in the unnecessary recording of trivial items. Similarly, the purchase of a cheap metal ashtray would also be charged as an expense in the period it was bought because it is not a material item, even though it may last 20 years. It would not be worth calculating depreciation on it.

A motor lorry would be deemed to be a material item. We then calculate depreciation to charge each period, with the cost consumed in each period of its use.

You can see that small amounts are not material, while larger amounts are material. The question is, at what figure does an item become material? There is no fixed rule for this.

Firms make all sorts of rules to say what is material and what is not. There is no law that says what these should be. What is material and what is not depends upon judgement. A firm may decide that all items under £100 should be treated as expenses in the period in which they were bought, even though they may be in use in the firm for the following ten years. Another firm, especially a large one, may put the limit at £1,000. Different limits may be set for different types of items.

The size and type of firm will affect the decisions as to what is material, and what is not.

Prudence

Very often an accountant has to use his judgement to decide which figure he will take for an item. Suppose a debt has been owing for quite a long time, and no one knows whether it will ever be paid. Should the accountant be an optimist in thinking that it will be paid, or should he be more pessimistic?

It is the accountant's duty to see that people get the proper facts about a business. He should make certain that assets are not valued too highly. Similarly, liabilities should not be shown at values too low. Otherwise, people might inadvisedly lend money to a firm, which they would not do if they had the proper facts.

The accountant should always be on the side of safety, and this is known as prudence. The prudence convention means that normally he will take the figure which will understate rather than overstate the profit. Thus he should choose the figure which will cause the capital of the firm to be shown at a lower amount rather than at a higher one. He will also normally make sure that all losses are recorded in the books, but profits should not be anticipated by recording them before they should be. This concept used to be (and often still is) known as the 'conservatism' concept.

Consistency

Even if we do everything already listed under concepts and conventions, there will still be quite a few different ways in which items could be recorded.

Each firm should try to choose the methods which give the most reliable picture of the business.

This cannot be done if one method is used in one year and another method in the next year and so on. Constantly changing the methods would lead to misleading profits being calculated from the accounting records. Therefore the convention of consistency is used. This convention says that when a firm has once fixed a method for the accounting treatment of an item, it will enter all similar items that follow in exactly the same way.

However, it does not mean that the firm has to follow the method until the firm closes down. A firm can change the method used, but such a change is not taken without a lot of consideration. When such a change occurs and the profits calculated in that year are affected by a material amount, then either in the profit and loss account itself or in one of the reports with it, the effect of the change should be stated.

37.7 Accounting Terminology

Unfortunately many of the terms used in the description of Accounting theory mean quite different things to different people. Things described as concepts and conventions in this book may well be called principles by someone else. They might be called concepts without any attempt to distinguish between concepts and conventions. Provided that the reader realises this, there is no problem.

Probably the most recent attempt to change a term is the use of the word *prudence* instead of **conservatism**. As most accounting books now use the word prudence, this is the one used in this book. Both of these words can be taken to mean the same.

Quantifiability means the ability to make a proper measure of the transaction. This must take place if the transaction is to be measured in money.

New Terms

Objectivity (p 334): Using of a method that everyone can agree to.

Subjectivity (p 334): Using of a method which other people may not agree to.

Going Concern Concept (p 335): Where a business is assumed to continue for a long time.

Business Entity Concept (p 335): Concerning only transactions which affect the firm, and ignoring the owner's private transactions.

Realisation Concept (p 335): The point at which profit is treated as being earned.

Dual Aspect Concept (p 335): Dealing with both aspects of a transaction.

Accrual Concept (p 336): Where net profit is the difference between revenues and expenses.

Materiality (p 337): To record something in a special way only if the amount is not a small one.

Prudence (p 337) or **conservatism**: To ensure that profit is not shown as being too high, or assets shown at too high a value.

Consistency (p 338): To keep to the same method, except in special cases.

Exercises

37.1 Which accounting concept is used in each of the following accounting treatments? Explain.

(a) The cost of a tape dispenser has been charged to an expense account, although in fact it could still be in use in ten years' time.

(b) A sole proprietor has sold his private house, but has not recorded anything about it in the business records.

(c) A debt has been written off as a bad debt even though there is still a chance that the debtor eventually may be able to pay it.

(d) A machine has been bought for an exceedingly low figure, and has been entered in the asset account at that figure even though it is worth more.

(e) An expert says that the value of the management team to the company is worth well over a million pounds, yet nothing is entered for it in the books.

(f) A motor van broke down in December 19–1, but the repairs bill for it was not paid until 19–2 yet it has been treated as a 19–1 expense.

(g) A customer saw a carpet in 19–1 and said he might well buy it. He phoned in 19–2 to ask us to deliver the carpet. The item was not treated as a sale in 19–1 but was treated instead as 19–2 sales.

(h) The final day of the financial year saw the passing of a law which would render trading in our sort of goods illegal, and the business will have to close. The accountant says that our stock figure cannot be shown at cost in the balance sheet.

(i) We have been told that we cannot show our asset of motor cars at cost one year and at cost plus the next year when the manufacturer increases prices of all cars, which also includes our unsold stock.

(j) We have shown all items of machinery costing less than £100 as machinery operating expenses.

37.2X When preparing the final accounts of your company, name the accounting concepts you should follow to deal with each of the following:

(a) Electricity consumed during the accounting period is still unpaid at the year end.

(b) The owner of the company has invested his private assets in the company.

(c) A debtor who owes the company a large amount has been declared bankrupt. The outstanding amount due to the company is now considered to be irrecoverable.

(d) The company has suffered substantial losses in the past few years. It is extremely uncertain whether the company can continue to operate next year.

(e) The company has suffered a loss in the current year. The owner believes that a better result could be presented if the straight line depreciation method were adopted to calculate the depreciation of its fixed assets instead of the reducing balance method which is used at present.

Multiple-choice Questions

Each multiple-choice question has four suggested answers, either letter (A), (B), (C) or (D). You should read each question and then decide which choice is best, either (A) or (B) or (C) or (D). On a separate piece of paper you should then write down your choice. Unless the textbook you are reading belongs to you, you should not make a mark against your choice in the textbook.

Set No 1: 20 questions

Answers on page 355.

MC1 Which of the following statements is incorrect?
(A) Assets – Liabilities = Capital
(B) Capital – Liabilities = Assets
(C) Assets = Capital + Liabilities
(D) Assets – Capital = Liabilities.

MC2 Which of the following is not an asset?
(A) Debtor
(B) Motor Vehicle
(C) Creditor
(D) Stock of Goods.

MC3 Which of the following is a liability?
(A) Cash balance
(B) Loan from J Owens
(C) Debtor
(D) Buildings.

MC4 Which of the following is incorrect?

	Assets	*Liabilities*	*Capital*
	£	£	£
(A)	9,460	2,680	6,780
(B)	7,390	1,140	6,250
(C)	6,120	2,490	4,630
(D)	8,970	3,580	5,390

MC5 Which of the following statements is incorrect?

	Effect upon	
	Assets	*Liabilities*
(A) Paid creditor by cheque	– Bank	+ Creditors
(B) Bought goods on credit	+ Stock	+ Creditors
(C) Received cash from debtor	+ Cash – Debtor	
(D) Sold goods for Cash	+ Cash – Stock	

MC6 Which of the following are correct?

	Accounts	*To record*	*Entry in the account*
(i)	Assets	a decrease	Debit
		an increase	Credit
(ii)	Capital	a decrease	Debit
		an increase	Credit
(iii)	Liabilities	a decrease	Debit
		an increase	Credit

(A) (i) and (ii)
(B) (i) and (iii)
(C) (ii) and (iii)
(D) None of them.

MC7 Which of the following are correct?

	Account to be debited	*Account to be credited*
(i) Bought motor van by cheque	Motor Van	Bank
(ii) Paid a creditor, T Allen, by cheque	Cash	T Allen
(iii) Loan repaid to C Kirk by cheque	Loan from Kirk	Bank
(iv) Sold goods for cash	Sales	Cash

(A) (i) and (ii) only
(B) (ii) and (iii) only
(C) (iii) and (iv) only
(D) (i) and (iii) only.

MC8 Which of the following are incorrect?

	Account to be debited	*Account to be credited*
(i) Sold goods on credit to P Moore	P Moore	Sales
(ii) Bought Fixtures on credit from Furnishers Ltd	Fixtures	Furnishers Ltd
(iii) Introduce more capital in cash	Capital	Cash
(iv) A debtor, L Sellars, pays by cheque	Cash	L Sellars

(A) (iii) and (iv) only
(B) (ii) and (iii) only
(C) (i) and (iv) only
(D) (i) and (iii) only.

MC9 Which of the following should not be called 'Sales'?
(A) Goods sold, to be paid for in one month's time
(B) Goods sold, cash being received immediately
(C) Item previously included in Purchases, now sold on credit
(D) Sale of a Motor Lorry not now required.

MC10 Which of the following should not be called 'Purchases'?
(A) Items bought for the prime purpose of resale
(B) Goods bought on credit
(C) Office Stationery Purchased
(D) Goods bought for cash.

MC11 Which of the following are incorrect?

	Account to be debited	*Account to be credited*
(i) B Ash returns goods to us	Returns Inwards	B Ash
(ii) Goods bought on credit from L Thomas	L Thomas	Purchases
(iii) Motor Van bought on Credit from X L Garages	Purchases	X L Garages
(iv) Goods sold for cash	Cash	Sales

(A) (i) and (ii) only
(B) (i) and (iii) only
(C) (ii) and (iii) only
(D) (iii) and (iv) only.

MC12 Of the following, which are correct?

	Account to be debited	*Account to be credited*
(i) Surplus office furniture sold for cash	Cash	Sales
(ii) We returned goods to F Ward	F Ward	Returns Inwards
(iii) Goods bought for cash	Purchases	Cash
(iv) Goods sold on credit to F Clarke	F Clarke	Sales

(A) (i) and (ii) only
(B) (iii) and (iv) only
(C) (ii) and (iii) only
(D) (ii) only.

MC13 What is the amount of Capital, given the following information? Buildings £30,000, Stock £5,600, Bank £750, Creditors £2,200, Loan from K Noone £7,000:
(A) £29,150
(B) £36,350
(C) £41,150
(D) None of the above.

MC14 Which of these statements is incorrect?
(A) Profit is another word for Capital
(B) A loss decreases Capital
(C) Profit increases Capital
(D) Drawings decreases Capital.

MC15 Which of the following are incorrect?

	Account to be debited	Account to be credited
(i) Paid insurance by cheque	Insurance	Bank
(ii) Paid telephone bill by cash	Telephone	Cash
(iii) Received refund of part of motor expenses by cheque	Cash	Motor Expenses
(iv) Took cash out of business for personal use	Drawings	Capital

(A) (i) and (iii) only
(B) (ii) and (iv) only
(C) (iii) and (iv) only
(D) (iv) only.

MC16 Of the following, which are correct?

	Account to be debited	Account to be credited
(i) Paid rent by cheque	Rent	Cash
(ii) Received commission in cash	Commissions	Cash
(iii) Introduced extra capital in cash	Cash	Capital
(iv) Sold surplus stationery for cash	Cash	Stationery

(A) None of them
(B) (i) and (iv) only
(C) (ii) and (iii) only
(D) (iii) and (iv) only.

MC17 What is the balance on the following account on 30 June 19–5?

N Garth

19–5	£	19–5	£
June 18 Bank	400	June 1 Purchases	870
" 22 Returns	44	" 15 Purchases	245
		" 29 Purchases	178

(A) A debit balance of £849
(B) A credit balance of £829
(C) A credit balance of £849
(D) There is a nil balance on the account.

MC18 What was the balance on the account of N Garth, in MC17, on 20 June 19–5?
(A) A credit balance of £671
(B) A debit balance of £715
(C) A credit balance of £715
(D) A debit balance of £671.

MC19 Of the following which *best* describes a Trial Balance?
(A) Is the final account in the books
(B) Shows all the asset balances
(C) Is a list of balances on the books
(D) Discloses the financial position of a business.

MC20 When should the trial balance totals differ?
(A) Only when it is drawn up by the accountant
(B) When drawn up before the Profit and Loss Account is prepared
(C) If drawn up half way through the financial year
(D) Never.

Set No 2: 20 questions

Answers on page 355.

MC21 Gross Profit is:
(A) Excess of cost of goods sold over sales
(B) Purchases + Sales
(C) Net Profit less expenses
(D) Excess of sales over cost of goods sold.

MC22 Net Profit is calculated in the
(A) Trial Balance
(B) Trading Account
(C) Profit and Loss Account
(D) Balance Sheet.

MC23 The credit entry for Net Profit is shown in the
(A) Capital Account
(B) Profit and Loss Account
(C) Balance Sheet
(D) Trading Account.

MC24 The value of closing stock is found by
(A) Adding opening stock to Purchases
(B) Deducting Purchases from Sales
(C) Looking in the stock account
(D) Doing a stocktaking.

MC25 Which of the following are *not* part of the double entry system?
(i) Trading Account
(ii) Balance Sheet
(iii) Trial Balance
(iv) Profit and Loss Account

(A) (i) and (ii)
(B) (i) and (iii)
(C) (ii) and (iii)
(D) (ii) and (iv).

MC26 Which is the *best* definition of a balance sheet?
(A) A list of balances after calculating net profit
(B) A statement of all liabilities
(C) A trial balance at a different date
(D) A list of balances before calculating net profit.

MC27 The descending order in which current assets should be shown in the balance sheet are:
(A) Debtors, Bank, Stock, Cash
(B) Stock, Debtors, Bank, Cash
(C) Stock, Debtors, Cash, Bank
(D) Cash, Bank, Debtors, Stock.

MC28 Carriage Inwards is charged to the Trading Account because:
(A) It is not a balance sheet item
(B) It is not part of our motor expenses
(C) Returns Inwards also goes in the Trading Account
(D) It is basically part of the cost of buying goods.

MC29 Given figures showing: Sales £28,500; Opening Stock £4,690; Closing Stock £7,240; Carriage Inwards £570; Purchases £21,360; the cost of goods sold figure is:
(A) £19,830
(B) £19,380
(C) £18,810
(D) Another figure

MC30 In the Trading Account the Returns Inwards should be
(A) Added to Cost of Goods Sold
(B) Deducted from Purchases
(C) Deducted from Sales
(D) Added to Sales.

MC31 The Purchases Journal is *best* described as
(A) A list of purchases bought on credit
(B) Containing suppliers' accounts
(C) A list of purchases bought for cash
(D) Part of the double entry system.

MC32 Customers' personal accounts are found in
(A) The private ledger
(B) General Ledger
(C) Purchases Ledger
(D) Sales Ledger

MC33 Which of the following are *not* personal accounts
(i) Debtors
(ii) Drawings
(iii) Rent
(iv) Creditors

(A) (iii) only
(B) (i) and (ii) only
(C) (i) and (iv) only
(D) (ii) and (iii) only.

MC34 A credit balance of £500 on the cash columns of the cash book would mean
(A) The book-keeper has made a mistake
(B) We have £500 cash in hand
(C) We have spent £500 cash more than we have received
(D) Someone has stolen £500 cash.

MC35 £200 withdrawn from the bank and placed in the cash till is entered:
(A) Debit bank column £200: Credit bank column £200
(B) Debit cash column £200: Credit bank column £200
(C) Debit bank column £200: Credit cash column £200
(D) Debit cash column £400: Credit cash column £400.

MC36 A contra item is where
(A) Cash is banked before it has been paid out
(B) Where double entry is completed within the cash book
(C) Where the proprietor has repaid his capital in cash
(D) Where sales have been paid by cash.

MC37 An invoice shows a total of £3,200 less $2\frac{1}{2}$ per cent cash discount. If this was paid in time, the amount of the cheque paid would be for
(A) £2,960
(B) £3,040
(C) £3,120
(D) £2,800.

MC38 The total of the Discounts Received column in the Cash Book is posted to
(A) the credit of the Discounts Received Account
(B) the credit of the Discounts Allowed Account
(C) the debit of the Discounts Allowed Account
(D) the debit of the Discounts Received Account.

MC39 A bank overdraft is *best* described as
(A) a firm wasting its money
(B) having more receipts than payments
(C) a firm having bought too many goods
(D) a firm having paid more out of its bank account than it has put in it.

MC40 A cash discount is *best* described as a reduction in the sum to be paid
(A) if goods are bought on credit and not for cash
(B) if either cheque or cash payment is made within an agreed period
(C) if cash is paid instead of cheques
(D) if trade discount is also deducted.

Set No 3: 20 questions

Answers on page 355.

MC41 If a sales invoice shows 12 items of £250 each, less trade discount of 20 per cent and cash discount of 5 per cent, then the amount to be paid, if the payment is made within the credit period, will be for
(A) £2,440
(B) £2,360
(C) £2,280
(D) £2,500.

MC42 The total of the Sales Journal is entered on
(A) The debit side of the Sales Day Book
(B) The credit side of the Sales Account in the General Ledger
(C) The debit side of the Sales Account in the General Ledger
(D) The debit side of the Sales Day Book.

MC43 A trade discount is *best* described as
(A) A discount given if the invoice is paid
(B) A discount given for cash payment
(C) A discount given to suppliers
(D) A discount given to traders.

MC44 The Sales Journal does not contain
(A) Credit sales made without deduction of trade discount
(B) Credit sales made to overseas customers
(C) Cash sales
(D) Credit sales which eventually turn out to be bad debts.

MC45 The Purchases Journal consists of
(A) Cash purchases
(B) Suppliers' ledger accounts
(C) A list of Purchase invoices
(D) Payments for goods.

MC46 The total of the Purchases Journal is transferred to the
(A) Debit side of the Purchases Account
(B) Credit side of the Purchases Journal
(C) Debit side of the Purchases Day Book
(D) Debit side of the Purchases Ledger.

MC47 The balances in the Purchases Ledger are usually
(A) Credit balances
(B) Contras
(C) Nominal account balances
(D) Debit balances.

MC48 Debit notes are entered in our
(A) Returns Outwards Journal
(B) Returns Inwards Journal
(C) Purchases Account
(D) Returns Outwards Account.

MC49 A statement of account
(A) Is used instead of an invoice
(B) Means that our customers need not keep accounts
(C) Saves us sending out invoices
(D) Acts as a reminder to the purchaser of the amount owed.

MC50 Originally we bought 80 items at £60 each, less trade discount of 25 per cent. We now return 5 items, so we will issue a debit note amounting to
(A) £270
(B) £240
(C) £225
(D) £220.

MC51 Straight Line Method of Depreciation consists of
(A) Unequal amounts of depreciation each year
(B) Increasing amounts of depreciation each year
(C) Reducing amounts of depreciation each year
(D) Equal amounts of depreciation each year.

MC52 Depreciation is:
(A) The cost of a current asset wearing away
(B) The cost of a replacement for a fixed asset
(C) The salvage value of a fixed asset plus its original cost
(D) The part of the cost of the fixed asset consumed during its period of use by the firm.

MC53 A firm bought a machine for £50,000. It is expected to be used for 6 years then sold for £5,000. What is the annual amount of depreciation if the straight line method is used?
(A) £7,000
(B) £8,000
(C) £7,500
(D) £6,750.

MC54 When a separate Provision for Depreciation Account is in use then book-keeping entries for the year's depreciation are
(A) Debit Profit and Loss: Credit the Balance Sheet
(B) Debit Profit and Loss: Credit Asset Account
(C) Debit Asset Account: Credit Provision for Depreciation Account
(D) Debit Profit and Loss: Credit Provision for Depreciation Account.

MC55 In the trial balance the balance on the Provision for Depreciation Account is
(A) shown as a credit item
(B) not shown, as it is part of depreciation
(C) shown as a debit item
(D) sometimes shown as a credit, sometimes as a debit.

MC56 If a provision for depreciation account is not in use then the entries for the year's depreciation would be
(A) debit Asset Account, credit Profit and Loss Account
(B) credit Asset Account, debit Provision for Depreciation Account
(C) credit Profit and Loss Account, debit Provision for Depreciation Account
(D) none of the above.

MC57 A Provision for Bad Debts is created
(A) When debtors become bankrupt
(B) When debtors cease to be in business
(C) To provide for possible bad debts
(D) To write off bad debts.

MC58 When the final accounts are prepared the Bad Debts Account is closed by a transfer to the
(A) Balance Sheet
(B) Profit and Loss Account
(C) Trading Account
(D) Provision for Bad Debts Account.

MC59 These questions relate to the following assets and liabilities:

	£		£
Stock	1,000	Machinery	750
Cash at Bank	750	Debtors	750
Cash in Hand	50	Fixtures	250
Creditors	500	Motor vehicle	750
Capital	3,800		

(i) The balance sheet totals are:
(A) £4,800. (B) £4,300. (C) £4,000. (D) £4,500.
(ii) Current liabilities are:
(A) £1,750. (B) £500. (C) £3,800. (D) £2,550.
(iii) Working capital is:
(A) £3,050. (B) £2,050. (C) £500. (D) £800.
(PEI)

MC60 If we take goods for own use we should
(A) Debit Drawings Account: Credit Purchases Account
(B) Debit Purchases Account: Credit Drawings Account
(C) Debit Drawings Account: Credit Stock Account
(D) Debit Sales Account: Credit Stock Account.

Set No 4: 22 questions

Answers on page 355.

MC61 A debit balance brought down on a Packing Materials Account means
(A) We owe for packing materials
(B) We have no stock of packing materials
(C) We have lost money on packing materials
(D) We have a stock of packing materials unused.

MC62 A credit balance brought down on a Rent Account means
(A) We owe that rent at that date
(B) We have paid that rent in advance at that date
(C) We have paid too much rent
(D) We have paid too little in rent.

MC63 Working Capital is a term meaning
(A) The amount of capital invested by the proprietor
(B) The excess of the current assets over the current liabilities
(C) The capital less drawings
(D) The total of Fixed Assets + Current Assets.

MC64 If someone owns a grocery store, which of the following are *not* Capital Expenditure?
(i) Rent
(ii) Motor Van
(iii) Fixtures
(iv) Fire Insurance

(A) (ii) and (iii)
(B) (i) and (ii)

(C) (i) and (iii)
(D) (i) and (iv).

MC65 If £750 was added to Rent instead of being added to a fixed asset
(A) Gross Profit would not be affected
(B) Gross Profit would be affected
(C) Both Gross and Net Profits would be affected
(D) Just the balance sheet items would be affected.

MC66 A cheque given to you by a customer and banked by you, but for which he has proved not to have enough funds to meet it, is known as
(A) A dishonoured cheque
(B) A debit transfer
(C) A standing order
(D) A bank error.

MC67 Which of the following are not true? A Bank Reconciliation Statement is
(i) Drawn up by the bank monthly
(ii) Not part of the double entry system
(iii) Part of the double entry system
(iv) Drawn up by our cashier.

(A) (i) and (ii)
(B) (i) and (iii)
(C) (ii) and (iv)
(D) (iii) and (iv).

MC68 Of the following, which should *not* be entered in The Journal?
(i) Cash payments for wages
(ii) Bad Debts written off
(iii) Credit purchases of goods
(iv) Sale of fixed assets.

(A) (i) and (ii)
(B) (i) and (iii)
(C) (ii) and (iii)
(D) (iii) and (iv).

MC69 The Journal is
(A) Part of the double entry system
(B) A form of Sales Day Book
(C) A form of diary
(D) A supplement to the Balance Sheet.

MC70 Given a desired cash float of £700, if £541 is spent in the period, and the opening cash float has been £700, how much will be reimbursed at the end of the period?
(A) £541
(B) £700
(C) £159
(D) None of the above.

MC71 A petty cash book
(A) Is used only in limited companies
(B) Is used when we have a bank overdraft
(C) Is used for small cheque payments
(D) Will keep down the number of entries in the general ledger.

MC72 Which of the following do *not* affect trial balance agreement?
(i) Purchases £585 from C Owens completely omitted from the books.
(ii) Sales £99 to R Morgan entered in his account as £90.
(iii) Rent account added up to be £100 too much.
(iv) Error on sales invoice of £14 being entered in the books.

(A) (i) and (iv)
(B) (i) and (ii)
(C) (i) and (iii)
(D) (iii) and (iv).

MC73 Which of the following *are* errors of principle?
(i) Rent entered in Buildings account
(ii) Purchases £150 completely omitted from books
(iii) Sale of machinery £500 entered in Sales account
(iv) Cheque payment to R Kago entered only in Cash Book.

(A) (ii) and (iii)
(B) (iii) and (iv)
(C) (i) and (ii)
(D) (i) and (iii).

MC74 When the trial balance totals do not agree, the difference is entered in
(A) The Balance account
(B) A Suspense account
(C) An Errors Account
(D) The Profit and Loss Account.

MC75 Which of these errors would be disclosed by the Trial Balance?
(A) Error on a Purchase Invoice
(B) Purchases from T Morgan entered in C Morgan's account
(C) Carriage outwards debited to Sales account
(D) Overcast of total on Sales account.

MC76 All these questions refer to the following Trading and Profit and Loss Account

Trading Account

	£	£		£	£
Opening stock		700	Sales	24,770	
Purchases	18,615		less Returns	270	24,500
less Returns	280	18,335			
Carriage in		320			
		19,355			
Closing stock		980			
		18,375			
Gross profit carried down		6,125			
		£24,500			£24,500

Profit and Loss Account

Wages		1,420	Gross profit b/d		6,125
Rent Paid	360				
Accrued	90	450			
General expenses		220			
Carriage out		360			
Net profit		???			
		£6,125			£6,125

(i) The missing net profit figure should be:
(A) £1,675. (B) £21,675. (C) £3,675. (D) £4,675

(ii) Total expenses were:
(A) £210. (B) £2,450. (C) £810. (D) £2,575.

(iii) The cost of goods sold totalled:
(A) £18,375. (B) £19,500. (C) £24,500. (D) £24,770.

(iv) The expense item of Rent totalled:
(A) £360. (B) £270. (C) £90. (D) £450.

(v) The turnover is:
(A) £24,770. (B) £24,500. (C) £19,355. (D) £18,375.

(vi) The net cost of purchases is:
(A) £18,615. (B) £18,335. (C) £18,655. (D) £18,375.

(vii) Purchases returned totalled:
(A) £360. (B) £320. (C) £280. (D) £270.

(viii) Gross profit as a percentage on net sales is:
(A) 20%. (B) 30%. (C) 25%. (D) $33\frac{1}{3}$%.

(ix) Net profit as a percentage on net sales is:
(A) 10%. (B) 20%. (C) 25%. (D) 15%.

(x) The value of unsold goods was:
(A) £980. (B) £24,500. (C) £6,125. (D) £19,355.

(PEI)

MC77 Answer the following questions using the following trial balance and the information given below:

Trial balance as at 31 December

	£	£
Capital		5,600
Furniture and Fittings	5,880	
Stock January 1	700	
Drawings	1,200	
Bank overdraft		1,260
Salaries	3,560	
General expenses	190	
Purchases/Sales	4,020	9,840
Discount All'd/Rec'd	150	130
Rent and rates	820	
Returns In/Out	90	80
Trade Debtors/Creditors	1,500	1,070
Bad debt provision		130
	£18,110	£18,110

(a) Salaries owing at 31 December – £140
(b) Rent and rates paid in advance – £220
(c) Depreciate furniture and fittings by 10% pa
(d) Closing stock valuation – £800
(e) Increase the bad debt provision to bring it up to 10% of debtors' balances.

(i) What will be the yearly depreciation charge?
(A) £5,292. (B) £6,468. (C) £588. (D) £5,886.

(ii) What will be the salaries figure shown on the profit and loss account?
(A) £140. (B) £3,700. (C) £3,420. (D) £3,560

(iii) The rent and rates figure shown on the profit and loss account will be:
(A) £600. (B) £820. (C) £220. (D) £1,040.

(iv) The new bad debt provision will be:
(A) £1,650. (B) £1,450. (C) £150. (D) £110.

(v) What will be the gross profit on the trading account?
(A) £5,910. (B) £5,830. (C) £4,630. (D) £4,430.

(vi) The net profit on the profit and loss account will be:
(A) £1,420. (B) £792. (C) £1,400. (D) £812.

(vii) The book value of furniture and fittings on the balance sheet will be:
(A) £5,292. (B) £6,000. (C) £6,368. (D) £5,880.

(viii) What will be the turnover for the year?
(A) £9,840. (B) £3,840. (C) £9,750. (D) £4,640.

(ix) Using the adjusted sales figure, the stock turnover for the year will be:
(A) 10. (B) 11. (C) 12. (D) 13.

(x) What will be the capital figure at end of year?
(A) £4,100. (B) £5,600. (C) £5,192. (D) £6,392.

(PEI)

MC78 Given last year's Capital as £57,500, this year's Capital as £64,300, and Drawings as £11,800, then Profit must have been
(A) £18,600
(B) £18,100
(C) £16,600
(D) £19,600.

MC79 Given last year's Capital as £74,500, closing Capital as £46,200, and Drawings of £13,400, then
(A) Profit for the year was £14,900
(B) Loss for the year was £14,900
(C) Loss for the year was £15,900
(D) Profit for the year was £16,800.

MC80 Given this year's closing Capital as £29,360, the year's net profit as £8,460 and Drawings as £5,320, what was the Capital at the beginning of the year?
(A) £29,360
(B) £26,220
(C) £34,680
(D) None of the above.

MC81 In a commercial firm an 'Accumulated Fund' would be known as
(A) Fixed Assets
(B) Total Assets
(C) Net Current Assets
(D) Capital.

MC82 A Receipts and Payments Account does not show
(A) Cheques paid out during the year
(B) The Accumulated Fund
(C) Receipts from sales of assets
(D) Bank balances.

Answers to Multiple-Choice Questions

1 B	2 C	3 B	4 C	5 A
6 C	7 D	8 A	9 D	10 C
11 C	12 B	13 D	14 A	15 C
16 D	17 C	18 C	19 C	20 D
21 D	22 C	23 A	24 D	25 C
26 A	27 B	28 D	29 B	30 C
31 A	32 D	33 D	34 A	35 B
36 B	37 C	38 A	39 D	40 B
41 C	42 B	43 D	44 C	45 C
46 A	47 A	48 A	49 D	50 C
51 D	52 D	53 C	54 D	55 A
56 D	57 C	58 B	59 (i) B (other possibility of deducting Current Liabilities to give £3,800 cannot work). (ii) B (iii) B	
				60 A
61 D	62 A	63 B	64 D	65 A
66 A	67 B	68 B	69 C	70 A
71 D	72 A	73 D	74 B	75 D
76 (i) C (ii) B (iii) A (iv) D (v) B (vi) B (vii) C (viii) C (ix) D (x) A				
77 (i) C (ii) B (iii) A (iv) C (v) A (vi) B (vii) A (viii) C (ix) None of them (x) D				
78 A	79 B	80 B	81 D	82 B

Answers to Exercises

Chapter 2

2.1

(a) 10,700 *(b)* 23,100 *(c)* 4,300 *(d)* 3,150 *(e)* 25,500 *(f)* 51,400

2.3

(i) Asset *(ii)* Liability *(iii)* Asset *(iv)* Asset *(v)* Liabilities *(vi)* Asset

2.5

Wrong: Assets: Loan from C Smith; Creditors; Liabilities: Stock of Goods; Debtors.

2.7

Assets: Motor 2,000; Premises 5,000; Stock 1,000; Bank 700; Cash 100 = total 8,800: Liabilities: Loan from Bevan 3,000; Creditors 400 = Total 3,400. Capital 8,800 – 3,400 = 5,400.

2.9

A Foster
Balance Sheet as at 31 December 19–4

Fixtures	5,500	Capital	23,750
Motor Vehicles	5,700	Creditors	2,450
Stock of Goods	8,800		
Debtors	4,950		
Cash at Bank	1,250		
	26,200		26,200

2.11

	Assets	*Liabilities*	*Capital*
(a)	– Cash	– Creditors	
(b)	– Bank		
	+ Fixtures		
(c)	+ Stock	+ Creditors	
(d)	+ Cash		+ Capital
(e)	+ Cash	+ Loan from J Walker	
(f)	+ Bank		
	– Debtors		
(g)	– Stock	– Creditors	
(h)	+ Premises		
	– Bank		

2.13

C Sangster
Balance Sheet as at 7 May 19–4

Assets		Capital and Liabilities	
Fixtures	4,500	Capital	18,900
Motor Vehicle	4,200	Loan from T Sharples	2,000
Stock	5,720	Creditors	2,370
Debtors	3,000		
Bank	5,450		
Cash	400		
	23,270		23,270

Chapter 3

3.1

	Debited	*Credited*		*Debited*	*Credited*
(a)	Motor Van	Cash	*(b)*	Office Machinery	J Grant & Son
(c)	Cash	Capital	*(d)*	Bank	J Beach
(e)	A Barrett	Cash			

3.2

	Debited	*Credited*		*Debited*	*Credited*
(a)	Machinery	A Jackson & Son	*(b)*	A Jackson & Son	Machinery
(c)	Cash	J Brown	*(d)*	Bank	J Smith (Loan)
(e)	Cash	Office Machinery			

3.5

Cash

(1) Capital	1,000	(14) Office Mach	60
		(31) Speed & Sons	698

Motor Lorry

(3) Speed & Sons	698		

Capital

		(1) Cash	1,000

Speed & Sons

(31) Cash	698	(3) M Lorry	698

Office Machinery

(14) Cash	60		

3.6

Bank

(1) Capital	2,500	(2) Office F	150
		(5) Motor Van	600
		(15) Planers	750
		(31) Machinery	280

Capital

		(1) Bank	2,500

Office Furniture

(2) Bank	150	(8) J Walker	60

Machinery

(3) Planers Ltd	750		
(31) Bank	280		

Cash

(23) J Walker	60		

Planers Ltd

(15) Bank	750	(3) Machinery	750

Motor Van

(5) Bank	600		

J Walker & Sons

(8) Office F	60	(23) Cash	60

3.8

Bank

(1) Capital	5,000	(2) Motor Van	1,200
(25) Cash	800	(12) Cash	100
		(19) Super Motors	800
		(30) Office Fixtures	300

Office Fixtures

(5) Young Ltd	400		
(15) Cash	60		
(30) Bank	300		

Capital

		(1) Bank	5,000

Cash

(12) Bank	100	(15) Office Fixtures	60
(21) Loan: Jarvis	1,000	(25) Bank	800

Motor Van

(2) Bank	1,200		
(8) Super Motors	800		

Young Ltd

		(5) Office Fixtures	400

Super Motors

(19) Bank	800	(8) Motor Van	800

Loan from Jarvis

		(21) Cash	1,000

Chapter 4

4.1

(a) Dr Purchases, Cr Cash
(b) Dr Purchases, Cr E Flynn
(c) Dr C Grant, Cr Sales
(d) Dr Cash, Cr Motor Van
(e) Dr Cash, Cr Sales

4.3

	Debited	*Credited*		*Debited*	*Credited*
(a)	Purchases	J Reid	*(b)*	B Perkins	Sales
(c)	Motor Van	H Thomas	*(d)*	Bank	Sales
(e)	Cash	Sales	*(f)*	H Hardy	Returns Outwards
(g)	Cash	Machinery	*(h)*	Returns Inwards	J Nelson
(i)	Purchases	D Simpson	*(j)*	H Forbes	Returns Outwards

4.5

Cash

(1) Capital	500	(3) Purchases	85
(10) Sales	42	(25) E Morgan	88
(31) A Knight	55		

Purchases

(3) Cash	85		
(7) E Morgan	116		
(18) A Moses	98		

Sales

		(10) Cash	42
		(24) A Knight	55

Returns Outwards

		(14) E Morgan	28
		(21) A Moses	19

A Knight

(24) Sales	55	(31) Cash	55

E Morgan

(14) Returns	28	(7) Purchases	116
(25) Cash	88		

A Moses

(21) Returns	19	(18) Purchases	98

Capital

		(1) Cash	500

4.6

Cash

(1) Capital	1,000	(2) Bank	900
(19) Sales	28	(7) Purchases	55

Purchases

(4) S Holmes	78		
(7) Cash	55		

Returns Outwards

		(12) S Holmes	18

S Holmes

(12) Returns	18	(4) Purchases	78
(29) Bank	60		

D Moore

(10) Sales	98		

Bank

(2) Cash	900	(5) Motor Van	500
(24) D Watson (Loan)	100	(29) S Holmes	60
		(31) Kingston Eqt	150

Sales

		(10) D Moore	98
		(19) Cash	28

Fixtures

(22) Kingston Eqt	150		

Motor Van

(5) Bank	500		

D Watson (Loan)

		(24) Bank	100

Kingston Equipment

(31) Bank	150	(22) Fixtures	150

Capital

		(1) Cash	1,000

4.7

Bank

(1) Capital	10,000	(25) F Jones	1,070
(6) Cash	250	(29) Manchester M	2,600

Sales

		(4) Cash	200
		(8) C Moody	180
		(10) J Newman	220
		(14) H Morgan	190
		(14) J Peat	320
		(24) Cash	70

Cash

(2) T Cooper (Loan)	400	(6) Bank	250
(4) Sales	200	(20) Purchases	220
(24) Sales	70	(31) Office Furn	100
(28) Capital	500		

Purchases

(3) F Jones	840		
(3) S Charles	3,600		
(11) F Jones	370		
(20) Cash	220		

Returns Inwards

(12) C Moody	40		
(26) H Morgan	30		

Motor Van

(17) Manchester M	2,600		

Office Furniture

(18) Faster S	600	(27) Faster S	160
(31) Cash	100		

Capital

		(1) Bank	10,000
		(28) Cash	500

J Newman

(10) Sales	220		

H Morgan

(14) Sales	190	(26) Returns	30

C Moody

(8) Sales	180	(12) Returns	40

J Peat

(14) Sales	320		

Returns Outwards

		(15) F Jones	140
		(19) S Charles	110

Manchester Motors

(29) Bank	2,600	(17) Motor Van	2,600

Faster Supplies Ltd

(27) Office Furn	160	(18) Office Furn	600

F Jones

(15) Returns	140	(3) Purchases	840
(25) Bank	1,070	(11) Purchases	370

S Charles

(19) Returns	110	(3) Purchases	3,600

T Cooper (Loan)

		(2) Cash	400

Chapter 5

5.1

	Account to be debited	Account to be credited		Account to be debited	Account to be credited
(a)	Rates	Bank	(b)	Wages	Cash
(c)	Bank	Rent Received	(d)	Bank	Insurance
(e)	General Exps	Cash			

5.2

	Account to be debited	Account to be credited		Account to be debited	Account to be credited
(a)	Rent	Cash	(b)	Purchases	Cash
(c)	Bank	Rates	(d)	General Exps	Bank
(e)	Cash	Commissions Recd	(f)	T Jones	Returns Out
(g)	Cash	Sales	(h)	Office Fixtures	Bank
(i)	Wages	Cash	(j)	Drawings	Cash

5.5

Bank

(1) Capital	200	(5) Motor Van	250
(2) U Surer (Loan)	1,000	(12) Insurance	22
		(31) Electricity	17

Capital

		(1) Bank	200

U Surer (Loan)

		(2) Bank	1,000

Motor Van

(5) Bank	250		

Insurance

(12) Bank	22		

Electricity

(31) Bank	17		

Motor Expenses

(7) Cash	15		

Cash

(6) Sales	105	(7) Motor Exps	15
(15) Commission	15	(8) Wages	18

Purchases

(3) T Parkin	296		
(10) C Moore	85		

Sales

		(6) Cash	105

T Parkin

		(3) Purchases	296

C Moore

		(10) Purchases	85

Commission

		(15) Cash	15

Wages

(8) Cash	18		

5.6

Bank

(1) Capital	2,000	(3) Fixtures	150
(21) Rent	5	(24) Motor Van	300

Cash

(5) Sales	275	(10) Rent	15
		(12) Stationery	27
		(30) Wages	117
		(31) Drawings	44

Purchases

(2) D Miller	175		
(6) S Waites	114		

Sales

		(5) Cash	275
		(23) U Henry	77

Fixtures

(3) Bank	150		

Rent

(10) Cash	15		

Capital

		(1) Bank	2,000

M Mills

(18) Returns Out	23	(2) Purchases	175

S Waites

		(6) Purchases	114

U Henry

(23) Sales	77		

Rent Received

		(21) Bank	5

Stationery

(12) Cash	27		

Returns Out

		(18) M Mills	23

Motor Van

(24) Bank	300		

Wages

(30) Cash	117		

Drawings

(31) Cash	44		

5.7

Cash

(1) Capital	1,500	(3) Rent	28
(11) Sales	49	(4) Bank	1,000
		(20) B Repairs	18
		(28) Purchases	125
		(30) Motor Exps	15

Capital

		(1) Cash	1,500

Rent

(3) Cash	28		

Building Repairs

(20) Cash	18		

Bank			
(4) Cash	1,000	(7) Stationery	15
		(27) A Hanson	279
		(29) M Van	395

Purchases			
(2) A Hanson	296		
(28) Cash	125		

Sales			
		(5) E Linton	54
		(11) Cash	49
		(17) S Morgan	29

Stationery			
(7) Bank	15		

Returns Outwards			
		(14) A Hanson	17

Fixtures			
(31) A Webster	120		

Motor Expenses			
(30) Cash	15		

Motor Van			
(29) Bank	395		

A Hanson			
(14) Returns Out	17	(2) Purchases	296
(27) Bank	279		

E Linton			
(5) Sales	54	(22) Returns In	14

S Morgan			
(17) Sales	29		

Returns Inwards			
(22) E Linton	14		

A Webster			
		(31) Fixtures	120

Chapter 6

6.1

H Harvey			
(1) Sales	690	(10) Returns	40
(4) Sales	66	(24) Cash	300
		(31) Balance c/d	416
	756		756
(1) Balance b/d	416		

L Masters			
(4) Sales	418	(31) Balance c/d	621
(31) Sales	203		
	621		621
(1) Balance b/d	621		

N Morgan			
(1) Sales	153	(18) Bank	153

J Lindo			
(1) Sales	420	(10) Returns	20
		(20) Bank	400
	420		420

6.2

J Young			
(10) Returns	55	(1) Purchases	458
(28) Cash	250	(15) Purchases	80
(30) Balance c/d	233		
	538		538
		(1) Balance b/d	233

G Norman			
(10) Returns	22	(1) Purchases	708
(30) Balance c/d	686		
	708		708
		(1) Balance b/d	686

L Williams			
(30) Returns	17	(1) Purchases	120
(30) Balance c/d	180	(3) Purchases	77
	197		197
		(1) Balance b/d	180

T Harris			
(19) Bank	880	(3) Purchases	880

6.3

H Harvey

19–6		Dr	Cr	Balance	
May 1	Sales	690		690	Dr
May 4	Sales	66		756	Dr
May 10	Returns		40	716	Dr
May 24	Cash		300	416	Dr

N Morgan

19–6		Dr	Cr	Balance	
May 1	Sales	153		153	Dr
May 18	Bank		153	0	

J Lindo

19–6		Dr	Cr	Balance	
May 1	Sales	420		420	Dr
May 10	Returns		20	400	Dr
May 20	Bank		400	0	

L Masters

19–6		Dr	Cr	Balance	
May 4	Sales	418		418	Dr
May 31	Sales	203		621	Dr

6.5

D Williams			
(1) Sales	458	(24) Bank	300
		(28) Cash	100
		(30) Balance c/d	58
	458		458
(1) Balance b/d	58		

J Moore			
(1) Sales	235	(12) Returns	26
(8) Sales	444	(20) Balance c/d	653
	679		679
(1) Balance b/d	653		

G Grant			
(1) Sales	98	(12) Returns	9
		(30) Balance c/d	89
	98		98
(1) Balance b/d	89		

F Franklin			
(8) Sales	249	(30) Bank	249

A White			
(20) Bank	77	(2) Purchases	77

H Samuels			
(17) Returns	24	(2) Purchases	231
(30) Balance c/d	219	(10) Purchases	12
	243		243
		(1) Balance c/d	219

P Owen			
		(2) Purchases	65

O Oliver			
(17) Returns	12	(10) Purchases	222
(26) Cash	210		
	222		222

Chapter 7

7.1

Cash

(1) Capital	250	(6) Rent	12
		(15) Carriage	23
		(31) Balance c/d	215
	250		250

Bank

(9) C Bailey	43	(12) K Gibson	25
(10) H Spencer	150	(12) D Ellis	54
		(31) Rent	18
		(31) Balance c/d	96
	193		193

Capital

		(1) Cash	250

Rent

(6) Cash	12		
(31) Bank	18		

Carriage

(15) Cash	23		

D Ellis

(12) Bank	54	(2) Purchases	54

C Mendez

		(2) Purchases	87
		(18) Purchases	43

K Gibson

(12) Bank	25	(2) Purchases	25

D Booth

		(2) Purchases	76
		(18) Purchases	110

L Lowe

		(2) Purchases	64

C Bailey

(4) Sales	43	(9) Bank	43

B Hughes

(4) Sales	62		
(21) Sales	67		

H Spencer

(4) Sales	176	(10) Bank	150

Purchases

(2) D Ellis	54		
(2) C Mendez	87		
(2) K Gibson	25		
(2) D Booth	76		
(2) L Lowe	64		
(18) C Mendez	43		
(18) D Booth	110		

Sales

		(4) C Bailey	43
		(4) B Hughes	62
		(4) H Spencer	176
		(21) B Hughes	67

Trial Balance as at 31 May 19–8

	Dr	Cr
Cash	215	
Bank	96	
Capital		250
Rent	30	
Carriage	23	
C Mendez		130
D Booth		186
L Lowe		64
B Hughes	129	
H Spencer	26	
Purchases	459	
Sales		348
	978	978

7.2

Bank

(1) Capital	800	(17) M Hyatt	84
(24) J Carlton	95	(21) Betta Ltd	50
		(31) Motor Van	400
		(31) Balance c/d	361
	895		895

Cash

(5) Sales	87	(6) Wages	14
(30) J King (Loan)	60	(9) Purchases	46
		(12) Wages	14
		(31) Balance c/d	73
	147		147

Capital

		(1) Bank	800

Motor Van

(31) Bank	400		

Wages

(6) Cash	14		
(12) Cash	14		

Shop Fixtures

(15) Betta Ltd	50		

J King (Loan)

		(30) Cash	60

H Elliott

(7) Sales	35		

L Lane

(7) Sales	42		
(13) Sales	32		

J Carlton

(7) Sales	72	(24) Bank	95
(13) Sales	23		

K Henriques

(27) Returns	24	(2) Purchases	76

M Hyatt

(17) Bank	84	(2) Purchases	27
		(10) Purchases	57

T Braham

(18) Returns	20	(2) Purchases	56
		(10) Purchases	98

Betta Ltd

(21) Bank	50	(15) S Fixtures	50

Sales

		(5) Cash	87
		(7) H Elliott	35
		(7) L Lane	42
		(7) J Carlton	72
		(13) L Lane	32
		(13) J Carlton	23

Purchases

(2) K Henriques	76		
(2) M Hyatt	27		
(2) T Braham	56		
(9) Cash	46		
(10) M Hyatt	57		
(10) T Braham	98		

Returns Outwards

		(18) T Braham	20
		(27) K Henriques	24

Trial Balance as on 31 March 19–6

	Dr	Cr
Bank	361	
Cash	73	
Capital		800
Motor Van	400	
Wages	28	
Shop Fixtures	50	
J King (Loan)		60
H Elliott	35	
L Lindo	74	
K Henriques		52
T Braham		134
Sales		291
Purchases	360	
Returns Outwards		44
	1,381	1,381

7.3

Bank

Dr		Cr	
(1) Capital	600	(5) Motor Van	256
(25) P Potter	43	(7) Motor Exps	12
		(12) N Moss	62
		(21) O Hughes	46
		Balance	267
	643		643

Cash

Dr		Cr	
(1) Capital	50	(4) Purchases	23
(23) H Henry	66	(15) Motor Exps	5
(26) Sales	34	(20) Drawings	10
		(27) Drawings	24
		(29) Postages	4
		Balance	84
	150		150

Capital

Dr		Cr	
		(1) Bank	600
		(25) Cash	50

Drawings

Dr		Cr	
(20) Cash	10		
(27) Cash	24		

Sales

Dr		Cr	
		(3) H Henry	66
		(3) N Neita	25
		(3) P Potter	43
		(9) B Barnes	24
		(9) K Lyn	26
		(9) M Moore	65
		(26) Cash	34
		(30) N Neita	43
		(30) M Edgar	67
		(30) K Lyn	45

Purchases

Dr		Cr	
(2) C Jones	500		
(4) Cash	23		
(11) C Jones	240		
(11) N Moss	62		
(11) O Hughes	46		

Returns Inwards

Dr		Cr	
(19) N Neita	11		

Returns Outwards

Dr		Cr	
		(13) C Jones	25
		(28) C Jones	42

Motor Van

Dr		Cr	
(5) Bank	256		

Motor Expenses

Dr		Cr	
(7) Bank	12		
(15) Cash	5		

Postages

Dr		Cr	
(29) Cash	4		

H Henry

Dr		Cr	
(3) Sales	66	(23) Cash	66

N Neita

Dr		Cr	
(3) Sales	25	(19) Returns In	11
(30) Sales	43		

P Potter

Dr		Cr	
(3) Sales	43	(25) Bank	43

B Barnes

Dr		Cr	
(9) Sales	24		

K Lyn

Dr		Cr	
(9) Sales	26		
(30) Sales	45		

M Moore

Dr		Cr	
(9) Sales	65		

M Edgar

Dr		Cr	
(9) Sales	67		

C Jones

Dr		Cr	
(13) Returns	25	(2) Purchases	500
(28) Returns	42	(11) Purchases	240

N Moss

Dr		Cr	
(21) Bank	62	(11) Purchases	62

O Hughes

Dr		Cr	
(21) Bank	46	(11) Purchases	46

Trial Balance 30 June 19–7

	Dr	Cr
Bank	267	
Cash	84	
Capital		650
Drawings	34	
Sales		438
Purchases	871	
Returns Inwards	11	
Returns Outwards		67
Motor Van	256	
Motor Expenses	17	
Postages	4	
N Neita	57	
B Barnes	24	
K Lyn	71	
M Moore	65	
M Edgar	67	
C Jones		673
	1,828	1,828

Chapter 8

8.1

B Webb

Trading & Profit & Loss Account for the year ended 31 December 19–6

Purchases	14,629	Sales	18,462
Less Closing Stock	2,548		
Cost of Goods Sold	12,081		
Gross Profit c/d	6,381		
	18,462		18,462
Salaries	2,150	Gross Profit b/d	6,381
Motor Expenses	520		
Rent & Rates	670		
Insurance	111		
General Expenses	105		
Net Profit	2,825		
	6,381		6,381

8.2

C Worth

Trading & Profit & Loss Account for the year ended 30 June 19–4

Purchases	23,803	Sales	28,794
Less Closing Stock	4,166		
Cost of Goods Sold	19,637		
Gross Profit c/d	9,157		
	28,794		28,794
Salaries	3,164	Gross Profit b/d	9,157
Rent	854		
Lighting	422		
Insurance	105		
Motor Expenses	1,133		
Trade Expenses	506		
Net Profit	2,973		
	9,157		9,157

Chapter 9

9.1

B Webb
Balance Sheet as at 31 December 19–6

Fixed Assets			Capital		
Premises		1,500	Balance at 1.1.19–6	5,424	
Motors		1,200	Add Net Profit	2,825	
		2,700		8,249	
Current Assets			Less Drawings	895	7,354
Stock	2,548				
Debtors	1,950		Current Liabilities		
Bank	1,654		Creditors		1,538
Cash	40	6,192			
		8,892			8,892

9.2

C Worth
Balance Sheet as at 30 December 19–4

Fixed Assets			Capital		
Buildings		50,000	Balance at 1.7.19–3	65,900	
Fixtures		1,000	Add Net Profit	2,973	
Motors		5,500		68,873	
		56,500	Less Drawings	2,400	66,473
Current Assets					
Stock	4,166		Current Liabilities		
Debtors	3,166		Creditors		1,206
Bank	3,847	11,179			
		67,679			67,679

Chapter 10

10.1

R Graham
Trading & Profit & Loss Account for the year ended 30 September 19–6

Opening Stock		2,368	Sales	18,600	
Add Purchases	11,874		Less Returns In	205	18,395
Less Returns Out	322	11,552			
Carriage Inwards		310			
		14,230			
Less Closing Stock		2,946			
Cost of Goods Sold		11,284			
Gross Profit c/d		7,111			
		18,395			18,395
Salaries & Wages		3,862	Gross Profit b/d		7,111
Rent & Rates		304			
Carriage Out		200			
Insurance		78			
Motor Expenses		664			
Office Expenses		216			
Lighting & Heating		166			
General Expenses		314			
Net Profit		1,307			
		7,111			7,111

Balance Sheet as at 30 September 19–6

Fixed Assets			*Capital*	
Premises		5,000	Balance at 1.10.19–5	12,636
Fixtures		350	Add Net Profit	1,307
Motor Vehicles		1,800		13,943
		7,150	– Drawings	1,200
Current Assets				12,743
Stock	2,946		*Current Liabilities*	
Debtors	3,896		Creditors	1,731
Bank	482	7,324		
		14,474		14,474

10.2

Trading Account for the year ended 31 December 19–3

Opening Stock		6,924	Sales	38,742	
Add Purchases	26,409		Less Returns In	890	37,852
Less Returns Out	495	25,914			
Carriage Inwards		670			
		33,508			
Less Closing Stock		7,489			
Cost of Goods Sold		26,019			
Gross Profit		11,833			
		37,852			37,852

Balance Sheet as at 30 April 19–7

Fixed Assets			*Capital*		
Fixtures		600	Balance as at 1.5.19–6		12,844
Motors		2,400	Add Net Profit		2,732
		3,000			15,576
Current Assets			Less Drawings		2,050
Stock	4,998				13,526
Debtors	4,577				
Bank	3,876		*Current Liabilities*		
Cash	120	13,571	Creditors		3,045
		16,571			16,571

10.3

B Jackson
Trading & Profit & Loss Account for the year ended 30 April 19–7

Opening Stock		3,776	Sales	18,600	
Add Purchases	11,556		Less Returns In	440	18,160
Less Returns Out	355	11,201			
Carriage Inwards		234			
		15,211			
Less Closing Stock		4,998			
		10,213			
Gross Profit c/d		7,947			
		18,160			18,160
Salaries & Wages		2,447	Gross Profit b/d		7,947
Motor Expenses		664			
Rent		576			
Carriage Out		326			
Sundry Expenses		1,202			
Net Profit		2,732			
		7,947			7,947

Chapter 11

11.1

(a)

	Accounts		
	Personal	*Real*	*Nominal*
(1) Customer account balance	2,620		
(2) Drawings			4,210
(3) Sales			36,340
(4) Wages & Salaries			8,310
(5) Supplier account balances	1,730		
(6) Fixed assets at net book value		14,500	
(7) Cash in hand		15	
(8) Capital			17,365
(9) Cost of Goods Sold			18,185
(10) Rates & Other Taxes			1,720
(11) Insurances			680
(12) Stock		1,836	
(13) Depreciation			1,010
(14) General Expenses			550
(15) Bank		1,799	

(b)

Roger Craig
Profit & Loss Account for the year ended 31 December Year 3

Wages & Salaries	8,310	Gross Profit	
Rates etc	1,720	(36,340 – 18,185)	18,155
Insurance	680		
General Expenses	550		
Depreciation	1,010		
Net Profit	5,885		
	18,155		18,155

(c)

Balance Sheet as at 31 December Year 3

Fixed Assets			*Capital*	
At Net Book Value*		14,500	Balance as at 1 January,	
			Year 3	17,365
Current Assets			Add Net Profit	5,885
Stock †	1,836			23,250
Debtors	2,620		Less Drawings	4,210
Bank	1,799			19,040
Cash	15	6,270		
			Current Liabilities	
			Creditors	1,730
		20,770		20,770

* This is *after* depreciation 1,010.
† As Cost of Goods sold (9) already calculated, the stock (12) must be the closing stock.

Chapter 13

13.1

Cash Book

	Cash	*Bank*		*Cash*	*Bank*
(1) Capital	100		(2) Rent	10	
(3) F Lake (Loan)		500	(4) B McKenzie		65
(5) Sales	98		(9) B Burton	22	
(7) N Miller		62	(16) Bank C	50	
(11) Sales		53	(19) F Lake (Loan)		100
(15) G Moores	65		(26) Motor Expenses		12
(16) Cash C		50	(30) Cash C		100
(22) Sales		66	(31) Wages	97	
(30) Bank C	100		(31) Balances c/d	184	454
	363	731		363	731

13.2

Cash Book

	Cash	*Bank*		*Cash*	*Bank*
(1) Balances b/d	56	2,356	(2) Rates		156
(5) Sales	74		(3) Postages	5	
(7) Cash C		60	(7) Bank C	60	
(12) J Moores	50	100	(8) T Lee		75
(20) P Jones		79	(10) C Brooks	2	
(22) Bank C	200		(17) Drawings	20	
(31) Sales		105	(22) Cash C		200
			(24) Motor Van	195	
			(28) Rent		40
			(31) Balance c/d	98	2,229
	380	2,700		380	2,700

Chapter 14

14.1

Cash Book

	Disct	*Cash*	*Bank*		*Disct*	*Cash*	*Bank*
(1) Capital			6,000	(1) Fixtures			950
(3) Sales		407		(2) Purchases			1,240
(5) N Morgan	10		210	(4) Rent		200	
(9) S Cooper	20		380	(7) S Thompson & Co	4		76
(14) L Curtis			115	(12) Rates			410
(20) P Exeter	2		78	(16) M Monroe	6	114	
(31) Sales			88	(31) Balance c/d	—	93	4,195
	32	407	6,871		10	407	6,871

In General Ledger:
Debit Discounts Allowed 32: Credit Discounts Received 10.

14.2

Cash Book

	Disct	Cash	Bank		Disct	Cash	Bank
(1) Balance b/d		230	4,756	(4) Rent			120
(2) R Burton	7		133	(8) N Black	9		351
(2) E Taylor	11		209	(8) P Towers	12		468
(2) R Harris	15		285	(8) C Rowse	20		780
(6) J Cotton: loan			1,000	(10) Motor Expenses		44	
(12) H Hankins	3		74	(15) Wages		160	
(18) C Winston	13		247	(21) Cash			350
(18) R Wilson				(24) Drawings		120	
& Son	17		323	(25) T Briers	7	133	
(18) H Winter	23		437	(29) Fixtures			650
(21) Bank		350		(31) Balances c/d		123	4,833
(31) Commission			88				
	89	580	7,552		48	580	7,552

Discounts Received

		(31) Total for month	48

Discounts Allowed

(31) Total for month	89		

14.3

	Disct	Cash	Bank		Disct	Cash	Bank
(1) Balances b/f		211	3,984	(2) T Adams	4		76
(4) C Potts			98	(2) C Bibby	13		247
(6) Sales			49	(2) D Clarke	22		418
(9) R Smiley	4		156	(7) Insurance		65	
(9) J Turner	16		624	(12) Motor Expenses		100	
(9) R Pimlott	13		507	(21) Salaries			120
(18) Sales		98		(23) Rent		60	
(28) R Godfrey				(31) Stationery			27
(Loan)			500	(31) Balances c/d		84	5,030
	33	309	5,918		39	309	5,918

14.6*(a)* Depending on the exact nature of the transaction, and whether the provider of goods or services will accept the method of payment.

Any three from:

(i) By handing over an asset at an agreed value, e.g. a motor car to cancel a debt.
(ii) By contra, e.g. an amount owing by him to you may be set off against what he owes.
(iii) By credit card
(iv) By direct debit
(v) By standing order
(vi) By a postal order or money order
(vii) By credit transfer

(b)

Cash Book

	Disct	Cash	Bank		Disct	Cash	Bank
(1) Balances b/d		419	3,685	(6) Wages		102	
(2) A Wood			296	(9) C Hill	13		211
(12) Sales		146		(12) T Jarvis	28		1,023
(17) Atlas & Co			500	(13) Wages		104	
(23) Bank C		200		(19) Postages		21	
(28) T Phillips	8		317	(20) Wages		102	
(31) Cash			260	(23) Cash C			200
				(25) W Moore			429
				(26) Wages		105	
				(31) Bank C		260	
				(31) Balances c/d		71	3,195
	8	765	5,058		41	765	5,058

Chapter 15

15.1

Sales Journal

(1) J Gordon	187
(3) G Abrahams	166
(6) V White	12
(10) J Gordon	55
(17) F Williams	289
(19) U Richards	66
(27) V Wood	28
(31) L Simes	78
	881

Sales Ledger

J Gordon

(1) Sales 187
(10) Sales 55

G Abrahams

(3) Sales 166

V White

(6) Sales 12

F Williams

(17) Sales 289

U Richards

(19) Sales 66

V Wood

(27) Sales 28

L Simes

(31) Sales 78

General Ledger

Sales Account

(31) Total for month 881

15.3

Workings of invoices:

(1) F Gray	3 rolls white tape × 10 =	30		
	5 sheets blue cotton × 6 =	30		
	1 dress length × 20 =	20	80	
	less Trade Discount 25%		20	60
(4) A Gray	6 rolls white tape × 10 =	60		
	30 metres green baize × 4 =	120	180	
	less Trade Discount × 33⅓%		60	120
(8) E Hines	1 dress length black silk × 20 =			20
(20) M Allen	10 rolls white tape × 10 =	100		
	6 sheets blue cotton × 6 =	36		
	3 dress lengths black silk × 20 =	60		
	11 metres green baize × 4 =	44	240	
	less Trade Discount × 25%		60	180
(31) B Cooper	12 rolls white tape × 10 =	120		
	14 sheets blue cotton × 6 =	84		
	9 metres green baize × 4 =	36	240	
	less Trade Discount 33⅓%		80	160

Sales Journal

(1) F Gray	60
(4) A Gray	120
(8) E Hines	20
(20) M Allen	180
(31) B Cooper	160
	540

Sales Ledger

F Gray

(1) Sales	60

A Gray

(4) Sales	120

E Hines

(8) Sales	20

M Allen

(20) Sales	180

B Cooper

(31) Sales	160

General Ledger

Sales Account

(31) Total for month	540

15.5*(a)*(i)

Sales Day Book

Yr 4	Invoice No	Details	List (£)	Trade Discount (£)	Net (£)
Jan	1040	Cash	80	—	80
"	1041	Debtor	420	105	315
"	1042	Cash	30	—	30
"	1043	PH Ltd	860	215	645
"	1044	Debtor	110	11	99
"	1045	PH Ltd	1,040	260	780
"	1046	Cash	15	—	15
"	1047	Cash	32	—	32
"	1048	Debtor	320	16	304
"	1049	Debtor	100	10	90
					2,390

(ii)

Sales Account

	Year 4			
	Jan 31 Credit Sales	2,233		
	" 31 Cash Sales	157	2,390	

(b)

PH Ltd

Year 4		*Year 4*	
Jan Sales	645.00	Jan Bank	638.55
" "	780.00	" Discount	6.45
		" Balance c/d	780.00
	1,425.00		1,425.00

Chapter 16

16.1

Workings of purchases invoices

(1) K King	4 radios × 30 =	120		
	3 music centres × 160 =	480	600	
	less Trade Discount 25%		150	450
(3) A Bell	2 washing machines × 200 =	400		
	5 vacuum cleaners × 60 =	300		
	2 dish dryers × 150 =	300	1,000	
	less Trade Discount 20%		200	800
(15) J Kelly	1 music centre × 300 =	300		
	2 washing machines × 250 =	500	800	
	less Trade Discount 25%		200	600
(20) B Powell	6 radios × 70 =		420	
	less Trade Discount 33⅓%		140	280
(30) B Lewis	4 dish dryers × 200 =		800	
	less Trade Discount 20%		160	640

Purchases Journal

(1) K King	450
(3) A Bell	800
(15) J Kelly	600
(20) B Powell	280
(30) B Lewis	640
	2,770

General Ledger

Purchases Account

(31) Total for month	2,770

Purchases Ledger

K King

(1) Purchases	450

A Bell

(3) Purchases	800

J Kelly

(15) Purchases	600

B Powell

(20) Purchases	280

B Lewis

(30) Purchases	640

16.3

Purchases Journal

(1) Smith Stores	90
(23) C Kelly	105
(31) J Hamilton	180
	375

Sales Journal

(8) A Grantley	72
(15) A Henry	240
(24) D Sangster	81
	393

Purchases Ledger

Smith Stores

		(1) Purchases	90

C Kelly

		(23) Purchases	105

J Hamilton

		(31) Purchases	180

Sales Ledger

A Grantley

(8) Sales	72		

A Henry

(15) Sales	240		

D Sangster

(24) Sales	81		

General Ledger

Sales Account

		(31) Total for month	393

Purchases Account

(31) Total for month	375		

16.4

(a)	Product A	Product B
Manufacturers Recommended Retail Price	1,500	4,000
less Trade Discount	(20%) 300	(25%) 1,000
Price paid per product	1,200	3,000
(b) Profit per product (equals Trade Discount when sold at MRRP)	300	1,000
(c)	$\frac{300}{1,200} \times \frac{100}{1} = 25\%$	$\frac{1,000}{3,000} \times \frac{100}{1} = 33\frac{1}{3}\%$

16.6(a)

Purchases Day Book

Aug 4 G Mann	300
" 11 B Jollie	200
	500

Sales Day Book

Aug 5 B Allen	240
" 12 G Parker	360
" 21 E Todd	243
	843

Cash Book

	Discount	Bank		Discount	Bank
Aug 18 G Parker	36	324	Aug 15 B Jollie	10	190
" 31	12	228	" 29 G Mann		300

(b) Discount allowed to traders as a means of calculating net sales price.

(c) To speed up payments of debtors' accounts.

Chapter 17

17.1

Purchases Journal

(1) H Lloyd	119
(4) D Scott	98
(4) A Simpson	114
(4) A Williams	25
(4) S Wood	56
(10) A Simpson	59
(18) M White	89
(18) J Wong	67
(18) H Miller	196
(18) H Lewis	119
(31) A Williams	56
(31) C Cooper	98
	1,096

Returns Outwards Journal

(7) H Lloyd	16
(7) D Scott	14
(25) J Wong	5
(25) A Simpson	11
	46

General Ledger

Purchases Account

(31) Total for month	1,096		

Returns Outwards Account

		(31) Total for month	46

Sales Ledger

H Lloyd

(7) Returns	16	(1) Purchases	119

D Scott

(7) Returns	14	(4) Purchases	98

A Simpson

(25) Returns	11	(4) Purchases	114
		(10) Purchases	59

A Williams

		(4) Purchases	25
		(31) Purchases	56

S Wood

		(4) Purchases	56

M White

		(18) Purchases	89

J Wong

(25) Returns	5	(18) Purchases	67

H Miller

		(18) Purchases	196

H Lewis

		(18) Purchases	119

C Cooper

		(31) Purchases	98

17.3

Sales Book

(3) E Rigby	510
(3) E Phillips	246
(3) F Thompson	356
(8) A Green	307
(8) H George	250
(8) J Ferguson	185
(20) E Phillips	188
(20) F Powell	310
(20) E Lee	420
	2,772

Purchases Book

(1) K Hill	380
(1) M Norman	500
(1) N Senior	106
(5) R Morton	200
(5) J Cook	180
(5) D Edwards	410
(5) C Davies	66
(24) C Ferguson	550
(24) K Ennevor	900
	3,292

Returns Inwards Book

(14) E Phillips	18
(14) F Thompson	22
(31) E Phillips	27
(31) E Rigby	30
	97

Returns Outwards Book

(12) M Norman	30
(12) N Senior	16
(31) J Cook	13
(31) C Davies	11
	70

Sales Ledger

	E Rigby		
(3) Sales	510	(31) Returns In	30
	E Phillips		
(3) Sales	246	(14) Returns In	18
(20) Sales	188	(31) Returns In	27
	F Thompson		
(3) Sales	356	(14) Returns In	22
	A Green		
(8) Sales	307		
	H George		
(8) Sales	250		
	J Ferguson		
(8) Sales	185		
	F Powell		
(20) Sales	310		
	E Lee		
(20) Sales	420		

Purchases Ledger

	K Hill		
		(1) Purchases	380
	M Norman		
(13) Returns Out	30	(1) Purchases	500
	N Senior		
(12) Returns Out	16	(1) Purchases	106
	R Morton		
		(5) Purchases	200
	J Cook		
(31) Returns Out	13	(5) Purchases	180
	D Edwards		
		(5) Purchases	410
	C Davies		
(31) Returns Out	11	(5) Purchases	66
	C Ferguson		
		(24) Purchases	550
	K Ennevor		
		(24) Purchases	900

General Ledger

	Sales		
		(31) Sales Book	2,772
	Purchases		
(31) Purchases Book	3,292		
	Returns Inwards		
(31) Returns In Book	97		
	Returns Outwards		
		(31) Returns Out Book	70

17.4

	M Jones		Page 62
Jan 3 Sales	60	Jan 21 Returns	12
Jan 10 Sales	70		
Jan 21 Sales	70		
	B Buston		
Jan 7 Sales	180		
	M White		
Jan 15 Sales	162		

17.7

(Sales Ledger)

	A Birch		
(1) Balance b/d	4,251	(7) Bank	4,100
(9) Sales	1,095	(7) Discount	151
		(31) Balance c/d	1,095
	5,346		5,346
	H Jameson		
(1) Balance b/d	1,260	(23) Bank	900
(15) Sales	740	(24) Returns	140
(19) Sales	205	(31) Balance c/d	1,165
	2,205		2,205

(General Ledger)

	Capital		
		(1) Balance b/d	9,151
	Sales		
		(31) Sales Book	2,040
	Purchases		
(31) Purchases Book	1,604		
	Returns Inwards		
(31) Return In Book	140		
	Returns Outwards		
		(31) Returns Out Book	80
	Discounts Allowed		
(31) Cash Book	151		
	Discounts Received		
		(31) Cash Book	187

(Purchases Ledger)

	S Franklin		
(18) Bank	1,080	(1) Balance b/d	1,780
(18) Discount	120	(12) Purchases	206
(19) Returns	80		
(31) Balance c/d	706		
	1,986		1,986
	P Greenbank		
(2) Bank	603	(1) Balance b/d	670
(2) Discount	67		
	670		670
	E Oliver		
(29) Bank	1,110	(1) Balance b/d	1,110
(31) Balance c/d	1,398	(8) Purchases	348
		(23) Purchases	1,050
	2,508		2,508

Cash Book

	Discount	Bank		Discount	Bank
(1) Balance b/d		7,200	(2) P Greenbank	67	603
(7) A Birch	151	4,100	(18) S Franklin	120	1,080
(23) H Jameson		900	(29) E Oliver		1,110
			(31) Balance c/d		9,407
	151	12,200		187	12,200

Chapter 18

18.1(*a*) Style of invoice will vary.

Calculations:	£
3 sets of Boy Michael Golf Clubs × £270	810
150 Watson golf balls at £8 per 10 balls	120
4 Faldo golf bags at £30	120
	1,050
Less Trade Discount $33\frac{1}{3}$%	350
	700
Add VAT 10%	70
	770

(*b*)

D Wilson Ltd Ledger
G Christie & Sons

	£		£
19–7			
May 1 Sales	770		

G Christie & Son Ledger
D Wilson Ltd

	£		£
		19–7	
		May 1 Purchases	770

18.2

Sales Book

19–5	*Net*	*VAT*
Aug 1 M Sinclair & Co	150	15
" 8 M Brown & Associates	260	26
" 19 A Axton Ltd	80	8
" 31 T Christie	30	3
	520	52

Sales Ledger

M Sinclair & Co

(1) Sales	165		

M Brown & Associates

(8) Sales	286		

A Axton Ltd

(19) Sales	88		

T Christie

(31) Sales	33		

General Ledger

Sales

		(31) Credit Sales for the month	520

Value Added Tax

		(31) Sales Book: VAT content	52

18.3

Sales Book

	Net	*VAT*
(1) B Davies & Co	150	15
(4) C Grant Ltd	220	22
(16) C Grant Ltd	140	14
(31) B Karloff	80	8
	590	59

Purchases Book

	Net	*VAT*
(10) G Cooper & Son	400	40
(10) J Wayne Ltd	190	19
(14) B Lugosi	50	5
(23) S Hayward	60	6
	700	70

Sales Ledger

B Davies & Co

(1) Sales	165		

C Grant Ltd

(4) Sales	242		
(16) Sales	154		

B Karloff

(31) Sales	88		

Purchases Ledger

G Cooper & Son

		(10) Purchases	440

J Wayne Ltd

		(10) Purchases	209

B Lugosi

		(14) Purchases	55

S Hayward

		(23) Purchases	66

General Ledger

Sales

		(31) Credit Sales for month	590

Purchases

(31) Credit Purchases for month	700		

Value Added Tax

(31) VAT Content in Purchases Book	70	(31) VAT Content in Sales Book	59
		(31) Balance c/d	11
	70		70

18.5

C Hills

(8) Bank	154	(1) Balance b/d	154
(31) Balance c/d	275	(13) Purchases	110
		(20) Purchases	165
	429		429
		(1) Balance b/d	275

L Lowe

(31) Balance c/d	341	(1) Balance b/d	275
		(21) Purchases	66
	341		341
		(1) Balance b/d	341

K Harris

(1) Balance b/d	330	(16) Bank	594
(11) Sales	264	(31) Balance c/d	88
(15) Sales	88		
	682		682
(1) Balance b/d	88		

Printing

(15) Bank	20		

Value Added Tax

(31) Purchases Book	31	(31) Sales Book	32
(31) Balance c/d	1		
	32		32
		(1) Balance b/d	1

Bank

(1) Balance b/d	740	(8) C Hills	154
(16) K Harris	594	(15) Printing	20
		(31) Balance c/d	1,160
	1,334		1,334
(1) Balance b/d	1,160		

Capital

		(1) Balance b/d	641

Purchases

(31) Day Book	310		

Sales

		(31) Day Book	320

Trial Balance as at 31.12.19–9

	Dr	Cr
C Hills		275
L Lowe		341
K Harris	88	
Printing	20	
Value Added Tax		1
Bank	1,160	
Capital		641
Purchases	310	
Sales		320
	1,578	1,578

18.7*(a)*

19–4			19–4		
Jan 31	Tax on Inputs	2,000	Jan 31	Tax on Outputs	2,100
Jan 31	Balance c/d	100			
		2,100			2,100
Feb 28	Tax on Inputs	2,100	Feb 1	Balance b/d	100
			Feb 28	Tax on Outputs	2,000
		2,100			2,100
Mar 31	Tax on Inputs	2,200	Mar 31	Tax on Outputs	1,500
			Mar 31	Balance c/d	700
		2,200			2,200
Apr 1	Balance b/d	700			

(b) The balance of 700 on 31 March 19–4 is the amount owing by Customs & Excise (VAT) to the firm. This will be cleared by Customs & Excise sending a remittance for 700

Chapter 19

19.1

Straight Line		*Reducing Balance*	
Cost	4,000	Cost	4,000
Yr 1 Depreciation	700	Yr 1 Depn 40% of 4,000	1,600
	3,300		2,400
Yr 2 Depreciation	700	Yr 2 Depn 40% of 2,400	960
	2,600		1,440
Yr 3 Depreciation	700	Yr 3 Depn 40% of 1,440	576
	1,900		864
Yr 4 Depreciation	700	Yr 4 Depn 40% of 864	346
	1,200		518
Yr 5 Depreciation	700	Yr 5 Depn 40% of 518	207
	500		311

4,000 − 500 = 3,500 ÷ 5 = 700

19.2

(a) Straight Line		*(b) Reducing Balance*	
Cost	12,500	Cost	12,500
Yr 1 Depreciation	1,845	Yr 1 Depn 20% of 12,500	2,500
	10,655		10,000
Yr 2 Depreciation	1,845	Yr 2 Depn 20% of 10,000	2,000
	8,810		8,000
Yr 3 Depreciation	1,845	Yr 3 Depn 20% of 8,000	1,600
	6,965		6,400
Yr 4 Depreciation	1,845	Yr 4 Depn 20% of 6,400	1,280
	5,120		5,120

$$\frac{12{,}500 - 5{,}120}{4} = 1{,}845$$

19.3

(a) Reducing Balance		*(b) Straight Line*	
Cost	6,400	Cost	6,400
Yr 1 Depn 50% of 6,400	3,200	Yr 1 Depreciation	1,240
	3,200		5,160
Yr 2 Depn 50% of 3,200	1,600	Yr 2 Depreciation	1,240
	1,600		3,920
Yr 3 Depn 50% of 1,600	800	Yr 3 Depreciation	1,240
	800		2,680
Yr 4 Depn 50% of 800	400	Yr 4 Depreciation	1,240
	400		1,440
Yr 5 Depn 50% of 400	200	Yr 5 Depreciation	1,240
	200		200

$$\frac{6{,}400 - 200}{5} = 1{,}240$$

19.7

		Machines A	Machines B	Machines C
	Bought 1.1.19–4	3,000		
19–4	Depreciation 10% for 12 months	300		
		2,700		
	Bought 1.4.19–5		2,000	
19–5	Depreciation 10% × 2,700	270		
	" 10% for 9 months		150	
		2,430	1,850	
	Bought 1.7.19–6			1,000
19–6	Depreciation 10% × 2,430	243		
	" 10% × 1,850		185	
	" 10% for 6 months			50
		2,187	1,665	950

19–6 Total Depreciation 243 + 185 + 50 = 478

Chapter 20

20.1*(a)*

Motor Delivery Van

Date			£	Date			£
19–2				19–3			
Jul 1	Bank		2,000	Jun 30	Depreciation		400
				Jun 30	Balance c/d		1,600
			2,000				2,000
19–3				19–4			
Jul 1	Balance b/d		1,600	Jun 30	Depreciation		320
				Jun 30	Balance c/d		1,280
			1,600				1,600
19–4				19–5			
Jul 1	Balance b/d		1,280	Jun 30	Depreciation		256
				Jun 30	Balance c/d		1,024
			1,280				1,280
19–5				19–6			
Jul 1	Balance b/d		1,024	Jun 30	Depreciation*		205
				Jun 30	Balance c/d		819
			1,024				1,024

* rounded off to nearest £

(b) per text

20.2*(a)*

(Straight line method)

Delivery Van

Year 1	Bank	1,500	Year 1	Depreciation	150
				Balance c/d	1,350
		1,500			1,500
Year 2	Balance b/d	1,350	Year 2	Depreciation	150
				Balance c/d	1,200
		1,350			1,350
Year 3	Balance b/d	1,200	Year 3	Depreciation	150
				Balance c/d	1,050
		1,200			1,200

(b)

(Diminishing balance method)

Year 1	Bank	1,500	Year 1	Depreciation	150
				Balance c/d	1,350
		1,500			1,500
		1,350	Year 2	Depreciation	135
				Balance c/d	1,215
		1,350			1,350
		1,215	Year 3	Depreciation	121
				Balance c/d	1,094
		1,215			1,215

20.3

(Showing modern method only)

(a) Straight-line Method

Delivery Van

19–7		
Nov 1	Bank	1,200

Provision for Depreciation: Delivery Van

19–8			19–8		
Oct 31	Balance c/d	120	Oct 31	Profit & Loss	120
			19–8		
			Nov 1	Balance b/d	120
19–9			19–9		
Oct 31	Balance c/d	240	Oct 31	Profit & Loss	120
		240			240
			19–9		
			Nov 1	Balance b/d	240
19–0			19–0		
Oct 31	Balance c/d	360	Oct 31	Profit & Loss	120
		360			360
			19–0		
			Nov 1	Balance b/d	360

(b) Reducing Balance Method

Delivery Van

19–7					
Nov 1	Bank	1,200			

Provision for Depreciation: Delivery Van

19–8			19–8		
Oct 21	Balance c/d	120	Oct 31	Profit & Loss	120
			19–8		
			Nov 1	Balance b/d	120
19–9			19–9		
Oct 31	Balance c/d	228	Oct 31	Profit & Loss	108
		228			228
			19–9		
			Nov 1	Balance b/d	228
19–0			19–0		
Oct 31	Balance c/d	325	Oct 31	Profit & Loss	97
		325			325
			19–0		
			Nov 1	Balance b/d	325

20.6(*a*)

Machinery (both methods)

Year 1					
Jan 1	Bank	10,000			

(b)

Machine Depreciation (Straight Line Method)

Year 1			Year 1		
Dec 31	Accumulated Provision	3,100	Dec 31	Profit & Loss	3,100
Year 2			Year 2		
Dec 31	Accumulated Provision	3,100	Dec 31	Profit & Loss	3,100
Year 3			Year 3		
Dec 31	Accumulated Provision	3,100	Dec 31	Profit & Loss	3,100

Machine Depreciation (Reducing Balance Method)

Year 1			Year 1		
Dec 31	Accumulated Provision	6,000	Dec 31	Profit & Loss	6,000
Year 2			Year 2		
Dec 31	Accumulated Provision	2,400	Dec 31	Profit & Loss	2,400
Year 3			Year 3		
Dec 31	Accumulated Provision	960	Dec 31	Profit & Loss	960

(c)

Accumulated Provision for Machine Depreciation (Straight Line)

			Year 1		
			Dec 31	Machine Depreciation	3,100
Year 2			Year 2		
Dec 31	Balance c/d	6,200	Dec 31	Machine Depreciation	3,100
		6,200			6,200
Year 3			Year 3		
Dec 31	Balance c/d	9,300	Jan 1	Balance b/d	6,200
			Dec 31	Machine Depreciation	3,100
		9,300			9,300

Accumulated Provision for Machinery Depreciation (Reducing Balance)

			Year 1		
			Dec 31	Machine Depreciation	6,000
Year 2			Year 2		
Dec 31	Balance c/d	8,400	Dec 31	Machine Depreciation	2,400
		8,400			8,400
			Year 3		
Year 3			Jan 1	Balance b/d	8,400
Dec 31	Balance c/d	9,360	Dec 31	Machine Depreciation	960
		9,360			9,360

Chapter 21

21.1

D Plim

Jan 1	Balance b/f	200	Feb 1	Cash	150
			Feb 1	Bad Debts	50
		200			200

C Mike

Jan 1	Balance b/f	120	Mar 10	Cash (30p in £)	36
			Mar 10	Bad Debts	84
		120			120

Bad Debts

Feb 1	D Plim	50			
Mar 10	C Mike	84	Jun 30	Profit & Loss	134
		134			134

21.2*(a)*

Provision for Doubtful Debts

19–8			19–7		
Sept 30	Profit & Loss	186	Sept 30	Profit & Loss	1,186
Sept 30	Balance c/d	1,000			
		1,186			1,186

(b)

Profit & Loss Account

19–7	Bad Debts	140	19–8	Reduction in Provision for Doubtful Debts	186
	Provision for Doubtful Debts	1,186			

(c)

Balance Sheet as at 30 September 19–

19–7	Debtors	11,860	
	Less Provision DD	1,186	10,674
19–8	Debtors	10,000	
	Less Provision DD	1,000	9,000

21.3

Date 31 Dec	*Total Debtors* £	*Profit & Loss* £	*Dr/Cr*	*Final Figure for Balance Sheet* £
19–3	7,000	70	Dr	6,930 (net)
19–4	8,000	10	Dr	7,920 (net)
19–5	6,000	20	Cr	5,940 (net)
19–6	7,000	10	Dr	6,930 (net)

Chapter 22

22.1

Motor Expenses

19–6		19–6	
Dec 31 Cash & Bank	744	Dec 31 Profit & Loss	772
" 31 Owing c/d	28		
	772		772

Insurance

19–6		19–6	
Dec 31 Cash & Bank	420	Dec 31 Prepaid c/d	35
		" 31 Profit & Loss	385
	420		420

Stationery

19–6		19–6	
Dec 31 Cash & Bank	1,800	Jan 1 Owing b/f	250
" 31 Owing c/d	490	Dec 31 Profit & Loss	2,040
	2,290		2,290

Rates

19–6		19–6	
Jan 1 Prepaid b/f	220	Dec 31 Prepaid c/d	290
Dec 31 Cash & Bank	950	" 31 Profit & Loss	880
	1,170		1,170

Rent Received

19–6		19–6	
Jan 1 Owing b/f	180	Dec 31 Cash & Bank	550
Dec 31 Profit & Loss	580	" 31 Owing c/d	210
	760		760

22.3

(a)(i)

Rent Payable

Year 1		Year 2	
Aug 1 Bank	600	Jul 31 Profit & Loss	2,400
Nov 4 Bank	600		
Year 2			
Mar 31 Bank	600		
Jul 31 Accrued c/d	600		
	2,400		2,400
		Year 2	
		Aug 1 Accrued b/d	600

(ii)

Rates

Year 1		Year 2	
Aug 31 Bank	75	Jul 31 Profit & Loss	475
Oct 22 Bank	220	" 31 Prepaid c/d	90
Year 2			
Apr 17 Bank	270		
	565		565
Year 2			
Aug 1 Prepaid c/d	90		

(iii)

Electricity

Year 1		Year 2	
Oct 17 Bank	310	Jul 31 Profit & Loss	1,480
Year 2			
Jan 21 Bank	390		
Apr 10 Bank	360		
Jul 31 Accrued c/d	420		
	1,480		1,480
		Year 2	
		Aug 1 Accrued b/d	420

(b)

Balance Sheet as at 31 July Year 2 (extracts)

Current Assets		*Current Liabilities*	
Prepayment (b)	90	Accrued Expenses (a) + (c)	1,020

22.5

Rates

19–2		19–2	
Nov 4 Bank	60	Nov 1 Owing b/f	10
19–3		19–3	
Apr 11 Bank	72	Oct 31 Profit & Loss	134
Oct 26 Bank	72	Oct 31 Prepaid c/d	60
	204		204

22.6

(a)

Rates

Bank	500	Prepayment c/d	100
		Profit & Loss	400
	500		500

Rent

Profit & Loss	300	Bank	225
		Owing c/d	75
	300		300

Insurance

Bank	450	Transfer to Drawings	50
		Profit & Loss	400
	450		450

Wages

Bank	5,200	Profit & Loss	5,500
Owing c/d	300		
	5,500		5,500

(b)

Bilton Potteries
Profit & Loss Account for the year ended 31 January 19–0

Wages	5,500	Gross Profit b/d	11,507
Rates	400	Rent Receivable	300
Insurance	400		
Net Profit	5,507		
	11,807		11,807

Balance Sheet as at 31 January 19–0

Fixed Assets			Capital		
Premises		5,000	Balance at 1.1.19–0		7,000
Current Assets			Add Net Profit		5,507
Stock	1,000				12,507
Debtors	434		less Drawings		3,850
Prepaid & Accrued	175				8,657
Bank	3,218	4,827	Current Liabilities		
			Creditors	870	
			Wages Owing	300	1,170
		9,827			9,827

Note.

As you have now been introduced to vertical style accounts, some of the final accounts in the remainder of the answers will be shown using that style.

22.7

George Holt

Trading & Profit & Loss Account for the year ended 31 October 19–6

Sales			9,620
Less Cost of Goods Sold:			
Opening Stock		1,970	
Add Purchases		5,930	
		7,900	
Less Closing Stock		1,780	6,120
Gross Profit			3,500
Add Discounts Received			90
			3,590
Less Expenses:			
Wages		1,520	
Rent		240	
Bad Debts		110	
Discounts Allowed		130	
General Expenses		190	
Depreciation		100	2,290
Net Profit			1,300

Balance Sheet as at 31 October 19–6

Fixed Assets			
Fixtures		400	
Less Depreciation		100	300
Current Assets			
Stock		1,780	
Debtors		2,350	
Prepayment		40	
Cash		30	
		4,200	
Less Current Liabilities			
Creditors	1,680		
Bank Overdraft	260	1,940	
Working Capital			2,260
			2,560
Financed by:			
Capital			
Balance as at 1.11.19–5			2,700
Add Net Profit			1,300
			4,000
Less Drawings			1,440
			2,560

22.8

John Brown

Trading & Profit & Loss Account for the year ended 31 December 19–7

Sales		40,000	
Less Returns Inwards		500	39,500
Less Cost of Goods Sold:			
Opening Stock		10,000	
Add Purchases	35,000		
Less Returns Outwards	620	34,380	
		44,380	
Less Closing Stock		12,000	32,380
Gross Profit			7,120
Less Expenses:			
Wages		3,500	
Rates		550	
Telephone		122	
Bad Debts		20	
Provision for Bad Debts		18	
Depreciation: Fittings	400		
Van	600	1,000	5,210
Net Profit			1,910

Balance Sheet as at 31 December 19–7

Fixed Assets			
Fittings		4,000	
Less Depreciation		400	3,600
Motor Van		3,000	
Less Depreciation		600	2,400
			6,000
Current Assets			
Stock		12,000	
Debtors	980		
Less Provision for Bad Debts	98	882	
Prepayment		50	
Bank		300	
		13,232	
Less Current Liabilities			
Creditors	700		
Expenses Owing	522	1,222	12,010
			18,010
Financed by:			
Capital			
Balance at 1.1.19–7			17,900
Add Net Profit			1,910
			19,810
Less Drawings			1,800
			18,010

22.10

Jane Jones
Profit & Loss Account for the year ended 31 December 19–7

Revenue			10,400
Less Expenses:			
Rates (140 – 30)		110	
Telephone		110	
Advertising		230	
Cleaning		50	
Motor Car Expenses (480 – 160)		320	
Sundry Expenses		1,200	
Depreciation: Equipment	112		
Motor (*see* workings)	176	288	2,308
Net Profit			8,092

Balance Sheet as at 31 December 19–7

Fixed Assets		
Freehold Premises		6,000
Equipment at cost	1,120	
Less Depreciation	512	608
Motor Car at cost	1,800	
Less Depreciation*	744	1,056
		7,664
Current Assets		
Prepaid Expenses	30	
Bank	5,400	
Petty Cash	40	
	5,470	
Less Current Liabilities		
Expenses owing	50	
Working Capital		5,420
		13,084
Financed by:		
Capital		
Balance at 1.1.19–7		9,740
Add Net Profit		8,092
		17,832
Less Drawings*		4,748
		13,084

Workings:

Depreciation Motor Car 1,320 × 20% =	264
Of this charge to Profit & Loss $\frac{2}{3}$ rds	176
charge to Drawings $\frac{1}{3}$ rd	88
	264

Drawings: per Trial Balance	4,500
$\frac{1}{3}$ Depreciation of Motor Car	88
$\frac{1}{3}$ Motor Car Expenses	160
	4,748
Depreciation: Motor Car	
To start of year (Cost 1,800 – 1,320)	480
For the year (including private part)	264
	744

22.12

Thomas Williams
Trading & Profit & Loss Account for the year ended 31 March 19–9

Sales		13,990	
less Returns Inwards		270	13,720
Less: Cost of Goods Sold:			
Opening Stock		1,720	
Purchases	7,620		
less Returns Outwards	190	7,430	
		9,150	
less Closing Stock		1,430	7,720
Gross Profit			6,000
Add: Discounts Received			310
			6,310
Less: Expenses			
Wages & Salaries		3,050	
Rent, Rates & Insurance		520	
Discounts Allowed		480	
Carriage Outwards		720	
General Office Expenses		150	
Provision for Bad Debts		50	
Depreciation:			
Fixtures & Fittings	40		
Delivery Van	100	140	5,110
Net Profit			1,200

Balance Sheet as at 31 March 19–9

Fixed Assets		
Fixtures & Fittings	400	
Less Depreciation	40	360
Delivery Van	700	
Less Depreciation	100	600
		960

Current Assets			
Stock		1,430	
Debtors	3,970		
less Provision	270	3,700	
Prepayments		60	
Cash		30	
		5,220	
Less *Current Liabilities*			
Creditors	2,020		
Expenses Accrued	70		
Bank Overdraft	1,450	3,540	
Working Capital			1,680
Financed by:			2,640
Capital			
Balance as at 1.4.19–8			2,400
Add Net Profit			1,200
			3,600
Less Drawings			960
			2,640

22.16

(a)(i) 'as at' means that the capital, assets and liabilities are shown at their book values at the close of the balance sheet date.

(ii) Because the Trading & Profit & Loss Account for the year ended 31 October 1990 has already been drawn up. This is why the net profit of £12,970 is shown. The only balance, therefore, remaining on the stock account is for the stock at 31 October 1990, as the opening stock on 1 November 1989 was transferred to the debit of the Trading Account.

(b)

G Williams
Balance Sheet as at 31 October 19–0

Fixed Assets			*Capital*		
Premises		27,400	Balance at 1.11.19–9	(C)	45,330
Furniture & Fittings		3,075	Add Net Profit		12,970
Plant & Machinery		13,840		(B)	58,300
Vehicles		6,100	Less Drawings		10,800
		50,415		(A)	47,500
Current Assets			*Loan*		
Stock	3,073		5 year loan Loamshire Finance		7,500
Trade Debtors	5,127		*Current Liabilities*		
Prepayment	50		Trade Creditors	2,065	
Cash	500	8,750	Bank Overdraft	1,875	
			Expenses Owing	225	4,165
		59,165			59,165

(A) is figure needed to balance
(B) is 47,500 + 10,800 = 58,300
(C) is 58,300 less 12,970 = 45,330

(c)

Capital

19–0		19–9	
Oct 31 Drawings	10,800	Nov 1 Balance b/d	45,330
" 31 Balance c/d	47,500	19–0	
		Oct 31 Net Profit	12,970
	58,300		58,300

Chapter 23

23.1

Bank Reconciliation as on 31 December 19–6

Cash at bank as per cash book		678
Add Unpresented cheques	256	
Credit transfers	56	312
		990
Less Bank Lodgements		115
Cash at bank as per bank statement		875

Note for teachers.
Both in theory and in practice you can start with the cash book balance working to the bank statement balance, or you can reverse this method. Many teachers have their preferences, but this is a personal matter only. Examiners sometimes ask for them using one way, sometimes the other. Students should, therefore, be able to tackle them both ways.

23.3

Bank Reconciliation Statement as on 31 March 19–9

Balance as per cash book		787
Add Traders' credit	73	
Unpresented cheques	127	200
		987
Less Standing order	25	
Bank lodgement	112	137
Balance per bank statement		850

23.6

Mitchell: Bank Reconciliation Statement as on 31 December 19–

Balance per cash book		2,200
Add unpresented cheques		250
		2,450
Less Standing order	40	
Credit transfer	175	
Bank charges	40	255
Balance per bank statement		2,195

23.7

A Brook: Bank Reconciliation as on 30 June–

Balance per cash book	1,523
Add unpresented cheque	34
	1,557
Less bank lodgement not credited	400
Balance per bank statement	1,157

Chapter 24

24.1

(a)	Motor Vehicles	Dr	6,790	:	Kingston	Cr	6,790
(b)	Bad Debts	Dr	34	:	H Newman	Cr	34
(c)	Unique Offices	Dr	490	:	Office Furniture	Cr	490
(d) (i)	Bank	Dr	39	:	W Charles	Cr	39
(ii)	Bad Debts	Dr	111	:	W Charles	Cr	111
(e)	Drawings	Dr	45	:	Purchases	Cr	45
(f)	Drawings	Dr	76	:	Insurance	Cr	76
(g)	Machinery	Dr	980	:	Systems Accelerated	Cr	980

24.3

(a) *The Journal (dates omitted)*

	Dr	*Cr*
Freehold Premises	45,000	
Fixtures & Fittings	12,500	
Motor Vehicles	9,500	
Bank (Overdraft)		2,800
Cash	650	
Stock	1,320	
F Hardy	160	
A Derby		270
Capital		66,060
	69,130	69,130
Assets & Liabilities entered to open the books		
Discounts Allowed	7	
Parker		7
Being discount allowed to Parker		
Motor Van	4,500	
Supervans Ltd		4,500
Being purchase of van		
Supervans Ltd	1,125	
Bank		1,125
Being payment of deposit on van		
Bank	50	
I M Broke		50
Being final payment by Broke		
Bad Debts	200	
I M Broke		200
Being bad debt written off		

(b)

Bad Debts

I M Broke	200		

I M Broke

Balance b/d	250	Bank	50
		Bad Debts	200
	250		250

24.5

The Journal (narratives omitted)

		Dr	Cr
(a) **July 1**	**James Crawford**	1.80	
	Interest Receivable (6% × 120 × $\frac{3}{12}$)		1.80
(b) **Aug 30**	**Weighing Machines**	1,350.00	
	Mechweights		1,350.00
	Mechweights	400.00	
	Weighing Machines		400.00
(c) **Sept 10**	**Bank**	52.50	
	Bad Debt Recovered		52.50

24.6

The Journal

(1) Premises	2,000	
Motor Van	450	
Fixtures	600	
Stock	1,289	
Debtors: N Hardy	40	
M Nelson	180	
Bank	1,254	
Cash	45	
Creditors: B Blake		60
V Reagan		200
Capital		5,598
	5,858	5,858
(14) Motor Van	300	
Better Motors		300

Returns Inwards Journal

(11) K O'Connor	16
(11) L Staines	18
	34

Returns Outwards Journal

(19) N Lee	9

Purchases Journal

(2) B Blake	20
(2) C Harris	56
(2) H Gordon	38
(2) N Lee	69
(22) J Johnson	89
(22) T Best	72
	344

Sales Journal

(3) K O'Connor	56
(3) M Benjamin	78
(3) L Staines	98
(3) N Duffy	48
(3) B Green	118
(3) M Nelson	40
(9) M Benjamin	22
(9) L Pearson	67
	527

Cash Book

	Disct	Cash	Bank		Disct	Cash	Bank
(1) Balances		45	1,254	(1) Rent			15
(16) N Hardy	2		38	(4) Motor Expenses		13	
(16) M Nelson	11		209	(7) Drawings		20	
(16) K O'Connor	2		38	(24) B Blake	4		76
(16) L Staines	4		76	(24) V Reagan	10		190
				(24) N Lee	3		57
				(27) Salaries			56
				(30) Rates			66
				(31) Better Motors			300
				(31) Balance c/d		12	855
	19	45	1,615		17	45	1,615

B Blake

(24) Bank	76	(1) Balance	60
(24) Discount	4	(2) Purchases	20
	80		80

V Reagan

(24) Bank & Disct	200	(1) Balance b/d	200

C Harris

		(2) Purchases	56

H Gordon

		(2) Purchases	38

N Lee

(19) Returns	9	(2) Purchases	69
(24) Bank & Disct	60		
	69		69

M Benjamin

(3) Sales	78
(9) Sales	22

L Staines

(3) Sales	98	(11) Returns	18
		(16) Bank & Disct	80
	98		98

N Duffy

(3) Sales	48

B Green

(3) Sales	118

L Pearson

(9) Sales	67

Better Motors

(31) Bank	300	(14) Motor Van	300

General Ledger

Capital

		(1) Balance	5,598

Rent

(1) Bank	15

Motor Expenses

(4) Cash	13

Drawings

(7) Cash	20

Salaries

(27) Bank	56

Rates

(30) Bank	66

Sales

		(31) Total for month	527

Purchases

(31) Total for month	344

Returns Inwards

(31) Total for month	34

Returns Outwards

		(31) Total for month	9

Premises

(1) Balance	2,000

Motor Vans

(1) Balance	450
(14) Better Motors	300

Fixtures

(1) Balance	600

Stock

(1) Balance	1,289

J Johnson

		(22) Purchases	89

T Best

		(22) Purchases	72

N Hardy

(1) Balance	40	(16) Bank & Disct	40

M Nelson

(1) Balance	180	(16) Bank & Disct	220
(3) Sales	40		
	220		220

K O'Connor

(3) Sales	56	(11) Returns	16
		(16) Bank & Disct	40
	56		56

Discounts Allowed

(31) Total for month	19		

Discounts Received

		(31) Total for month	17

Trial Balance as at 31 May 19–6

C Harris		56
H Gordon		38
J Johnson		89
T Best		72
M Benjamin	100	
N Duffy	48	
B Green	118	
L Pearson	67	
Capital		5,598
Rent	15	
Motor Expenses	13	
Drawings	20	
Salaries	56	
Rates	66	
Sales		527
Purchases	344	
Returns Inwards	34	
Returns Outwards		9
Premises	2,000	
Motor Vans	750	
Fixtures	600	
Stock	1,289	
Discounts Allowed	19	
Discounts Received		17
Bank	855	
Cash	12	
	6,406	6,406

Chapter 25

25.1

Petty Cash Book

			Total	Wages	Stationery	Postage	Ledger
4.67	(1)	Balance b/f					
45.33	(1)	Cash					
	(3)	Wages	8.76	8.76			
	(7)	Postages	2.94			2.94	
	(10)	Wages	9.11	9.11			
	(14)	Envelopes	2.28		2.28		
	(17)	Wages	8.84	8.84			
	(20)	J Smith	4.16				4.16
	(21)	Stationery	2.75		2.75		
	(24)	Wages	8.48	8.48			
			47.32	35.19	5.03	2.94	4.16
	(28)	Balance c/d	2.68				
50.00			50.00				
2.68	(1)	Balance b/d					
47.32	(1)	Cash					

25.3

Bank Cash Book

	Disct	Bank		Disct	Bank
(3) N Etheridge		5,602.50	(1) Balance b/d		1,125.50
(3) Cash Sales		506.75	(1) Petty Cash		89.55
(10) J Holland	3.00	57.00	(22) Drawings		150.00
(22) P Coleman	9.00	91.00	(22) Purchases		150.00
(28) Cash Sales		234.75	(28) G Ford		50.00
(30) J Holland		25.00	(28) D White		75.00
			(31) Balance c/d		4,876.95
	12.00	6,517.00			6,517.00

Petty Cash Book

Dr		Cr	Total	Cleaner	Motor Exps	Insurance	Sundries
(1) Balance b/f	10.45	(3) Cleaner	15.00	15.00			
(1) Bank	89.55	(3) Motor Exps	6.00		6.00		
		(15) Sundries	4.25				4.25
		(15) Insurance	15.00			15.00	
		(22) Cleaner	15.00	15.00			
		(28) Sundries	3.50				3.50
			58.75	30.00	6.00	15.00	7.75
		(31) Balance c/d	41.25				
	100.00		100.00				

Chapter 26

To economise on space, all narratives for journal entries are omitted.

26.1

(a)	J Harkness	Dr	678	:	J Harker	Cr	678
(b)	Machinery	Dr	4,390	:	L Pearson	Cr	4,390
(c)	Motor Van	Dr	3,800	:	Motor Expenses	Cr	3,800
(d)	E Fletcher	Dr	9	:	Sales	Cr	9
(e)	Sales	Dr	257	:	Commissions Received	Cr	257

26.4

D Martin: Corrected net profit calculation

Profit originally calculated		8,975
Add (B) Sales not recorded	28	
(E) Rent receivable	50	
(G) Rent for next year	10	88
		9,063
Less (A) Rates not recorded	200	
(C) Closing stock overvalued	48	
(D) Depreciation	200	
(F) Sales Returns	22	
(H) Provision for bad debts	20	490
Corrected figure of net profit		8,573

26.6*(a)*

R James
Computation of Correct Net Profit
for the year ended 31 December 19–6

Net Profit per accounts		3,040
Add (i) Purchases overstated		140
		3,180
Less (ii) Depreciation omitted	280	
(iii) Bad Debts written off	41	
(iv) Closing stock overvalued	124	445
Corrected Net Profit		2,735

(b)

R James
Balance Sheet as at 31 December 19–6

Fixed Assets		
Furniture & Fittings		1,680
Motor Vehicles	2,980	
Less Depreciation	280	2,700
		4,380
Current Assets		
Stock	2,600	
Debtors	1,200	
Bank	1,235	
	5,035	
Less Current Liabilities		
Creditors	1,850	
Working Capital		3,185
		7,565
Financed by:		
Capital		
Balance as at 1.1.19–6		7,690
Add Net Profit		2,735
		10,425
Less Drawings		2,860
		7,565

Chapter 27

27.1*(a)*

T Boyd: Computation of correct net profit

Net Profit originally calculated		1,170
Add (b) Shelves – capital expenditure	76	
(a) Purchases overstated	60	136
		1,306
Less (c) Discount allowed incorrectly entered: to eliminate double the error		194
Corrected net profit figure		1,112

(d) has no effect on profit calculation

(b) (i) Excess debit 60 (ii) No effect (iii) Debit side understated 97, Credit side overstated 97 (iv) Credit side understated 48.

27.2

The Journal

	Dr	Cr
(i) Suspense	60	
Purchases		60
(ii) Fittings	76	
Wages		76
(iii) Discount Allowed	194	
Suspense		194
(iv) Suspense	48	
S Lewis		48

27.3

Trial Balance as on 31 January 19–9

	Dr	Cr
Capital 1.2.19–8		5,500
Drawings	2,800	
Stock 1.2.19–8	2,597	
Trade Debtors (2,130 – 6)(ii)	2,124	
Furniture & Fittings (1,750 + 120)(iii)	1,870	
Cash	1,020	
Trade Creditors (2,735 – 75)(i)		2,660
Sales (7,430 + 108*)*564 – 456(v)		7,538
Returns Inwards	85	
Discounts Received		46
Discounts Allowed (iv)	38	
Business Expenses	950	
Purchases (4,380 – 120)(iii)	4,260	
	15,744	15,744

Chapter 28

28.1

Sales Ledger Control

(1) Balance b/f	4,560	(31) Returns Inwards	460
(31) Sales Journal	10,870	(31) Cheques & Cash	9,615
		(31) Discounts Allowed	305
		(31) Balances c/d	5,050
	15,430		15,430

28.2

Sales Ledger Control

(1) Balances b/f	6,708	(31) Discounts	300
(31) Sales Journal	11,500	(31) Cash & Cheques	8,970
		(31) Bad Debts	115
		(31) Returns Inwards	210
		(31) Balances c/d	8,613
	18,208		18,208

28.5

Sales Ledger Control

(1) Balances b/f	6,840	(31) Discounts	420
(31) Sales	46,801	(31) Bad Debts	494
		(31) Receipts	43,780
		(31) Returns In	296
		(31) Balances c/f	8,651
	53,641		53,641

Some of the answers to Chapters 29 and 30 are shown in the horizontal style. This is simply for ease of illustration.

Chapter 29

29.1

J Jackson: Trading Account for the year ended 31 July 19–3

Stock 1.8.19–2		4,936	Sales	30,000
Add Purchases	(D)	25,374		
	(C)	30,310		
Less Stock 31.7.19–3		6,310		
Cost of Goods Sold	(B)	24,000		
Gross Profit	(A)	6,000		
		30,000		30,000

(A) Mark-up is 25%, therefore margin is 20%. Gross Profit is therefore 20% × 30,000 = 6,000
(B) Is missing figure, i.e. 30,000 – (A) 6,000 = 24,000
(C) and (D) also found by missing figure deduction in that order.

29.2

P R Match: Trading Account for the year ended 31 August 19–9

Stock 1.9.19–8		2,000	Sales	(D)	21,000
Add Purchases		18,000			
		20,000			
Less Stock 31.8.19–9	(A)	6,000			
Cost of Goods Sold	(B)	14,000			
Gross Profit	(C)	7,000			
		21,000			21,000

(A) To find, we know average stock is 4,000. Therefore (Opening Stock 2,000 – Closing Stock?) ÷ 2. Therefore Closing Stock must be 6,000, i.e. (2,000 + 6,000) ÷ 2 = 4,000
(B) can then be found, i.e. simply 20,000 – 6,000 = 14,000
(C) As mark-up is 50%, this figure therefore 14,000 × 50% = 7,000
(D) is then missing figure, i.e. (B) + (C)

Chapter 30

30.1

S Pea: Balance Sheet as at 31 July 19–7

Fixed Assets			Capital			
Furniture	900		Cash Introduced			1,000
Less Depreciation	100	800	Add Net Profit	(C)		
Motor Vehicles	2,100			(B)		
Less Depreciation	500	1,600	Less Drawings			3,000
		2,400		(A)		
Current Assets			Loan from B Smith			200
Stock	2,700		Current Liabilities			
Debtors	1,600		Creditors		3,300	
Cash	50	4,350	Bank Overdraft		1,000	4,300
		6,750				6,750

(A) (B) & (C) found in that order by filling in figures needed to balance the balance sheet figures, i.e. (A) is 6,750 – 4,300 – 200 = 2,250. (B) – 3,000 = 2,250, so (B) is 5,250 Profit (C) + 1,000 = 5,250 so Net Profit is 4,250

30.2*(a)*

Sales Ledger Control

Balances b/f	1,490	Cash	5,410
Sales	5,760	Balances (Difference) c/d	1,840
	7,250		7,250

Purchases Ledger Control

Cash	3,890	Balances b/f	940
Balances c/d	1,110	Purchases	4,060
	5,000		5,000

(b)

Statement of Affairs as at 31 March 19–8

Fixed Assets			Capital (Difference)	2,770
Office Furniture		300		
Current Assets				
Stock	1,160		Current Liabilities	
Debtors	1,490		Creditors	940
Bank	730			
Cash	30	3,410		
		3,710		3,710

(c)

Statement of Affairs as at 31 March 19–9

Fixed Assets			Capital		
Office Furniture		250	Balance at 31.3.19–8		2,770
Current Assets			Add Net Profit	(C)	1,700
Stock	1,310			(B)	4,470
Debtors	1,840		Less Drawings		1,270
Bank	870			(A)	3,200
Cash	40	4,060	Current Liabilities		
			Creditors		1,110
		4,310			4,310

(A) (B) & (C) found in that order by filling in missing figures to make balance sheet totals agree

30.3

C Cat: Statement of Affairs as at 31.12.19–1

Fixed Assets			Capital		
Machinery		2,000	Cash Introduced		4,000
Furniture		1,500	Add Net Profit	(B)	900
		3,500		(A)	4,900
Current Assets					
Stock	1,000		Current Liabilities		
Debtors	350		Creditors		350
Bank	400	1,750			
		5,250			5,250

(A) & (B) found in that order, by filling in missing figures

30.4*(a)*

Sales Ledger Control

Balances b/fwd	7,250	Cash	22,460
Sales (Difference)	24,370	Discounts	670
		Bad Debts	410
		Balance c/d	8,080
	31,620		31,620

(b)

Purchases Ledger Control

Cash	17,190	Balances b/fwd	4,140
Discounts	470	Purchases (Difference)	19,150
Balances c/d	5,630		
	23,290		23,290

(c)

J Adams: Trading Account for the year 31 May 19–8

Opening Stock	1,980	Sales	24,370
Add Purchases	19,150		
	21,130		
Less Closing Stock	2,160		
Cost of Goods Sold	18,970		
Gross Profit c/d	5,400		
	24,370		24,370

Chapter 31

31.1

Town Society

Income & Expenditure Account for the year ended 30 June 19–1

Income		
Subscriptions		320
Sale of Refreshments	30	
Less Cost	20	10
Sale of Dance Tickets	80	
Less Expenses	45	35
		365
Expenditure		
Rent (10 + 10)	20	
Printing & Stationery (15 – 5)	10	
Sundry Expenses	15	45
		320

31.3

(a) Accumulated Fund 1.6.19–6:

Bar Stocks	88	
Equipment	340	
Bank	286	
		714

(b)

Down Town Sports & Social Club

Income & Expenditure Account for the year ended 31 May 19–7

Income			
Subscriptions			149
Net proceeds of jumble sale			91
Net proceeds of dance			122
Contribution from Bar:			
Bar Takings		463	
Less Cost of Supplies:			
Opening Stock	88		
Add Purchases	397		
	485		
Less Closing Stock	101	384	79
			441
Less Expenditure			
Wages		198	
Hire of Rooms		64	
Loss on Equipment		12	
Depreciation		30	304
Surplus of Income over Expenditure			137

31.4*(a)*

Deepdale Church Youth Centre

Receipts & Payments Account for the year ended 31 December 19–4

Balance 1.1.19–4	460	Light & Heat	205
Subscriptions	800	Expenses of Fete	310
Donation	80	New Games Equipment	160
Sale Fete Tickets	540	Cleaner's Wages	104
		Repairs & Renewals	83
		Motor Van Repairs	126
		Balance 31.12.19–4	892
	1,880		1,880

(b)

Income & Expenditure Account for the year ended 31 December 19–4

Income		
Subscriptions		800
Donation		80
Profit on Fete: Sale of Tickets	540	
Less Expenses	310	230
		1,110
Less Expenditure		
Light & Heat (205 + 45)	250	
Cleaner's Wages	104	
Repairs & Renewals	83	
Motor Van Repairs	126	563
Surplus of Income over Expenditure		547

Balance Sheet as at 31 December 19–4

Fixed Assets		
Furniture & Fittings		1,500
Games & Equipment		800
Motor Van		1,000
		3,300
Current Assets		
Cash & Bank	892	
Less Current Liabilities		
Electricity Owing	45	
Working Capital		847
		4,147
Financed by:		
Accumulated Fund: Balance at 31.12.19–3		3,600
Add Surplus		547
		4,147

Chapter 32

32.1

E Smith

Manufacturing & Trading Accounts for the year ended 31 March 19–7

Stock of raw material 1.4.19–6		2,400	Production cost of goods completed c/d	44,756
Add Purchases		21,340		
Carriage inwards		321		
		24,061		
Less Stock of raw mats 31.3.19–7		2,620		
Cost of raw materials consumed		21,441		
Manufacturing wages		13,280		
Prime cost		34,721		
Factory overhead expenses:				
Rent & rates	2,300			
Power	6,220			
Other expenses	1,430	9,950		
		44,671		
Add Work-in-Progress 1.4.19–6		955		
		45,626		
Less Work-in-Progress 31.3.19–7		870		
		44,756		44,756
Stock finished goods 1.4.19–6		6,724	Sales	69,830
Add Production cost of goods completed b/d		44,756		
		51,480		
Less Stock finished goods 31.3.19–7		7,230		
		44,250		
Gross profit		25,580		
		69,830		69,830

32.3

T Shaw
Manufacturing, Trading & Profit & Loss Account for the year ended 31 December 19–7

Stock of raw materials			Production cost of goods	
1.1.19–7		18,450	completed c/d	152,185
Add Purchases		64,300		
Carriage inwards		1,605		
		84,355		
Less Stock of raw materials				
31.12.19–7		20,210		
Cost of raw materials consumed		64,145		
Direct labour		65,810		
Prime cost		129,955		
Factory overhead expenses:				
Rent $\frac{2}{3}$	1,800			
Fuel & Power	5,920			
Depreciation:				
Machinery	8,300	16,020		
		145,975		
Add Work-in-Progress				
1.1.19–7		23,600		
		169,575		
Less Work-in-Progress				
31.12.19–7		17,390		
		152,185		152,185
Stock finished goods				
1.1.19–7		17,470	Sales	200,600
Add Production cost of				
goods completed b/d		152,185		
		169,655		
Less Stock finished goods				
31.12.19–7		21,485		
		148,170		
Gross profit c/d		52,430		
		200,600		200,600
Office salaries		16,920	Gross profit b/d	52,430
Rent $\frac{1}{3}$		900		
Lighting & heating		5,760		
Depreciation: Office equipment		1,950		
Net profit		26,900		
		52,430		52,430

32.4

Excelsior Pressings
Manufacturing, Trading & Profit & Loss Account for year ended 31 December Year 8

Cost of Raw Materials Consumed:			Production Cost of	
Stock 1 Jan Year 8		28,315	Goods Completed c/d	459,395
Add Purchases		172,300		
		200,615		
Less Stock 31 Dec Year 8		30,200		
		170,415		
Direct Wages		194,500		
Prime Cost		364,915		
Factory Overhead Expenses				
Indirect Wages	45,820			
Factory Expenses	3,700			
Heating & Lighting	2,760			
Rent & Rates	12,300			
Salaries	10,800			
Depreciation	20,000	95,380		
		460,295		
Add Opening				
Work-in-Progress		6,200		
		466,495		
Less Closing				
Work-in-Progress		7,100		
		459,395		459,395
Cost of Goods Sold:			Sales	652,500
Opening Stock of Finished				
Goods		33,700		
Production Cost of				
Goods Completed b/d		459,395		
		493,095		
Less Closing Stock of				
Finished Goods		37,500		
		455,595		
Gross Profit c/d		196,905		
		652,500		652,500
Rent & Rates		4,100	Gross Profit b/d	196,905
Heating & Lighting		690		
Salaries		21,600		
Advertising		60,800		
Administration Expenses		27,500		
Depreciation of Office				
Equipment		4,000		
Net Profit		78,215		
		196,905		196,905

Chapter 33

33.1

H Smith: Wages calculations

40 hours × £1.50 : Gross Pay		60.00
Less Income Tax	8.00	
National Insurance 5% × 60.00	3.00	11.00
Net Pay		49.00

33.2

M Marchand
Payslip week ended 28 April 19–0

(a)	Gross pay 40 × 4.40 (basic)	176.00	
	10 × 6.60 (overtime)	66.00	242.00
(b)	Less National Insurance 10% × 242.00	24.20	
	" Pension 8% × 176.00	14.08	
	" Income Tax 30% × (242.00 – 30.00)	63.60	
	" Union Contributions	2.00	103.88
(c)	Net Take-home Pay		138.12

33.3

J Brown: Payslip week ended 25 May 19–0

Gross Earnings 200 units × 120p		240.00
Less: Pension Scheme	4.80	
National Insurance	24.00	
PAYE 25% × (240 – 75)165	41.25	70.05
		169.95

A White: Payslip week ended 25 May 19–0

Gross Earnings: 40 hours × 410p	164.00	
4 hours × 410p × $1\frac{1}{4}$	20.50	184.50
Less: Pension Scheme	3.69	
National Insurance	18.45	
PAYE 25% × (184.50 – 75) 109.50	27.37	49.51
		134.99

Note: for J Brown the pay is on piecework, as piecework £240.00 exceeds hourly earnings of (40 × 375p) £150.00. For A White pay is on hours worked. Piecework earnings would have been less at 140 × 130p = £182.00.

33.4

	Wages	*£10*	*£5*	*£1*	*50p*	*20p*	*10p*	*5p*	*2p*	*1p*
1	112.86	10	1	7	1	1	1	1		1
2	97.19	9		7			1	1	2	
3	128.47	12		8		2		1	1	
4	134.75	12	1	9	1	1		1		
5	84.77	7	1	9	1	1		1	1	
	558.04	50	3	40	3	5	2	5	4	1

33.5

	Wages	*£10*	*£5*	*£1*	*50p*	*20p*	*10p*	*5p*	*2p*	*1p*
1	99.68	9		9	1		1	1	1	1
2	119.43	11		9		2			1	1
3	122.55	11	1	7	1			1		
4	94.77	8	1	9	1	1		1	1	
5	104.35	9	1	9		1	1	1		
	540.78	48	3	43	3	4	2	4	3	2

33.6

	Wages	*£10*	*£5*	*£1*	*50p*	*20p*	*10p*	*5p*	*2p*	*1p*
1	96.99	9		6	1	2		1	2	
2	133.46	12	1	8		2		1		1
3	128.86	12		8	1	1	1	1		1
4	112.36	10	1	7		1	1	1		1
5	101.26	9	1	6		1		1		1
	572.93	52	3	35	2	7	2	5	2	4

Chapter 34

34.1

(a) Category method.

A	Lowest of (280 + 440 + 390) 1,110 or (330 + 370 + 480) 1,180	= 1,110
B	Lowest of (170 + 210) 380 or (250 + 310) 560	= 380
C	Lowest of (400 + 860) 1,260 or (350 + 600) 950	= 950
D	Lowest of (570 + 770) 1,340 or (660 + 990) 1,650	= 1,340
		3,780

(b) Article method: 280 + 370 + 390 + 170 + 210 + 350 + 600 + 570 + 770 = 3,710

34.3

(a) (i) FIFO 6 × £13 = £78 (you should show full workings)

(ii) LIFO

	Received	Issued	Stock after each transaction		
Jan	24 × £10		24 × £10		240
Apr	16 × £12.50		24 × £10 =	240	
			16 × £12.50 =	200	440
June		14 × £10			
		16 × £12.50	10 × £10		100
		30			
Oct	30 × £13		10 × £10 =	100	
			30 × £13	390	490
Nov		4 × £10			
		30 × £13	6 × £10		60
		34			

(iii) AVCO

	Received	Issued	Average cost per unit of stock	No. of units in stock	Total value of stock
Jan	24 × £10		£10	24	£240
Apr	16 × £12.50		£11	40	£440
Jun		30	£11	10	£110
Oct	30 × £13		£12.50	40	500
Nov		34	£12.50	6	£75

(b)

Trading Accounts for the year ended 31 December 19–0

	FIFO	*LIFO*	*AVCO*			*(All methods)*
Purchases	830	830	830	Sales 30 × £16	480	
Less Closing stock	78	60	75	34 × £18	612	1,092
	752	770	755			
Gross profit	340	322	337			
	1,092	1,092	1,092			1,092

34.6

Chung Ltd
Computation of Stock as at 31 December 19–8

Total per stock sheets				198,444
Add	*(b)* Sales to 11.1.19–9	6,960		
	Less profit $33\frac{1}{3}\%$	2,320	4,640	
	(c) Undercast		50	4,690
				203,134
Less	*(c)* Overcast		1,000	
	(d) Incorrect extension 560 – 528		32	
	(e) Goods on approval		3,000	
	(f) Incorrect total carried forward 106,850 – 105,680		1,170	5,202
				197,932

34.7

Ceramics Ltd
Computation actual Stock at 30 June 19–6

Stock: 5 July 19–6			15,705
Add	Cost of goods sent on approval: $66\frac{2}{3}\%$ of 630	420	
	Cost of sales for the period 1 to 4 July 19–6: $66\frac{2}{3}\%$ of 993	662	
	Cost of goods returned and still in transit: $66\frac{2}{3}\%$ of 540	360	1,442
			17,147
Less	Stock overvalued: 500 – 390	110	
	Fixed asset (generator) wrongly included in stock	500	
	Error in carry forward: 420 – 240	180	
	Error in casting	100	
	Stock overvalued	350	1,240
	Stock at 30 June 19–6		15,907

Note: Items *(c)* and *(f)* do not affect stock.

34.8

Business 1	15,600 – margin $\frac{1}{6}$th = 15,600 – 2,600 =	13,000
Business 2	Closing Stocks:	
	Raw Materials	14,700
	Finished Goods	28,910
	Work in Progress	17,390
		61,000
Business 3	Stock at 26 Dec Year 4	24,280
	Add Purchases	870
		25,150
	Less Sales at cost 500 – 20% margin =	400
	Stock at cost 31 Dec Year 4	24,750
Business 4	Reduce to net realisable value	2,780

34.9

Item no 24

Date	*Ref*	*In*	*Out*	*Balance*
19–9				
May 1	Opening balance			500
May 2	Starlight Co Ltd	300		800
May 8	740		173	627
May 8	Moonbeam & Sons	200		827
May 10	810		294	533
May 14	976		104	429
May 24	Starlight Co Ltd	350		779
May 28	981		206	573

34.10

19–9 Jan 1	Stock			8,000	
	Received deliveries				
Jan 8			6,000		
Jan 16			8,000		
Jan 24			12,000	26,000	
	Total gallons available for sale			34,000	
	less sold	56,609			
		35,609		21,000	
	Gallons in stock 31.1.19–9			13,000	

(a) 13,000 gallons

(b)

12,000 gallons at Jan 24 price × 64p	7,680
1,000 gallons at Jan 16 price × 62p	620
	8,300

(c) No. of gallons sold 56,609 – 35,609 = 21,000

(d)

Sales 8,000 (of opening stock) × 60p + 25% =	6,000
6,000 (of Jan 8 delivery) × 60p + 25% =	4,500
7,000 (of Jan 16 delivery) × 62p + 25% =	5,425
	15,925

(e)

Trading Account for January 19–9

Sales			15,925
Opening Stock 8,000 × 60p		4,800	
Add Purchases 6,000 × 60p =	3,600		
8,000 × 62p =	4,960		
12,000 × 64p =	7,680	16,240	
		21,040	
Less Closing Stock		8,300	12,740
Gross Profit			3,185

Chapter 35

35.1

Date	*Supplier*	*Invoice no*	*Total*	*A–G*	*H–M*	*N–Z*
19–9						
Feb 1	F Archer	21	960	960		
Feb 2	J Potter	22	360			360
Feb 3	J Harris	23	575		575	
Feb 4	C Clay	24	106	106		
Feb 5	B Sidwell	25	91			91
Feb 6	F Lake	26	450		450	
			2,542	1,066	1,025	451

35.3

Sales Analysis Book

		Total	*UK*	*Far East*	*USA*
(1)	Hiram K Hiram	119			119
(3)	P Osaki	288		288	
(5)	B Hardcastle	249	249		
(10)	A Smith	44	44		
(15)	T Roosevelt	387			387
(17)	L Nakamura	84		84	
(19)	C Rockefeller	219			219
(28)	I Aoki	188		188	
(31)	S Chang	572		572	
		2,150	293	1,132	725

35.5*(a)*

Purchases Day Book

Year 6		*Fol*	*Total*	*Kitchen Hardware*	*Elect*	*Garden*
Jun 4	Grofast Seeds Ltd		60			60
" 6	E Gaze		192	192		
" 16	Light & Shade Ltd		350		350	
" 20	E Gaze		225	200		25
" 26	Lightning Wire Co		108		108	
" 29	Rich Loam Co		360			360
			1,295	392	458	445

(b)

Purchases: Kitchen Hardware

Year 6		
Jun 30	Purchases for month	392

Purchases: Electrical

Year 6		
Jun 30	Purchases for month	458

Purchases: Garden

Year 6		
Jun 30	Purchases for month	445

Chapter 36

36.1

Capital *(a) (c) (d) (f) (j) (l)*
Revenue *(b) (e) (g) (h) (i) (k)*

36.3

Capital *(a), (b), (e)*
Explanation – *see* text.

36.4

Capital £1,500 of *(a)*: £500 of *(b)*: £2,300 of *(c)*: £100 of *(e)*: *(f)*
Revenue £6,500 of *(a)*: £1,500 of *(b)*: £200 of *(c)*:*(d)*: £700 of *(e)*

36.7

Nature	Reason
(a) Revenue Expenditure	Used up in the short term
(b) Revenue Expenditure	Used up in the short term
(c) Question is not too clear	
(i) If spent on improving building construction	
Capital Expenditure	Adds to fixed asset value
(ii) If spent on extra wages for security guards	
Revenue Expenditure	Used up in the short term
(d) Revenue Expenditure	Used up in the short term
(e) Capital Expenditure	Adds to value of computer

Chapter 37

37.1

(a) Materiality
(b) Business Entity
(c) Prudence
(d) Cost
(e) Money Measurement
(f) Accrual
(g) Realisation
(h) Going Concern
(i) Consistency
(j) Materiality

Index

M